AN INTRODUCTION TO

LITERARY CRITICISM

....

Marlies K. Danziger HUNTER COLLEGE

W. Stacy Johnson HUNTER COLLEGE

D. C. HEATH AND COMPANY

BOSTON

PN
81
.D 37

Printed October 1968

Introduction

Literary criticism is traditionally defined as the art of judicious condemnation or praise: Samuel Johnson, for instance, describes the critic as "a man able to distinguish the faults and beauties of writing." But in our own time, the term has taken on wider significance, to include the analysis, elucidation, and interpretation of literature. With his awareness of how complex the literary work is, the modern critic usually recognizes that he may have to give close attention to detail, consider some of the relevant historical background, and even reinterpret the essential meaning of a piece of writing before he can pass judgment upon it.

Not only the professional critic but also the serious student of literature is obliged to recognize the complicated nature of such a critical process. The aim of this book is to help him do so, and to describe for him some ways of looking at a work, both in itself and in its larger context. We begin by considering various definitions of literature and, without dwelling at length on esthetic theory, trying to observe which of these definitions seem to be the most useful for the critical reader. The second chapter is devoted to the meanings of technical terms and to techniques for analyzing the literary work; and then, since one may narrow and distort the meaning of a poem, play, or novel when viewing it only by itself, we go on in the third chapter to a consideration of traditions and conventions. The fourth chapter deals with two quite different uses of extra-literary material, examining the biographical, historical, and social backgrounds upon which writers may draw, and also the psychological, philosophical, and social ideas which some critics apply to literature. Finally, we turn to the actual judgment of literary works and consider the validity of various criteria. As even so brief an outline will suggest, the text proceeds on certain assumptions about the best ways to study and evaluate literature. We are, however, interested primarily in showing the problems which a critical reader may encounter, rather than in arriving at solutions for every problem.

As a final section we reprint a series of essays that illustrate speculative or theoretical approaches to literature as well as several types of practical criticism. In some of the essays the student will find critics debating and disagreeing with each other on important issues; in such cases, whether or not he decides upon his own position, he will be able to recognize the critics' premises and terms, many of which are defined and discussed in our text.

We hope that students will read this book along with stories, plays, and poems, so as to apply the techniques described and illustrated here and consciously to formulate their own judgments of specific works. For it is the ultimate purpose of the book to encourage not so much the study of criticism as the critical study of literature.

M. K. D.
W. S. J.

Contents

An Anthology of Critical Essays

An Introduction to Literary Criticism

CHAPTER ONE

The Definition of Literature

What, we may begin by asking, *is* literature, and how can we best define it? The answer is not at all self-evident, for the term can be used in several different senses. It can mean anything written in verse or in prose. It can mean only those works which have a certain distinction. Or it can refer to mere verbiage: "all the rest is literature." For our purposes, it may be best to start by defining it in as broad and neutral a way as possible, simply as a verbal art; that is, literature belongs traditionally to the arts as opposed to the sciences or to practical knowledge, and its medium is the word, as opposed to the visual signs of painting and sculpture or the tones of music.

The Verbal Nature of Literature

When we say that its medium is the word, we are going beyond the root meaning of *literature,* which is derived from the Latin *littera,* "letter," and therefore seems to refer primarily to the written or printed word. But many civilizations, from the ancient Greek to the Scandinavian, French, and English, have produced important oral traditions. Even such lengthy narrative poems as Homer's *Iliad* and *Odyssey,* the Icelandic sagas, and the Old English *Beowulf* were presumably sung or chanted by professional bards centuries before they were written down. In order to include these and other oral works, it is useful to consider literature broadly as a verbal art, leaving open the question of whether the words are written or spoken.

The fact that literature has a verbal basis raises a number of problems. The written word is different from the visual sign in drawing, as the spoken word is different from the tones produced by music, because it embodies meaning in a special sense. This verbal meaning constitutes the importance of literature, for even a beautifully printed poem cannot compete as a purely visual work with a great painting, and even a beautifully spoken poem cannot equal as sound a fine piece of music. To put it in another way, there are no dictionaries to define the generally received significance of a red triangle or a musical chord, as there are to define words like *armchair, hallucination,* and *divine.* Each of these words has an abstract, "intellectual" significance, and to some extent this is true of all words. Nevertheless, because language is a highly complex medium, the same word may have several distinct meanings: in the phrases "a divine vacation" and "divine love" the one adjective suggests two quite dissimilar experiences. So we are always faced with the question of just what the words in a poem or a story really mean.

For one thing, language is subject to historical change. The modern reader cannot rely on a dictionary several hundred years old. Ancient Greek is no longer immediately understandable to a modern Greek; neither is Old English to a native Englishman. To know that "þaes ofereode, þisses swa maeg," the refrain of "Deor's Lament" in which the Anglo-Saxon *scop* or bard consoles himself for the hardships of his life, means "That came to an end, so may this," requires a real effort of translation. Reading even the Middle English used by Chaucer, though it is much closer to our own speech than Old English, demands either special knowledge or the help of glossaries. To understand fully the well-known description of the knight in the Prologue of *The Canterbury Tales*—"He was a verray, parfit, gentil knyght"—we must know that *verray* has the meaning not of the modern *very* but rather of "true" (as in *verity*) and that *gentil* refers not to maidenly docility but to good breeding, to excellence of birth and character (as in *gentleman*).

Not only is language subject to historical change; it is also by its very nature complex and ambiguous, often having more than one meaning either because the words are used metaphorically or because they have several overtones. The question again arises of how we are to know which particular meaning or multiple meanings to assign to the words. When Chaucer says of the Wife of Bath, "For she koude of that art the olde daunce," he clearly does not mean "the olde daunce" literally; what she knows is not a folk dance but the game of love. The phrase suggests on the one hand the long standing and universality of the game, and on the other the gusto or *joie de vivre* of the Wife. Thus the metaphor has two distinct associations which enrich the meaning. Furthermore, a word or phrase may have several very different meanings which are played off against each other. When Hamlet says bitterly of Claudius, his uncle, who has recently married his mother and is therefore also his stepfather, that he is "A little more than kin and less than kind," he means *kind* in two senses simultaneously: kindred or near relation and friendly or sympathetic. Hamlet feels that Claudius is not really his near relative, nor is he friendly and affectionate.

The English language is peculiarly rich in overtones and complexity because, along with the possibilities for such metaphors and puns, it abounds in synonyms. Often one English word has a Latinate or French form, and its synonym an Old English, and thus Germanic, origin. The implications of the French and Latinate words are likely to be, at best, more serious, more impressive, and, at worst, more pretentious than those of the Anglo-Saxon words. Thus, *profound* carries a more abstract and more weighty sense than *deep,* and *ennui* has a more elegant sound than *boredom.* But we cannot always be certain of the extent to which such distinctions are significant in the literature of an earlier period— say, in that of the fourteenth century.

Of course the overtones of words change, as yesterday's slang becomes today's received usage, and the elegance of a century ago comes to sound in modern ears like vulgar false gentility. And as associations change, they can also become so intense as to dominate the literal meaning of a word: a *villain* was once merely a farm servant, and at one time the words *wonderful* and *awful* were commonly used in their simple senses (full of wonder, full of awe), not as antonyms but as virtual synonyms. Obviously, the implication of a word can come to be its explicit meaning. Still, we must beware of giving modern overtones or modern and too limited meanings to all the words we read.

To the vexing question of how one can know precisely what the words really mean, two contrasting answers are frequently given. One is that only the author knows; the other, that each reader must decide on the meaning for himself. Plausible as these sound in theory, both answers actually leave us helpless. For the author—Chaucer, Spenser, or Shakespeare—may no longer be available for comment. Or, when he has left explanatory statements, as Milton has in his prefaces to *Paradise Lost* and *Samson Agonistes,* or Keats in his various letters, these may help to explain only certain limited aspects of the work. In any case, they show what the writer thought he was doing or intended to do rather than what he has actually achieved. Finally, if the author is our contemporary and can be asked about his work, he may be reluctant to comment, or he may even take a certain diabolic pleasure in making confusing and contradictory statements. As for leaving the decision to each individual reader, this answer presents the problem that innumerable different readings may result, some perhaps very full, perceptive, and knowledgeable, others rather more private and associative, and still others actual misinterpretations. How, then, is one to distinguish the partial or erroneous from the valid readings?

Under the circumstances, it seems best to discard both these theoretical answers and to take a frankly pragmatic position. We can recognize the difficulty of determining the precise meaning of the words, but we can nonetheless aim at more than a private or haphazard reading. We can, first of all, make an effort to find out the meaning a word may have had at the time of its use by the writer, if this differs from its present meaning. Here the monumental *New English Dictionary on Historical Principles* (*N.E.D*), often called the *Oxford English Dictionary* (*O.E.D.*), is most helpful, since it traces the history of English words, telling not only when they first came into the language and from what sources, but also what changes in meaning they have undergone. For example, when we read the description of man in George Herbert's "The Window"—"He is a brittle, crazy glass"—we may be puzzled by the word *crazy,* which we know to mean "insane." But the *N.E.D.* shows that its original sense is "full of cracks or flaws," so that Herbert is quite appropriately comparing man to a piece of glass which is not only brittle but already cracked or damaged. We can also try to discover and keep in mind the special implications a word may have had at an earlier time, if that differs from its modern significance. When the lover of Marvell's "To His Coy Mistress" mockingly assures his beloved that if it were possible,

> My *vegetable* love should grow
> Vaster than empires, and more slow,

we can recognize that he is not presenting himself as incapable of human or animal love, as worse than a cold fish, but that he is rather alluding to one of the three powers of the soul (vegetable, sensible, and rational) accepted in medieval and Renaissance philosophy, and that he wishes to suggest mainly the great, slow, and inevitable growth of his love, comparable perhaps to that of a giant oak.

Secondly, we can discriminate between different meanings which the same word may have in different contexts. For instance, when Milton calls Satan's eyes "carbuncle" in the temptation scene of *Paradise Lost* (IX, 500), he has in mind their fiery-red and jewel-like quality, but when T. S. Eliot in *The Waste Land* calls an amorous real-estate agent "the young man carbuncular," he is alluding to the gentleman's pimply complexion. Here again, we can try to become aware of the full and varied connotations of the words. Milton's "carbuncle his eyes" suggests the glitter, richness, and intensity appropriate to the description of Satan as a splendid, towering serpent, who is capable of attracting, fascinating, and eventually tempting the weak and hapless Eve. Eliot's phrase "young man carbuncular," indicating a very bad complexion and perhaps poor health, suggests, in contrast, the seediness and the lack of vitality of the young man, who is, as it turns out, quite unable to arouse any response in the woman he is seducing.

The Problem of the Text

Another major problem which has to do with the fact that literature is a *verbal* art emerges when we ask about the nature of the text we read. We cannot simply take it for granted, especially in the case of older works, that the text has passed smoothly and without great changes from the author to the printer to the reader. For many different reasons, a work may have a complicated and confusing history. The manuscript which records it may be much later in time than the original composition, or incomplete, or otherwise unreliable. *Beowulf,* for example, thought to have been originally an oral poem of the second half of the seventh or first half of the eighth century, is preserved in a single manuscript, Cotton Vitellius A, xv, which is attributed to a tenth-century scribe but was rediscovered only in the seventeenth century in the great collection of Sir Robert Bruce Cotton. Furthermore, parts of this single manuscript have been damaged by fire and by unskillful rebinding. *The Canterbury Tales,* on the other hand, presents bibliographical problems because an extraordinary number of manuscripts exist. Professors Manly and Rickert have studied 82, of which 58 are "relatively complete." Some of these are derived one from another, so that complicated family trees have to be worked out, but a few of them seem to represent different versions, whose relative validity it is sometimes not easy to establish. Even with so many available manuscripts, the very order of the tales which Chaucer completed remains a matter of controversy and doubt.

Printed texts may present as many difficulties as manuscripts. This is especially true in the case of Elizabethan drama, since several of the major playwrights had little or nothing to do with the publication of their works. The first surviving printed edition of Marlowe's *Doctor Faustus,* for example, is dated 1604; a somewhat different, considerably expanded text was brought out in 1616. But the play is believed to have been written in 1588–1589, and Marlowe died in 1593. How reliable is each of the two texts, separated as they are from the date of composition and from each other by so many years? *Hamlet* likewise presents textual problems because it exists in several versions: two quartos of 1603 and 1604, and the folio of 1623. Curiously enough, it is the first quarto which seems to be the least reliable; it is very short and includes a number of garbled passages. The theory has been advanced that this is a "pirated" or unauthorized version, possibly based on what a minor actor could remember of the lines. The second quarto is almost twice as long as the first, and is thought to have been put out by Shakespeare's company to correct the pirated text. But it, too, has certain unclear passages, and it is probably too long to be an actual stage version. The folio, finally, has about 200 lines fewer than the second quarto but reintroduces two long passages found only in the unreliable first quarto. Thus the precise nature of each text and the relationship among the three remains something of a puzzle.

Even when the author has had a say in the publication of his work, textual problems may arise. An obvious instance is the matter of revision. When there is a wide gap between the original composition and the revised version, which one should be preserved in print? Henry James' *Portrait of a Lady* was first published in 1881, but James added most of the illuminating and memorable metaphors when he revised the novel for the New York edition of 1908. Which text should be read? Wordsworth's *Prelude* exists in a manuscript of 1805 and an extensive revision published in 1850. Most editors reprint the 1850 version, but scholars have argued that the 1805 version is clearer and more vivid, and that this should be used as the basic text. In our own time, W. H. Auden omits a climactic stanza of "September 1, 1939," the one before the last, from his *Collected Poems* (1945) and his *Collected Shorter Poems, 1930–1944* (1950), but the editors of popular anthologies, Louis Untermeyer and Oscar Williams, continue to print the full text as it appeared in *Another Time* (1940), and Joseph Warren Beach, who draws attention to this anomaly in his book *The Making of the Auden Canon,* feels that the omission leaves the poem truncated. Here both editors and a well-known scholar disapprove of the decision of the author, and the former even ignore his wishes.

Still other problems may arise because of certain public pressures. A number of serious and now admired works have at one time or another suffered from censorship, either because they expressed unpopular political and religious opinions or because they were thought to undermine public morals. Rousseau's *Émile,* his great work of educational philosophy, was condemned by the Archbishop of Paris and officially burned; the publication of Shelley's *Queen Mab,* a philosophical poem about human misery and the means of overcoming it, was prohibited by a jury trial; Joyce's *Ulysses,* his brilliant representation of modern life in Dublin ironically contrasted with classical myths, was banned from the United States from 1922, when it was first published in Paris, to 1933, when a special court order reversed an earlier legal decision and declared that it was free from obscenity. Even more problematic than the total suppression of certain works is the publication of expurgated versions, for here the reader may not be aware of what has been left out. For years, D. H. Lawrence's *Lady Chatterley's Lover* was available only in an abridged form, from which the frank and sensual love scenes were omitted; not until 1959 did a court order enable publishers to put out the full text. Restoration comedies are frequently reprinted in editions which quietly omit some of the more salacious dialogue. Even Shakespeare underwent such treatment at the hands of Dr. Thomas Bowdler, a nineteenth-century editor who systematically ruled out supposedly offensive lines. It is from his name that we now have the term **to bowdlerize,** meaning to remove passages of a book which might be considered objectionable.

As many of these examples suggest, establishing an authentic text may be a difficult and delicate task. The editor may have to track down various existing manuscripts or printed texts, and patiently compare or **collate** them in order to ascertain which ones are merely offspring of an earlier version, which ones are genuinely different versions, and of these, which one would provide the best foundation for his edition. In theory, that text is usually chosen which the author is known to have worked on last. That is why the revised New York edition of James' novels is usually reprinted, and why—to cite an earlier example—Pope's expanded version of *The Rape of the Lock* (1714), in which he introduces the sylphs, is read in preference to his first version of 1712, in which he concentrates on the adventures of the human figures. If it cannot be ascertained on which text the author worked last, as in the case of some Elizabethan plays, that one is usually chosen which is closest in time to the original. But sometimes the situation is so complicated, as it is with Marlowe's *Doctor Faustus,* that special decisions have to be made or a composite text combining readings from several versions is adopted.

Nor does the editor's task end here. It includes eliminating any obvious inconsistencies of spelling, capitalization, and punctuation, the so-called **normalizing** of the text, and often extends to a modernizing of these mechanics. Finally, if he has found unclear or garbled passages, the editor may introduce his own corrections or **emendations**—his guesses about how the passage read in the original or what the author intended. A classic example is the eighteenth-century emendation by Lewis Theobald of the incomprehensible line in *Henry V* in which Mistress Quickly says of the dying Falstaff: "his Nose was as sharpe as a pen, and a Table of greene fields." For the last words Theobald substituted "and 'a [he] babbled of green fields," a reading which is still being debated by scholars. Another disputed emendation has to do with the line in the second *Hamlet* quarto: "Oh that this too, too *sallied* flesh would melt." The key phrase appears in the folio as *"solid* flesh," but many scholars prefer *"sullied* flesh," since the second quarto elsewhere misprints *sullies* as *sallies* and since *sullied* is a better emendation than *solid* in the first quarto reading, "grieved and sallied flesh," in view of the adjective with which *sallied* is there paired.

What is noteworthy about the processes of editing is how many stages of work may come between the original and the text we finally have in our hands. As critical readers, we should be aware of the fact that printed texts are not infallible. All are not equally authentic and prepared with the same scholarly care. On the other hand, there seem to be no simple, definite rules which can be applied to the establishing of every text. Each one may present special problems, and each one can be taken only on its own terms.

Literature as Art: The Theory of Imitation

Coming back to our definition of literature as a verbal art, we must now consider another basic question: in what sense, specifically, is it an art? Various answers to this question have been offered since classical antiquity, and we shall begin by considering three of the main traditional explanations. Each of these, as M. H. Abrams has pointed out in his extensive analysis and historical survey in *The Mirror and the Lamp,* tends to describe literature in relation to something outside itself.

Perhaps the oldest and most venerable way of describing literature as an art is to regard it as a form of **imitation.** This defines literature in relation to life, seeing it as a way of reproducing or recreating the experiences of life in words, just as painting reproduces or recreates certain figures or scenes of life in outline and color. Sophocles' *Oedipus,* we might say, "imitates" or recreates the inner struggles of a proud and powerful man who is slowly forced to recognize and come to terms with the terrible truth that he has been unintentionally guilty of murdering his father and marrying his mother. Trollope's *Barchester Towers,* George Eliot's *Middlemarch,* and Thackeray's *Vanity Fair* in very different ways "imitate" or recreate middle-class life in nineteenth-century England.

Historically, the concept of art as imitation goes back to Plato and Aristotle. Plato introduced this concept in the *Republic* when he described literature and painting in derogatory terms as imitations twice removed from reality. Since reality, for him, was an ideal form, essence, or absolute—the One behind the many, the light whose shadows only are visible to mankind in its cave—anything in this world and particularly anything man-made, even a chair or a bed, seemed to be only a copy at one remove from the real. And the arts, which Plato thought of as copies of man-made objects, were only copies of a copy. With Aristotle, however, the negative sense of *imitation* dropped out. Unlike Plato, he did not regard this world as a mere shadow of another. And in any case, he believed that the instinct of imitation was an important one, implanted in men from childhood and distinguishing them from beasts. When Aristotle, at the beginning of his *Poetics,* called epic poetry, tragedy, comedy, dithyrambic poetry (which we would call the lyric), and even the music of the flute and lyre "modes of imitation" (*mimesis*), he meant simply the copying or, to use more positive terms, the representation or recreation of life. It is this more positive sense that was taken over in succeeding ages. Sir Philip Sidney, in his "Apology for Poetry," stated firmly: "Poesy therefore is an art of imitation, for so Aristotle termeth it in his word *mimesis,* that is to say, a representing, counterfeiting, or figuring forth: to speak metaphorically, a speaking picture. . . ." More common than Sidney's metaphor of a "speaking picture," which likens literature to painting, is that of a mirror. It is to the idea of imitation that Hamlet alludes when he explains to the actors that their art should "hold as 'twere the mirror up to nature" (III, ii); and Dr. Johnson also does so in his famous "Preface to Shakespeare" when he says that the great dramatist "holds up to his readers a faithful mirror of manners and of life."

If we try to evaluate this interpretation of literature, we must acknowledge that it touches on at least two important points. Taken at face value, it suggests that it is life which literature imitates or mirrors; in other words, the subject matter of literature is the manifold experiences of living people. No one would deny that this is true. But the trouble is that in saying so, we are not saying much about literature, since we are not taking into account what happens to the subject matter —which we might actually call the raw material—once it is part of a poem, play, or novel.

Quite apart from this objection, a serious difficulty arises because the very term *life* is so ambiguous as to be open to several quite different interpretations. Hamlet, we have seen, says that it is "nature" which is to be imitated, using a term so broad that it includes not only the great outdoors but also human nature on the one hand and the whole universe or cosmos on the other. Dr. Johnson alludes to "manners," thereby including social behavior as well. But these are not the only possible interpretations. Fundamentally, two very different ways of conceiving of life have been adopted at various times. One way is to think of it as all the varied and particular experiences which make up man's daily existence—what we mean when we exclaim, "What an eventful life he leads!" The other is to think of it in the much broader sense of human life in its general and enduring aspects—what we mean when we shrug our shoulders and say, "Well, that's life!" It is, then, not at all clear in what sense life is to be imitated by literature.

The second important point suggested by the theory of imitation is that life is being imitated in the sense of being reinterpreted and recreated. Here the main emphasis seems to be on *how* life is imitated—what kind of counterfeiting or figuring forth, to use Sidney's terms, will be chosen, or what kind of mirror will be used to reflect man's experiences. This view takes us closer to one of the essential facts about literature, that the raw material is reshaped and even transformed in the literary work.

But here again, it is not at all clear just what constitutes such an imitation, since much depends on how one conceives of "life" in the first place. When this is thought of as all the particular experiences of daily living, life as it usually is, the imitation is likely to be a very faithful, almost photographic reproduction, as detailed and particularized as possible. It is best exemplified by the "slice of life" which the naturalists have tried to present. When, on the other hand, life is thought of as the general and enduring aspects of existence—not as it usually is but as it ought to be—two further kinds of imitation may result. There is the conscious representation of what is typical—the description in mid-eighteenth-century poetry of "the ploughman," "the housewife," or "the village preacher," each carrying out predictable and generally recognizable tasks. And then there is the highly idealized recreation of life, whereby unusually noble or elevated figures undergo somewhat extraordinary experiences, as they do in classical drama, particularly in Greek tragedy. It was to this sort of idealizing that Aristotle first applied the term *imitation.* In either of the two cases, particulars and confusing details are avoided in order to present the broad, clear outlines of experience. Dr. Johnson described such imitation vividly when he observed, in his *Rasselas,* that "The business of a poet is to examine, not the individual, but the species; to remark general properties and large appearances; he does not number the streaks of the tulip, or describe the different shades in the verdure of the forest."

But since the concept of imitation can be interpreted in such varied and contrasting ways, we must acknowledge that it tends to be too loose a description of literature for our purposes. In any case the very term *imitation* is not entirely desirable, for the modern reader may attribute to it some of the negative sense it had for Plato—the sense that literature is *only* an imitation, not true or not the real thing. There have, of course, been times when plays or novels were looked upon with distrust because they took the attention away from supposedly more serious and "real" aspects of the world. But since few of us nowadays accept this puritanical view of literature, it would be well to avoid a term which, to modern ears at least, has such misleading connotations.

The Theory of Effect

The second traditional way of defining literature regards it in relation to its public. Since the main emphasis here is on the effect that literature may have on its readers or, in the case of drama, on its spectators, theories of this kind are sometimes called **pragmatic** (having to do with practical results), and since the effect is often thought to be mainly emotional, they are also sometimes called **affective** (the noun *affect* being synonymous, in psychology, with *emotion, feeling,* or *mood*).

The interest in the psychological experience of the audience again goes back to classical antiquity. Certainly Aristotle revealed it when he described, however ambiguously, the state of catharsis, the purging of pity and fear which he believed the audience undergoes in the course of a tragedy. Teachers of rhetoric or public speaking, notably Quintilian, showed a similar interest when they emphasized that the major aim of literature is to move the audience, to arouse a strong emotional response and thereby to give pleasure. Since that time, many different affective and pragmatic theories have been proposed. At one extreme are those which suggest that the reader or spectator becomes wholly involved with the characters and their fate, that he may identify himself so fully with them that he loses his own sense of identity. At the other extreme is the theory that the reader or spectator remains detached, with a "psychical distance" between him and the work, so that he always remains aware of the fact that he is faced not with life but with a work of art. In addition, there is frequently discussion of whether literature is purely a psychological experience or also, ultimately, a moral one. Horace provided the classical formula for this discussion when he stated, in his *Ars Poetica,* that poets either teach or delight ("Aut prodesse volunt aut delectare poetae"), at their best combining the useful and the beautiful ("Omne tulit punctum, qui miscuit utile dulci"). Since then, some critics have emphasized the element of pure delight, some the element of instruction. But the majority have felt that literature both delights and instructs, and that the two elements are, in actual fact, interrelated: to instruct, literature must delight; or, alternatively, to delight, it must also instruct.

No one, of course, would deny that literature does indeed have an effect on its readers. But the pragmatic and affective theories, no less than the mimetic ones we considered earlier, are open to several objections. For one thing, it is very hard to say just what the reader or spectator actually experiences, and much more testing and experimenting is needed in order to reach any definitive conclusions. In fact, it is unlikely that any single description will do justice to the immensely varied experiences which literature can offer. Different people may have quite different psychological responses to the same work; that is, a naïve reader may become wholly involved with the characters of a story, whereas a more sophisticated reader may remain detached. Or, on the other hand, different kinds of literature may bring about quite different experiences; one is more likely to become at least partly involved with the characters of a drama or a novel, for instance, than with the subject matter of lyric poetry. Furthermore, it is by no means easy to say in what sense, if any, literature can offer instruction; this is a problem we will have to consider in more detail later. In any case, in trying to arrive at a valid description of what the reader or spectator experiences, one is working in the difficult and as yet hardly explored field of the psychologist, which is not really that of the literary critic.

The Theory of Expression

The third traditional way of looking at literature is to relate it to its creator. In this case, it is seen as the product of the poet, dramatist, or novelist. Two chief conceptions of the poet and his work have come down from classical times. One is that the poet is divinely inspired, a prophet (*vates*), "possessed" by a muse or divinity who speaks through him. At the moment of creation, therefore, the poet is supposedly almost out of his senses, in the power of what Plato describes as a divine madness. According to this view, literature is the profoundest, divinely inspired wisdom—a testament or prophecy—created spontaneously in an ecstatic state. The other conception of the poet is that he is fundamentally a craftsman (*poeta*, "maker"), who is fully conscious of what he is doing both at the moment of composition and afterwards, when he is willing to polish and repolish his work. To use Horace's phrase, he does not spare "the labor of the file." In this case, the literary work is regarded as a piece of art in the literal sense—as something man-made which can be labored over, changed, and refined. Historically, this second view was dominant in the seventeenth and eighteenth centuries, the age of neoclassicism. But a new version of the first view became popular in the late eighteenth and nineteenth centuries, the age of romanticism. According to this version, the poet, though not literally in the possession of a divine madness, is capable of extraordinary inspiration. He is a genius who, through his imagination and emotions, is able to grasp and record truths about man which ordinary people may not recognize or feel. Literature, in this case, is regarded as a form of expression—and expression in the basic sense of a process whereby strong and irrepressible feelings are forced out. It is this process which Wordsworth describes when he calls poetry "the spontaneous overflow of powerful emotion." For obvious reasons, theories of this kind are known as **expressive**.

Naturally, we would not want to deny that literature is the product of a poet—that, whatever its ultimate source of inspiration, it is created by one particular person. But to this third view of literature, as to the first two, certain objections can be raised. Is there sufficient evidence, we might ask, to support the conceptions of the poet and his work which we have just reviewed? Are the two chief conceptions mutually exclusive? And are there not, perhaps, still other and quite different interpretations of the creative process? For just as the pragmatic and affective theories tended to focus on the psychology of the audience, so these theories focus on the psychology of the poet, and, to be tenable, they should be tested by experimentation. Once again we must recognize that we are forsaking the field of literary criticism for that of psychology.

The three traditional ways of regarding literature, then, even though they draw attention to certain undeniable qualities of a literary work, are, in the long run, incomplete and unsatisfactory. Whereas they emphasize the relationship between literature and something else—its subject matter, its audience, or its originator—we are looking for ways of describing the special and distinctive quality of a literary work *per se*.

The Idea of Fictionality

One such way has been suggested by critics who speak of the fictionality or of the virtual world one finds in literature, in order to suggest what happens *within* a literary work. For though the work is usually, in one way or another, a reflection or recreation of the world and of life —what earlier critics called an imitation—we are certainly aware of the fact that it is not, after all, the world and not real life. The drama and the novel offer the best examples of this virtual world, a world which seems to be but is not the real one. They present characters undergoing recognizable human experiences, whether ordinary or extraordinary, usually at some definite time and in an identifiable place. We may even feel, occasionally, that we know the characters so well that they seem like old acquaintances, and we may then be tempted to wonder what kind of life they led before the play or novel opens. What did Hamlet study in Wittenberg, and what sort of wife did King Lear have? If we recognize that these speculations are as absurd as asking what is on the other side of a hedge shown in a landscape painting, we are acknowledging that however lifelike the characters may seem, they are not moving in the real world but in a fictional world of their own. The same is true even of short lyrics. In these, the poet often seems to be speaking in his own voice and of his personal experiences. But in another sense, he is usually presenting himself only in a single mood—as a languishing lover, or a mourner bidding farewell to a departed friend, or a wedding guest hymning the praises of the bride and groom. Thus he is already a fictional character in incipient form, and he is moving about in a fictional world, which may resemble ours but is not, after all, the world in which we move.

The Idea of Structure

The concept of fictionality or of a virtual world is a useful way of distinguishing literature from actuality and the real world of experience. But it does not, by itself, adequately suggest what happens to the material within the literary work. To do so, a second concept has been proposed, that a piece of literature is to be regarded as a **structure**. Although this idea has been interpreted in several rather special senses, it means, fundamentally, that each work is a highly complex organization and that its many components or facets are interrelated in such a way that the whole is greater than its parts. Used in this sense, the term does not refer only to the formal aspects—the parallels or contrasts of scenes, the climactic or anticlimactic ordering of the plot—but includes the whole of a literary work. In other words, each work not only has a structure but is a structure. In the romantic period, a similar idea was expressed by saying that a poem, novel, or drama has "organic form," thereby comparing it with a living organism, none of whose parts can be destroyed without crippling the rest. But since pieces of literature do not grow or develop as plants and animals do, it seems better to use the other metaphor—provided we think of a structure not just as the mechanical putting together of assorted ingredients but as a vital and dynamic interrelationship of plot, character, tone, style, and all the other component parts.

If we look at literature in this way, we become aware of the unity or integrity of each work, a quality which is vividly illustrated by what happens when haphazard changes are attempted. In the eighteenth century, for instance, Nahum Tate brought out what he considered a superior version of *King Lear,* in which the fool is omitted and the play ends happily. But these changes make all the difference to the tone and the meaning. Without the fool's seemingly mad but actually wise and moving lines, much of the bitter comment on Lear's plight is lost. Without the shocking murder of Cordelia in prison, there is no sense of what has been called "tragic waste"—the lamentable loss of the good in the final great upheaval along with the unregretted destruction of the wicked. And without the death of King Lear, which comes as a merciful release from all his suffering, the long and hard process of Lear's physical downfall but moral regeneration remains incomplete, or, at least, does not end with the appropriate finality. All that Tate manages to accomplish is to dramatize the much simpler process of poetic justice, whereby the good are rewarded when Lear and Cordelia are reunited and regain the kingdom, whereas the wicked characters are suitably punished. Not only these larger elements of plot and character, however, but also the style, the very way in which the meaning is expressed in words, is an integral part of the whole. Matthew Arnold, speaking in the 1880's, touched on this point when he complained of the student who paraphrased the line from *Macbeth,* "Canst thou not minister to a mind diseased?" with the words "Can you not wait upon the lunatic?" Shakespeare's line is elevated enough to suggest the dignity of Macbeth and the importance of the scene. The student's version, in contrast, is so flat as to sound almost flippant.

The idea that a literary work is a verbal structure—that it has a complex unity or integrity—has important ramifications. Once we accept it, we will not be satisfied with interpretations which are based only on parts of a work instead of taking the whole into account. *Gulliver's Travels* provides a classic example of how quite different interpretations can result, depending on whether one isolates the ending or relates it to the preceding action. Taken by itself, the ending seems to be unmitigatedly pessimistic. On his last voyage, Gulliver has learned to respect and admire the Houyhnhnms, the noble and completely rational horses, and to despise the Yahoos, the filthy and completely irrational creatures who resemble men. Once he is back in England, Gulliver is so revolted by his own kind that he can hardly bear their company and yearns to be back among the horses. The revulsion against mankind which he experiences has been assumed by some critics to express Swift's own feelings. But when the ending is seen in relation to the rest of the book, it no longer seems so wholly bitter. Throughout, Swift has been working with extremes, of which he does not necessarily approve. The tiny people of Lilliput, the giants of Brobdingnag, the mad scientists of Laputa—these are greatly exaggerated views of certain aspects of human life which Swift is satirizing. It is more than likely that the Houyhnhnms, too, are an extreme, just as the Yahoos are, and that Swift does not consider the former's perfect wisdom and rationality attainable or even desirable ideals for man. Furthermore, throughout the book Gulliver is a comic hero, whose reactions are often foolish and misguided; there is no guarantee that his extreme position at the end is Swift's last word on his fellow men.

The idea of structure also makes us distrust the old-fashioned division into form and content, or form and subject matter. Such a division is not just undesirable but impossible, if we accept the idea that the subject matter is patterned, reshaped, and ultimately transformed in a piece of literature. For how can we say where the subject matter ends and the form begins? To quote W. B. Yeats' tantalizing question, "How can we know the dancer from the dance?" Furthermore, if we recognize that we cannot isolate the subject matter, we will not be tempted to equate this with the total meaning of a work. One could describe Milton's *Samson Agonistes* as if it were the same as the Bible story, since both have as their subject matter the antagonism experienced by Samson, Delilah, and the Philistines, and both end with Samson's pulling down of the temple. But this description comes nowhere near the essence of Milton's dramatic poem. Taking the almost anecdotal folk story of the Book of Judges, Milton has transformed it into a classical tragedy by imposing on it the unities of time, place, and action, by adding a chorus to comment on Samson's experiences, and above all, by concentrating not on the physical exploits but on the moral struggles of his hero. He shows the blind and captive Samson in his final hours, in which he resists various temptations, learns to submit to God's will with patience, and thereby makes himself worthy of carrying out his task, the destruction of the Philistine temple. Thus the story of Judges, which glorifies the strength and virility of a legendary hero, becomes, in Milton's hands, the very different story of how a tragic hero achieves moral and spiritual regeneration.

Nor will we be tempted to equate the total meaning of a poem, play, or story with its apparent purpose or "message," any more than with its subject matter. The moral of Chaucer's "Pardoner's Tale" is that love of money is the root of all evil, and this moral is stated explicitly by the Pardoner a number of times in the course of his lengthy sermon. But the moral is ironically qualified, and the narrative is given a larger meaning, because this sermon is really a story within a story, and because it is preached by a man who himself would lie, cheat, and do almost anything for money. Not only is Chaucer emphasizing the sin of avarice by such a twist; he is also brilliantly satirizing the sins of hypocrisy and ruthlessness, simply by letting the Pardoner's words and actions speak for themselves. In a less obvious example, the explicit moral of Hawthorne's story "Ethan Brand" is that when a man loses his sympathy for fellow creatures, loses "hold of the magnetic chain of humanity," he commits the unpardonable sin. But the meaning of "Ethan Brand" is much more complex than this moral. It includes a series of carefully established contrasts—between the experiences of an innocent but sensitive child, who instinctively recognizes something strange and terrible in Brand, and the child's experienced but obtuse father, who is interested only in keeping his lime-kiln going; between the natural darkness of the setting and the diabolical light thrown by the kiln; between the laughter, the comic and the grotesque elements in the story and the essentially terrible events that are referred to or occur—failures, acts of cruelty, and, at last, a suicide. These contrasts make us feel the moral much more vividly than the simple statement of this moral, but more than that, they extend the meaning by bringing in the related experiences of the minor characters and even the collusion of the forces of nature or the universe. Certainly, then, the total meaning may be greater than any explicitly stated message.

Just as the idea of fictionality or of a virtual world is a useful way of distinguishing literature from actual experience, so the idea of structure enables us to distinguish literature from other uses of language. Most documents are interesting chiefly for what they say, for how accurately they express something that has happened or is about to happen. A telegram states as clearly and concisely as possible the time of someone's arrival, the answer to an urgent query, or some other item of important information; a legal document sets down as unambiguously as possible the facts of an accident or crime, or the testator's disposition of his property. Since accuracy, clarity, and conciseness are the main qualities we look for in such statements, we might well be equally satisfied with a paraphrase which had these virtues. In literature, on the other hand, we are interested not only in what is being said but also in how the language is used. For one thing, the plot and the characters owe their very existence to the words which recount them—they have no other being than in these words. For another, the style is, as we shall see, quite as much an integral part of the whole as the larger elements of plot, character, or setting. In this case, we would not be satisfied with a paraphrase, which tends to reduce a poem, novel, or drama to its bare outlines. Finally, we may be less concerned with how accurately one of these works transcribes an actual occurrence—often there can be no real question of such transcription, anyway, since the characters and action are invented—than with the kind of world or vision or interpretation of life that has been achieved within the work. It is, in fact, a distinctive feature which literature shares with the other arts but which differentiates it from other uses of language that, rather than making us look from what is being expressed to what is being referred to, it makes us look squarely at itself, at its internal relationships. Like the other arts, literature can be studied and appreciated for its own sake, as a value in itself.

CHAPTER TWO

The Analysis of Literature

Our discussion of literary works as structures has suggested that we want to focus attention first and foremost on the poem, play, or story, and that we are interested primarily in how the manifold parts contribute to the total meaning. This is not, however, to say that the total meaning is merely a summing-up of components, or that even the simplest lyric is a blandly homogeneous object: the various parts of a work are not absorbed into the whole. One of the most pervasive ideas in contemporary criticism is that a literary piece of any value is a complex unity, that it includes within itself various *tensions*—contrasts, oppositions, even apparent contradictions. It may exhibit, for example, tension between strict artifice of form (rhyme, meter, stanza) and naturalness of language, or between a cool, detached manner of writing and a subject matter that includes violence and passion, or between the apparent significance of a character's speech and its less obvious, quite different meaning. The contrasts within Hawthorne's story "Ethan Brand," between wise innocence and dull experience, between grimly comic and ironically tragic events, are further instances of tension. The elements strain against each other, but in doing so they help to hold the story together.

Analysis of parts and details, then, as well as generalization on the total effect of a story or poem, regularly enters into critical reading. This analysis is a delicate task, for if we agree that the whole is likely to be greater than the sum of its parts and that we cannot always know the dancer from the dance, we will want to avoid any mechanical "taking apart" of a work for fear of murdering to dissect. We can take comfort in the thought that probably no one ever grasps the whole meaning of a great poem. Still, we must recognize that it is our business, and our pleasure, as critical readers to try. We will want to be careful not to simplify or falsify what we read by taking the part for the whole; we will want to read conscientiously; and we will want to use our terms with care.

Plot and Character

No critical words call for more care in use than the familiar ones *plot* and *character*. E. M. Forster is inclined to regard the two as potential rivals, in the novel at least, so that a well-planned plot, clearly posing some conflict and resolving it, may have to be achieved at the expense of completely believable characters. But when he writes of this conflict, Forster seems to be thinking of decisions to be made by the novelist and not of discriminations required of a reader. From the reader's point of view, plot and characterization cannot be clearly distinguished in most stories, for the plot (including dialogue) amounts simply to how the characters act and react. It is true that some stories tend to emphasize the actions of a character, so that we know more of the way he behaves than of how he thinks or feels, and that others tend to make outward actions minimal and subsidiary to the persons' motives and states of mind. This difference in emphasis can be described, in striking instances, as the difference between a highly plotted story—say, a murder mystery—and a character study, such as Virginia Woolf's *Mrs. Dalloway*. But the murder mystery must have some characterization, and *Mrs. Dalloway* has a real if tenuous plot.

Essentially, the **plot** is a narrative of motivated action, involving some conflict or question which is finally resolved. "A narrative" does not necessarily mean a simple sequence of events; although the normal mode of development in fiction is chronological, this pattern of movement in time (the pattern of "and then . . . and then") is often altered for special purposes. For instance, the novelist may bring into the narrative sequence scenes that literally occurred earlier, using a device to which the motion-picture term **flashback** is often given. Some writers, notably William Faulkner, even use a technique that might be called the "flash forward," interrupting the flow of time to describe what is going to occur years after the events now being narrated. Strictly speaking, the flashback is a shifting of focus, not just an extended reference by either the characters or the narrator to past occurrences, but sometimes the same effect can be achieved by the writer's introducing a story within his story. This technique allows one character to tell other characters about what happened earlier, at such length and in such detail that we become more fully conscious of the past actions being described than of the narrative present in which the person is speaking. All such devices—the flashback, interpolated narrative, and extensive reference to past events—are especially useful to the author of any work that follows the epic formula by starting *in medias res,* in the middle of things. Virgil's *Aeneid,* for instance, begins in the middle of Aeneas' journey from Troy to Italy and refers later to the occasion for the journey and its progress up to this point.

The plot is a narrative, then, not necessarily chronological but often varying the normal pattern of sequence in time, and a narrative of motivated action. When we speak of motivated action, it should be evident again, from another vantage point, why there can be no true plot without some characterization. Forster himself, writing on "Plot" in *Aspects of the Novel,* illustrates the importance of the characters' motivation when he says that a plot differs from a simple story by including causality.

> "The king died and then the queen died" is a story. "The king died and then the queen died of grief" is a plot. The time-sequence is preserved, but the sense of causality overshadows it. Or again: "the queen died, no one knew why, until it was discovered that it was through grief at the death of the king." This is a plot with a mystery in it, a form capable of high development.[1]

Forster's third example introduces the element of **suspense,** which is essential to the mystery story. Along with this piquing and sustaining of our curiosity will sometimes go a counterbalancing use of hints as to the outcome of an action, called **foreshadowing.** Foreshadowing may take the form of verbal prophecies, often cryptic, or of significant events or objects. One instance is that of the woman in Henry James' "The Pupil," whose soiled gloves are the only initial hint of her soiled character, which is later to reveal itself fully. A more dramatic one is the series of prophecies uttered by the three witches in *Macbeth,* which augur of greatness for Macbeth and yet sound ominous:

> Macbeth shall never vanquished be, until
> Great Birnam wood to high Dunsinane Hill
> Shall come against him.

Later the boughs of Birnam wood are carried by the forces which attack Dunsinane.

Both of these terms, *suspense* and *foreshadowing,* imply the arousing of a question in the mind of the reader and possibly in the minds of the characters. It may be a simple question of fact directly posed by the plot: Who killed the beautiful heiress? Did John steal the money? Or the question may take the form of a conflict that is central to the story: Will Hamlet kill the king? Will John decide to steal the money? The king and Hamlet are struggling to answer the first question, and the struggle to answer the second goes on in John's mind. Such a question may be very slight: Will the boy kiss the girl good-night or not? And it may be very subtle: What will this character's emotional reaction be to an inevitable event? But, regardless of subtlety or the lack of it, there would seem

[1] From *Aspects of the Novel* by E. M. Forster, copyright 1927 by Harcourt, Brace & World, Inc.; renewed 1955 by E. M. Forster. Reprinted by permission of Harcourt, Brace & World, Inc.

Jones are; or, infrequently, they will prove to be misleading. What one character says about another may also be a means of characterizing a person who has not yet revealed himself. And the narrative account of the actions and speeches of a fictional person, which we consider as a part of the plot, can provide the characterization of the speaker or actor, showing more perhaps than the person himself is supposed to realize of his nature—although the contrived speeches of a villain like Iago in *Othello* may be in direct contrast to his actions. In general, of course, characters who prove themselves by talking and acting before our eyes are more likely to seem complex and convincing than those about whom we are only told.

But in certain novels of ideas and moral tales this complexity is not the point; the characters are not conceived so as to seem particular or unique. They are, instead, **types** representing categories of men. Allegorical figures are almost always of this kind. So are the embodiments of the "humors" in Renaissance stage comedy, those characters who demonstrate one of the four temperaments, sanguine, phlegmatic, choleric, and melancholy. More familiar, and often less defensible, are the **stock characters** of popular literature: the stage Irishman, the tough but sentimental private detective, the prostitute with a heart of only slightly alloyed gold. Quite full and rich stories, nevertheless, which are neither allegorical nor conventionally comic can include so-called **flat characters.** In fact, the contrast between such a figure and a **round character** is one among the many sorts of contrasts and parallels which characters can provide, and it may amount to an important element in the structure of a story. The least interesting examples would be those of "round" heroes or protagonists and "flat" villains or antagonists. But there are also "flat" central characters like Melville's Billy in the long story *Billy Budd,* who is complemented, as he is judged, by the more fully realized character Captain Vere.

One of the problems raised by *Billy Budd* is the question of which of these men, Billy and "Starry" Vere, is the central character. A possible answer is that they are both central because they represent two opposed ways of viewing the human personality: one which sees man as essentially innocent and as transcending in his purity both the past and the legal constraints of society; one which sees man as essentially imperfect, as the product of history who must discipline his impulses in order to preserve society and himself. Because the story presents a contrast between these two conceptions, its central tension would be lost if either character were subordinated to the other. In this and in other stories the term *protagonist* is difficult to apply. Indeed, a very significant fact in the structure of some modern plays and novels is that there is no single hero or main character. Chekhov, for instance, usually presents a group of

to be two kinds of questions, or problems, that a plot can pose. One is the problem of what has in fact happened or will happen; the other is the problem of how some tension or opposition within the lives of the characters will be resolved. Only the second kind, strictly speaking, involves a conflict—either a conflict between two people, or, on the other hand, a conflict within one person's mind between alternative ways of acting. A single story may include all of these, questions of fact, conflicts between characters, and conflicts within the minds of characters, as *Hamlet* does. But there are plots, like those of detective tales and some stories by O. Henry, in which suspense derives entirely from questions of what has occurred or will occur, not from any active opposition of character against character or of motive against motive. These are plots for which the ending, often a surprise ending or "twist," is all-important, providing the final answer, plausible or not, to one question. Sometimes, then, the essence of a plot can be described as conflict, but for other plots the term *problem* would seem to be more appropriate.

Certain works of fiction display, not a single major question to be resolved, but a succession of more or less equally significant ones. This is especially true of stories that have what is called an **episodic** construction, by which is meant the stringing together, as it were, of a series of episodes or events, very often events that could be isolated and told as separate tales. A pattern may be worked out or themes may recur in this series of episodes, but often the only apparent unity in such a novel lies in each adventure's involving the same main character, the effect being that of a series of related plots. There are also stories in which each question, as soon as it is resolved, gives way to a larger question, until a climax is reached. And, especially in the drama, the narrative may be complicated by a **double plot,** the secondary plot or **subplot** being related to the main action either as a **contrast** or as a parallel and complement. The plot problem or conflict, then, can be either tenuous or multiple and extremely complicated.

Most of the elaborate analyses of plot have tried to account for rather complicated single structures, excluding subplots. Aristotle, whose emphasis on unity of action has had an enormous influence on critics, regards that unity as resulting when an action is single and continuous, with a beginning, middle, and end. The Renaissance and neoclassical critics, elaborating on Aristotle, often insist upon a literal observance of **the three unities** of action, time, and place, so that a play should represent actions that cover no more than two or three hours and occur in a single place. But the unity of action is the most important kind of unity in the *Poetics,* and it is a criterion that applies to other kinds of literature as well as to the drama. Aristotle also analyzes the complex tragic plot in greater detail, as including a **reversal,** or **peripeteia,** of the protagonist's (the main character's) fortunes, his **recognition** of this change, and a conclusion in suffering, or a catastrophe. And he refers to the part of the tragedy which precedes the critical change in fortune as the **complication** and that which follows as the unraveling, or **denouement**. Similarly, a nineteenth-century analysis of dramatic plot, proposed by Gustav Freytag, uses the terms **rising action, climax,** and **falling action.** But perhaps the most elaborate pattern of all is that which includes seven parts or stages. These are the **exposition,** the explaining of the situation in which a main action is to occur; the **inciting moment,** at which the nature of the problem first appears; the **development;** the **climax,** the turning point when the crucial question or conflict in the story is presented directly, to be solved one way or another; the **denouement,** the working out of a solution; **final suspense;** and the **conclusion.** Rigid as these categories may seem, they can be enlarged, reduced, and reordered: clearly, some stories have almost no "final suspense," and many give us the necessary exposition during the development, after the problem that is to lead to the climax of the story has been introduced. But, like other terms for analysis, these may be useful. They may provide a means of indicating what elements in a story are especially significant. If, for instance, we were to apply them to such a familiar matter for fiction as the tale of Cinderella, we would have to recognize at once how many different treatments of a subject are possible. In one that emphasized the fairy-tale magic of the material, the inciting moment would be the appearance of the fairy godmother, but in a modern psychological version the inciting moment might well be Cinderella's hearing about the ball and wanting to attend it.

Resolution, falling action, and *denouement* are all rather unsatisfactory words for the rounding-off of a plot. *Resolution* suggests a too neat ending, whereas the proper conclusion of a story may be a person's coming to realize that no resolution is possible for his difficulty; the plot question, then, is how he will face his situation, and the resolution for the reader is, in effect, that there is no resolution for the character. *Falling action* makes the ending sound both easy and anticlimactic. And *denouement* seems to signify the unraveling of a mystery and not to allow for the more subtle answering of a psychological problem. Nevertheless, all of these terms imply the artistic necessity that a plot shall realize its own implicit conclusion. None of them could be applied to the ending frowned upon by Aristotle, in which a **deus ex machina** appears, a god lowered from the heavens to solve all conflicts, or to other such easy, arbitrary, and implausible ways of neatly finishing the story.

The saving coincidence of any kind has been disdained by most critics, on the reasonable grounds that fiction cannot afford to be as strange as truth. But the great English novelist who dares most frequently to use coincidence, Charles Dickens, makes it part of his intensifying and

exaggerating of actual life, which is full of odd chances an The coincidences belong within Dickens' world of complex int ships partly hinted and partly hidden, and they do not appear t as crucial coincidences in the naturalistic stories of Hardy do. (objection to coincidence, then, is one not so much to improbab inconsistency: when a plot is resolved by such an event, the cc is likely to be irrelevant to, and of a different order from, the the work. The form has been violated, the rules implied and have been broken. We may reject the neoclassical version of th unities but still recognize that in one sense the criterion of unity vant: the beginning, middle, and end are to be of a piece.

Finally, the problem of analyzing the plot of a literary w never wholly solved by the mechanical use of any set of terms or d Under the large heading of *development,* for instance, we still h consider the various ways of sustaining an action and leading it climax, including the method which produces a series of revela about matters of fact and that which shows psychological changes character. These two sorts of development are combined by Dicken *Great Expectations,* where Pip comes to learn about his origins an the same time gradually changes as a person. One has to observe, the peculiar natures of particular narrative patterns. The events in a sto may have a symmetry like that in Homer's *Iliad,* which begins with foreign father's attempt to ransom his living daughter from the haugh Achaeans and ends with another foreign father's attempt to ransom dead son from the same Achaeans. It may follow the linear moveme in space of a quest, like Dante's *Divine Comedy,* which spirals direct from earth through hell and purgatory to heaven, or Mark Twain *Huckleberry Finn,* which progresses toward its conclusion down th Mississippi River. And it may move not through space but backward i memory and then slowly forward again in time, like Proust's seven-vo ume *Remembrance of Things Past* or Faulkner's short story "Was." O the movement of a work may appear to be aimless and loose, rather thar planned or symmetric: in Goethe's *Faust,* for instance, there is an un predictable, fluid, dreamlike treatment of events in time and space, pro ducing what has been called an **open form.** As these examples suggest, the plot involves both the point of view and the setting of a work. But it also involves, and is most clearly related to, the nature of the characters.

The subject of **character** is no more simple in itself than that of plot. There are, first of all, several means by which a writer may characterize his people. He may, in the role of narrator, describe and pass judgment on these creatures of his imagination before he allows us to see them in action. Sometimes the descriptions and judgments will be not literally intended but ironic, as Fielding's comments on the people in *Tom*

people who are involved with one another in various ways, and no one of whom wholly dominates the scene.

Another version of this problem of identifying the protagonist occurs when a story is presented as being written or spoken by a character who is himself involved in the narrative. Conrad's *Heart of Darkness* is a tale told by a man named Marlow about his experiences in Africa, including the death in his presence of the corrupted and crazed white man Kurtz. These experiences have filled Marlow with a despairing sense of the darkness underlying civilization, of the moral darkness in the hearts of all men. *Heart of Darkness* can be read as the story of Kurtz, upon which Marlow gives the author's commentary, or as the story of Marlow, an idealist who has been shattered by his disillusionment; or, again, it may be that the two characters are of equal importance.

Point of View

Now, with the reference to a narrator, we find ourselves considering the new subject of point of view and the question of whose words or minds we are reading when we read a poem or a story. Sometimes the answer seems to be easy: in this novel, Daniel Defoe is writing; in that poem, Alfred Tennyson. And, according to one meaning of the phrase, the points of view are Defoe's and Tennyson's. *Moll Flanders* is written from the view of a middle-class journalist turned novelist, and it reveals his interests as well as his style; *Maud* is written by a Victorian poet who is fascinated by morbid states of mind and is inclined to be fearful of passions. But in a stricter and more technical sense—and this is the sense in which the phrase **point of view** is usually employed by critics—the term refers to the eyes and mind through which actions are represented as being screened. Moll Flanders herself is writing her story, and the former lover of Maud is telling his.

Perhaps the most familiar point of view in fiction is that of the **omniscient author**, who takes us from place to place with ease and even moves freely into and out of the minds of his characters. The writer who uses this device may or may not introduce his own comments into the narrative: the extreme, and rather old-fashioned, instance of his doing so would be the use of such a phrase as "I must warn the reader. . . ." Another common point of view might be called the **third person limited**, in which the narrator again tells the story conventionally, using third-person pronouns, but limits himself and his reader to whatever knowledge or feelings one character would have. Henry James often employs this method. Or the writer can use a **first-person** narrator, already illustrated by our references to Defoe's Moll Flanders and to Tennyson's morbid lover of Maud. Sometimes, by the way, this narrator is not a central figure in the action but, like Conrad's Marlow in *Lord Jim* (if not in *Heart of Darkness*), is primarily an observer.

A modern variation on the first-person point of view is the device called **stream of consciousness**, by which not the spoken or written words of a character but his very thoughts become the medium of the story. This device, used by James Joyce in *Ulysses*, by Virginia Woolf, and sometimes by Faulkner, is not common and should not be confused with a narrator's extended account of the character's thoughts. A passage which applies the third-person pronoun to its subject ("he remembered," "he imagines") is not an example of this technique. "Stream of consciousness" can be called the ultimate attempt by a writer to absorb plot into character. It represents a nearly total abdication of the writer's explicit point of view in favor of the character's, so that the mode of development is neither strictly logical nor strictly chronological but purely psychological. In it, the exposition of fact and the development of theme proceed as they would in a person's mind, according to association of ideas. A more conventional story can make arbitrary but rational transitions: "Even at the end of this long day, standing alone in the rose garden and thinking of how tired she was, Margaret stood erect, as her maiden Aunt Helen had taught her to when she was eleven and a very unladylike orphan." But the stream of consciousness has to provide transitions that are as irrational (and lacking in formal syntax) as the flow of impressions in the mind: "Overblown roses like the ones on Aunt Helen's old hat when she made me stand up good Lord fifteen years ago already just after Mother died. . . ." With its advantage for probing into a character's personality and suggesting his half-conscious associations and motives, the device is nevertheless a difficult one for writers to use, so that the thoughts transcribed are neither too neat and plotted to seem real, on the one hand, nor, on the other, too chaotic and free-flowing to serve the economy of a plot, in which every detail should be somehow relevant to the whole meaning.

To some extent, all highly imaginative writing involves a point of view that is not merely or literally the author's. The "I" of a poem or story is never quite identical with the personality of the writer but is in part a projection of his mind, a *persona* or mask through which he speaks. Although we may be tempted to read certain poems as primarily personal statements, we must remember that all art is oblique and not perfectly direct, that it embodies and does not only state its meaning. It is a difficult and subtle problem, sometimes, to distinguish between the voice of a poem and the voice of the poet. But we should be careful not to confuse Shakespeare with his character Polonius, for instance. We cannot assume that the advice in *Hamlet*, "This above all, to thine own self be true," is necessarily the playwright's message to us.

Setting

The writer's point of view allows him to select what he wishes to observe about people and give emphasis to the motives of certain characters. Another way in which he emphasizes significant details is the description, either by the narrator himself or by a character, of the setting. The word **setting**, when it is applied to the drama, means the visible background and furnishings of a stage. But it is also taken in a larger sense, especially when applied to a novel or a poem, so as to include the times and places in which the action occurs. The setting for Jane Austen's *Pride and Prejudice,* for instance, is early nineteenth-century England, or, more specifically, the country houses of minor English gentry in that period; the setting for Hawthorne's *Scarlet Letter* is colonial Boston and its vicinity, including the town and countryside, the homes of high and low, the pulpit and the prison. The narrow range of life provided by Jane Austen's setting, including only one level of society in one small area in one brief period, suggests her concern with the nice observation of particular people and actions. But setting takes on a different significance in Hawthorne, to reveal his large vision of symbolic places and objects and moral behavior.

Setting, then, is a term that can apply to the furniture of one room or to a whole era and nation. The setting of a story may be important in that it affects action and character: Jane Austen's people are the product of their world and would be out of place, with their dances and diversions, in Hawthorne's Puritan New England. Or it may act primarily to reflect rather than to define action and character: the disarray of a bedroom or the ramshackle state of a house often display the qualities of the resident, and sometimes they hint at a story. Or, finally, setting may embody a larger meaning in the work, a theme or idea that is implied in other elements of structure as well. The fog which is described at length in Dickens' *Bleak House* serves as an image for the fog of legal confusion which hangs about the novel. The snow in James Joyce's story "The Dead" suggests to the characters, as it does to the reader, a cold and deathlike quality in themselves and in their world. And the house called Howard's End, in Forster's novel with that title, can be taken to represent the English nation.

There are other stories, and poems, in which some place holds our attention as the center of the work, virtually playing the role of a main character. A famous example from fiction is Egdon Heath in Thomas Hardy's *Return of the Native.* And it is evident that the scene is all-important in such a poem as Wordsworth's "Tintern Abbey." In a less obvious sense, "Wessex," a part of England that is the setting for most of Hardy's fiction, becomes as important an element in that fiction as the

English Lake Country does in so much of Wordsworth's poetry. When a novel or story derives a good deal of its peculiar quality from the evocation of some less familiar or more picturesque area than even "Wessex" or the Lake Country, it may be called an instance of **local-color** fiction. George Washington Cable's stories of Creole Louisiana might be included in this category; or Sarah Orne Jewett's *Country of the Pointed Firs,* tales about the coast of Maine; or Rumer Godden's novels describing life in India. But the term *local color* is somewhat arbitrary and relative, because a setting may seem strange and colorful to an American and not to an English reader, to a native of California and not to a native of South Dakota. Furthermore, in using the phrase one may seem to suggest that the work so described is interesting mainly for its transcription of local peculiarities rather than for such profound qualities as the greatest literature displays; and partly for this reason, men like Hardy and Mark Twain are not often included among the local-color writers.

Symbolism and Allegory

A number of the settings mentioned by way of example—Hardy's Egdon Heath, Forster's Howard's End, Joyce's snow, and Dickens' fog— might be referred to as symbolic. Indeed, the subject of setting in fiction, like that of imagery in verse, is very likely to lead into the more difficult problem of literary symbolism, a problem which we have now to consider.

Because the term is applied in various ways, there is probably no single neat definition for it that is quite satisfactory. A **symbol** may be any object that suggests a larger meaning than itself: in this sense all literary works are symbolic and so is every word. Or the term can refer, more precisely, to any object that has been given conventional significance by a history of general usage, like the cross, a symbol of Christianity. Or, in the sense that applies especially to literature, a symbol may be any object or even action that embodies the nature of a class of things or an abstract idea—the white whale in Melville's *Moby-Dick,* for instance, and perhaps the character of Christian in Bunyan's *Pilgrim's Progress.* But this definition is not final, for it would include, under the still very general heading of symbolism, allegorical figures like Bunyan's hero; and critics since the time of Coleridge have been interested in distinguishing the symbolic, given a more particular and limited meaning, from the allegorical.

Until the period of romantic criticism, however, the word *symbol* was used in this way when it was used at all, often with emphasis upon what modern readers would call the device of **allegory.** This literary device, although it is not now fashionable, has a long and honorable history, running in English literature from medieval drama—*Everyman* is a good example—through such Renaissance works as Spenser's *Faerie Queene* down (in spite of fashion) to the present. There are distinct allegorical elements, for example, in the religious fantasies of Charles Williams and C. S. Lewis. In the traditional allegory every major character is likely to be a personification of at least one quality or idea, and, very often, the settings are typical rather than particular. Bunyan's Christian represents the Christian soul and does not have to be taken literally as a human being in order to make sense; his slough of despond means the despairing state of mind and need not be thought of as a slough at all. Another way of putting it is to describe a simple allegory as only the extension of a metaphor. Instead of saying that the Christian soul is like a wanderer in this world, beset by temptations and trials, the allegorist tells a story of this wanderer and shows him being attacked by personified temptations or frustrated by projections of his own weakness and folly. It is difficult for a writer of allegory to maintain an exact parallel, so that, for instance, everything Britomart, or Chastity, does in *The Faerie Queene* can be said to represent something that the virtue of chastity "does." In effect, if a story is at all complicated, this so-called one-to-one relationship of the personification to the idea cannot be perfectly consistent. But the result is often failure, as with Tennyson's treatment of Arthur in *Idylls of the King,* when it appears to be radically inconsistent—when a character is sometimes strictly and merely allegorical and sometimes not.

In the most complex allegories, furthermore, there is something more than a one-to-one relationship, because the story operates on several levels. Spenser's Britomart represents Queen Elizabeth in one aspect as well as the abstraction Chastity. And the greatest of allegories, Dante's *Divine Comedy,* provides a one-to-four relationship of image and idea in certain passages, for the poet indicates that he has drawn from a medieval tradition of interpreting events upon four levels at once—the literal, the political, the moral, and the anagogical or mystical. In Dante, the form of an eagle can be literally composed of flames representing human spirits, but also signify politically the legitimate imperial power, morally the virtue of justice, and mystically the heavenly state of souls which are unified in their beatitude. The allegory becomes so complicated in this instance that it is very close to what is commonly called symbolism. And in fact many allegorical works, like Dante's, include elements that must be considered symbolic according to even the most rigorous definition.

There are several ways of defining symbolism so as to distinguish it from allegory. In allegory, some critics have said, the meanings of the tale are meant to be clear, whereas symbolism provides overtones and suggestions of meaning rather than keys; or, according to another formulation, the characters in allegory are cardboard-flat, but in a symbolic work the characters seem to be complicated people. Still another way of making the distinction is to define a literary symbol as being first of all an object (a thing or place) which is represented so that it seems real; and, second, an object which embodies special significance as the result of the way it acts upon or is acted upon by other objects, and especially the characters, in a story, a poem, or a play. The two crucial ideas in this definition are reality and relationship: the symbol takes on more than literal significance by being what it literally is and by being related to other things. To illustrate the first point, we might observe that an allegorical eagle is likely to speak poetry and even theology but is not likely to fly and almost certainly will not moult feathers, whereas a symbolic eagle would probably fly and quite certainly could not speak, because real eagles cannot. To illustrate the second point, we can refer to the whale called Moby-Dick. Unlike the whale in a medieval bestiary that is explicitly identified as signifying the devil, Moby-Dick is given extraordinary significance only because characters in Melville's novel react to him more intensely than men usually would, as if he were the embodiment of evil or of some ultimate mystery.

As this instance suggests, there are difficulties and dangers in interpreting symbols. The wide range of possible meanings for Moby-Dick is not unlimited, and the critical reader will not accept every interpretation as valid. But how does one control the reading of symbols and avoid the "reading in" of purely personal and irrelevant meanings? When an object in a story or poem appears to be more important than it would normally or literally be, either because of repetition and emphasis or the characters' reactions to it, can we be fairly sure of its nature? Not always —and the critic should beware of pressing explication beyond a reading which he can reasonably defend—but sometimes, yes, if we are willing to give interpretations that we understand to be partial and not exhaustive. Suppose we look at Blake's "The Sick Rose" for an example:

> O Rose, thou art sick!
> The invisible worm,
> That flies in the night,
> In the howling storm,
>
> Has found out thy bed
> Of crimson joy;
> And his dark secret love
> Does thy life destroy.

There is something very strange about the rose in this poem, some sense of its being more than an ordinary flower. That sense results, in part, from the way the speaker is related to the rose: he addresses it, as if it were animate and could hear him, and he refers to its being sick; to him, apparently, it means more than a blossom ordinarily would. Furthermore, it is related to an "invisible worm," a mysterious thing that secretly loves and slowly is killing it. Surely we can agree that this strange flower is symbolic—but of what? Without referring to specific aids that exist outside the poem, we might answer that the rose embodies vitality ("joy," "life") which is inevitably destroyed; and this may be as far as we can go in agreeing upon an interpretation. But many readers will find that this sense of the poem is deepened and enlarged because of associations they have with the image of the rose: familiar associations that derive from scores of poems and songs in which this flower is identified with vivid beauty, very often with feminine beauty, and especially with a fragile physical beauty that is fleeting. These associations are legitimate only if they are disciplined by close attention to what Blake says of his rose. It would be very dubious, in this instance, to insist upon the flower's being a woman, and much too far-fetched to suppose that the poem has to do specifically with a loss of virginity. The point is that this symbol embodies some sense of the ephemeral and vulnerable beauty of life's most vivid forms and emotions.

The associations with roses which may help us to understand Blake's poem are literary and conventional, and many symbols draw upon such associations. Robert Frost's "The Road Not Taken," for example, suggests the familiar image of the crossroads at which man must choose one path or the other, although Frost avoids stating the cliché and allows his roads to be symbolic by describing them literally and letting them only suggest the idea of a crucial decision. But there are other kinds of symbols, too, which might be called the archetypal and the personal.

Some literary symbols are associated with what seem to be universal human experiences, and they act as **archetypes** of these experiences: day and night, for instance, or summer and winter, representing vitality and stillness, youth and age. Great typical images like these are the stuff of **myths,** ancient stories of such important events in the lives of man and nature as birth, initiation, trial, death and rebirth. In many mythical tales the ocean provides the origin of life—Venus rises from the sea—and in many it is the means and the symbol of death. And in literature of all periods these associations with the waters of the sea recur, as if they were fixed deep in the human imagination. Melville's symbolic novel *Moby-Dick* explores the real ocean, which is also the ocean of myth, to reveal again how it represents for men a great unknown, a power that can be beneficent or malignant, a source of vitality but an alien and destructive element. Mythical objects, then, like the sea, the seasons, and the earth itself with its yearly renewal of life, and mythical acts like the rites associated with birth, puberty, and marriage, may be parallel with the objects and acts in a modern poem or play and, whether either the writer or his audience is fully conscious of the parallel, may sometimes suggest what profound human significance these symbols and symbolic gestures possess.

But certain poets, instead of drawing upon these psychological and mythical resources, develop private symbols, the meanings of which are revealed by wide reading within the work of the individual writer. William Butler Yeats, for example, has a symbolic system of his own, and the image of a tower in his poetry is to be associated with other such images from other poems of his. Writers may even create their own myths, stories about the universe that embody new symbolic terms, as William Blake does in his mystical books.

By using the symbolic method, whether the symbols draw upon conventional or universal or limited and special associations, the writer can suggest general human experiences in a concrete form, and he can appeal to ideas and emotions of which the reader is not fully conscious. The careful reader tries to clarify these overtones, but he has to be exceedingly wary lest he draw upon personal reactions rather than generally felt and more or less verifiable associations, such as those provided by literary tradition, psychological analysis, and myth. He has, furthermore, to test the relevance of such associations by referring to the whole structure of the work being interpreted. For the careful reader the use of these sources may provide insights into the story or poem that are consistent with its structure, that illuminate rather than distort it. The myth of Oedipus, who killed his father and married his mother, a myth interpreted by psychologists as the acting out of the male child's incestuous desire and guilt, can help us to understand the intensity of Hamlet's emotions toward his mother and stepfather. But we must remember that Hamlet is neither a Greek king nor Mr. H. in a case history, that his oedipal reactions are only a part of the play and not the whole significance of it. Similarly, when we refer to the mythical quality of a symbolic thing or act in literature, like the deer in Faulkner's story "The Old People" which is like a primitive totem figure, we are trying to suggest one quality in the symbol and not to reduce it to a neat categorical meaning.

For, without being vague about the limited range of meanings which a literary symbol suggests, the critic should not imagine that he has found and fixed the only meaning. He should not, in other words, turn symbolism into allegory. It may be useful, finally, to remember that whereas the strictly allegorical writer begins with precise ideas to which some objective form must be given, the writer of symbolism begins with the object and lets it act so as to imply its own significance—a significance that no one reading is likely to exhaust.

Style

One reason for feeling that there is something strange, some implied significance, in Blake's "The Sick Rose" is that the words describing its subject are peculiarly chosen and arranged. Not only does the speaker address a rose in the phrase "thou art," but the terms he uses to describe the destroying worm and its motive are *invisible, dark,* and *secret,* adjectives suggesting mystery. Furthermore, the statement about rose and worm is made in short poetic lines, so that each line is given unusual emphasis, while some of the words—*joy* and *destroy,* and, less precisely, *worm* and *storm*—rhyme. A paraphrase that ignores these words, sounds, and rhythms—"Rose, you're diseased: some night bug has been eating your petals and slowly killing you"—would probably not strike anyone as being symbolic or, indeed, very interesting. The qualities which this paraphrase lacks and which do much to give Blake's poem its special significance are elements of *style.* And, although prose writers rarely use rhyme and never make an arbitrary division of lines, some such qualities as these, including the connotations and the sounds of words, their order in sentences, and the lengths of sentences and paragraphs, also constitute what is called *prose style.*

The term *style,* whether applied to prose or to poetry, should not be confused with the more general word *technique.* By the technique of a writer we ordinarily mean all the ways he uses to produce the whole literary structure, including the ordering of the plot, means of characterization, establishment of and shifts in point of view, use of setting, and introduction of allegorical or symbolic devices, as well as style. When we speak of style, however, we are concerned specifically with what might be called the texture of writing, with such matters of verbal detail as diction, imagery, syntax, and sound.

Diction

Diction, the first of these elements that make up style, means simply the writer's choice of words. The difference between the *worm* of Blake's poem and the *bug* of our paraphrase is one of diction, and one that illustrates the importance of this matter. *Worm* conveys the impression of something lowly and disgusting, with overtones of death and decay, suggesting the conventional idea that worms feed on the flesh of corpses. Perhaps it hints, too, at some sense of guile and of natural evil: in the language of Shakespeare, the *worm* is a serpent. *Bug,* on the other hand, has a less complex and probably a less disagreeable meaning. A flying worm is certainly more weird than a flying bug.

This difference between one word and another that appears to have

the same or a similar meaning can be a difference between the pleasant
and the unpleasant, the serious and the humorous, the dignified and the
common. In comparing two such words, we sometimes distinguish **denotation,** the simplest explicit definition for each term, from **connotation,**
the sum of associations and implied attitudes that each carries. The rather
subtle contrast already cited between *ennui* and *boredom* is one of connotation; so is the more obvious contrast between the verb *transform* and
its synonym *transmogrify,* which carries a comic and even a grotesque
sense. The connotation of a term may be so distinct that it becomes at
last the denotation—as *wonderful* has come to mean "excellent," not
"full of wonder," in common speech—but the connotative quality may
sometimes, too, be rather tenuous and difficult to analyze. Obvious or not,
the effect of a writer's diction derives largely from his choice of words
for their connotative value, their "feeling." When John Crowe Ransom,
for instance, refers to a "transmogrifying bee" in his poem "Janet Wak-
ing," he gives an odd and slightly ironic touch to the death of a chicken
that has been stung—a death that might otherwise, because of a little
girl's reaction to it, seem to be treated with sentimentality.

Occasionally writers use words that are highly technical or archaic
or taken from a special dialect in order to achieve some such effect of
strangeness, as when T. S. Eliot begins a satirical poem about self-conscious piety, his "Sunday Morning Service," with the very pompous adjective *polyphiloprogenitive,* or when Gerard Manley Hopkins uses ob-
solete words like the verb *brandle* (shake) for their sounds and for their
peculiar flavors. The use of both archaic and dialectal language in English literature goes back at least as far as the sixteenth century and Edmund Spenser, whose poetry includes many words that were no longer
current in the speech of his day—words such as *thilke* (that) and
whilom (formerly). But the influence upon writers and speakers that
has tended most to preserve a special vocabulary distinct from ordinary
speech is that of the King James Bible, the translation of 1611. This
great version is familiar enough to provide, along with the commonplace
images and phrases, a source for the heightening and dignifying of language, the language especially of poetry and of poetic prose like that of
Thomas Carlyle, whose *Sartor Resartus* is filled with Biblical echoes.

A danger for the poet in using words from the vocabulary of Chaucer
or Shakespeare or the English Bible is that he will seem to be pretentious
and not so much elevated or ironic as simply odd. Nevertheless, in one
way or another the writer may well have to risk absurdity in order to
achieve his art. Although the degree and kind of difference between literary or poetic language and the language of common speech have varied
from age to age, there is almost always some difference. The phrase

poetic diction can be used pejoratively, to describe the sort of uncommon and pretentious language to which a critic objects; but in fact poetry is by its nature likely to have a slightly if subtly uncommon diction, and so is most imaginative prose. When Wordsworth declares in his Preface to the second edition of *Lyrical Ballads* that he has attempted to write poetry in the "real language of men," he is reacting against the highly conventional, generalized, and cliché-ridden diction of the later and lesser Augustans, with their refusal to write "fish" when they could substitute "the finny tribe" or "birds" when they could refer to "feathered flock." This elegant circumlocution, called **periphrasis**, Wordsworth usually avoids. (Pope himself, the greatest of Augustan poets, ridicules the abuse of periphrasis when he translates "Shut the door" into its pseudopoetic equivalent, "The wooden guardian of our privacy/Quick on its axle turn.") Even so, Wordsworth's own poetry often displays a special language, with its use of philosophical terms and of technical words from the psychology of his day, which is far from being flatly colloquial. His language is only less obviously artificial than that of his predecessors.

Among the modern poets who have been especially conscious of this matter, W. H. Auden gives the impression of being perfectly colloquial in such titles as "Which Side Am I Supposed to Be On?" and "We All Make Mistakes." He can also use special and abstract language, as in this prayer:

> Confirm it that thy Primal Love
> May weave in us the freedom of
> The actually deficient on
> The justly actual.[1]

And he can shift abruptly from the distinctly poetic to the most commonplace phrasing: "Over the heather the wet wind blows,/I've lice in my tunic and a cold in my nose." Auden has been accused by some critics of being inappropriately flippant, in similar passages, and of using the language of the wisecrack for a cheap effect. Whether the criticism is just or not—for the best of Auden's work it is not—it raises the question of the appropriateness to his subject of a writer's language. In a sense, of course, the language creates the subject: but we may still reasonably object to certain combinations of terms if they seem not to be justified by the serious total meaning of a work. When Wordsworth's ode on "Intimations of Immortality" describes a child not only as priest, prophet, and seer, but as "a six years' Darling of a pigmy size," the shift to a sentimental, even coy, diction strikes many readers as a flaw. The matter of appropriateness or **decorum** of language was especially important to the

[1] From *The Collected Poetry of W. H. Auden;* copyright 1945, Random House, Inc. Reprinted by permission.

neoclassical poets of the eighteenth century. And, although we rarely use the term *decorum* in this sense, the same critical problem has still to be considered.

Often, however, and especially in more modern writers like Auden, the contrast between several levels of diction—formal and very ordinary, even slangy, speech, or sentimental and scientifically cold language— becomes an essential pattern in a literary work. So T. S. Eliot, in *The Waste Land,* contrasts the echoes of the Shakespearian language that describes great Cleopatra on her "burnished throne" with the vulgar debasement of words like *elegant,* used in the 1920's to describe everything from clothes to dance-steps:

> O O O O that Shakespeherian Rag—
> It's so elegant
> So intelligent.[1]

It becomes apparent that diction is an element of literary structure when we notice the connotations of a series of words in a single play or poem or story. Often some pattern or new dimension of meaning is implied by these connotations. Such a pattern occurs in *The Rape of the Lock,* Pope's mock-epic about a fashionable coquette and one of her admirers, who offends the young lady by clipping a lock of her hair to keep as a memento. In telling this tale, Pope uses, along with various fanciful and heroic devices, a series of words that have religious meanings, words such as *mystic, pious, angel powers, heaven, prayers,* and *soul.* These words predict and reflect the scenes in which his heroine is described as a priestess who worships her own divine image in the mirror, and the beau enacts the ritual of burning old *billets-doux* upon an altar of love. By applying such serious language to frivolous matters, the poet establishes his ironic contrast between grand pretensions and petty reality. The result is pointed satire. Wordsworth's Immortality Ode, however, uses a series of just such religious terms with a quite different result. For this poem deals with the serious subject of a man's recognizing his immortal nature through recalling the intuitions of childhood. In it, the terms *celestial, visionary, priest, prophet,* and *benediction* provide a virtually religious sense of the sacredness of life. The ode would remain personal and "philosophical" without the connotation carried by this language, but it would lack the full emotional impact and a dimension of meaning that these words communicate.

We have already observed that language is by its very nature both complex and ambiguous; this complexity and ambiguity can be found in a single line or sentence or even in a single term. In various ways,

[1] From *Collected Poems 1909–1935* by T. S. Eliot, copyright 1936 by Harcourt, Brace & World, Inc., and reprinted with their permission.

and consciously or not, writers may exploit the overtones of words so as to
make them carry more than one meaning. Shakespeare does this when
Hamlet describes his uncle as "more than kin and less than kind." In that
line, by the way, and often in ambiguous language, the two senses of the
crucial word (*kind*) are etymologically related, for both derive from the
Old English *cynn*. The ordinary pun is another instance, usually drawing upon coincidence of sound rather than historical relationship of
words, in which a term has several meanings at once. John Donne plays
upon the sound of his own name and its homonym *done* to tell God in
his hymn of confession that, even after counting over numbers of the
poet's sins, "When thou hast done, thou hast not done"—i.e., you have
not yet summed me up. Shakespeare is especially fond of such punning,
too: the dying Mercutio in *Romeo and Juliet* says, "Look for me tomorrow
and you shall find me a grave man" (that is, *in* the grave). Sometimes
writers use titles that can have several meanings at once. Conrad's *Heart
of Darkness* refers both to the savagery in the heart of Africa, the Dark
Continent, and to the darkness in the hearts of men. The title of an adventure story by Richard Connell, "The Most Dangerous Game," can be
interpreted in two ways, both of them justified by the language and action
of the tale: *game* may mean a game that is played or the object of a hunt
(in the sense that deer and bear are called game). In fact, the phrase
has both meanings and they are not incompatible, for this story suggests
that the most dangerous game is playing with other men's lives, because
the most dangerous game that can be hunted is man.

The most thoroughgoing treatment of multiple meanings in literature, of **ambiguity, or plurisignation,** to use a term some critics prefer,
is William Empson's *Seven Types of Ambiguity*. Empson offers examples
of ambiguity in the syntax as well as the diction of various poets. As he
demonstrates by some extremely subtle (and sometimes far-fetched) analysis, the texture of a literary work can be enriched, and its meaning enlarged, by integral ambiguity; this is, in fact, one very important way in
which a writer may achieve intensity along with economy. More recent
writers, in particular, have been quite conscious of this possibility of
verbal condensation, and various kinds of word-play have been systematically exploited by modern poetry and fiction. James Joyce's difficult
experiment *Finnegans Wake,* for example, is constructed not only of ambiguous but of **portmanteau** words: such words as *rugaby,* meaning both
the game *rugby* and *rockabye,* a cradle song; or *amuckst,* combining the
senses of *amongst* and *amuck*. As Humpty Dumpty explains to Alice,
slithy (another of these words) means both "lithe" and "slimy," and so
"it's like a portmanteau—there are two meanings packed up into one
word."

One must distinguish between a word or phrase that has several meanings at once, all of them consistent with each other—as in the examples given—and a word or phrase that can have one, but only one, of several contradictory meanings. The teacher who praises the ambiguity of a line in Shakespeare, which is of the first kind, may condemn the ambiguity in a paper written by one of his students, which is of the second kind. If the student writes, "There can be no serious question of Swift's being a misanthrope," he means either, "Unquestionably Swift was a misanthrope," or "Unquestionably Swift was not a misanthrope," but he cannot mean both. This "either/or" ambiguity can of course occur in literary works, as it sometimes does, for instance, in the condensed and elliptical poetry of Hopkins. But when it occurs in straightforward narrative or lyric, most readers would regard it as a flaw rather than a virtue. On the other hand, such equivocal phrasing might perhaps be justified in a dramatic work where the uncertainty of meaning can express the mixed and uncertain attitudes of the character who is speaking.

Imagery

Another aspect of a writer's style, and one which often seems especially important in verse, is **imagery**. The term *image* is as difficult to define as any in the critic's vocabulary. First of all, even though the word would literally suggest a visual impression, it ordinarily means the evoking of any experience of the senses. The vivid description of an odor or a melody, according to this larger meaning, could be an image, and so could the description of how a surface feels to the touch. The most comprehensive definition of a literary image is simply the communication in words of a particular sense impression. This definition would allow us to say that many pieces of descriptive writing, and descriptive poetry in particular, consist wholly of images. In fact, critics have held that the essence of a poem is imagery, although this view will appear questionable if we accept as poetry such reflective and discursive verse as Dryden's *Religio Laici* or Pope's *Essay on Man*.

But this very large sense for the word *image* is not the only one possible. Many writers, when they refer to imagery, are concerned with metaphorical objects. From their point of view, the evocation of sights and sounds in figures of speech is a part of imagery, but the description of literal sights and sounds in a novel or poem is something else: when Hamlet speaks of taking arms against a sea of troubles, he is making a poetic image, but, in this sense, the literal sea upon which he sails from Denmark would not be an image.

The difficulty with this sometimes useful distinction is that we may not always be sure of the extent to which literal objects carry more than literal meanings. Just as the setting and the symbolism of a work can be

identical, so the real objects may be related to the metaphors in a play or
poem, or even a novel, and may themselves be as clearly symbolic as
Blake's rose and worm are. The possible merging of literal images with
metaphorical images is illustrated by Matthew Arnold's poem "Dover
Beach," in which, again, the sea is used both as a setting and for a comparison. The poem is a dramatic monologue, spoken by a man looking
out upon the beach, to a woman in the room with him.

> The sea is calm to-night.
> The tide is full, the moon lies fair
> Upon the straits; — on the French coast the light
> Gleams and is gone; the cliffs of England stand,
> Glimmering and vast, out in the tranquil bay.
> Come to the window, sweet is the night-air!
> Only, from the long line of spray
> Where the sea meets the moon-blanch'd land,
> Listen! you hear the grating roar
> Of pebbles which the waves draw back, and fling,
> At their return, up the high strand,
> Begin, and cease, and then again begin,
> With tremulous cadence slow, and bring
> The eternal note of sadness in.
>
> Sophocles long ago
> Heard it on the Aegean, and it brought
> Into his mind the turbid ebb and flow
> Of human misery; we
> Find also in the sound a thought,
> Hearing it by this distant northern sea.
>
> The Sea of Faith
> Was once, too, at the full, and round earth's shore
> Lay like the folds of a bright girdle furl'd.
> But now I only hear
> Its melancholy, long, withdrawing roar,
> Retreating, to the breath
> Of the night-wind, down the vast edges drear
> And naked shingles of the world.
>
> Ah, love, let us be true
> To one another! for the world, which seems
> To lie before us like a land of dreams,
> So various, so beautiful, so new,
> Hath really neither joy, nor love, nor light,
> Nor certitude, nor peace, nor help for pain;
> And we are here as on a darkling plain
> Swept with confused alarms of struggle and flight,
> Where ignorant armies clash by night.

The ocean that is a literal image at the beginning of the poem becomes a figure of speech, and, finally, takes on symbolic quality. In the first section of the monologue, it is described as a setting. This setting immediately suggests two metaphors to the speaker: the one that Sophocles is said to have used, comparing the ebb and flow of human suffering to that of water, and a new one, which compares the sea to Faith, presumably religious faith but perhaps any faith at all in the larger meaningfulness of human existence. How are the two metaphors related? One refers to a negative and personal "sea" of emotions that all men sometimes feel, the other to a positive and general "sea" of belief that is now ebbing away. The first comparison, however, is not simply negative, for all its sad quality. It is associated with the musical "note of sadness" of the far Aegean and also with the imagination of a great poet, Sophocles. Sophoclean tragedy gives a beautiful form to men's sufferings by such poetic means as the use of imagery; faith, whether an orthodox religious faith or a Romantic faith in man's harmony with nature, is another way of giving interest and dignity to our lives. But for the speaker in this poem, Greek tragic dignity is something distant, and philosophical or religious faith is rapidly dying. In effect, he cannot accept in either of these senses a belief that the fascinating and the often lovely sea is an image relevant to the human situation, the situation of man here and now. The poem ends with another metaphor, that of the darkling plain, a dry-land metaphor that suggests discord rather than cadence, limitation rather than vastness. Even so, one might argue that the rhythmic sound of the literal sea is echoed throughout the ebbing and flowing of the poetic lines; and that there is in the poem, over and above the distinct meanings of the several metaphors, a feeling of greater significance in that literal sea. The sea at Dover, according to this argument, would be for the speaker a symbol that he is unable to explain. He denies its possibility as a metaphor. But it still fascinates him and perhaps still implies a mysterious power in nature which, for all his moving denial of its value, impresses him profoundly. The central image in this short poem, then, is a quite literal one to begin with, a part of the setting, but it is also metaphorical, and perhaps it can be called at last a symbol.

We have been using **metaphor** in a broad sense, as distinct from literal image—for a metaphor is a figure of speech that compares objects instead of only evoking them—and distinct also from symbol—for a metaphor expresses its meaning in so many words instead of only suggesting it. The word *metaphor* is often used in this way, so that it is virtually synonymous with **trope**, meaning a "turn" by which words are made to say something more than, or other than, what is literally true. But there is a more limited sense of the term also, which identifies as metaphor only one sort of trope. When the speaker in "Dover Beach" refers to the "Sea of Faith," meaning that faith *is* a sea, he is making a metaphor in this narrow sense; but if Sophocles tells us that emotion is *like* the waves of the sea, that is a **simile**, a figure that explicitly compares two terms instead of equating them. Ordinarily a simile uses the word *as* or the word *like*. There are other tropes as well, although metaphor in even its limited sense is the most common, for all language is to some extent metaphorical: we speak in *buried* or *submerged* metaphors of space, about moving ahead or looking backward, about falling into debt or rising above difficulties (but we never rise above debt or fall below our troubles).

Another very common trope is **synecdoche**, the use of a part to stand for the whole: a farm worker is called a hand, and for Wordsworth the young child is an "Eye among the blind." Equally familiar is **metonymy**, making a name or thing represent another thing or person: the critic who writes that Keats was influenced by Spenser means that Keats was influenced by his reading of Spenser's poetry, not directly by the man himself; similarly, the broadcaster who says, "The White House has just announced . . ." means not that a house has spoken but that a representative of the President has. Yet another figure of speech, **hyperbole**, or exaggeration, is familiar in Renaissance love lyrics; Pope makes light ironic use of it when he insists that his Belinda's eyes "eclipse the day," are brighter than the very sun! Less common is the use of **oxymoron**, the combining of words with apparently contradictory meanings: Romeo utters a series of oxymorons when he complains about his "Loving hate," his "heavy lightness, serious vanity," "cold fire, sick health," and so on; and there is a similar series in Chaucer's *Book of the Duchess*: "My wit is folye, my day is night,/My love is hate, my sleep wakinge." This figure is closely related to **paradox**, the deliberate statement of what seems to be absurd if not impossible. Oscar Wilde is celebrated for his witty paradoxes: "The amount of women in London who flirt with their own husbands is perfectly scandalous." "Ignorance is like a delicate fruit; touch it and the bloom is gone." And the metaphysical poets of the seventeenth century, Donne, Marvell, Herbert, and others, often use an extreme form of logical paradox or apparent self-contradiction. This figure is one kind of **conceit**, a term used for any extensive and witty comparison or bringing together of radically dissimilar things. John Donne, in his famous "A Valediction: Forbidding Mourning," works out an elaborate analogy between two lovers and the two legs of a compass, and T. S. Eliot, to cite a more modern example, begins "The Love Song of J. Alfred Prufrock" with an unexpected image:

> Let us go then, you and I,
> When the evening is spread out against the sky
> Like a patient etherised upon a table. . . .[1]

[1] From *Collected Poems 1909–1935* by T. S. Eliot, copyright 1936 by Harcourt, Brace & World, Inc., and reprinted with their permission.

Dr. Johnson, who disapproved of such far-fetched comparisons, vividly described their chief characteristic when he said that in them "the most heterogeneous ideas are yoked by violence together."

Paradoxes and paradoxical qualities have fascinated many modern critics, most notably Cleanth Brooks. But there is among critics an even more widespread interest in the way patterns of images, whether literal or figurative, can be recognized within narrative works and can suggest new or deeper meanings within these works. The concern with recurrent metaphor that Caroline Spurgeon's book on *Shakespeare's Imagery* inaugurated has become largely an interest in the working out of themes within plays, poems, and novels (whereas Miss Spurgeon was inclined to draw inferences about Shakespeare's life and personal opinions from her study), and especially of themes that are not apparent from a casual reading. Thus, although it is perfectly obvious that Carlyle in his *Sartor Resartus* uses the metaphor of clothing as a unifying device, expanding on the metaphor to include certain real clothes which he regards as symbolic, it is not so obvious what the recurrent dramatic images of clothing in *Macbeth* reveal: that the murderer and usurper is falsely robed in his ill-fitting royal garments, that he cannot at last successfully disguise or symbolically alter his naked humanity.

There are dangers in the method that focuses attention upon imagery, especially the imagery of metaphor. The greatest of these is that one will distort the meaning, say, of a novel or play by failing to observe how the implications of metaphorical language are contained and controlled by the plot, by the characterization—is it Othello or Iago who uses the images of animal lust?—and by all the elements of the whole structure. But at best the examination of these patterns when they exist can add to our conscious grasp of a literary work by qualifying our sense of its total meaning.

Just as modern interest in patterns of imagery can sometimes lead to an unbalanced interpretation, so modern taste for particular kinds of image and not for others can sometimes result in a distorted judgment. To cite an extreme example, most sophisticated readers are accustomed to find some order in a poet's imagery and to dislike mixed metaphor. The *New Yorker* magazine warns writers to "Block That Metaphor"; and we can agree about the absurdity of such passages as "Those red herrings that my opponent has thrown in the face of the voters will now come home to roost." Here, the figurative language is far enough from original observation to make the images *clichés,* phrases so familiar as to be hackneyed. And of course they are comically incompatible. Still, there may be rare instances when the conflict of images is justified. Shakespeare mixes metaphors in Hamlet's lines, already cited, about taking arms against a sea of troubles, and the strange conjunction there occurs as a startling means of embodying the strained and mixed state of the speaker's mind. Perhaps the idea of using weapons against a sea (although heroes in folktales and epics have done it) is as absurd as the idea of herrings flying home to roost. But Shakespeare's language is both fresh and dramatically appropriate, for Hamlet is afraid that he alone cannot control the "sea of troubles" that is Denmark any more than he could affect the literal sea with his sword. His tragedy is characterized by such unusual, even unnatural conjunctions, and its language throughout is that of strangeness, even of madness.

We are likely, also, to dislike hyperbole and to prefer its opposite, **understatement**—perhaps in most instances with good reason. An attempt to communicate deep emotion is more likely to succeed if it appears to be simple rather than elaborate. Nevertheless, a poem may be concerned with something other than, or more complicated than, the expressing of a simple sincere emotion. The writer may delight in elaborating for the sake of his art, as Auden insists in "The Truest Poetry Is the Most Feigning," where he urges the virtues of extravagant hyperbole. The difference between artful understatement and such exaggeration is suggested by the contrast between Wordsworth's lines on the death of Lucy—

> She lived unknown, and few could know
>   When Lucy ceased to be;
> But she is in her grave, and, oh,
>   The difference to me!—

and Milton's "Lycidas," where everyone from the sea nymphs and the shepherds to Saint Peter is said to know about and mourn the death of Edward King, in the most extreme language and gestures. Dr. Johnson blames "Lycidas" for failing to persuade the reader that "the difference" King's death made to Milton was a matter of great personal grief. But even if we agree that the poem does not communicate a profound sense of personal loss, we need hardly condemn it. "Lycidas" concerns itself with art and large ideas rather than intimate feelings; it is more conventional than the later elegy. But it is not for those reasons a less valuable poem, as we shall see.

Finally, certain conventions may strike us as so old-fashioned that we have to adjust our minds to their use. **Personification,** for instance, writing of an inanimate object or an abstraction as if it were a person— Father Time, Mother Earth, Sorrow as a woman or Death as a man—is a familiar device. And it seems dull and obvious when a dull and obvious poet writes, "Earth my fair mother, let me lie upon your bosom." But Auden makes it work beautifully in his lines from the elegy for Yeats, "Earth, receive an honored guest,/William Yeats is laid to rest." Both of these phrases exemplify another familiar convention as well, that of

apostrophe, directly addressing an abstraction or inanimate being, or someone who is absent.

Now, however, we are speaking not of imagery but of a related subject, the use of rhetorical devices. Although **rhetoric** can be a very inclusive term meaning the artful and expressive use of language, it is often applied in both a limited and a negative sense to suggest mere verbal embellishment. No doubt this sense is related to a modern suspicion, inherited from the Romantic movement, of artifice or elegance in expression. Rhetorical devices, in principle, are not now favored by many poets. Few modern writers use such traditional forms of apostrophe, for instance, as the **invocation** of the muse which is found sometimes in older lyrics and invariably in the epic. As Virgil at the beginning calls upon his poetic muse for aid, so Milton invokes the "Heavenly Muse" in the first lines of *Paradise Lost;* but there are no such obvious examples from the last century or so of English or European literature. Certain other rhetorical figures are also more familiar from instances in the earlier periods. Even the **rhetorical question,** which ordinarily implies a negative answer, is now used mostly in political speeches rather than in poetry, although the rhetoric of the orator's "Shall this corruption be countenanced in public office?" (audience: "No!") is related to the rhetoric of Shelley's question, "If Winter comes, can Spring be far behind?" Certainly, there are various kinds of playing upon syntax and grammar which are likely to be associated with the literature of the English eighteenth century, not with that of any later time. John Gay's line about his life in the city, declaring that he has "respir'd its smoke, and all its cares endur'd," is a typical Augustan use of **chiasmus,** the reversing of elements in an otherwise parallel construction (the perfect parallel, without this device, would be, "respir'd its smoke and endur'd all its cares"). Gay's greater contemporary Pope demonstrates **zeugma,** the yoking of two words that are in the same grammatical relation to another word but in two different senses, when he writes of his coquette Belinda, who fears to "stain her honour, or her new brocade" (the meaning of *stain* is altered, is made literal, by the second object). So does Dr. Johnson in his line "And now a rabble rages, now a fire." Both *rage,* but in different senses.

Such wit as this may now seem very artificial, very mannered, but a truly critical reader will try not to limit himself narrowly by the prejudices of his time. We are likely today to prefer complexity of implication to complexity of verbal structure, so that a wine-stained brocade symbolizes a woman's stained honor and the rabble is described metaphorically in the language that suggests a holocaust. Or, rather than the allegory of colors, seasons, and sounds, we may prefer the device of **synesthesia,** which describes one sensation in the language of another (the taste of darkness, the odor of deep purple): so Wallace Stevens in his "Domination of Black" writes of "the tails of the peacock/Tuned in the loud fire." [1] This example, by the way, recalls the synesthesia of ordinary speech, when we call bright colors "loud," as if we could hear them. But the opposition of symbolic imagination to verbal wit, of the implied to the stated, is not very precise and cannot be pursued too strictly. Pope's witty control of language is not incompatible with a wisdom deeper than wordplay; the mysterious power of Blake's language is not, at best, divorced from technical control. All literary art, we have to recognize, whether we label it formal and classical or expressive and romantic, combines some fervor with some artifice and gives the order of a conscious mind to the matter which may have sources and significance deeper than we can analyze.

This ordering and artifice is most evident in highly concentrated forms of poetry. Even in the lyric, often thought of as the most intensely personal and emotional type of writing, the careful and sometimes arbitrary choice of words dictated by the meter and rhyme scheme gives evidence of *poeta,* the craftsman, as well as *vates,* the prophet or visionary. But the ordinary structure of prose, too, which may be elaborated on in extraordinary ways by the writer, is proof of control, of art. The order of words in sentences, along with the lengths of sentences and paragraphs, makes up an important part of prose style, the element called syntax—from a Greek word meaning "to put in order."

Syntax

The various traditional styles named **Attic, Isocratic, Ciceronian,** and **baroque** are recognizable by their various kinds of syntax, as the following sentences will illustrate. The Attic employs mostly simple sentences. As the Isocratic sentence runs to greater length, so it involves greater complexity; where the Attic would move forward clearly and directly, the Isocratic uses parallel clauses to balance and oppose the parts. Less artificial, and more likely to reveal its full meaning only after a series of details and interpolations, is the Ciceronian or **periodic sentence.** As for the baroque sentence, though it is pithy in its parts and dramatic in its total effect, its construction lacks the perfect symmetry of parallelism, for it develops gradually and by additions or modifications as it unfolds. Most writers of prose today want to achieve variety in style rather than to follow any one of these models. In good modern writing a long periodic sentence, reaching a climax only at its conclusion, may be followed by a short simple one. Nevertheless, these syntactically consist-

[1] From *Collected Poems of Wallace Stevens;* quoted by permission of the publisher, Alfred A. Knopf, Inc.

ent styles are able, if subtly managed, to communicate the distinct individual quality of a work.

A writer's syntax can also be a striking means of communicating mood or attitude, or even of establishing characterization. Two passages of apparently simple narrative may suggest something of the variety of effect which syntax can achieve. These three sentences introduce Ernest Hemingway's story "The Undefeated": [1]

> Manuel Garcia climbed the stairs to Don Miguel Retena's office. He set down his suitcase and knocked on the door. There was no answer.

Henry James' story "The Lesson of the Master" begins with this sentence:

> He had been told the ladies were at church, but this was corrected by what he saw from the top of the steps—they descended from a great height in two arms, with a circular sweep of the most charming effect—at the threshold of the door which, from the long bright gallery, overlooked the immense lawn.

The first sentences reveal that tendency to a fairly simple syntax which characterizes Hemingway's style, with few complex sentences and few modifying elements; and the second passage is almost unmistakably from James. But these introductions do more than notify the experienced reader of whose work the stories are. They suggest at once profound differences between the mind and mood of Manuel Garcia, to whom the stark declarative sentences are appropriate, and the intelligence and subtlety of observation that we can expect of James' "he." Hemingway's syntax, which is adaptable, indicates here a literal-minded emphasis on life as a series of actions no one of which is at the moment qualified or judged by being subordinated to other actions. James' style, which can also be adapted to different characters and situations, now suggests that "he" is a man who observes matters and relates them to each other, qualifying, correcting, and defining the various impressions which are made almost simultaneously upon him. The effect of each passage changes when only the syntax is changed:

> At the top of the stairs he had climbed to Don Miguel Retena's office, Manuel Garcia, his suitcase set down beside him, stood and waited for an answer to his knocking at the door.

Now we lack the clues which Hemingway's original sentences gave to Manuel Garcia's nature and way of living. A less subtle version can be made of James' sentence:

[1] From *Men Without Women;* reprinted by permission of the publisher, Charles Scribner's Sons.

> The ladies were not at church, as he had been told. He saw them from the top of the steps. He was standing in the long bright gallery, at the threshold of the door that looked out over the immense lawn. They descended from a great height in two arms, and the effect they made of a circular sweep was most charming.

The rhythm is more choppy than in James, and the main character seems to be a less complicated man. He is charmed not incidentally but emphatically, and he does not appear now to take in the whole picture at once as an esthetic experience.

Syntax is likely, in spite of such examples, to be an element in style that is hard to analyze without reference to other matters such as diction and imagery. Very long complex-compound sentences are recognizably different in quality from very short sentences. The rhythm of sentences varied in structure and length can be distinguished from the monotonous chopping that results when a series of sentences repeat the same length and the same word order. But there are dangers in assuming that certain constructions invariably carry certain implications. Although we think of the compound sentence as a childishly simple form, stringing clauses together with *ands* and *buts* rather than subordinating some and emphasizing others, extremely subtle writers use this very sentence to produce a feeling of tension or of balance. Furthermore, even though we feel that the inverted phrase "Home is the hunter" has a lyric sense that makes it different from "The hunter is home," the difference made by syntax alone is at least difficult to define.

Some of the rhetorical devices already mentioned are obviously devices of syntax: chiasmus, for instance, which is simply the altering of word order in an otherwise parallel phrase or clause. We have also had to touch on this subject earlier in commenting on ambiguity, for some examples of double or uncertain meaning, especially in verse, derive from the ambiguity inherent in the structure of the English sentence. When Keats addresses his "Grecian Urn" as a "still unravish'd bride of quietness," the phrase can mean "quiet bride" (*of* used in that sense with *quietness* may seem strange, but the idiomatic phrase "lady of mystery" is comparable); or it can mean "bride married to Quietness," personifying the abstraction (and the syntax then would seem more normal, and parallel with the next phrase, "foster child of silence and slow time," although the personification is still very odd); or it can mean both at once.

These examples show not only that the subject of syntax is related to the larger ones of rhetoric and diction, but also that syntax is quite as important in the style of poetry as in that of prose. The length and degree of complexity in the sentences of a poem establish one pattern which works along with, and sometimes in contrast with, the more obviously artificial patterns of meter and sound. It is a combination of syntax, diction, and sound that produces the typical effect of **balance** and **antithesis** in Augustan or neoclassical poetry. The sense of balance is achieved by the parallel structure of several phrases or clauses and by the repetition of words; and this very balance heightens the sense of antithesis when the meanings of key words in the parallel phrases are precisely opposed one to the other. The device is apparent when Pope describes man as a being

> With too much knowledge for the Sceptic side,
> With too much weakness for the Stoic's pride.

Here we notice not only the emphasis given to *knowledge* versus *weakness* and *Sceptic* versus *Stoic,* but the arbitrary importance lent to the final two words, *side* and *pride,* by the fact of the couplet rhyme.

Whereas syntax and poetic form work together in Pope's verse, where all the elements reinforce the feeling of neat duality, they can also be used to modify each other. One very famous illustration is Milton's description in *Paradise Lost* of how Satan fell from the heavenly kingdom:

> Him the Almighty Power
> Hurled headlong flaming from the ethereal sky
> With hideous ruin and combustion down
> To bottomless perdition, there to dwell
> In adamantine chains and penal fire,
> Who durst defy the Omnipotent to arms.

The word order is certainly not colloquial or even usual for poetic language. But this long elaborate sentence with its initial emphasis on *Him* and its suggestion of a long and writhing fall, is contained in poetic lines that quite lack the further elaborate and artificial qualities of strict scansion and rhyme. If a hack versifier were to revise these lines to make their metrical pattern somewhat stricter and to add rhyme, the result might be something like this:

> Him the Almighty One
> Hurled headlong flaming from the fields of sun,
> With ruin hideous, and burning, where
> Perdition has no bottom, dwelling there
> To stay in chains of adamant, and fire,
> Who dared call down the Mighty Father's ire.

This unfortunate version would lose not only a sense of vastness, of freedom, and of uninterrupted movement, but also the interaction between artful syntax and apparently simple prosody.

Prosody

Prosody, the poetic pattern of meter, rhyme, and stanza, is another and sometimes a more striking aspect of poetic style. Rhythm and sound are important, certainly, in prose as well as verse, but the stricter rhythm of meter and the use of alliteration, assonance, and rhyme are associated with the art of the poet. Of the prose writer we ask at least a certain grace, avoiding choppiness and such awkward repetition of sound as we hear in "the probity and dignity of his view of the possibility of infinity" or, to take a bad example from a good writer, in Alfred North White-head's "Education is the acquisition of the art of the utilization of knowl-edge." In poetry we expect, as well, a positive aural structure to be im-plied, whether the verse has an irregular rhythm or a definite scansion, whether it is written in couplets or, like Milton's epic blank verse, is unrhymed.

Sometimes, in fact, we speak of metrical and certain sound effects as **versification**, the giving of verse form, poetic form, to language. Under this heading would be included, first of all, the various metrical schemes that English has borrowed, or the names of which it has borrowed, from classical Greek. Actually, the classical **feet**, or metrical units, are measures of **quantity**, of the length of a syllable or the time required to pronounce it. English feet are based rather upon stress or accentuation. Clear exam-ples of the difference between quantity and stress are not easy to find, for most of us are much less aware of the length of a sound than we are of whether or not it has to be accented. But we can invent an instance: in the phrase "Not downstairs but upstairs," the stress for the word *upstairs* is on the first syllable, but the second syllable is "longer," is quantitatively heavier. Although writers who are sensitive to rhythm and sound may be conscious of quantitative differences—Tennyson claimed to know the quantities of every word in English except perhaps *scissors* —the patterns that we are most aware of and analyze derive from arbi-trary stress. So the classical terms *iambic, trochaic, spondaic, dactylic,* and *anapestic* are used to describe feet of two or three syllables each that combine stressed and unstressed syllables in various ways. Stressed syl-lables are often shown by the acute accent mark (´) and unstressed by ×.

The two matters of the metrical foot and length of line can be summed up neatly. An **iambic** foot is marked ×´ : alóne. A **trochaic** foot is marked ´× : lónely. A **spondaic** foot is marked ´´ : nó, nó. A **dactylic** foot is marked ´×× : lóneliness. An **anapestic** foot is marked ××´ : in the séa.[1] Lines of verse may be said to consist of these feet, and are named in accordance with the number and kind of feet they contain. **Monometer** is a line of one foot: "Alóne!" (iambic monometer), "Cónstantly" (dac-

---

[1] A foot of two syllables is called a **duple** foot; one of three syllables, a **triple** foot. A foot ending with a stressed syllable is called a **rising** foot; one ending with an unstressed syllable, a **falling** foot. Thus, for example, an iambic foot is duple and rising; a dactylic foot, triple and falling.

tylic monometer). **Dimeter** has two feet: "Sóftly, sóftly" (trochaic dimeter), "Óff agáin, ón agáin" (dactylic dimeter). **Trimeter** has three
feet: "Laméntátion, and móurning, and wóe" (anapestic trimeter). **Tetrameter** has four feet: "Wáke: the váulted shádow shátters" (trochaic
tetrameter). **Pentameter** lines have five feet: "The cúrféw tólls the knéll
of párting dáy" (iambic pentameter—this is by far the commonest sort
of line in English poetry). **Hexameters** have six feet (iambic hexameters
are often called **alexandrines**); the rarer **heptameter** and **octameter** have
seven and eight feet respectively (an iambic heptameter line is sometimes called a **fourteener**).

First, But this neat summing up is not enough for a reading of poetry.
It may seem easy, once these terms are memorized, to **scan** a poem—that
is, to identify its metrical form and variations. In fact, scansion involves
even more technical observation, and it is not often so simple or even
satisfactory as might be supposed.

First of all, many lines of English verse do not lend themselves to
perfect scansion. Irregularities of various kinds abound. A line may have
a syllable more or a syllable less than normal. For example, in Milton's
line "Thát dúrst dislíke his réign, ánd me préférring," the last syllable
is extra in the normally iambic pentameter scheme of *Paradise Lost;*
such a line is said to be **hypermetrical**. Robert Herrick's line "Hére a
líttle chíld Í stánd" requires a final unaccented syllable to be normally
trochaic; such a line is called **catalectic**. Another sort of irregularity is
the **substitution** of one sort of foot for another—for example, of a trochaic foot for one of the iambic feet in an otherwise regular iambic line.
Examples of substitution are easy to find, for this device allows the poet
rhythmic variety and subtle emphasis. The following are lines from another seventeenth-century poet, George Herbert:

> Bút while Í bústled, Í might héar a fríend
>
> Whísper, Hów wíde is áll this lóng preténse?

The regular scansion given here for the first line could be debated, but
clearly the first two syllables of the second line cannot be read as an iamb
—one cannot say *whispér*—and so they work, in effect, a trochaic substitution.

Many examples of scansion could be debated, of course. In the
phrase "Óff agáin, ón agáin," the second syllable of *again* might easily

be given enough stress to produce the pattern ´ × ´ . It seems that there is some arbitrary judgment involved in scanning such lines. This is true because there are varying degrees of emphasis in any word, not simply strong and weak syllables. Probably no system of even five or six degrees in accent would be accurate enough to represent the way we actually speak, and certainly no system can be precise that distinguishes only weak and strong accents. But there is another, related reason for disagreement over scansion, one which has to do with the difference between **stress** and **accent.** We have been using these terms so far virtually as synonyms, without differentiating between the stress upon a syllable, or **ictus,** that results from a formal sense of meter, and, on the other hand, the normal accent that belongs to ordinary speech. A purely formal scansion of several lines from a poem with an iambic pentameter pattern might force the stress so that the final couplet of Arnold's sonnet on Shakespeare would be read,

> All weakness which impairs, all griefs which bow,
> Find their sole speech in that victorious brow.

Of course this sing-song rendering of the pattern, ignoring the sense, is absurd. But equally if more subtly false is a reading that recognizes only the normal accents of the words and the emphasis suggested by their sense, ignoring the poetic scheme:

> All weakness which impairs, all griefs which bow,
> Find their sole speech in that victorious brow.

Any satisfactory reading of the lines would involve awareness of both verse pattern and sense—giving, for example, much less emphasis to the third word, *which,* than the first and formal version would, but considerably more emphasis to the words *their* and *that* than our second, prosaic version does. It would probably give nearly equal accents to *sole* and *speech,* too, so that they share what is sometimes called a **hovering accent,** one that falls equally on two syllables. The impression of a formal pattern is produced by the tendency of normal rhythms to approximate it: although some lines in Arnold's sonnet are not strict iambic pentameter, the strong over-all impression, soon established, is one of that meter. And once the pattern is established, it modifies the rhythm that a prosaic reading would give to any single line.

Still other irregularities have sometimes to be considered. **Syncopation,** for example, is the alternating of very emphatic and less emphatic syllables in stressed positions, as in Poe's "The Raven": And the lamplight o'er him streaming throws his shadow on the floor" (here the weaker accents are shown by the grave mark `). The **metrical silence,** to mention another useful term, results when unaccented syllables that a metrical pattern would lead us to expect are omitted; the reader is likely to pause, as if compensating for the lost syllable, with an effect like that of a "pause" in music. This pause or metrical silence can be indicated by parentheses ( ):

> Ah, what can ail thee, wretched wight,
> Alone and palely loitering;
> The sedge is wither'd from the lake,
> And no ( ) birds ( ) sing.

Scansion of poetry is complicated, then, by the evident irregularity of many verses; by the necessity of the reader's being sometimes arbitrary in the designation of strong and weak syllables (when many are not very strong and not very weak); and by the need to recognize metrical form along with the rhythms of conventional pronunciation and ordinary sense. Even if a system could be devised to account for all irregularities, represent subtle gradations of emphasis, and compromise accurately between meter and prose rhythm, it would have to indicate that no two poetic lines, and certainly no two poems, have precisely the same rhythmic form. The task appears impossible. Nevertheless, the principles of meter are worth knowing, and worth using in the close analysis of poetry, if we remember that they are approximate and not absolute—that the extreme irregularity of some verse is to be defined but not necessarily condemned in these terms.

Just as the accomplished dancer has gone beyond the point of consciously counting "one, two, three" when he waltzes, so the experienced reader may not be conscious of scanning metrical patterns as he reads, of observing *numbers,* to use the old-fashioned term. But he will certainly have a sense of poetic rhythm that results in part from these patterns. Even when the conventional metrical terms are not applicable, some formal means of achieving rhythm are implicit in the reading of poetry. In Anglo-Saxon poetry, which lacks both meter, as we ordinarily think of it, and rhyme, there is formality provided by the fact that each line can be divided into halves, with two strongly accented words in either half, three of these words (usually) beginning with the same sound. (Hence the name **alliterative poetry.**) The Old English epic *Beowulf* is composed in this kind of verse, and there are examples of it as late as the fourteenth and early fifteenth centuries. A few lines in a modernized version of the fourteenth-century alliterative *Morte Arthur* will suggest the effect:

> Then *d*raws he to Dorset   and *d*elays no longer,
> Doleful, *d*readless,   with *d*rooping tears,
> Comes into Cornwall   with *c*are in his heart.[1]

In our own time some poets have become interested once more in the rhythmic possibilities of such verse as this. And in the Victorian period Gerard Manley Hopkins attempted an unconventional pattern somewhat like that of the old alliterative poetry, which he called **sprung rhythm**. Again in his poetry, one counts not all the syllables but only accented ones to understand the formal principle:

> The world is charged with the grandeur of God.
> It will flash out like shining from shook foil;
> It gathers to a greatness, like the ooze of oil
> Crushed.

In this passage, the four sense-stresses provide the metrical pattern, and these are separated by varying numbers of unstressed syllables. The effect is usually more abrupt than in conventional poetry, but also tends to be more forceful.

Both early English poets and modern experimenters in rhythm are likely to rely on other formal devices in place of conventional meter: on the **caesura**, or very distinct pause dividing a line into two or three parts, and on such repetition of sounds as alliteration. These devices are often included in a discussion of prosody, for they are evidently related to the matters we have just been considering. The formal poets of the eighteenth century, especially conscious of all technical problems of versifying, often use such effects along with a strict meter and rhyme scheme. The feeling of duality we remarked in Pope, whether a duality of oppositions or one of harmonies, can be communicated not only by the syntax of balance and antithesis, and by the diction that produces witty contrasts, but also by the use of a strong **medial caesura**, the pause that breaks a line at the very middle, into two equal parts, and by the characteristic rhyme of the **couplet**, *aa, bb, cc,* and so on. Again, there are two equals, two sides, one echoing the other.

> Awake, my St. John! // leave all meaner things
> To low ambition, // and the pride of Kings.

(Notice that *St. John* is pronounced *Sin-jun,* and that the *and* is taken to be ironically emphatic.) These first lines of the *Essay on Man* illustrate

[1] From *Medieval English Verse and Prose in Modernized Versions,* by Roger S. Loomis and Rudolph Willard; copyright 1948 by Appleton-Century-Crofts, Inc.

the point, breaking exactly in the middle, with the caesura in each line emphasized by a mark of punctuation; the lines include two imperative verbs, *awake* and *leave,* and two objects, *ambition* and *pride;* finally, they make a pointed comparison of two terms in the couplet, rhyming mere *things* with the ordinarily impressive word *Kings*—which is, after all, a smaller thing than the word *Man.*

Although English poets from Chaucer onward have used iambic pentameter lines rhyming in pairs, the distinctly balanced and artificial **heroic couplet,** represented at its highest development by Pope, is a version of this form associated with the Augustan or neoclassical period that begins in the seventeenth century of Waller and Dryden and ends in the early nineteenth century with minor poets like George Crabbe. The heroic couplet is characterized not only by various rhetorical and rhythmic devices we have already observed, but also by a tendency away from **enjambment,** or the running on of a sentence from one couplet into the next, and toward that **end-stopping** illustrated by the period after *Kings* in the lines just quoted. These lines make a **closed couplet:** one sentence is enclosed within it. (The other terms, by the way, can as well be applied to any lines of verse; a line is enjambed, or **run-on,** if it ends without ending a clause, and it is end-stopped if it has a period, semicolon, or colon at the end.) The greatest examples of the heroic couplet are likely to be excellent examples of how all technical means, the use of sound, syntax, and rhythm, work together to qualify diction and produce a witty effect.

There are many other forms as well that illustrate the importance of verse technique in creating the total sense of a poem. Byron's satirical and comic verse, especially in his *Don Juan,* takes advantage of purely arbitrary resemblances between words to rhyme *Aristotle* with *bottle, hero* with *zero;* and, to emphasize the ludicrous aspects of life, he can use even more outrageous rhymes:

> But oh! ye lords of ladies intellectual,
> Inform us truly, have they not henpecked you all?

These lines supply an example of **triple rhyme;** that is, the rhyme embraces the last three syllables in each line. A rhyme like that of *numbers* with *slumbers* is a **double rhyme.** These last rhyme words are **feminine:** the stressed syllable is followed by an unstressed one. A **masculine ending** for a line, the ending on a stressed syllable, is likely to sound strong and serious instead of suggesting either a "dying fall" or the comic effect that Byron has managed.

In considering meter and related subjects, we have necessarily dealt with sound, and in particular with terminal rhyme and with **alliteration,** or the repetition of initial sounds in important words. There are, of course, other sound effects to be recognized. **Consonance,** first of all, occurs when

consonant sounds are repeated, as in Tennyson's line "The *m*oan of doves
in *im*me*m*orial *e*l*m*s." A contrasting device is **assonance**, the repetition of
accented vowels or diphthongs within words, as in another line of Tennyson's, "Than t*i*red *eye*lids upon t*i*red *eyes*." Another effect is **onomatopoeia**,
the imitation of sounds being described, as in the verbs *crack* and *hiss*.
This is in fact a rare device in poetry and one too often mistakenly
ascribed. The less precise term **cacophony** is given to a harsh and heavy-
sounding phrase, and **euphony** to one that sounds more light and easy to
pronounce. The first line of Arnold's sonnet "To a Friend" exemplifies
cacophony—"Who prop, Thou ask'st, in these bad days, my mind?"—
but the last lines achieve a contrasting euphony: "The mellow glory of
the Attic stage,/Singer of sweet Colonus, and its child." If cacophony is
not justified, it may mar or ruin verse, as, for example, in the line from
Browning's "Rabbi Ben Ezra": "Irks care the crop-full bird? Frets doubt
the maw-crammed beast?" But poets may successfully use heavy and
slow-moving lines to give a sense of straining, such as Donne achieves in
his prayer, "Bend/Your force, to break, blow, burn and make me new."
On the other hand, they may choose to combine easy sounds with regular rhythm for a trancelike effect, as Coleridge does in his fragmentary
"Kubla Khan":

> The shadow of the dome of pleasure
> Floated midway on the waves;
> Where was heard the mingled measure
> From the fountain and the caves.

When we think of the importance of sound in poetry, however, we
are likely to think first of rhyme. There are obvious rhymes, like the song-
writer's *moon* and *June,* and subtle ones like the imperfect echoes sometimes called **slant rhymes:** *even, heaven; hearth, earth.* (We have to remember, in speaking of slant rhyme, that pronunciations change, and that
although Pope's rhyming of *obey* and *tea* is not perfect now, it was in his
own period when *tea* was pronounced *tay.*) There are accidental and
musical rhymes that only delight the ear, and there are rhymes that intensify meaning by suggesting a relationship, as the echoing of mere
things by mere *Kings* does. Finally, there are **internal rhymes** as well as
the usual terminal rhymes. Hopkins uses both in "Spring," when he describes how the song of the thrush

> Through the echoing timber does so rinse and wring
> The ear, it strikes like lightning to hear him sing.

The rhyme of *wring* and *sing* is apparent, but that of *ear* and *hear* is no
less carefully planned or less important.

The effect of terminal rhyme is strikingly exemplified by the couplet,
whether heroic or not. But more complicated schemes of terminal rhyme

are also familiar. The **triplet**—three rhyming lines—is most often encountered as a variation in a poem of couplets, but it can be sustained
(*aaa, bbb, ccc,* etc.) throughout a work, as it is in Tennyson's "The Two
Voices." Another uncommon scheme is **terza rima**, rhyming *aba, bcb, cdc,*
etc., which Dante employs for the *Divine Comedy;* probably the most celebrated English version of this form is Shelley's "Ode to the West Wind":

> Make me thy lyre, even as the forest is:
> What if my leaves are falling like its own!
> The tumult of thy mighty harmonies
>
> Will take from both a deep autumnal tone,
> Sweet though in sadness. Be thou, Spirit fierce,
> My spirit! Be thou me, impetuous one!

This passage introduces the subject of the **stanza**, as we notice the
break after every third line of Shelley's. A stanza is a section in the poem
that has a given meter and rhyme scheme; it can be distinguished from a
less formal division according to subject only, called a **verse paragraph.**
The stanzaic poem may have three main logical sections—beginning, middle, and end—but five stanzas, with the logical conclusion beginning in
the middle of, say, the fourth stanza. In contrast, the less formally organized poem with three logical divisions would have three verse paragraphs.
Terza rima, as the passage quoted indicates, has the effect of making its
units interlock; the second line of every stanza is echoed in the first line
of the next. A poem in triplets, on the other hand, has no such inter-
locking.

Any three-line stanza is called a **tercet.** A more familiar stanza is the
quatrain, composed of four lines. Quatrains may be written in a variety
of rhyme schemes and meters, including the **heroic quatrain**, with iambic
pentameter lines rhyming *abab;* the **In Memoriam stanza**, with iambic
tetrameter lines rhyming *abba;* and the **ballad stanza.** Ballad stanzas, the
most common of all, normally alternate tetrameter and trimeter lines,
rhyming *abcb,* as the familiar folk ballads do.

> There lived a wife at Usher's Well;
>   A wealthy wife was she.
> She had three stout and stalwart sons,
>   And sent them o'er the sea.

There are, however, possible variations on this form. Emily Dickinson,
most of whose verse is in one version or another of the ballad stanza, alters
the conventional scheme by using slant rhymes—*room* and *storm, hills*
and *feels, begun* and *afternoon*—or by keeping the rhyme but changing
the length of lines:

> This quiet dust was Gentlemen and Ladies,
>   And lads and girls;
> Was laughter and ability and sighing,
>   And frocks and curls.

Here the lines are pentameter (with an added syllable) and dimeter, instead of tetrameter and trimeter.

Some longer stanza forms are familiar enough, too, so that they bear distinctive names. **Rhyme royal**, a stanza used by Chaucer and later by the poet King James I of Scotland, consists of seven iambic pentameter lines that rhyme *ababbcc*. The eight iambic pentameter lines of **ottava rima**, the stanza used by Byron in *Don Juan,* rhyme *abababcc*. The **Spenserian stanza**, the form of *The Faerie Queene,* has eight lines of iambic pentameter and a final alexandrine, rhyming *ababbcbcc*.

Unlike these stanzaic forms, which are repeated in a poem, the fourteen lines of the **sonnet** constitute a whole poem. The sonnet has been a favorite short lyric form with English poets since the sixteenth century. The **Italian** or **Petrarchan sonnet**, used by Milton and Wordsworth, is divided into an **octave**, a first section of eight lines, and a **sestet**, the final six lines; the octave rhymes *abbaabba,* the sestet, commonly *cdecde,* sometimes *cdcdcd* or some other variant. The **Elizabethan** or **Shakespearean sonnet** consists of three quatrains and a couplet: *abab cdcd efef gg.* (A rare version is the **Spenserian sonnet**, rhyming *abab bcbc cdcd ee.*) Ordinarily, the English sonnet has an iambic pentameter line. This fourteen-line form, in any of its several versions, offers scope along with formal discipline, and so it has been used by a great variety of poets over five centuries, for a great variety of subjects. In the sixteenth and nineteenth centuries and in our own time, poets have produced sonnet sequences, often no doubt with the great Shakespearean sequence in mind; longer works like Rossetti's *House of Life* and Auden's *Quest* consist entirely of sonnets.

To suggest some of the advantages of the sonnet form, let us look at one example, from Shakespeare:

> That time of year thou mayst in me behold,
> When yellow leaves, or none, or few, do hang
> Upon those boughs which shake against the cold,
> Bare ruin'd choirs, where late the sweet birds sang.
> In me thou seest the twilight of such day,
> As after sunset fadeth in the west,
> Which by and by black night doth take away,
> Death's second self, that seals up all in rest.
> In me thou seest the glowing of such fire,
> That on the ashes of his youth doth lie,

As the death-bed whereon it must expire,
Consum'd with that which it was nourish'd by.
   This thou perceiv'st, which makes thy love more strong,
   To love that well, which thou must leave ere long.

Here, the three quatrains consist of a single sentence each, the second
and third beginning with an echo of the phrase "in me," from the first
line. Both this coincidence of syntax with metrical form and this repetition help to emphasize the metaphorical structure of the poem. Each of
the one-sentence quatrains presents a single image for growing old: autumn, twilight, the dying embers, all suggesting loss of light and warmth.
Only in the couplet, however, used to give a striking turn, do we discover
the point of the sonnet. It becomes at last a kind of love poem. Incidentally, Shakespeare likes to use the couplet as a dramatic concluding device in all his work. In his plays, soliloquies and whole scenes often end
with a striking double rhyme. In the sonnets, the couplet does more than
provide a strong final note; it is likely to begin with words like *yet* or *but,*
words that introduce a dramatic reversal and therefore often a witty
or surprising conclusion.

   Although rhythm and sound effects can give pleasure to the ear and
can even in themselves be interesting, these technical matters of meter,
rhyme, and stanza are important primarily as they are relevant to the full
sense communicated by a play or poem. To note the metrical and rhyme
scheme of a Shakespeare sonnet without observing what the sonnet means
and how it achieves its meaning, this is to stop short of critical reading
and to miss the main object of analysis. The verse scheme of a poem
often intensifies or qualifies the stated meaning so as to produce a fuller
meaning. Arnold's rhythm in "Dover Beach" echoes the ebb and flow of
waves. Dante's *terza rima* reflects that threefold order, evident everywhere
in the *Divine Comedy,* that symbolizes the Trinity. Tennyson's triple
rhymes in "The Two Voices" anticipate the climax to a dialogue between
the voice of despair and the voice of resignation, when a third voice of
hope is made possible by the sight of man, wife, and child, a group of
three that represents love in the present and promise for the future; the
rhyme scheme, in contrast with the title of the poem, suggests a resolution with three rather than an unresolved dialogue of two. But most verse
forms qualify the sense of a poem more subtly than in these examples. A
poet can evoke the formal world and ordered manner of speech that seem
appropriate to Augustan satire. Or he can eschew the artifice of rhyme as
Milton does in *Paradise Lost* to attain the higher dignity of **blank verse,**
iambic pentameter lines unrhymed, a form congenial to epic and other
very serious matter. Or he can go as far as Walt Whitman in abandoning
both rhyme and regular meter, to produce lines embodying the spontaneity
and individual freedom that *Leaves of Grass* celebrates:

> I celebrate myself, and sing myself,
> And what I assume you shall assume,
> For every atom belonging to me as good belongs to you.

This unrhymed poetry of irregular rhythms is called **vers libre,** or **free verse** (not to be confused with blank verse), and it obliges the poet to justify the ending of each line according to a break in the phrasing or the sense. In each of these instances, the form or informality of the poem becomes part of its whole meaning.

Tone

Here we are touching on a larger subject, one that involves all the elements of style, including diction, imagery, syntax, sound, and rhythm. This is the subject of **tone.** Although the word is now and then used loosely as if it were a synonym for atmosphere or mood, the usual and more precise sense of literary tone is the expression of attitude, the equivalent in written language of a tone of voice. If we ask in what voice, with what intonation, a lyric or a scene or a passage from a story should be read aloud to communicate the speaker's or the character's or the narrator's attitude, then we are asking about the tone. Some critics commenting on this term have wanted to limit it so as to imply only a speaker's attitude toward his auditor. But when we read narrative prose or verse, the story-teller must be considered to speak to us as auditors; and in the language of many narrators, at least, there seems to be no definite feeling toward the reader, the "listener." To be sure, older novelists, like Fielding, address their readers as their pupils or their peers, but other writers assume the level of their audience without cajoling, condescending, sympathizing, or otherwise showing an attitude toward us. It may be more useful, then, to broaden the definition and to think of literary tone as the expression of attitude toward objects specified or implied. One of the objects attended to may indeed, in a narrative or dramatic work, be another character whom the speaker addresses. Or it may be the mistress to whom a lyric is devoted. Or it may be death, Napoleon, a small town, even the whole universe.

A group of poems about death, for instance, will vary in tone from the darkly solemn to the lightly mocking. Donne's bold lines in defiance, "Death, be not proud!" contrast with the beginning of Shakespeare's song,

> Fear no more the heat o' the sun,
>   Nor the furious winter's rages;
> Thou thy worldly task hast done,
>   Home art gone and ta'en thy wages.
> Golden lads and girls all must,
> As chimney-sweepers, come to dust.

The tone here is neither defiant nor despairing, but a calmly serious one—serious and yet not solemn, for the pun on "come to dust," meaning both "come in order to dust the chimney" and "turn into dust"—does not seem inappropriate. This tone is established by diction, by rhythm, even by the rhyme: *sun* is followed by *done, rages* by *wages,* and the couplet neatly ends the matter.

A literary tone, like a tone of voice, can be formal or easy, arrogant or modest, detached or sentimental, straightforward or ironic. There may even be a variety of tones within one work. Certainly this will be true in a dramatic piece as the scenes and speakers change. But we must distinguish between the shifting tones of characters' speeches and the over-all or controlling tone, especially of less dramatic works. Shakespeare's Iago, in *Othello,* speaks with bitter cynicism, but Othello's final agonizing speech is in a very different voice, and the attitude at last implied toward the events of the play is a tragic one of pity and awe. When the essayist's tone or the narrator's tone in a work of fiction shifts too far or too often, however, the result can easily be confusion, even incoherence. Tennyson's long poem *The Princess* suffers from this failure, because at certain points the main characters and the main actions of the story are treated lightly, with almost a comic effect, and again at other times these people and their actions are described in highly serious language.

In fact, the faults in Tennyson's poetry are usually faults of tone: an extremely and inappropriately serious manner mars the speech of Galahad when he says, "My strength is as the strength of ten,/Because my heart is pure." A narrator might say this about Galahad, but he cannot say it of himself without being pompous. Another difficult tone to control is the sentimental; if such a tone is not fully justified by its subject, the result is **sentimentality,** an indulging in emotion primarily for its own sake. We may well be impatient of this indulgence when a character in a sentimental novel weeps and swoons over the death of a pet, or when we are invited by sad violins to weep if not to swoon over the heroine's unhappiness in a movie "tear-jerker."

Probably the most difficult tone to deal with is the ironic. Irony of tone, or **verbal irony,** should not be confused with irony of event, or **dramatic irony,** although both are means of sharply contrasting appearance with actuality. Dramatic irony occurs when characters on the stage or on the page act upon assumptions so far opposite to the truth that there is a striking discrepancy between what they believe and what the reader or the audience recognizes to be the fact. We know that Sophocles' Oedipus will not triumph by discovering the murderer of King Laius, but he remains unaware that he himself is the slayer, or that Laius was his father. Things are not as they seem to be, and the tragic irony is underlined when a blind man sees the truth to which a sharp-eyed ruler is blind—a ruler who, as soon as *he* sees, loses his power and blinds himself. Verbal irony also results from the contrast of seeming with being, of statement with actuality. The man who says "Oh, great!" in disgust, when he means the opposite, is being ironic. So is Swift when he calls his account of an ugly, aging, overpainted frump "The Progress of Beauty."

There are several kinds of verbal irony. **Sarcasm** means an extreme form of irony, not particularly frequent in literature, that is cutting, personally insulting, and quite unmistakable; it is thus closely related to the direct insult of name-calling or invective. The irony of understatement, **meiosis**, can be illustrated by the common phrase "not bad," meaning "very good." **Socratic irony**, by contrast, is the very sophisticated assumption of ignorance, or uncertainty, by a man who in fact knows his own mind; it is a familiar teaching device, used by Socrates in the dialogues of Plato, and it often involves asking apparently innocent questions that oblige another person to recognize the inconsistencies or absurdities in his own thought. A literary device related to Socratic irony is the use by a sophisticated narrator of a naive commentator or hero, who gullibly accepts the apparent meanings of things when the reader can see that the real meanings are very different: Swift's Gulliver, Voltaire's Candide, and Johnson's Rasselas are all of this species; they are all optimists who must gradually be educated to the hard realities of human life. A further extension of this contrast between illusion within the work and a controlling skepticism, or at least sophistication, is the **Romantic irony** that characterizes some works of the late eighteenth and early nineteenth century. Romantic irony exploits the simultaneous sense of the lovely and the ludicrous, the sublime and the ridiculous. It is a way of being at one and the same time serious and deprecating about a subject. Thus Mephistopheles, in Goethe's *Faust,* is a wisecracking and flippant devil, but still, in another sense, the devil. Many of his paradoxes and witticisms sound purely frivolous, and yet they suggest all sorts of indisputable truths about human nature; or, rather, many of his sayings express the truth, but only in a light and frivolous way. Byron in *Don Juan* produces a similar effect by indulging in the most moving sentiments and then with a wry phrase undercutting them.

The term *irony* has come more recently to take on rather larger meanings than any yet mentioned. A philosophical sense of so-called **cosmic irony** pervades the work of certain late Victorian and early modern writers, especially Thomas Hardy, for whom the world seems always to hold frustration and emptiness precisely when men believe they can find fulfillment. But perhaps this is not strictly a matter of tone so much as one of belief. An even more extended sense of the word that refers at least in part to literary tone is favored by those contemporary critics who use *irony* as a term of praise. Most great literature, according to their view, involves some double awareness, some recognition that every truth is only partial and is qualified by its opposite. This sense of irony, which is really an extension of the Romantic irony we have just observed, does not oppose what is apparent to what is real, but a partial reality to another partial reality; the ironic tone, according to this meaning, is a refusal of complete commitment to any single view of things as too simple. It can be illustrated by a witty song from the musical comedy *Gentlemen Prefer Blondes.*

> I'm just a little girl from Little Rock.
> We lived on the wrong side of the tracks,
> But a gentleman took me out one night,
> And after he taught me wrong from right,
> We moved to the right side of the tracks.[1]

These words are sung by a girl who was started on her very agreeable life of luxury by being seduced. Throughout the lyrics, social and practical *right* equals moral *wrong;* but this is no piece of morality, and the song ironically refuses to commit itself to one set of values or the other, the practical or the moral.

The critical reader has not only to recognize the tone of a passage as cool or sentimental, ironic or solemn, but also to judge its consistency, subtlety, and appropriateness. Some of the finest examples of tone, certainly, are the most subtle. Here, for one, is a fairly complex passage about a young Irish boy falling in love from James Joyce's story "Araby."

> Her image accompanied me even in places the most hostile to romance. On Saturday evenings when my aunt went marketing I had to go to carry some of the parcels. We walked through the flaring streets, jostled by drunken men and bargaining women, amid the curses of labourers, the shrill litanies of shop-boys who stood on guard by the barrels of pigs' cheeks, the nasal chanting of street-singers, who sang a *come-all-you* about O'Donovan Rossa, or a ballad about the troubles in our native land. These noises converged in a single sensation of life for me: I imagined that I bore my chalice safely through a throng of foes. Her name sprang to my lips at moments in strange prayers and praises which I myself did not understand. My eyes were often full of tears (I could not tell why) and at times a flood from my heart seemed to pour itself out into my bosom. I thought little of the future. I did not know whether I would ever speak to her or not, or if I spoke to her, how I could tell her of my confused adoration. But my body was like a harp and her words and gestures were like fingers running upon the wires.[2]

In this paragraph the diction and rhythm, especially important for the tone, produce a nice balance between romantic and matter-of-fact. Such evocative words as *romance, sensation, strange, bosom,* even *harp,* echo the language of sentiment, and another group of words adds religious heightening to the emotions described: *image, litanies, chanting, chalice, prayers, praises, adoration.* (The parallel between religious feelings and the young boy's most personal emotion is suggested elsewhere in the story.) Associated with this romantic and elevated diction, the rhythm of almost all the sentences is lyrical, like that of a series of very short poems. And yet the tone of the whole passage is not purely rhapsodic, as it would be if there were not other elements involved. Against the romantic diction is posed another group of words: *curses, pigs' cheeks, nasal,* perhaps even *the future.* At least one sentence is distinctly prosaic: "I thought little of the future." And although the individual sentences may sound like lyrics, the paragraph is not a poem: read together, the sentences often begin abruptly, and there are more breaks, more separate sentences, than there would be in an emotional outburst. After all, the feeling is controlled and modified; it is the tone of a mature man, not that of an adolescent boy, of reminiscence, not of pure ecstasy.

Clearly, in dealing with literary tone, we are once more dealing at the same time with other subjects. Sometimes writing and talking about literature seems rather like trying to describe the god Proteus, who had the disagreeable habit of changing constantly from one shape to another. First we find that *structure* can mean just the poem itself, and then, as soon as we look at the various elements of structure, each one of them appears to merge into another until everything equals everything else: *diction,* or the choice of words in a poem, is literally the whole poem (which is nothing but words), but in another sense the *plot* or argument is the poem, and diction becomes part of a logic; and they all amount in turn to what is called *tone,* the expression of an attitude toward a subject. Of course it is not the poem itself—or the novel or the play—that is always changing, but our way of looking at it, when we use these various terms to describe what makes up its structure. We must recognize that these are our terms and not separate parts of a literary work, like the ingredients of a stew. It is, after all, possible to use such necessary words with some exactness but with a modest discretion, too.

CHAPTER THREE

Literary Traditions and Conventions

Important as it is to analyze a novel, play, or poem in and for itself, it is often just as important to know to what group or family it belongs. We are interested in such classification not just for the sake of tidiness, but rather because it is helpful to know the background, the traditions or conventions a writer is either using or consciously playing against. We may, in fact, limit or actually distort the meaning of a work if we ignore its literary background.

But determining to what group or class a work belongs is no simple matter. Even the distinction between poetry and prose, obvious as it appears at first glance, is a complex and debatable subject, not to be dismissed with the pronouncement of Molière's bourgeois gentleman that whatever is not prose is poetry, and whatever is not poetry is prose.

Poetry and Prose

One difference between these two forms which is frequently mentioned has to do with the language or diction they use. As we have seen, poetry is commonly associated with images, with concrete descriptive phrases and the figurative language of similes and metaphors—and sometimes also with that special "poetic diction" whereby fish become "the finny tribe," birds are elevated into "the feathered flock," and rats are unmentionable unless disguised as "the whiskered vermin race." Prose, in contrast, is associated with plain, straightforward statements, unadorned by imagery and close to everyday or colloquial speech. Lord Chesterfield explained to his son that in prose one says "the beginning of the morning" or "the break of day"; in poetry, "Aurora spread her rosy mantle." Though we would certainly acknowledge that the language of poetry is more consciously chosen, with more attention to precision and suggestiveness than the language of common speech, it is not clear that there is always a very sharp dividing line between the language of poetry and that of good literary prose. Shakespeare's sonnets or Keats' odes are indeed richly imagistic, but

there are lines which seem hardly to use images at all—for example, John
Dryden's forthright statement in his *Religio Laici* that the ordinary per-
son need not trouble himself about the fine points in the doctrine of the
Incarnation:

> Shall I speak plain, and in a nation free
> Assume an honest layman's liberty?
> I think (according to my little skill,
> To my own Mother Church submitting still)
> That many have been sav'd, and many may,
> Who never heard this question brought in play.

As for the refined and elevated "poetic diction," this was cultivated only
at certain periods, notably in the eighteenth century, and it was character-
istic mainly of certain literary types such as the heroic epic or the pastoral.
We have observed how modern poets, particularly T. S. Eliot and W. H.
Auden, at times quite consciously choose colloquial and even slangy dic-
tion. On the other hand, there are prose passages, in John Donne or Sir
Thomas Browne, for example, which are extremely ornate and figurative.
And even in more simple, utilitarian prose—John Locke's or John Stuart
Mill's—explanatory similes or metaphors are used from time to time for
emphasis. Any difference in language, then, would be only one of degree.

The same comment can be made about the commonly held assumption that meter and rhythm distinguish poetry from prose. On the one
hand, meter is not characteristic of all poetry; and although poetry does
indeed tend to have a strongly marked rhythm, certain poems, such as
those written in free verse, have what might almost be considered prose
rhythms. On the other hand, prose may have such strongly marked
rhythm, as in the incantatory passages of the King James Bible or some
of Ahab's speeches in *Moby-Dick*, that it can be scanned as if it were
poetry. Again, no hard-and-fast lines can be drawn.

Another possible distinction between poetry and prose seems at first
glance to be too obvious to be worth mentioning. It is that poetry is presented in lines of arbitrary length, whereas prose is written in a continuous flow. There is, to be sure, the intermediate form of **prose poetry**, in
which the words are arranged as if they made up a prose paragraph but
have the pronounced rhythm of poetry. Charles Baudelaire, who experimented with this form, significantly entitled his collection *Little Poems in
Prose*. But on the whole, it seems fair to say that poetry and prose simply
look quite different on the printed page. Although this may sound like a
very superficial distinction, it suggests a more fundamental point. Poetry,
we might say, submits to a tighter, more arbitrary form than does prose; it
is, in other words, the product of greater craftsmanship, of greater attention to detail. And this point suggests still another and even more fundamental distinction—that poetry expresses meaning in a more concise and

concentrated fashion than prose, using many more of the possibilities of verbal art. It is to achieve such concentration, presumably, that it uses the devices of allusion or multiple connotation, leaving it to the reader to catch the full significance, and it is to this end, too, that the sound may be made to echo the sense. Prose, in contrast, tends to be more discursive, to spell out the full meaning by making clear whatever undertones or implications there may be.

Genre and Convention

But more useful than the very broad classification of poetry and prose is the study of the more specific literary types, the so-called *genres*. The term **genre** comes from the French, and is derived from the Latin *genus, generis,* meaning "kind," "sort," or "type." Indeed, before this term was taken over into English, critics used to speak only of the literary **kinds** or the literary **types**, using terms still current today. *Genre* is related to such terms as *genus, generation,* and *general,* a fact which indicates that it refers to certain general categories or subdivisions of literature. It suggests an interest in classifying literary works by what they have in common, by what distinguishes one group from another.

As in the case of poetry and prose, the classification poses something of a problem. What makes a genre a genre, what characteristics distinguish one from the other, may vary considerably. In one case, it may be chiefly a matter of verse form: fourteen lines organized according to a certain meter and rhyme scheme constitute a sonnet. In another case, the decisive factor seems to be the subject matter: the description of an ideal society, invented in order to suggest what might be improved in existing societies, is the chief characteristic of literary **utopias.**

There are, furthermore, certain conventions which have come to be the distinctive features of some of the genres. The term **convention** refers to any arbitrary device or rule of conduct which we agree to accept (Latin *convenire* means "to come together" or "to agree"), and as a matter of fact we accept so many of these in life and in literature that we sometimes have to remind ourselves that they really are only conventions. We take it for granted, for instance, that a fork can be put into one's mouth, but not a knife, and that when a gentleman wears tails and a top hat, he will not bicycle to his destination. In roughly the same way, we have no difficulty in assuming, at the theater, that we can look into a room, one of whose walls has apparently been removed, and we must make a conscious effort to realize that this convention would have to be explained to a spectator accustomed only to the Greek amphitheater. We also accept without qualm the novelistic device whereby the narrator moves freely from one character's mind to another's, or from place to place and from one moment of time to another, with a flexibility we certainly do not have in real life. Some conventions, to be sure, can easily seem somewhat old-fashioned and ridiculous: for instance, the long and loud aria of the tenor in grand opera when he is dying of a sword-thrust, or the aside in a play, supposedly heard only by the audience but obviously audible to the other characters on stage. But we accept innumerable other conventions without question, such as the soliloquy of Elizabethan tragedy, the speech of a character alone on stage, revealing his innermost thoughts, or the invocation and epic question at the beginning of most epics, whereby the poet calls on the Muses for help and asks a key question which introduces the main subject of the poem.

Ancient Genres: Drama, Epic, and Lyric

To cut through the seemingly impenetrable tangle of genre classification, we might begin by considering the oldest grouping, which has come down from classical antiquity. It consists of three basic literary types: drama, epic, and lyric. These three can be differentiated in a number of ways: according to rather obvious formal traits, general structure, tone, kind and source of subject, and, finally, relation of the narrator to the action.

The drama, first of all, comes to the spectators through the combined actions and speeches of characters as they move about on a stage. Northrop Frye, in his *Anatomy of Criticism,* describes it as words that are acted out in front of the audience. Furthermore, drama tends to be a concentrated form, in which action leads rather rapidly to a climax and denouement, usually without time to introduce wholly unrelated material. As for the subject matter, it ranges from that of tragedy—often the historical or legendary exploits of noble figures who may seem to be larger than life—to that of comedy—usually invented, fictitious versions of everyday life and the actions of more or less exaggerated people who tend to be ordinary rather than heroic. Finally, in drama the writer seems to be hidden behind the action, letting his characters do the acting and speaking, so that even when one of them is virtually a mouthpiece for the playwright's ideas, as Tanner in Shaw's *Man and Superman* and Undershaft in the same author's *Major Barbara* appear to be, that fact is qualified by the speaker's still being a dramatic person with a limited point of view.

The epic, being a long narrative poem, is more purely a form of speech. This is especially true of the older epics such as the *Iliad,* the *Odyssey,* and *Beowulf,* which were intended to be chanted by a *rhapsode* or *scop* before a group of listeners. The epic is also much longer than the drama; at the Pan-Athenaic festivals in the fifth century B. C. the rhapsodes had to take turns chanting the *Iliad* or *Odyssey,* since the task was too much for any one man. Being longer, the epic tends to have a less tight structure than the drama, sometimes even becoming episodic: presenting, that is, a series of loosely related incidents, as in the *Odyssey*. It is clear that in Virgil's *Aeneid* tightly and loosely constructed books are presented alternately, as if on the analogy of the *Iliad* on the one hand and the *Odyssey* on the other. Epic subject matter consists of the exploits of heroic figures, men of great stature and even gods; these exploits are given vast significance, affecting whole civilizations in the work of Homer and Virgil, and, finally, in Milton's *Paradise Lost,* affecting the whole of mankind. Like tragedy, the epic is likely to draw its subjects from history and myth instead of inventing new tales. As for the relation of the narrator to the action, he may intervene in his own voice to invoke a muse, to ask the traditional epic question—as Homer asks what god has brought about a quarrel between Agamemnon and Achilles—or, like Milton, to make moral comments on the action described. In this the epic poet is unlike the dramatist.

As the very name suggests, the lyric was originally intended to be sung, to the accompaniment of a lyre. It is usually much shorter than either the drama or the epic, taking only a matter of minutes to speak or to read. Being so much shorter, it tends to be more tightly constructed; in fact, it usually has great unity and may be restricted to exploring a single mood. Its subject matter consists of personal emotions, such as love or grief, or public emotions, such as the patriotic admiration of national heroes or reverence for the gods or God. The tone may be either serious or light. For the most part, the lyric makes use of neither historical and legendary nor fictitious material. It draws mainly on the immediate experience or mood of the poet, whether as a personal or a public individual. The lyric poet, finally, seems to speak purely as himself, in his own voice: he presents himself as being closely related to the objects and actions described, whether they are his mistress in her silks, the daffodils beside the lake, or his dead friend whom he mourns. As Professor Frye has observed, in this form the audience seems to be concealed from the poet, whereas in drama the poet seems to be concealed from the audience.

Romance and Novel

We have been considering so far only the three oldest and most general literary types and the main ways of distinguishing among them. But the situation is vastly more complicated because many more than the three basic genres have since become current and popular. Let us look, for example, at what has happened to the long narrative.

The Middle Ages saw the creation of the chivalric romance, the narrative of the strange and exciting adventures of knights errant and

damsels in distress. It is related to the epic because it is very long and
deals with rather noble or heroic figures. But its structure is much more
episodic, as one adventure after another is recounted; and in subject matter, love may be more important than war. Furthermore, the story is based
even less on history and more on legend than the plot of an epic, and much
of the material is wholly the result of invention. This is true especially of
the sensational elements—the so-called **marvelous**—which abound in
chivalric romance. Knights encounter monsters and giants; wicked spirits
transform themselves into seductive ladies; and a hero who falls into the
hands of a ruthless magician may end up as a tree in the midst of the
forest. In *Amadis of Gaul,* one of the most popular of the romances, these
and other improbable events follow one another with implausible speed.
Similar interests are prominent in *The Faerie Queene,* although they are
more controlled by the allegorical meaning Spenser wants to convey. It is
clear that this genre is well named: *chivalric* to suggest its subject of the
deeds and trials of knighthood; *romance* to suggest the largely invented
narrative of love and adventure.

The modern version of the long narrative is the **novel.** This genre
resembles the epic in length and in emphasis on the narrative, but differs
from it by being in prose, as well as by its choice and treatment of subject
matter. So flexible is the novel as a genre that it is best described simply
as a long narrative in prose. As a matter of fact, it embraces so many subtypes that one can hardly generalize about it further. Usually, we might
say, it deals with middle-class characters and ordinary life; that is, it seldom focuses on legendary heroes or royalty as do tragedy and the epic.
But there are no hard-and-fast limits. Defoe's Moll Flanders is a professional London thief, a low and classless creature who is even, at one point,
deported to America. The Baroness d'Orczy wrote about the French aristocracy in her Scarlet Pimpernel series, and a recent novel by T. H. White,
The Once and Future King, deals with King Arthur. On the whole, however, the characters of the novel are engaged in such ordinary, fundamental pursuits as trying to get married, going on travels, making money,
and advancing themselves in their society or profession—all this quite
apart from whatever psychological development they may be undergoing.

This kind of material is, quite obviously, based on invention rather
than on history or legend. Only in a certain type of historical novel, some
of the minor characters and some of the incidents are drawn from actual
fact. In *War and Peace,* for instance, Tolstoy includes Napoleon and the
Russian general Kutuzov among his characters; and in his Lanny Budd
series, Upton Sinclair lets his young hero have lengthy conversations with
Roosevelt and Churchill in order to depict the problems before and during
World War II. Still, this kind of reference is not common in the novel,
which usually tries to set up its own little world, its independent micro-

cosm. On the other hand, however much the material is the product of invention, the treatment it characteristically receives in the novel is realistic. The characters and incidents are usually described in such a way as to make them seem ordinary and even factually true. The narrator nearly always tries to give the impression that he is reporting the facts as they occurred, and to do so, he often gives a very full description of the ordinary things of life—so much so that Lionel Trilling feels that the novel, more than any other literary form, gives us "the hum and buzz" of a society. Even in *Robinson Crusoe,* which deals with the rather unusual situation of someone's being shipwrecked on a deserted island and having to build up his life anew, Defoe gives the impression of reality by a careful and matter-of-fact recording of all the steps Crusoe painstakingly takes to provide himself with food, shelter, and a satisfying routine of life. But in this respect, too, there are obvious exceptions. The so-called **Gothic novel,** which became popular in the eighteenth century and is an ancestor of the modern mystery story, fantasy, and science fiction, is full of implausible action, introduced for the sake of sensationalism. In Walpole's *Castle of Otranto,* to mention only one example, a young man is mysteriously crushed to death by a huge helmet belonging to an unknown giant; a family portrait sighs audibly; and at length the whole castle of Otranto is shattered as the ghostly giant rises to avenge himself and his family on the present owner, who has usurped the title and property. This kind of novel is still quite close to the romances we have just considered.

Subgroups

Not only have new genres such as the chivalric romance and novel sprung up which cannot readily be fitted in with the three basic types of drama, the epic, and the lyric, but there are also innumerable subgroups which we ought to recognize as such. In particular, the term *lyric,* which we have been using for any relatively short poem expressing the poet's private or public feelings, refers to a very broad category. Some of its subgroups are distinguished by a special subject matter and a set of recurring devices: the **elegy,** for example, is a song of mourning, and the **epithalamion** a wedding song, in both of which personifications of nature or classical and mythological figures are brought in to mourn or rejoice with the poet. Incidentally, when an elegy is elevated in tone or conceived as a choral chant, it may also be called a **threnody;** when it is very simple and songlike it may be known as a **dirge.** Other groups are held together by a special tone and versification, notably the **ode,** an elaborate, solemn celebration or "effusion," often in strikingly irregular verse-form.[1] The sonnet,

---

[1] The ode may be either **Pindaric** or **Horatian;** and Pindaric odes, in turn, may be either genuinely like those the Greek poet Pindar wrote to celebrate the

we have seen, is characterized by the particularly tight form of fourteen pentameter lines and a predetermined rhyme-scheme into which the sense is fitted. The **ballad** is a rather fully developed and distinct subgroup of the lyric. Quite apart from its special verse form, it tends to have a typical subject matter of its own, for it is commonly a simple but dramatic narrative based on a folk story, such as the adventures of that gallant sailor, Sir Patrick Spens, or the clashes between the Percies and Douglases on the borders of Scotland. It has a characteristic tone of pathos and understatement, particularly when the hero is drowned or killed in battle or, as in "Lord Randal," actually murdered. Often intended to be sung, the ballad may have a refrain; it may also use the special device of **incremental repetition,** the recurrence of a refrain or of some other element with slight changes at each reappearance, such that the narrative is carried forward. Many ballads are folk poetry or folk songs in the sense that their author is unknown and they may even be the product of a whole community; for a long time, they were passed on chiefly by word of mouth, and probably underwent gradual change in the process. A number of so-called **literary ballads** such as Coleridge's "The Ancient Mariner," Keats' "La Belle Dame sans Merci," and W. H. Auden's story of the life and death of Miss Edith Gee, are modeled on the folk ballad and use the same devices. Oddly enough, the broad category of the lyric even includes a special subgroup which we also call the **lyric:** a very short, songlike poem of no predetermined subject matter or verse form, such as Shakespeare's "Full fathom five," Herrick's "A sweet disorder in the dress," or Wordsworth's Lucy poems. In this case, the genus and species confusingly bear the same name.

The kinds of drama, too, have proliferated vastly in the course of time.[1] In the Middle Ages, when drama was closely related to the activities of the Church, three of the chief forms, all in verse, were the **miracle play,** dramatizing the life of a saint; the **mystery play,** presenting episodes of the Old and New Testaments; and the **morality play,** an allegory showing

---

winners of the Olympic and other national games, or only superficially so. Pindar created a pattern of three sections, named after the actions of the chorus which presented the ode: the **strophe** or "turn," with lines of varying length, was chanted as the chorus turned or danced to one side; the **antistrophe** or "counter-turn," repeating precisely the metrical form of the strophe, was chanted as the chorus moved to the other side; and the **epode** or "stand," in a different metrical form, was chanted, so far as we can tell, while the chorus stood still. Ben Jonson and Thomas Gray both used this form. Various other English poets, misunderstanding or disregarding Pindar's structural principles and imitating only his surface appearance of irregularity, have written odes which are irregular both in length of lines and in the number of lines within sections. Perhaps the most famous example is Wordsworth's "Intimations of Immortality" ode. In contrast to the Pindaric, the Horatian ode is more restrained in tone and uses a recurring stanzaic form. An example is Collins' "Ode to Evening."

[1] We postpone for the moment a consideration of the two chief dramatic genres, tragedy and comedy. See below, 90–116.

the struggle between vices and virtues in order to extol the Christian way of life. The mystery plays, performed by the craft guilds of various English towns, were often presented in series or "cycles" dramatizing Biblical incidents from the Creation to Judgment Day, the individual episodes being acted out at various "stages" or platforms in different parts of town. Strong and unmistakable as the religious and moral themes were in these genres, secular details were introduced in order to add realistic or comic touches. In *The Second Shepherds' Play,* a mystery play about the nativity belonging to the Wakefield cycle, much is made of a comic sheep-stealing incident, and in *Everyman,* the best-known of the morality plays, a cousin refuses to accompany Everyman on his journey into the next world with the thin excuse—delightfully chosen for its triviality and for its glimpse of an all-too-human selfishness—that he has a cramp in his toe.

The Renaissance brought a variety of dramatic genres. **Chronicle or history plays** dramatized the events recorded in the chronicles or historical accounts of Geoffrey of Monmouth, Holinshed, and others, usually with much attention to spectacular processions and violent battles presented on-stage. In following the chronicles, they tended to be episodic in structure, but the best of these plays have some sort of unifying feature. Marlowe's *Edward II* and Shakespeare's *Richard III* are compelling studies of character. *Richard II* actually approaches tragedy, and *Henry IV,* comedy. Designed to appeal to the patriotism of the Elizabethan audience, the history plays often had a serious theme, such as the danger of interrupting the succession to the throne and the desirability of a firm and stable rule. Another genre, **tragicomedy,** was developed by the Elizabethan and Jacobean playwrights not just as a mingling of tragic and comic elements—the introduction of the comic gravediggers in *Hamlet* or the drunken porter in *Macbeth*—but as a special type of highly sensational drama, in which the plot might easily end in catastrophe but is miraculously brought to a happy conclusion. Shakespeare's *Winter's Tale* and *Cymbeline* with their suspicious husbands and wronged wives, as well as Beaumont and Fletcher's *Philaster,* belong to this form, in which consistency of tone is sacrificed for the sake of thrills, surprises, and other strong assaults on the emotions of the audience. Still another genre that became popular in the Renaissance and continued through the seventeenth century is the **masque,** an elaborate courtly entertainment in which music and dance enliven a rather simple allegorical plot. Shakespeare introduces a masque of harvest and fertility toward the end of *The Tempest.* As a separate form it is beautifully worked out by Milton in his *Comus* and, in a lighter vein, by Dryden in his "Secular Masque."

Nearer to our own time, one of the popular genres is the **problem play,** in which serious moral, social, or political problems are explored in a more or less realistic manner. Ibsen was one of the first to present this kind of play; in his *Doll's House* he dramatizes the plight of the "new" woman (new in the nineteenth century) who is not content to lead the sheltered existence of a housewife and mother. Shaw's *Widowers' Houses* shows the dilemma of an earnest young man who disapproves of the wealth other people gain from tenement housing but suddenly discovers that his own income, from supposedly respectable investments, ultimately comes from the same disreputable source. The play becomes a witty and paradoxical criticism of capitalist society. The numerous current dramas about racial strife and political or ideological conflicts belong to the same category. It is characteristic of this kind of drama that little or no attempt is made to suggest a solution for the problem. Usually, none exists, and it would be simplifying the problem to present one.

When we turn from the drama to the novel, a staggering number of subgroups confront us. An early and relatively distinct type is the **picaresque** novel, so called because its hero is a picaro (the Spanish term for "rogue") seeking adventures on the highways and in the inns of his country, though he may also come into contact with high life. *Lazarillo de Tormes,* Lesage's *Gil Blas,* and Smollett's *Roderick Random* represent the type. Although the hero commonly begins as a naive and good-natured fellow, he is soon drawn into a world of opportunists and scoundrels and becomes as bad or almost as bad as the rest in order to survive. Fielding's Joseph Andrews and Tom Jones are significant variations of the picaro, since they retain their good natures in spite of the selfish, vain, and hypocritical people they meet. The picaresque novel tends to deal with middle-class or low life, to treat its subject either realistically or comically and satirically, and to have a distinctly episodic structure, as adventure after adventure is recounted. In several ways it is the counterpart on a lower level to the episodic chivalric romance, which deals with the adventures of knights errant on the roads of their country; and it was a bold stroke of Cervantes to combine and play off against each other the elements of both genres in his *Don Quixote.*

Another early type is the **epistolary novel,** consisting of the letters the characters write to each other. Samuel Richardson, master of this form, uses it not only to present elaborate analyses of the psychological and social situations in which his heroines Pamela and Clarissa find themselves, but also to create extensive plot complications. That is, he has some of the letters copied, forged, delayed, or missent. Other writers using the form, notably Rousseau in his *Nouvelle Héloïse* and Goethe in his *Werther,* pay more attention to the psychological revelations that can be achieved. Since letters can take us into the very minds of the characters, the epistolary novel has been considered a precursor of the modern stream-of-consciousness form.

From the nineteenth century on, one of the novel-forms popular especially in Germany was the so-called **Bildungsroman** or **Erziehungs-roman** (*Bildung* and *Erziehung* meaning "education" in its broadest sense of growing up and maturing). Starting with Goethe's *Wilhelm Meister,* a largish and distinctive group of novels, including Keller's *Green Henry,* Mann's *Magic Mountain,* Romain Rolland's *Jean Christophe,* and Maugham's *Of Human Bondage,* trace the maturing of a young man to the point where he reaches an understanding of himself and of his environment. Joyce's *Portrait of the Artist as a Young Man* belongs in a sense to this group, but since it deals specifically with the maturing of a young man who feels himself destined to be a writer, it may be assigned also to another genre, the so-called **Künstlerroman** (*Künstler* meaning "artist"), which concentrates on the problems of a writer or painter in relation to his art and his society. Mann's *Dr. Faustus,* Maugham's *The Moon and Sixpence,* and Joyce Cary's *The Horse's Mouth* are in the same group. In so far as these novels dwell on a complex psychological development, they belong, moreover, to still another genre, the **psychological novel,** along with *Madame Bovary, The Brothers Karamazov,* and all stream-of-consciousness novels.

When the emphasis is less on individual characters than on social problems, as in John Steinbeck's *The Grapes of Wrath,* one speaks of the **sociological novel,** and when the focus is on the working classes, also of the **proletarian novel. Novels of the soil,** as the very name implies, concentrate on country life, and usually more on its hardships than on its pleasures. The characters are likely to make up for their lack of polish by an unmistakable earthiness or vitality. The novel of the soil is delightfully parodied in Stella Gibbons' *Cold Comfort Farm.*

Still another distinctive modern type is the **novel of ideas,** in which the characters and situations are chosen less for their own sake than to illustrate certain intellectual or cultural trends. Huxley's *Brave New World* and *Point Counter Point,* Mann's *Magic Mountain,* Sartre's *Age of Reason,* and Orwell's *1984* immediately come to mind. Then, too, there is the so-called **roman à clef,** literally, the novel with a key, in which the characters stand for actual people and can be recognized as such by the initiated. In Huxley's *Point Counter Point,* the vitalist Rampion is clearly intended to represent D. H. Lawrence; in *The Magic Mountain,* the somewhat fatuous but impressive Mynheer Peeperkorn supposedly stands for the German playwright Gerhart Hauptmann. Many of the popular **political novels** (themselves a special group, descended from Trollope's *Phineas Finn* and Disraeli's *Coningsby*) thrive on the faint aura of scandal brought them by the impression that some of the characters are based on actual people. The Gothic novel we considered earlier, the historical novel, detective story, ghost story, Western, science fiction —each of these can be regarded as yet another species of the novel, with distinctive characters, situations, and even settings and moods. We should, however, bear in mind that the various categories we have been enumerating are not mutually exclusive. *Point Counter Point* is a novel of ideas which is also a psychological novel and, in a minor way, a *roman à clef*. *The Magic Mountain* is all three of these and also a *Bildungsroman*. *War and Peace*—to choose an earlier and still more complex example—is all of these, but a historical novel as well, and it has a number of features which relate it to the epic.

The novel is not by any means the only form dominated by narrative interest. In the Middle Ages, one of the popular genres was the fabliau, a short, realistic, and often bawdy tale, in either prose or verse, about the exploits of middle or lower class characters. Often dwelling on how a young scholar gets the better of a member of the clergy, or one kind of craftsman outwits another, this type of story is generally told simply for its own sake, and not for any possible moral. Chaucer's Miller in *The Canterbury Tales* is assigned a lively and memorable fabliau, dealing with a gullible carpenter who loses his young wife to a quick-witted student when he believes the latter's story that a new flood is imminent and that he had better spend the night in a tub suspended from the ceiling. Not to be confused with the fabliau is that other type of short narrative called the fable, again in either prose or verse, which features animals instead of human characters, but presents these animals in such a way as to point a moral clearly applicable to human behavior. La Fontaine's fly, who buzzes around the six straining horses and the coachman's nose, convinced that it is she alone who is making the heavy coach move up the hill, is an obvious example of the foolish and self-righteous busybody, even without the little moral the poet feels constrained to draw at the end.

More strictly a narrative in prose is the philosophical tale or conte, which came into vogue especially in the eighteenth century. As its name suggests, the characters and situations are presented chiefly to illustrate certain ideas, so that there is much less attention to character development or the details of life than there is in the novel. In Voltaire's *Candide,* everything is chosen to demonstrate the absurdity of the optimistic view of life; in Dr. Johnson's *Rasselas,* to show the vanity of human wishes and the need to accept life as it is. In our own day, this type of shorter narrative is represented by George Orwell's *Animal Farm* and by John Steinbeck's *Pippin IV,* both of which are also satiric allegories.

The dominant modern form of shorter prose narrative is the short story. The term is somewhat vague, since it refers to anything from one-page stories in popular magazines to lengthy pieces such as Conrad's *Heart of Darkness*. Whatever form the various stories may take—character study, dramatization of an exciting incident, sketching a certain mood or atmosphere—the main feature of the genre seems to be a certain unity of impression or unity of effect, as opposed to the greater diversity, more complicated action, greater variety of characters, or longer time-span one associates with the novel. To describe the kind of narrative which is so long as to defy being called a short story but which is not complex enough to warrant the name of novel (*Heart of Darkness,* James' *Turn of the Screw,* Mann's *Death in Venice*), the terms **long short story** and **novelette** are sometimes used.

Modern Genres: Drama, Poetry, and Fiction

Because of the many additional types and subtypes, some of which have just been reviewed, we tend nowadays to accept a basic scheme rather different from the traditional one of drama, epic, and lyric. If we were asked to name offhand the three obvious basic genres, we should almost without hesitation say drama, poetry, and fiction. Drama is still roughly what it was in ancient times, but more extensive in range, including tragedy, comedy, and the various other forms we have noted—the mystery, miracle, and morality plays, tragicomedy, the problem play, and so forth. Poetry includes all the forms we have considered under the heading of the lyric, along with the **epigram**, the short witty saying in verse; the **philosophical poem** expounding ideas, such as Lucretius' *Of the Nature of Things* or Pope's *Essay on Man;* and the **descriptive nature poem** such as Thomson's *Seasons.* It would also embrace the **dramatic monologue,** that form of soliloquy in which the speaker—Browning's Andrea del Sarto or Bishop of St. Praxed's, Tennyson's Ulysses, or T. S. Eliot's Prufrock—usually addressing another character as in a dramatic scene, reveals an interesting situation or problem and also, often unconsciously, an intriguing personality. Oddly enough, the epic, which was once considered important and distinctive enough to be regarded as a separate genre, would now be classified as one type of poetry. Or it might be placed under the larger heading of **fiction,** which can cover all lengthy narratives. Usually, however, except when it is applied to the epic, the term *fiction* is reserved for prose. The term is very broad, and seems to embrace any of the more or less elaborate narratives ranging from the short story to the novel.

Fiction and Non-Fiction

Sometimes we also speak of two other general categories: fiction and non-fiction. *Fiction* remains the loose term for narratives, usually in prose. **Non-fiction** includes a large group of writing: **biography,** the study of someone's life, brilliantly exemplified by Boswell's *Life of Samuel Johnson;* **autobiography,** such as that by John Stuart Mill, an account of the writer's own life; the **memoir** or personal reminiscence of a man or a period; the diary or journal, such as the famous one kept by Pepys; and letters, of which the collections of Horace Walpole's and John Keats' correspondence are highly praised examples. Memoirs, diaries, letters, and the like are sometimes known as familiar literature, since they illuminate the ordinary and even private lives of a period and may lack the formality of structure and often also of style associated with, say, the epic or tragedy. The eighteenth century is particularly rich in this type. Whereas all the foregoing kinds of non-fiction tend to focus on characters or personalities, other kinds concentrate on ideas. The essay is, literally, a "trial" of ideas (from French essayer, "try"). It may be subdivided into familiar essays, such as Montaigne's or Lamb's, and formal ones, such as Arnold's literary criticism, each kind depending on the structure, tone, or style the writer adopts. There are, furthermore, the philosophical dialogues, used by Plato, Berkeley, and others, in which two or more characters present different points of view and thereby again test certain ideas; and collections of maxims or reflections, the most famous being Pascal's Pensées.

Actually, it is a matter of debate to what extent these various kinds of non-fiction can still be regarded as literature in the sense in which we have defined it, as an imaginative recreation of life which involves the creation of a "virtual world." Some of the diaries and letters may have more historical than literary interest; some of the essays and dialogues may have a purely philosophical importance. And yet, we could argue that nearly all the well-known works we have just noted at least border on literature in our sense of the word. Quite apart from the unmistakable strength of style which most of these have, Boswell in his Life of Johnson and Montaigne in his Essays, for example, present brilliant characterizations of others and of themselves, as well as a teeming little world when they describe their surroundings. Plato, especially in his Symposium, pays close attention to the characterization and the setting; more than that, he works out a dramatic sequence of ideas and makes full use of parables and myths. From this point of view, the best of non-fiction can also presumably be regarded as part of the realm of literature.

Special Genres: Allegory, Pastoral, and Satire

To complicate matters still further, some of the terms for the various genres seem to overlap, or, rather, certain categories cut across the lines of genre classification we have just been discussing. An obvious example is allegory, a genre which is characterized, we have seen, by its presenting a story in such a way as to suggest a more than literal meaning. Distinctive as allegory is, it exists in such other genres as the chivalric romance (Spenser's Faerie Queene), the morality play (The Castle of *Perseverance, Mankind, Everyman*), the masque (*Comus,* Shelley's *Mask of Anarchy*), and the novel (Bunyan's *Pilgrim's Progress*).

Quite as striking is the case of the **pastoral**. Its name (from Latin *pastor,* "shepherd") suggests that this genre features shepherds and shepherdesses living in a rural setting. Another term sometimes used for this genre, **bucolic** poetry, has similar associations, since it is derived from Greek *boukolikos,* "herdsman." But instead of presenting a realistic picture of country life, with Tom, the farm hand, sweating over the turnip patch, or Betty, the milkmaid, getting calluses as she drags her pail from the barn to the kitchen, it limits itself to highly conventional characters: lovelorn shepherds and cold-hearted shepherdesses; sensitive and thoughtful shepherds who muse on death and the transitory nature of life; literary-minded shepherds who engage in singing matches in which they display a remarkable knowledge of various lyric forms. The mode of existence of these characters is purely idyllic, artificial, untouched by hunger or cold; and they tend to move in an idealized setting that is only mildly and picturesquely rustic, in a landscape decorated with a sheep or two, a few ornamental flowers, and perhaps a cascading brook. That is why still another version of the name for this genre is the **pastoral idyll.**

It is commonly said that the pastoral tradition, which goes back to the Greek poet Theocritus, is the product of a complex, sophisticated, and urbanized civilization, looking back nostalgically to a simpler way of life, a golden age. But recently William Empson, in *Some Versions of Pastoral,* has expressed the interesting idea that the shepherd tends by his very nature to be a symbolic figure. Being in charge of a flock, he can easily be made to stand for a clergyman (pastor) or a politician. More than that, being outside society, he can even, Empson suggests, become a Christlike figure (the good shepherd), for with his poverty and simplicity he is at once below and above other people, and he may suffer from, but also, in a sense, suffer for, society. Though this interpretation may be putting too much weight on the delicate little lyrics which feature shepherds and is better reserved for more serious pastorals, it suggests that the shepherd can be made an archetypal figure, symbolic of certain quite universal human experiences.

Highly developed and distinctive as the pastoral is, it can appear, no less than allegory, in a number of other genres. In the Renaissance, when it enjoyed its greatest vogue, whole prose romances (Guarini's *Il Pastor Fido*) and whole dramas (John Fletcher's *Faithful Shepherdess,* which is also a tragicomedy) were written in the pastoral mode. Other prose narratives and plays have pastoral episodes or interludes. Sidney's *Arcadia* begins with the shepherds Strephon and Claius lamenting the departure of their beautiful Urania; Don Quixote comes upon the funeral of a shepherd, really a gentleman who has assumed the shepherd's way

of life, and who has supposedly died because of the cruelty of his beloved; the idyllic retirement of the court to the Forest of Arden in *As
You Like It* and the Perdita–Florizel sequences in *The Winter's Tale*
both have a distinctly pastoral flavor.

Even more than with the romance, novel, and drama, however, the
pastoral is associated with the lyric. In a simple form, it may be used in
a little love poem, such as this one, in which Nicholas Breton mockingly
traces the course of love:

> In the merry month of May,
> In a morn by break of day,
> Forth I walked by the wood-side
> Whenas May was in his pride.
> There I spied all alone
> Phyllida and Corydon.
> Much ado there was, God wot!
> He would love and she would not.
> She said, never man was true;
> He said, none was false to you.
> He said, he had loved her long;
> She said, love should have no wrong.
> Corydon would kiss her then;
> She said, maids must kiss no men. . . .

In the few remaining lines, Phyllida is, needless to say, quickly won over,
and the lyric ends with her being garlanded and becoming "the lady of
the May."

In a more elaborate fashion, the pastoral may be used in the **epithalamion** or wedding song. It is usual in this form to dwell on the happenings of the bridal day, either by describing the bridal procession, as
Spenser does in his "Prothalamion," or by tracing the course of the day
from the awakening of the bride to the bedding of the young couple, as
Spenser does in his "Epithalamion" and Donne in some of his wedding
poems. Shepherds, nymphs, and appropriate mythological figures are introduced to express their good wishes, and garlands are presented to the
bride, giving the poet the opportunity to work out a charming little catalogue of flowers. Towards the end, the happy pair receives blessings, and
hope is expressed that their union will be fruitful.

Some of the same themes and devices recur in that other special
genre, the **pastoral elegy**. To mourn the death of their friend, shepherds,
nymphs, and mythological figures are brought in, this time, of course, in
a sad or bitter mood. Milton, who uses the genre to the fullest in his
"Lycidas," commemorates the death of young Edward King, unhappily
drowned in the Irish Sea, by describing King as a young shepherd-poet
and himself as another shepherd, "nurst upon the self-same hill" and

feeding "the same flock, by fountain, shade, and rill." Not only do the
speaker and other shepherds feel the loss of Lycidas, but so does old
Camus, the embodiment both of Cambridge University, where King studied, and of the river Cam, on the banks of which the university is located. Even St. Peter comes to express his sorrow. His introduction is
made plausible by the fact that King was studying to become a clergyman, and that there is in any case a traditional analogy between the shepherd and the clergyman. As in the epithalamion, a catalogue of flowers
may be introduced, this time to suggest grief. Milton works out a beautiful one:

> With cowslips wan that hang the pensive head,
> And every flower that sad embroidery wears:
> Bid Amaranthus all his beauty shed,
> And daffadillies fill their cups with tears,
> To strew the laureate hearse where Lycid lies.

A typical structure is discernible in this kind of elegy, moving from
a sense of loss and deep grief to some sort of consolation, a sense that the
dead has risen and is watching over those who remain. At the beginning
of "Lycidas," much is made of the fact that the young shepherd is dead:

> For Lycidas is dead, dead ere his prime,
> Young Lycidas, and hath not left his peer.

Towards the end, however, we hear that Lycidas, "sunk low but mounted
high," is walking among the saints in heaven, and has become "the genius
of the shore" near which he drowned. Corresponding to what happens to
the dead is the definitely patterned experience the speaker may undergo.
Milton, or the speaker in "Lycidas," is not only sorrowful but extremely
bitter through much of the poem, as he reflects on the injustices of life,
the problematic nature of fame, and the corruption that occurs even in
the Church. But at the end he comes to terms with these problems and,
still using the dominant metaphor of the pastoral, suggests his determination to face the future firmly:

> Tomorrow to fresh woods and pastures new.

The very use of the pastoral convention here is not merely a way of
achieving decorative effect, but rather, we might say, a means of trans-
muting the experience of one man's death and possible resurrection, and
another man's grief and final consolation, into a general and even universal human experience.

Still another of the forms that cut across the usual genre lines is satire.
Unlike the pastoral, this is distinguished not by easily identifiable characters nor by a special setting but rather by a certain tone, one of disparagement or ridicule. The aim of satire is, in Pope's phrase, to "shoot

folly as it flies," to expose man's weaknesses, his minor follies or major vices, in all possible spheres, from social to political to moral conduct. The tone may vary from the light and witty—one recalls W. S. Gilbert's amusing ridicule of the esthetic young man "with a poppy or a lily in his medieval hand"—to the savage indignation with which Swift's King of Brobdingnag calls all men "the most pernicious race of little odious vermin that nature ever suffered to crawl upon the surface of the earth." But since the aim is usually to expose human weaknesses to laughter, the tone is likely not to be merely solemn, nor does it rise to the intensity we associate with tragedy.

Furthermore, certain special techniques or devices are so characteristic of satire that they may be considered as the conventions, the generally accepted traits, of the genre. At one extreme, there is the outright ridiculing by the simple device of name-calling, the open but clever denunciation which is known as **invective** (related to *inveighing against* or attacking verbally). Dryden carries such violent verbal attack to a fine point, in his *Absalom and Achitophel,* when he refers to Achitophel's son as "that unfeather'd two-legg'd thing" and "a shapeless lump, like anarchy," thereby reducing him to less than an animal, to an inanimate object without form or purpose. In his *Epistle to Dr. Arbuthnot,* Pope brilliantly describes Sporus as "That mere white curd of ass's milk," bringing in the uncomplimentary association with the animal but reducing his man still further by likening him not to the ass but to its milk, or rather, worse still, to the mere white curd of this milk. At the other extreme from such outright denunciation are some of the forms of irony with which satire abounds. Someone may be praised resoundingly for traits he does not possess. Pope, for example, blandly praises George II for the good taste and love of literature that the King notoriously lacked. Or human follies may be presented as if they were highly desirable virtues. Dryden ridicules his fellow-poet Shadwell in *MacFlecknoe* by writing, with seeming approval:

> The rest to some faint meaning make pretense,
> But Shadwell never deviates into sense.

Between the extremes of invective and ironic praise is a wide middle ground, to which we might assign the device of **innuendo,** the mere suggestion of negative criticism, well used by Pope when he hints at the unpleasantly effeminate nature of Sporus by saying he "Now trips a Lady, and now struts a Lord," or the device of **ironic understatement,** used in a masterly fashion when Swift writes, without further comment, "Last week I saw a woman flayed, and you will hardly believe how much it altered her appearance for the worse."

Another highly effective way of making fun of something, as schoolboys seem to know instinctively, is to imitate it in such a way as to suggest its ridiculous side. In satire, the recognition of this fact has given rise to the various types of **burlesque**. That term is very broad and general, usually applied to any mimicking designed to ridicule. **Parody** is an obvious form of such mimicking, whereby the favorite subjects or techniques of a writer are imitated so as to be still recognizable, but are amusingly exaggerated or distorted. Max Beerbohm is famous for the witty stories in the manner of Conrad and of James that he includes in his *Christmas Garland.* Parodies of poetry also abound. James K. Stephens neatly suggests the power and the simple-mindedness one finds in different parts of Wordsworth's poetry when he writes:

> Two voices are there: one is of the deep;
> It learns the storm cloud's thunderous melody,
> Now roars, now murmurs with the changing sea,
> Now birdlike pipes, now closes soft in sleep;
> And one is of an old half-witted sheep
> Which bleats articulate monotony,
> And indicates that two and one are three,
> That grass is green, lakes damp, and mountains steep:
> And Wordsworth, both are thine. . . .

A more complex form of burlesque which is frequently used in satire is the **mock-heroic** or **mock-epic**, also known as **high burlesque**. In this, the characters and situations are treated more seriously, more heroically, than is warranted. The classic example is *The Rape of the Lock,* in which Pope describes the snipping of a lock of hair—an unfortunate accident that actually befell a Miss Arabella Fermor at the hands of a certain ill-bred Lord Petre—as if it were an event of epic significance. In a charmingly witty way, Pope uses all the devices of the heroic genre, commonly associated with problems of national importance. When Belinda adorns herself at her dressing table in the morning, it is as if an epic hero were preparing for battle: "Now awful Beauty puts on all its arms." When the Baron sees her shining locks, he prays in the manner of the Homeric heroes "Soon to obtain, and long possess the prize," and again in the manner of the *Iliad,* we hear that only half his prayer will be answered. The scissors with which he snips the lock are elevated into "a two-edged weapon," an "engine," and "a glittering forfex." Belinda is guarded by the sylphs, the airy little creatures who are parody-versions of the gods who intervene in the action of the epic, and there is even the traditional journey into the underworld when Umbriel goes to the Cave of Spleen for the fits of bad temper which are unleashed after the catastrophic event. Not one but two epic battles are included, the first in the metaphorical description of the card game at Hampton Court, the second in the dramatization of the great argument in which the whole company becomes involved. Eventually, when the lock is somehow mislaid and lost, Pope resorts to an elevation-passage (the lost hair having become, he suggests, a star) and consolation for those who remain, both of which suggest, though not the epic, the equally serious genre of the elegy. The effect of all these heroic and serious parallels is not so much to elevate the material as to inflate it—and to inflate it, really, in order to deflate it. What is suggested is that the scandal is not to be taken quite so seriously—and more significantly, that the whole society of beaux and belles, preoccupied as it is with cards, gossip, and the game of love, is singularly unheroic, and even singularly far removed from the essentials of life. To turn for a moment to an earlier example, we can see the same effect of inflation that deflates in Chaucer's "Nun's Priest's Tale" (which is also an animal-fable). Chauntecleer is presented as immensely learned and well-bred; but the more authorities he is allowed to cite, the more we are aware that he is only a cock in a common barnyard, and the more we are aware of the vanity of the corresponding human type.

Whereas the mock-heroic accomplishes ridicule by first inflating its subject, **travesty** or **low burlesque** simply deflates the subject. That is, it treats a subject of some importance much less seriously than it deserves. Fielding uses this form most amusingly in the opening love scenes (if such they can be called) of *Joseph Andrews*. Instead of the usual situation in which a young man approaches the girl of his choice, it is Joseph who is being hotly pursued by not one but two women; and by another reversal of the expected, he stoutly defends his honor against both. Far from being young and attractive, furthermore, the two ladies are superannuated in the extreme, and they bear the expressive names of Lady Booby and Mrs. Slipslop, which suggest the low-burlesque nature of the narrative. These scenes are also, by the way, an example of parody, since Fielding is making fun of Richardson's Pamela, who resisted the advances of her Squire B. beyond the bounds of plausibility. John Gay's *Beggar's Opera* is another brilliant travesty, in which the general corruption of society is suggested by the fact that all the characters are thieves, or receivers of stolen goods, or highwaymen, or corrupt jailers. When Mr. and Mrs. Peachum, the "fences," go over their books to decide which thieves it would be lucrative to employ for another season and which ones might be given up to the law for the sake of the reward, they make it clear that they are no worse than the rest of the disloyal and money-hungry world. Incidentally, the mock-epic and travesty are not mutually exclusive, but can be combined with striking effect. In *MacFlecknoe* (meaning "son of Flecknoe") Dryden shows in mock-heroic fashion how the poet Flecknoe, of whom Dryden obviously does not think much, chooses Thomas Shadwell, of whom Dryden thinks still less, as his successor to the throne of Nonsense, and how he arranges for his coronation.

Dryden then introduces elements of travesty by leading the triumphal procession through the filthiest parts of London, and by having Flecknoe depart, at the end, not by ascending to heaven but by falling through a trap door into some undisclosed nether region. Flecknoe and Shadwell, representing dull and self-satisfied poets in general, are doubly ridiculed by being granted a princely status they do not deserve and by being greeted by catcalls from the disreputable parts of town.

As our discussion so far will have suggested already, the special genre of satire, which attacks the foibles and follies of mankind by the devices of invective, ironic praise, or the various types of burlesque, can be found in a great many other genres. *The Rape of the Lock* is a narrative poem, which has also been called an **epyllion** or little epic, characterized by great attention to pictorial effects. *Joseph Andrews* is a novel, and it is easy to think of other satiric novels, from *Don Quixote* and *Vanity Fair* to Evelyn Waugh's *The Loved One* and George Orwell's *1984*. Gay's *Beggar's Opera* is an operetta, a light form of opera, and as such it is related by its very method of presentation to the drama, in which satire also abounds—for instance in Ben Jonson's *Volpone* and *The Alchemist,* and nearly all the plays of George Bernard Shaw. There is even a special genre of **verse satire**, with strongly marked characteristics, cultivated—like so much other satire—especially in the eighteenth century. Its models are either the urbane, detached, and witty satires of Horace, used particularly by Pope in his *Moral Essays,* or the bitter and indignant satires of Juvenal, used by Dr. Johnson in his *Vanity of Human Wishes.* In these, one or more follies are described in derisive terms, and special "characters"—little set character-sketches of Bufo, the despicable patron, or Wolsey, the great statesman whose life comes to nothing—may be included to exemplify the theme. A particular kind of structure is recognizable in many of these satires, moving from the ridicule of the foolish or vicious to a presentation of the ideal, of the kind of human conduct which ought to be maintained.

The Value of Genre Classification

Enough has been said to make it clear that classifying pieces of literature into genres is a knotty business; the types may overlap, and any one work may belong to several types at once. All this raises the interesting question of how seriously such categorizing should be taken. Certainly the Renaissance, and, even more, the neoclassical movement in the extreme form it reached in seventeenth-century France, took the genres very seriously indeed. It was generally believed that the chief genres had long been fixed, each with its own clearly defined characteristics, and that no good could come of mingling them. Tragicomedy was considered "a monster," and the introduction of the drunken porter in *Macbeth* a breach of good taste. The neoclassic critics thought it desirable to maintain the so-called **purity of the genres**, and they tended to judge a work by whether or not it observed the rules of its particular literary type. Nowadays our general approach is no longer so prescriptive. We have seen enough of the proliferation of genres and their overlapping, as well as of experimental works such as Goethe's *Faust* which combine a great many literary forms in a very loose way, to feel that genres, like marriages, are not made in heaven. They are simply a convenient way of grouping works by what they have in common.

Even if we take this purely descriptive, as opposed to the earlier prescriptive, approach, we can find the study of genres useful. We cannot, after all, ignore the fact that a good many writers have consciously chosen to work within certain genres, making use of the generally accepted traits or conventions of these rather than striking out on their own. Far from regarding such conventions as an obstacle or fetter, they seem to find it stimulating to work within a definite framework—a test of their skill and craftsmanship, and therefore to be welcomed as much as the difficulties of rhyme or of an intricate metrical pattern. Nor can we ignore the pleasant psychological experience we have all had at one time or another, of seeing a familiar form which has been used particularly well. Let us take something as minor as a limerick:

> There was a young fellow of Ennis,
> Who was very effective at tennis;
>   The way he said "love!"
>   Made each turtle-dove
> Think the racquet more mighty than pen is.

Quite apart from the amusing play on the often quoted "The pen is mightier than the sword," the very way in which the turn of thought has been fitted into the familiar five-line stanza, and the comic insistence on the rhyme, give us a mild thrill of recognition.

For our purposes, however, the main question to be raised is less what the writer or the reader may gain, than how the working within a genre may affect an individual poem, play, or story. Though no single answer can, obviously, encompass all the various cases, we can certainly say that in general, a work may gain yet another dimension, an additional complexity, and that its very meaning may, as a result, be in some way amplified or perhaps even qualified.

One way in which a piece of literature can be enriched by being written in a particular genre is by emphasis. Wordsworth's use of the sonnet is a case in point. "Scorn not the sonnet," the poet admonishes an unnamed critic, and using a combination of the Petrarchan and

Shakespearean forms (rhyming *abbaaccaefefgg*) he goes on to recall how many great poets—Shakespeare, Petrarch, Tasso, Camoëns, Dante, Spenser, Milton—have used the genre in a memorable way. Wordsworth has chosen the very form that echoes his sense and thereby emphasizes his theme. Sir Philip Sidney does something more complicated in his sonnet "Loving in truth, and fain in verse my love to show." He wittily describes his difficulty in trying to find the best literary models in order to express his love and impress his mistress, only to be told by his muse, at length, that he should look into his own heart and write. But here the sense— that one's own feeling is what counts—is flatly and amusingly contradicted by the poet's choice of the very narrow sonnet form, and by the additional fact that this form is made more difficult than usual by the substitution of hexameter (six-foot) lines for the conventional pentameter. The result is to suggest, subtly and indirectly, that *both* heart and craft are necessary to the poet. In other words, the very meaning has been qualified, and a more complex thought than the explicit one has been expressed.

Not infrequently, the choice of a certain genre colors the very presentation of a subject by relating it to earlier works. To put it another way, the poet aligns himself with a definite tradition, and thereby adds a further dimension to his play or poem. The epic form, for example, automatically elevates the material and suggests that it is of prime significance. In his *Aeneid,* Virgil consciously introduces the episodes of the funeral games and the night exploits of two young men, as well as the invocation to the muse, extended similes, and so forth, in order to relate his material to Homer's *Iliad* and *Odyssey*. What he achieves is the suggestion, never made explicit, that the early history of Rome is a subject that is quite as serious, quite as important, as the story of the Trojan War presented by the much-admired Homer. The same is true of *War and Peace.* Though this is primarily a realistic novel, concentrating on a certain society and the maturing of a number of leading characters, its immense scope, the alternation of wartime and peacetime incidents, and the consciously chosen extended similes relate it to the epic and again suggest that the story has a national significance, that it is, in fact, a symbolic representation of the Russian people. Furthermore, it is precisely because the epic treatment elevates the material that the mock-epic as we saw it in *MacFlecknoe* and *The Rape of the Lock* has such a deflating effect.

Just as a great deal can be gained by working within the conventions of the various genres, much can also be gained by the very opposite means, by breaking with such conventions. Once a genre has been clearly established, even a mild break is likely to be effective. For example, a well-known limerick goes:

> There was a young man from Japan,
> Whose poetry never would scan;
>> When asked why 'twas so,
>> He replied "I don't know,
> Unless it's because I always try to get as many words into the last line as
>> I possibly can."

The extension of the last line creates the comic effect simply because it is quite unexpected.

The conventions of a genre can also, however, be broken for more serious purposes. Tolstoy, having set up the various recognizable parallels between his novel *War and Peace* and the epic, quite intentionally does not make his chief characters resemble epic heroes. Far from giving them the stature of an Achilles, Hector, or Aeneas, their firmness of purpose and ability to swing the action one way or the other, Tolstoy makes his Pierre and Prince André complicated, confused, and slightly neurotic people, at times unsure of what they are doing and capable of obvious mistakes in their choice of wives or way of living. They observe and reflect on the disturbing events of the Napoleonic wars, but do not influence them. As for the characters drawn from actual political life, Napoleon is shown to be mistaken when he thinks he is making history by ordering a battle here and a withdrawal there, and only the Russian general Kutuzov, who sleeps much of the time and lets events take their course, is taken to be right in his outlook on life. These various characterizations serve to emphasize one of Tolstoy's main themes—the deterministic view that history is not made or altered by individuals but is, rather, a mighty force to which the individual, if he is wise, will simply submit. Not only does Tolstoy choose the non-heroic characters to reinforce his theme; he also states explicitly his opinion that "the ancients have left us model heroic poems in which the heroes furnish the whole interest of the story, and we are still unable to accustom ourselves to the fact that for our epoch histories of that kind are meaningless." His point becomes all the more vivid precisely because some of his other details recall the epics of the ancients.

The more unexpected the break with the conventions of a genre, the more striking the effect will, of course, turn out to be. This is a simple axiom, and one of which John Gay takes full advantage. At the end of his *Beggar's Opera,* when the highwayman Macheath has been caught and is about to be executed, Gay suddenly interrupts the natural course of events by having a player approach the beggar poet and complain that since this is an opera, the "taste of the town" will never tolerate a catastrophic, tragic ending. With only a moment of grumbling, the poet thereupon throws plausibility to the winds, produces a reprieved Macheath, and brings about the requested happy ending with a song and a dance. The conventions of the comic opera are seemingly maintained, but only by a startling breach of another convention of all drama which insists upon the dramatic illusion. This illusion is broken by a reminder that we are only watching a play and that the playwright may manipulate his characters in whatever way he likes. What Gay achieves by his maneuver is not just a momentary comic effect but also, as critics have recently pointed out, yet another suggestion of the general lack of values in his society; everyone, including in this case the poet, can be influenced or bought. A similar shattering of the most basic convention of the genre occurs in Laurence Sterne's *Tristram Shandy,* which ridicules the kind of novel that relentlessly traces the life and adventures of its hero from birth to marriage or to death. At one point, the narrator slyly accuses his lady-reader of having missed an essential piece of information and asks her to turn back a few pages. He then reveals that the supposedly vital point was made only in the most indirect fashion on the earlier page, and that he really wants to know whether the reader is still attentive. Quite apart from again breaking the dramatic illusion, Sterne is breaking the tacit agreement between the writer and the reader that the former will not play practical jokes on or otherwise antagonize the latter. In doing so, Sterne manages to ridicule the literal-minded as well as the inattentive reader.

It is impossible to do justice to the infinitely varied ways that writers have found to work against a genre. Only one more way can be considered here—the choice of a genre that is in some respect incongruous with the subject matter, so that an obvious tension is created. Quite often, this tension produces a comic effect, as in the case of the mock-epic, in which the devices of the serious epic are applied to conspicuously unheroic material. But the use of other genres brings about similarly striking results. When Gray chose to treat the death of a favorite cat, drowned in a goldfish bowl, in the form of an ode—a genre which is associated, as we have seen, with strong emotions and a lofty tone—he was putting himself into an excellent position for the mock-heroic treatment he wanted to give the subject. And when Sir John Suckling decided to write a ballad about a wedding, he, in turn, was getting into the best position for the low burlesque or travesty he wanted to make of this subject, usually treated in an elaborate epithalamion. The effect need not always, however, be comic or satiric. To express his indignation about the way in which the Manchester uprising had been brutally quelled by the authorities, Shelley chose the form of a masque. Using the allegorical pageant which is characteristic of this genre, he presents, in his "Mask of Anarchy," a grotesque procession which includes Murder, Fraud, and Hypocrisy, each one looking like one of the public officials involved, and culminating in the appearance of Anarchy, blasphemously proclaiming itself God and ruler of all England. Shelley's bitterness is reinforced by his choice of a genre that is commonly associated with a mild and agreeable courtly entertainment.

Occasionally, by the way, the very fact that no recognizable genre has been chosen is also significant. Whitman's refusal in *Leaves of Grass* to work within the established genres, as well as his choice of the very loose, incantatory lines, indicates a burning desire to assert his own individuality. The point to notice is that we will not be fully aware of the significance of his decision unless we know how many different genres he might have chosen, and how many other works have indeed been written within the framework of the established genres.

Considering how a piece of literature may work either with or against the conventions of a genre, we can readily see the danger of not recognizing what that genre is. At the worst, we might miss the very meaning. It is, for instance, essential to know when we are reading *The Faerie Queene,* with its errant knights, benevolent and malevolent ladies, and assorted monsters, that it is not just another chivalric romance but an allegory of the aspiring young Christian in Book I, or the trials of Temperance in Book II. Any kind of parody, furthermore, will be baffling unless we know what is being ridiculed. Sheridan's *The Critic,* a delightful spoofing of the worst excesses of eighteenth-century drama, will seem flat and uninteresting unless we know, when we see the heroine Tilburina entering "mad, in white satin," followed by her confidante, "mad, in white linen," that contemporary drama was swarming with mad heroines modeled on Shakespeare's Ophelia, and that the main character was invariably accompanied by a friend in whom she confided at tedious length. On her first entrance, the disconsolate Tilburina greets the dawn as follows:

> Now flowers unfold their beauties to the sun,
> And, blushing, kiss the beam he sends to wake them—
> The striped carnation, and the guarded rose,
> The vulgar wallflower, the smart gillyflower,
> The polyanthus mean—the dapper daisy,
> Sweet William, and sweet marjoram—and all
> The tribe of single and of double pinks!
> Now, too, the feather'd warblers tune their notes
> Around, and charm the listening grove. The lark!
> The linnet! chaffinch! bullfinch! goldfinch!
>   green finch!
> But O, to me no joy can they afford!
> Nor rose, nor wallflower, nor smart gillyflower,
> Nor polyanthus mean, nor dapper daisy,
> Nor William sweet, nor marjoram—nor lark,
> Linnet nor all the finches of the grove.

Amusing as it is to see the flat-footed phrasing, the repetitiveness, and the poet's growing desperation as he tries to bring in other suitable flowers and birds, we shall miss some of the fun of the passage unless we recall the popularity of the catalogue of flowers, which we have observed in the pastoral epithalamion and pastoral elegy.

An insufficient knowledge of genres may at times leave us in doubt about the structure of a certain poem, or about the significance of some of the details. It may also lead us to have false expectations or to make unreasonable demands. Few of us would object when the fox or the raven of La Fontaine's fables speaks in an all-too-human way, since we know that this genre does not pretend to give a realistic image of its animal-characters. But roughly comparable criticisms are sometimes made of other literary types. Readers have often agreed with Dr. Johnson, for example, that Milton could not have been sincere and was not expressing his grief spontaneously when he chose to mourn the death of Edward King in a pastoral elegy. Quite apart from the doubtful criterion of sincerity, which we will consider later, this criticism fails to take into account the many advantages, particularly the universalizing of the experience, which Milton gains from adopting this highly conventional form.

Now that we have reached some tentative conclusions about how literary works come to be classified into genres and what may be gained by working within or playing against the conventions of these, we can turn to a somewhat closer study of two of the most complicated literary types: tragedy and comedy. Well-defined and distinctive as these seem at first glance to be, they are actually so complex and encompass so wide a range of writing as to defy any single clear-cut definition.

The Nature of Tragedy

Tragedy, in particular, is a complicated and elusive form. Its very name is shrouded in mystery, for *tragoidia* is the Greek for "goat-song," and seems to have been derived either from the old custom of giving a goat as prize for the best play of this kind, or from the players' wearing goatskins in early times. In either case, it is clear that tragedy has its roots deep in the past.

One of the chief ways of approaching or defining tragedy is to focus on the outstanding traits of its plot and characters. Almost immediately, one thinks of an heroic figure involved in catastrophic events that bring him to utter disaster, usually death. Chaucer's monk describes it simply as the story of someone who has fallen from high degree. Brief and memorable as is Chaucer's comment about

> . . . hym that stood in great prosperite
> And is yfallen out of heigh degree,

it does not, of course, do justice to the complexity of the genre. A much fuller and more profound description, centuries older, is provided in Aristotle's *Poetics*. So widely known and influential has this commentary become that it is well to keep firmly in mind from the start the fact that Aristotle by no means intended to say the last word on tragedy or to provide rules for writing in this literary form; rather, he was describing as sensitively and imaginatively as he could the kind of tragedy he knew—mainly that of Aeschylus, Sophocles, and Euripides. We must therefore beware of making Aristotle's observations sound more rigid than they are, and also of blaming him for not taking into account the kind of drama that was written long after his time.

Aristotle considers the plot the most important feature of tragedy— more so than the hero—and thereby draws attention to the noteworthy fact that what happens in the play—the pattern of experience or of life—is ultimately more significant than the person to whom it happens. As we noted earlier, it is, however, so difficult to separate plot and character that we should try to keep the two in mind simultaneously. The course of action Aristotle finds typical of tragedy consists of a clearly defined and strongly shaped pattern governed by a change of fortune, either from bad to good or from good to bad; and, not surprisingly, he finds the change from good to bad fortune the superior pattern. He then describes two further elements of the plot which he regards as highly effective. One is the **reversal** of the character's situation (**peripeteia**), very often having the effect of dramatic irony—bringing about, that is, the opposite of what the character has intended or expected. Sophocles, as we have observed, uses this ironic device brilliantly when he confronts his Oedipus with a series of figures who come to cheer him with good news, only to achieve the very opposite effect of incriminating him more and more. The second plot-element favored by Aristotle is the discovery or **recognition** (**anagnorisis**) whereby the characters finally gain the essential knowledge they have lacked. In some plays it is only the identity of other characters that is suddenly recognized, but in others a profound insight, usually some form of self-knowledge, is achieved. Again, *Oedipus* provides a striking example, for the hero, whom the blind seer Tiresias has been calling blind in spite of his unimpaired eyesight, eventually gains a new kind of vision—the insight that he himself is the guilty one he has been seeking. He comes to this self-knowledge through one of the several reversals of the situation, since the messenger from Corinth with his "good news" about the death of Oedipus' supposed father begins the process of revealing the truth to him, and as Aristotle points out, the combination of the two plot-elements, the reversal and the recognition, has a particularly powerful impact. Following the discovery or recognition, there is likely to be, according to

Aristotle, the scene of suffering, a painful action which may take the form of death or, in less extreme cases, some sort of wounding. Oedipus, for instance, is not made to die at the end. Rather, once more with the devastating irony that is characteristic of Sophocles, the playwright brings on stage a kingly figure who has blinded himself at the very moment when he achieved true vision, sacrificing his sight to his insight as a sign of accepting his guilt. The last we hear of Oedipus in this play is that he will have to leave Thebes, a lonely and forsaken outcast.

The same pattern of reversal, recognition, and suffering can also be seen in other, later plays. Shakespeare's *King Lear,* to cite only one example, works with the startling reversal whereby the old king, the head of his kingdom and of his family at the beginning of the play, finds himself, as soon as he is foolish enough to give up his authority, progressively and relentlessly stripped of his followers, of his house, and of his very clothing. It is once he is naked, stripped of all the "superficies" of life and even, for a moment, robbed of his sanity, that Lear reaches his moment of recognition—a remarkably far-reaching one which includes not only the awareness of his own guilt but also a vision of the corruption and injustice in the world at large, and, still more profoundly, of the smallness and vulnerability of man in the universe. The scenes of the mad Lear roaming the heath and reaching this kind of insight are surely among the most powerful representations of tragic suffering.

As for the hero who undergoes these harrowing experiences, Aristotle finds that the most effective type is likely to be neither wholly good nor wholly bad, but somewhere between these extremes. Such a man will be better, on the whole, than most men, but with some sort of **tragic flaw** (**hamartia**). Aristotle does not, incidentally, say that this flaw is the cause of the hero's downfall; in Greek drama, either fate or the gods are likely to be responsible for that. The flaw is intended, rather, to reconcile us to the downfall, to spare us the distressing sight of a wholly good and innocent man being defeated or destroyed. Once more, it is Oedipus whom this description of the hero fits quite strikingly. On the one hand, he has extraordinary stature, skill, and quick-wittedness. Not only is he ruler of Thebes, but he has become so by his own abilities, mainly by solving the riddle of the sphinx; and he takes his duties with the utmost seriousness, determined as he is to uncover the murderer for the good of his people. Certainly, then, he is better than most men. On the other hand, he is quick to anger, as we see in his repeated choleric attacks on those who bring him adverse news, and it was this very trait which caused him, unwittingly, to kill his own father at the crossroads in the first place. More fundamentally, Oedipus has the kind of overweening pride, the arrogant reliance on himself and his "native wit," which the Greeks called **hubris** or **hybris**. This kind of presumptuousness or spiritual pride—the very opposite of the awareness that one occupies a rather minor place in the universe and ought to acknowledge certain superior powers, whether of fate or of the gods— has come to be seen as the classic tragic flaw. It is visible in various forms in many of the greatest figures of literature—in Homer's Achilles, with his arrogant refusal to fight for the Greeks because he feels slighted, until his friend Patroclus is killed in battle; in Lear, with his unreasonable insistence that he has the right to give up his kingdom and yet be treated with veneration; or, quite as strikingly, in Milton's Satan, with his staunch determination to rule in hell rather than take second place in heaven.

Illuminating as are Aristotle's comments on the tragic plot and tragic hero, they do not, of course, exhaust the subject. Certain elements not observed or emphasized by Aristotle are now often considered an integral part of the tragic pattern. The most noteworthy of these is the ending. Whereas Aristotle mentions only the suffering, by either bodily injury or death, modern critics have drawn attention to the important purgation or cleansing—the maturing or regeneration—which the tragic hero may experience as a result of his suffering. This is true, in a sense, of Oedipus, for, paradoxically enough, he is more genuinely a king in his bearing and outlook once he is the blind and lonely outcast than he was when he was at the height of his worldly power. It is even more strikingly true of Lear, who gains immeasurably in stature and dignity when his suffering has made him gentle and compassionate and wise. Indeed, the last two acts of the play deal not with his downfall but with what, as a human being, he gains from the experience, and his death at the very end is not so much an atonement for his guilt as a merciful release.

There are, furthermore, tragic heroes to whom Aristotle's famous description does not apply. Aeschylus' *Prometheus* and Euripides' *Trojan Women* focus on characters of considerable stature who suffer intensely, but who have no noticeable flaw. They are the victims of some great force—Prometheus of the powerful, brutal Zeus, who has bound him to the rock because he refuses to reveal his great secret; the Trojan women, of the Greek conquerors and of the gods. Alternatively, the kind of tragedy that became popular in the late seventeenth and the eight- eenth century presents characters who lack the elevated position and heroic stature traditionally associated with tragedy. In this so-called **domestic** or **bourgeois tragedy** (Lillo's *London Merchant,* Lessing's *Miss Sara Sampson,* or the Gretchen sequence in Part I of Goethe's *Faust*) the characters belong to the middle class and are faced with such personal problems as becoming involved in the theft of money, or having to dispose of an illegitimate child. In our own day, Arthur Miller's *Death* *of a Salesman* with its focus on the unheroic Willie Loman, destroyed by his pursuit of the elusive dream of success, belongs to this tradition of domestic tragedy.

Another rather common way of approaching or defining tragedy is by the effect it has on its audience. Although we saw earlier that this focus on audience psychology is less desirable than a focus on the work itself, it has become so integral a part of the theory of tragedy that we ought to give it some attention here. As with so much else related to the genre, Aristotle has been a decisive influence, for it is he who is responsible for the formula that tragedy arouses pity and fear. The audience feels pity for the suffering hero and fear, apparently, for itself. In other words, the spectator undergoes a strong emotional experience, which Aristotle calls **purgation** or **catharsis**: "through pity and fear effecting the proper purgation of these emotions."

Often mentioned as is this theory of tragic catharsis, it presents the problem that the very nature of the supposed purgation is far from clear. As a matter of fact, a number of startlingly different interpretations of Aristotle's rather ambiguous statement have been proposed at various times. In the sixteenth century, for example, it was thought to refer to a general hardening of the emotions. The spectator, by seeing the violence and misery which may occur in human life, becomes inured or hardened to these sights and overcomes what are considered the undesirable emotions of pity and fear. In the eighteenth century, amusingly enough, the very opposite view became popular—that the passage refers to a general softening of the emotions. The spectator, by seeing the violence and misery of life, becomes softened and increases his capacity to feel especially pity or sympathy (in this case considered highly desirable emotions). At times it was thought that pity and fear are the feelings that are purged in the process; at other times, that very different feelings are purged, that by experiencing pity and fear as we watch what happens to ambition and pride in the tragic hero, we are cured of false ambition or pride. The interpretation that seems to come closest to Aristotle's meaning is that a purging almost in the medical sense takes place: pity and fear are brought to such an intense pitch by the tragedy that they are driven out, leaving the spectator, to use the beautiful words with which Milton concludes his *Samson Agonistes,* in "calm of mind, all passion spent."

So flexible is Aristotle's formula of pity and fear that it has, interestingly enough, been used both to justify and to attack quite different kinds of tragedy. He himself obviously had in mind only the heroic drama of classical antiquity. But the admirers of domestic tragedy have argued that this genre arouses pity and fear still more effectively, since the middle-class characters and their problems are closer to the audience's own position in life and general experience than the kings and queens of earlier tragedies. Those who dislike domestic tragedy, on the other hand, have argued the opposite—that precisely because the characters are so close to ordinary life, they lack the stature and elevation needed to stimulate the tragic emotions. This kind of disagreement suggests once again the dangers of going beyond the field of literary criticism into that of psychology, where we are likely to be hampered by insufficient evidence and inadequate knowledge.

Although Aristotle's theory is, then, the most widely accepted and influential one of its kind, other psychological theories have been proposed, particularly in our own time. One of the most fascinating of these suggests that tragedy has its powerful effect because the audience participates in a community experience of a rather primitive kind. Especially when the hero is the ruler of a community and when, as in the case of Oedipus, his suffering is undergone in part for the sake of his people (to relieve the terrible blight that has hit Thebes because of the unatoned murder of King Laius), the audience, so this theory runs, watches the downfall of the hero as if it were participating in some of the early tribal rites, the periodic sacrifices of the rulers to insure the fertility of the crops. In other words, the audience is experiencing something akin to a primitive ritual—an acting-out of the suffering and regeneration of a whole community. This may well have been the case with the earliest audiences of tragic drama, and modern proponents of the ritual interpretation of tragedy believe that even our own much more sophisticated audiences momentarily become drawn into such an experience.

Still another way of approaching tragedy is to consider the ideas or outlook on life it embodies—ideas that may or may not be expressed but that are certainly implied by the kind of characters chosen and by the way in which the course of action is developed. This aspect, which has to do with the central themes or total meaning of tragedy, has been called the "tragic view of life" or the "tragic vision," and it is certainly the most elusive, the hardest of all the facets of tragedy to define.

Roughly speaking, we might say that the **tragic vision** gives attention to the most problematic parts of human life and presents these in their most serious form. The themes that seem to recur in tragedy have to do with the terrible precariousness of human existence, whether the hero is confronted by overwhelming odds or by impossible choices. Sometimes the hero is brought low by antagonistic gods, as Euripides' Hippolytus is because he has offended the goddess Aphrodite; or he is ruined by a curse on his house, as Agamemnon and Clytemnestra are, at least in part, because the house of Atreus is doomed. Sometimes the hero falls through the actions of a powerful opponent: Aeschylus' Prometheus suffers at the hands of Zeus, and Othello is Iago's pawn. Alternatively, the hero may be destroyed by a terrible weakness within himself, the classic instance being Macbeth with his overriding ambition. Or he may suffer from a combination of these opposing forces: Hamlet, for example, is faced with the ruthless, coldly calculating King Claudius, with his own inability to act, and also—to adopt an idea of A. C. Bradley—with some terribly *unlucky* combination of circumstances, something that makes us feel, however vaguely, that he has been singled out by an unnamed mischance or fate. In all these varied cases we are aware of the terrifyingly exposed position, the extraordinary vulnerability, of man, and, of course, the more elevated and seemingly secure the hero appears at first, the more we become aware of his vulnerability.

As is frequently pointed out, however, tragedy dramatizes not only man's pitiful and frightening weakness but also, in one way or another, his greatness. Many of the heroes exhibit an extraordinary nobility in the way they bear their suffering, notably Prometheus, Oedipus, Milton's Samson, and T. S. Eliot's Thomas à Becket in *Murder in the Cathedral.* Or they show themselves capable of an extraordinary change for the better, a growing and maturing, before they meet their death, as do Hamlet and King Lear. Some of the tragic heroes are admirable in still another way, in the very single-mindedness and intransigence with which they maintain their position, even when that is an impossible one. Sophocles' Antigone does so when she persists in her efforts to bury her brother in spite of Creon's prohibition, knowing that the penalty is death. This taking into account of the enormous potentialities of man which constitute his greatness is, for many critics, one of the essentials of tragedy, and the main feature which distinguishes the tragic vision from a merely pessimistic view of life. Instead of seeing man simply as a victim, the tragic vision gives a much more complex appraisal of his paradoxical position, seeing man, in Pope's phrase, as "the glory, jest and riddle of the world." The recurring paradoxes of the blind who see more profoundly than those who have eyes and the mad who are wiser than the sane also point, we might say, to this complex view of man and of life.

It is part of this tragic vision to be painfully aware of the great and terrible conflicts with which man is faced. As we have seen, some of the tragic heroes are in conflict with fate or the gods, some with evil as embodied in other men, and some with a weakness in themselves. Still another type of conflict has come to be associated with tragedy—the clash between two kinds of good. Much more problematic, much harder to accept than the clear-cut conflict between good and evil, this clash may take many forms. It may involve opposing duties to one's family, such as Orestes' problem of either leaving his father's death unavenged or killing his mother; it may be based on someone's opposing responsibilities as an individual and a citizen, such as Antigone's dilemma of either leaving her brother unburied or infringing upon the severest law of the state established by the ruler, Creon; or it may take the form of disobeying the demands of love or, on the other hand, of duty, as it does repeatedly in the tragedies of Corneille and Dryden. The German philosopher Hegel, who was fascinated by this type of conflict and considered it the essential one of tragedy, developed an elaborate metaphysical theory of the genre, suggesting that the conflict comes about when one of two different and partial goods is maintained to the exclusion of the other (duty to the exclusion of love or vice versa; the right of the individual to the exclusion of that of the state or vice versa). As a result, the great moral force of the universe, what Hegel called the "ethical substance," is momentarily torn apart. Ultimately, however, Hegel believed that the breach in the ethical substance is always healed, that some sort of reconciliation is achieved. He had in mind the last play of Aeschylus' Oresteian trilogy, called *The Eumenides,* in which the goddess Athena makes peace with the opposing factions and restores harmony to the universe, and we can see a similar process in some of the Shakespearean tragedies, in which the minor characters give the impression that in spite of the death of a Hamlet or a Lear, ordinary life will go on. It is the awareness not only of the conflicts, then, but also of a possible reconciliation that seems to be typical of the tragic vision.

Yet it may be too simple and too optimistic to emphasize the final reconciliation without taking into account what is lost in the process. A. C. Bradley has called the loss of so much that is good and valuable tragic waste, and he considers it a significant part of the tragic pattern. In *Hamlet,* it is all the nobility and hard-earned maturity of the hero that is wasted when he dies along with Claudius and the corrupt members of the court; in *King Lear,* it is the purity and goodness of Cordelia, quite apart from all that has become admirable in Lear, which is sacrificed; even in *Macbeth,* Bradley argues, all the positive strength, the vigor and bravery of Macbeth are lost as he experiences the downfall he has brought upon himself. Though this "tragic waste" is only one of the several elements of the tragic vision, it suggests once more the attention to the dark and problematic side of life.

Only one more of the many facets of the tragic vision can be indicated here: its complex view of moral responsibility. Certainly, this issue of responsibility is raised by the Aristotelian notion of the tragic hero as someone pre-eminently good but with a flaw. When there seems to be a direct relationship between the flaw and the downfall, as there is in *Macbeth* or *King Lear,* we see in terrible form how man is responsible for his actions, and how, very often, the consequences of a weakness far exceed what that weakness would seem to warrant. However despicable Lear's vanity, foolishness, and arrogance at the beginning may be, there is something disproportionate in their consequences: the disorder in the family, the state, and almost, it seems, in the whole universe, not to mention the death of Cordelia. When the relationship between the flaw and the downfall is less direct, as it is in much of Greek tragedy because fate or the gods are playing a greater part, we see in equally terrible form how man is not solely responsible for his actions but must nevertheless take the consequences. And when there seems to be very little flaw but great suffering for the sake of a definite principle, as there is when Aeschylus' Prometheus allows himself to be bound to the rock in stoic silence and resists all temptations to compromise with the brutal Zeus, we see how man is capable of defending a self-imposed responsibility, no matter what the cost, but also to what dreadful pain he may be subjected. In still another version of this tragic view of responsibility, that proposed by the modern existentialists, man is thought to have neither a particular flaw nor a divinity to guide or hinder him. Rather, he is supposedly confronted by an utterly absurd and senseless life; but he must meet it with the same heroic bearing with which a Prometheus withstood a Zeus. What all these views have in common and what makes them an indisputable part of the tragic vision is their emphasis on the extraordinary difficulties of moral responsibility, and on the extraordinary weakness and greatness that man reveals in facing these difficulties.

The various ways of getting at the essence of tragedy are not, we should bear in mind, mutually exclusive. In fact, a full and satisfactory definition of tragedy would have to take into account the plot, the characters, and the tragic vision. One other factor ought probably to be included as well, and that is the part played by the formal elements. Concentrating as it does on some of the most serious aspects of life, tragedy tends to make use of a style that is correspondingly dignified and elevated. It is no accident, surely, that most tragedies are written either wholly or in part in the form of poetry, using all the heightening devices of imagery, meter, and rhythm, and that the few that are written wholly in prose, such as Synge's *Riders to the Sea,* modulate from ordinary speech rhythms into much more measured, stark, and stately language at the high points of the drama. Interestingly enough, the contributing effect of the diction was noted already by Aristotle, who also drew attention to a second formal element, that of spectacle. Visual and sound effects can, without doubt, do much to help create the appropriate atmosphere for tragedy. The dancelike movements of the Greek chorus, the huge masks worn by the chief actors in Greek drama, the alternation of splendid court scenes and grim soliloquies in Elizabethan tragedies, and the predilection in these for a final funeral procession to the sound of martial music—these are not merely decorations but an integral part of the total atmosphere.

Important as the diction and spectacle are in intensifying the general effect of tragedy, they have still another and ultimately perhaps even more important function. They serve to remove the action from ordinary life and to dignify it. We can recognize just how necessary such a distancing is when we consider how we would feel if we thought that the experiences of Oedipus, or Hamlet, or Lear were real ones. We would, surely, find the pain and suffering these figures undergo quite unbearable. It is precisely because we are able to see the characters as part of a work of art that we can recognize their suffering as only one facet of the total pattern, and the tragedy not as life itself but, rather, as a profound and moving interpretation of one of the many aspects of life. The formal elements give beauty and larger meaning to the experiences of waste, desolation, and suffering.

So far, we have been considering only those characteristics which tragedies seem to have in common. There are, however, several different kinds of tragedy, each with its particular, well-marked conventions. Greek tragedy, for one, has a distinctive structure, consisting of a series of **episodes** or scenes, in each of which only two or three main characters are featured. In *Oedipus,* for example, every one of the early episodes dramatizes a clash between Oedipus and one other character—Tiresias, or Creon, or the messenger from Corinth, or the shepherd—although the presence of his wife Jocasta in some of the scenes brings the number of leading characters to three. The episodes are separated from each other by the highly stylized chants and dances of the chorus, subdivided into the **strophe** or "turn," **antistrophe** or "counter-turn," and **epode** or "stand" which we noticed earlier in connection with the Pindaric odes. The chorus, incidentally, not only links the episodes and comments on the action but may also, as modern critics have pointed out, actually suffer through the action experienced by the major figures, although it often does so on a lower level and with less understanding of the central issues.

Still other conventions of Greek tragedy have come to be known as "the rules," though they were by no means as strictly and universally enforced as that name would suggest. The chief of these has to do with the so-called **unities** of time, place, and action. Usually, in the classical drama no more than twenty-four hours elapse; everything happens in one place; and, most important, a single plot is developed, to the exclusion of subplots or irrelevant interludes. Furthermore, the so-called **decorum of action**—literally, "what is fitting"—is observed; that is, scenes of violence are not presented on stage but are reported, commonly by a messenger. This attention to decorum is not just for the benefit of the squeamish. As later critics have argued, the presentation of acts of violence on the stage can easily appear not pitiful or terrifying but merely ridiculous, whereas a report which leaves something to the audience's imagination can be highly effective. It would be hard, indeed, to show Hippolytus being killed by his own bolting horses, terrified by the monster bull of Poseidon; the description of this terrible fate which Euripides lets his messenger give is at once so vivid and so suggestive that it is an unforgettable presentation of the catastrophe.

These various conventions achieve a tightly knit, highly controlled work of art, with all the power that comes from starkness and concentration. *Oedipus* owes much of its impressiveness to the fact that everything happens with a relentless and horrifying speed, and that our attention is not for one instant diverted from the terrible central action.

Later writers have made full use of the possibilities of this very concentrated form. Milton, as we saw, used it to give shape and a new significance to the story of the legendary Samson. In our own time, T. S. Eliot has employed it in his *Murder in the Cathedral,* based on the history of St. Thomas à Becket, in which the chorus, the observance of the unities, and perhaps also certain characteristics of the hero derive from classical tradition. This play also provides an interesting example of what can be gained by breaking with conventions once these are firmly established. Immediately after Thomas has been killed, the four knights who have perpetrated the deed turn to the audience and, shattering both the anguished tone and the dramatic illusion, give a series of specious and eminently modern-sounding arguments to justify their deed, in the witty and ironic tone one associates not with tragedy but with Shaw's comedies. This is, of course, a startling device, intended to draw the audience into the action and to suggest, much as Shaw does at the end of his *Saint Joan,* that if we had lived at the time of the tragic event, we, too, might well have been on the side not of the martyrs but of the guilty world.

While recognizing what can be gained by the use of these various conventions of classical tragedy, we should also perhaps bear in mind their possible abuses. A good many dramas in the seventeenth and eighteenth centuries were written as if the mere observance of the unities and of decorum would assure their success. Addison's *Cato,* in which most of the characteristics of this type of tragedy are scrupulously reproduced, has become no more than a literary curiosity. The French, in particular, got into difficulties by adding a new "rule" of their own; dispensing with the chorus, they insisted on a liaison des scènes or linking of scenes so that the stage would never be empty and the unities of time and place would be clearly maintained. This convention led to a stream of minor characters with little to say except good-bye to one major character and hello to the next.

In almost diametric opposition to the controlled and concentrated drama which classical tragedy at its best can be, there is the kind of tragedy written in the Elizabethan and Jacobean periods; that is, in the late sixteenth and early seventeenth centuries in England. The action of this type of play, far from being confined to one place or to a short period of time, may move freely from one country to another, while months may pass between one scene and the next. Subplots are introduced at will, such as the painful upheaval in the Gloucester family which parallels and reinforces Lear's experiences; and so are the seemingly irrelevant comic scenes known as **comic relief.** The grave-diggers in *Hamlet* and the drunken porter in *Macbeth* have been mentioned already; an even more daring use of comic relief can be seen in *Antony and Cleopatra,* where a clownish old man brings Cleopatra the asps with which she intends to kill herself. Instead of serving merely as a "relief" or a sop to the less educated members of Shakespeare's audience, this kind of scene, by momentarily shattering the solemn mood, really intensifies the pathos of what follows.

A number of other conventions are typical of this kind of drama. Perhaps the best-known of these is the **soliloquy,** in which a character, alone on the stage, reveals his innermost thoughts. Others are the **dumb-show,** a little pantomime, and the **play within the play,** both of which may be introduced mainly for the sake of spectacle but can also, at their best, further the central action, as they do when Hamlet uses them "to catch the conscience of the king." Furthermore, scenes of violence are frequently presented with considerable relish. The blinding of Gloucester in *King Lear* takes place on stage, and when one of his eyes has been put out, the wicked Regan gruesomely insists, "One side will mock another. Th' other too!" Webster's *Duchess of Malfi* includes a hair-raising scene in which the Duchess thinks she is taking her brother's hand but is actually holding a severed hand, which she is led to believe belongs to her beloved husband, though it is actually a waxen replica. Such scenes are a far cry from the observance of classical decorum, but when they are well presented, their shock-effect is tremendous.

At its best, Elizabethan tragedy has an expansiveness and a vitality that make it as impressive in its own way as is the classical tragedy with its concentration and control. The subplots which parallel the main plot, the sudden shifts of mood, the great movements of time and space, these can give the impression not only that the whole world is involved in the action but also that all of life has been brought into the drama. But the conventions of Elizabethan tragedy, too, have been subject to abuse. The soliloquies can become mere set speeches or ranting rather than profound revelations of character, and the scenes of horror or violence can be heaped on each other as if they were ends in themselves. It is perhaps significant that few, if any, later dramas written in this vein have been successful. Perhaps it is still harder to achieve a memorable result in this free and flexible form than in the more clearly defined and artistically controlled form of classical tragedy.

So rich and complex is the genre of tragedy and so varied are the critical opinions about what constitutes its essence that it is almost impossible to say where it ends, or rather, which works should or should not still be included in this category. Bordering on it, and not always easily distinguishable from it, is **melodrama**, the kind of drama in which violent happenings are inflicted on rather flat, black-and-white characters, mainly for the sake of a highly sensational effect. The nineteenth-century stereotype of the beautiful and innocent heroine struggling on the railroad tracks with the mustachioed and mortgage-conscious villain would not, of course, be considered a tragedy. But other cases are less clear-cut. Thomas Kyd's *Spanish Tragedy,* for example, features characters of some stature in conflict with other wicked characters; it produces a fine catastrophe with a play-within-a-play scene, in which the just and unjust perish alike and provide the suitably bloody ending; and it touches on the serious problems of justice, man's general insecurity, and the difficulties of maintaining oneself in a wicked world. As its very title suggests, Kyd certainly considered it a tragedy. Yet one could also argue that the incredibly complicated plot is virtually melodramatic in its sensationalism, with the hanging of the innocent young Horatio in the garden, the brutal treatment of the beautiful Bel-Imperia by her wicked brother, the half-feigned and half-real madness of Horatio's father Hieronymo, and the gruesome execution of a minor courtier who mistakenly thinks to the last that he will be reprieved.

It is also quite hard, at times, to draw the line between tragedy and other forms of serious drama. The problem play, as we have seen, is commonly regarded as a distinct type; its emphasis on a special social or political problem usually prevents it from having the universality of theme we associate with tragedy, and the characters, drawn from ordinary life and portrayed in a realistic manner, tend to lack the stature or dignity of tragic heroes. Yet it has been argued that Ibsen's *Ghosts,* for example, which seems to deal primarily with the problem of hereditary illness, actually rises above this rather limited theme and suggests the more profound one of the sins of the father being visited on his children and almost, perhaps, the Greek theme of a curse on the house. It has also been argued that Mrs. Alving and Oswald, in the way they come to terms with their problem and bear their guilt and suffering, rise to the height of tragic figures.

In spite of such borderline cases, however, we usually wish to distinguish tragedy from one kind of serious drama that in some ways seems closest to it—the play with an unhappy end, the purely **pathetic** drama, so called because its chief aim or effect is the arousing of pity or sympathy. We are all familiar, perhaps less from the theater than from the related form of motion pictures, with the kind of drama in which purely helpless and ineffectual people are hounded until they come to a miserable end: the coal-miner who is trapped and perishes in his mine, while his wife and children wring their hands at the mine-shaft; the janitor who is driven to strangle his wife and then flees from the police until he topples from a suitably craggy roof-top. Sad as these stories unquestionably are, they had better not be regarded as tragic. Many reasons can be given for excluding them: not only do the characters lack stature and the subjects lack the universality of tragic themes, but what is being emphasized is purely man's weakness, without that further impression of man's greatness which also seems to be an essential part of the tragic vision.

While considering the limits of tragedy, we may also raise the question of whether this genre is necessarily confined to the drama. To be sure, it was restricted in this way to begin with, and one can argue that much of its powerful effect depends on the concentrated time-span and the possibility of creating strong and moving visual effects which are characteristic of a dramatic presentation. On the other hand, the tragic vision, in itself, is obviously not restricted to the drama: it can be found even in non-fictional material such as Pascal's *Pensées,* that masterly collection of thoughts and maxims which explores in a profound, poignant, and ironic fashion the grandeur and the misery of man. Furthermore, the kind of plot and characters as well as the general view of life that we have seen to be typical of tragic drama can also be found in the epic or the novel. The last part of the *Iliad,* dramatizing the final struggle of Hector and Achilles, is frequently called tragic, and so is the whole of Hardy's *Mayor of Casterbridge,* tracing the relentless and self-induced downfall of a man who has the stature and the flaw of a classical tragic hero, or the whole of Dostoevsky's *Brothers Karamazov,* showing the painful struggle of the leading characters in a complex and problematic world, with the terrible destruction of several of these characters in the process. In deciding whether to extend the term *tragedy* to the epic and the novel or to restrict it to a special type of drama, we had perhaps better keep in mind that we are, as always in the case of the genres, dealing with classifications that are man-made, and often only critic-made at that.

The Nature of Comedy

As for **comedy**, the genre that is almost automatically linked with and contrasted with tragedy, it is, if anything, an even more elastic and all-inclusive category. Its very name seems to come from the Greek for "banquet" and "singing," and is thought to be ultimately derived from the entertainment that a group of revelers (the *comos*) provided in early times at the village festivals in honor of Dionysus, the god of fertility. But it now embraces an extraordinarily wide variety of types.

At one extreme in the range of comedy, there is the highly sophisticated form of **high comedy,** exemplified by Congreve's *The Way of the World* or the scenes dominated by Viola in Shakespeare's *Twelfth Night,* in which much of the fun consists of the witty dialogue, and perhaps also of the fact that the leading characters are sufficiently intelligent to be quite aware of the follies or absurdities of others and even of themselves. At the other extreme, there is the far-from-subtle **low comedy** or **farce,** in which flat characters are involved in pie-throwing, slipping on banana peels, splitting the seat of their pants, and other types of slapstick or horseplay. In between are the various forms of satire and burlesque we have noticed earlier, as well as such special forms as **romantic comedy,** depending heavily on love-intrigue; **social comedy** or the **comedy of manners,** concentrating on social absurdities, usually in upper-class characters; or the **character comedy** or **comedy of humors,** focusing on certain eccentricities of character which may or may not result from an excess of what the Renaissance called *humors*—the phlegmatic, choleric, sanguine, or melancholic (e.g., Molière's *The Miser,* or Ben Jonson's *Every Man in His Humour*). To complicate matters, these forms are not mutually exclusive; though one or the other may be dominant, social and romantic comedy may be combined, as they are in Goldsmith's *She Stoops to Conquer,* and scenes of pure farce may be included even in high comedy, as they are when the superannuated but flirtatious Lady Wishfort in *The Way of the World* covers her cracking face with more and more cosmetics to meet the advances of Sir Rowland, whom we know to be the servant Waitwell in disguise. Even less than in the case of tragedy, furthermore, is the term *comedy* restricted to the drama. We speak of comic poems (Pope's *Rape of the Lock* or Byron's *Don Juan*), just as we do not hesitate to speak of comic novels (*Don Quixote* or Meredith's *Egoist,* or any of the major works of Evelyn Waugh).

What all these different forms of comedy have in common is by no means easily identified, and so a good many rather different definitions or interpretations have been proposed. The simplest of these, focusing purely on the plot, suggests that comedy is a play with a happy ending, and this is certainly true as far as it goes. Even the most complicated plots of romantic comedy, in which the young lovers are separated, may have to resort to disguise, and may have to employ rascally servants to act as go-betweens, inevitably end with the reunion of the young people and a suitable distribution of rewards and punishments for the other characters. This getting no more and no less than what one deserves is known as **poetic justice**—an absolute kind of justice whereby the good are always rewarded and the wicked are always punished.

But to say that comedy is a play with a happy ending does not take into account many of the other facets of the genre. Another way of defining it, which tries to consider both the plot and the characters, is to suggest that it shows low figures in an unheroic action. The action of comedy is, indeed, unheroic in the sense that it does not deal with events of national importance, as does the epic, nor with the ultimate problems of human responsibility and suffering, the weakness and greatness of man, as does tragedy. Instead, it emphasizes the absurdities of human behavior—sometimes, as in parts of *Gulliver's Travels,* the vices of mankind, but more often personal foibles and social follies, the passionate desire to eat the cucumber sandwiches intended for someone else, or to appear in the latest French fashion, or to keep one's money intact. As for the characters, they certainly tend to be lower in class and behavior than the heroes of both tragedy and the epic. In farce, they are frequently low indeed—ordinary working people or simple family members, such as the gullible husband, flighty and domineering wife, and opportunistic priest in the medieval *Johan Johan.* But other types of comedy feature characters from higher classes. Restoration comedy, such as *The Way of the World,* Etherege's *Man of Mode,* and Wycherley's *Country Wife,* deals with the sophisticated upper-class society of "the town"; Shakespeare's romantic comedies include dukes and, in *The Tempest,* even kings, though only of rather minor realms. In these cases, most of the characters are low not on the social scale but in the much broader sense of having shortcomings which reveal the lower aspects of man. This is what Aristotle seems to mean when he says that comedy is "an imitation of characters of a lower type." It is, in fact, often said that whereas tragedy represents men as better or greater than they are, comedy represents them as worse or more petty than they are.

This idea that comedy focuses on man's weaknesses, on his foibles, follies, and absurdities, is one we have seen already in the definition of satire, which is, of course, one of the many types of comedy. Not only has the idea been extended to comedy as a whole; it has also been developed into the more elaborate theory that comedy characteristically presents the deviations from a norm. The **norm**, meaning the pattern or standard for a group, may be either the conventional behavior of society or an ideal behavior, usually a combination of good sense, good heart, and good manners, and it may be either expressed by one of the characters or only implied in the play. As for the deviations, the greater or lesser departures from the generally accepted or the ideal, these are represented by all the other characters. If we apply this theory to *The Way of the World,* we will see that it offers a wide range of deviations from both social and moral norms. The social absurdities are wittily revealed by some of the minor characters: Petulant is so eager to be thought the popular man-about-town that he engages three women of questionable reputation to go around to the various coffee houses to call for him as if they were ladies of society passionately in love with him; Witwoud is convinced that he is the wittiest and most amusing man in London because he lards his speech with the first similes that come to mind; Sir Wilful, just up from the country, thinks he can take his boots off in the drawing room and becomes incoherent when he is supposed to propose to the heroine. What Congreve is mocking through these characters is the affectation of the town on the one hand, and, on the other, the lack of manners and polish of those who have lived too long in the country. In contrast to these and as the mean between the extremes, the young lovers Millamant and Mirabell represent the social norm of good manners, genuine wit, elegance, grace, and charm. Other characters in the play, however, seem to be deviations from a more serious norm. Mrs. Fainall has once "undervalued the loss of her reputation" and has had to pay for her weakness ever since by a loveless marriage; Mrs. Marwood is the passionate and scheming woman who is willing to do anything for her lover, and anything to spite whoever has rejected her advances; Lady Wishfort is the unrealistic older woman who is convinced that she is still irresistible, and who plans to become a shepherdess in the best pastoral mode once her matrimonial plans fall through; and lastly, Fainall is the ruthless and coldly calculating rake to whom money means more than honor, and love, like cards, is a game not worth playing unless the stakes are high. In contrast to all these, the heroine and the hero, Millamant and Mirabell, clearly represent the values of good sense, personal honor, the capacity for love (though they would die rather than admit it in public), and a realistic view of marriage, brilliantly revealed by the famous compact-scene in which they set forth in turn the conditions under which each would be willing to marry. It is perhaps well to keep in mind that the norms expressed in comedy are seldom likely to be startlingly novel, and that it is usually the way in which the deviations are worked out that accounts for the strength and individuality of a work.

The theory that comedy is essentially the representation of deviations from a norm is particularly useful in explaining the sort of comedy in which there seems to be little or no intrigue. Dylan Thomas' *Under Milk Wood,* to take a modern example, seems merely to trace in a humorous way the thoughts and experiences of a group of ordinary people during a typical day in a small Welsh town. On closer look, however, it becomes clear that Thomas is surveying the astonishing range of the foibles, follies, and absurdities of a richly varied cast of characters. The confirmed spinster and bachelor who carry on a passionate love relationship exclusively by mail; the henpecked husband who mentally strangles, poisons, and otherwise does away with his wife; the ladies' man who dreams of countless women lining up and claiming the right to marry him; the frigid widow and the repressed cobbler—these are chosen to show, among other things, an obvious and undesirable deficiency in love. In contrast, Thomas creates the figure of the Reverend Eli Jenkins, who clearly recognizes the shortcomings of his flock but is able to declare, both morning and night, that he still likes them so well that he would not change this town for any other. In a more secular vein, Thomas also creates the figure of Polly Garter, the loose woman of the town, who is warm, spontaneous, in love with life and her many babies. Delighting in the paradox, Thomas suggests that this far from saintly girl is closer to the roots of life than all the respectable townspeople who look down on her. By his choice of Polly as well as the Reverend Eli Jenkins to represent the positive values of his play, Thomas cleverly manages to present the norm of love in both its profane and sacred form.

This delight in paradox, which can be seen not only in *Under Milk Wood* but in a great many other comedies, suggests still another very broad and commonly accepted definition of the genre: that the essence of comedy is **incongruity,** the bringing together of incompatible or seemingly incompatible parts. There is no doubt that innumerable comic scenes depend on strikingly inappropriate and surprising combinations. The sight of the dignified gentleman in the top hat slipping on the banana peel is the standard example from farce, but much more subtle scenes are also based on the device of incongruity. It is possible to list a whole series of classic love-scenes that are comic because of the implausible combination of partners: Phebe, the conventional cruel mistress in *As You Like It,* suddenly declaring her passion for Ganymede, whom we know to be Rosalind in disguise; the duped and vainglorious Malvolio of *Twelfth Night* in yellow cross-garters and with a frenzied smile on his face, persuaded that his mistress Olivia is in love with him and is pleased by his odd behavior; the inarticulate and half-drunk Sir Wilful in *The Way of the World,* trying to propose to the highly articulate and thoroughly well-bred Millamant; Shaw's Eugene Marchbanks, the overly sensitive eighteen-year-old poet, wishing to carry off the practical and motherly Candida, aged thirty-three, who has not the slightest intention of leaving her husband and children. In fact, we might say that any of the numerous comic scenes dealing with disguise or misunderstanding is based on incongruity. Furthermore, the characters in comedy are often coupled for the sake of an incongruous effect. Quite apart from the oddly matched lovers we have just considered, there is the choice of the fat man and the thin man—Sir Toby Belch and Sir Andrew Aguecheek in *Twelfth Night*, Laurel and Hardy in motion pictures—which can become the basis for farce. In a more subtle vein, Shaw incongruously pairs a passionate young heroine with a highly rationalistic, skeptical elderly hero in his *Caesar and Cleopatra*, and by another witty incongruity suggests that whereas Cleopatra could easily fall in love with Caesar, the latter is much too sensible and much too preoccupied with the affairs of state to give her more than a passing thought.

The term *incongruity* can, furthermore, be extended to cover the various kinds of exaggeration or distortion which seem to be typical of comedy, and in which there is a marked discrepancy between what we see before us and what we know to be true. There is likely to be a pointed exaggeration of the witlessness of a Witwoud or the boorishness of a Sir Wilful in social comedy, and just as obvious an exaggeration in character comedy of whatever traits are being scrutinized—the miserliness of Molière's *L'Avare*, the hatred of society in the central figure of his *Misanthrope*. When the exaggeration takes the form of an extreme distortion of one particular character trait, it is known as **caricature**. Dickens is justly famous for his caricature of Uriah Heep in *David Copperfield*, epitomizing false humility by the way in which he constantly bows and rubs his hands; and Shaw, in *Widowers' Houses*, creates a memorable caricature of a ruthless Cockney rent-collector who bears the expressive name of Lickcheese.

All these examples have to do primarily with the choice of scenes and of characters. But if, as we easily can, we extend the term *incongruity* to include paradox, the unexpected linking of seemingly incompatible ideas, then we can see the element of incongruity also in some of the themes of comedy. We have just observed how Dylan Thomas plays with the paradox of the loose woman whose values are preferable to those of conventional society, but the master of this sort of comedy is without question George Bernard Shaw. In his *Major Barbara*, he tantalizingly lets the socialist doctrine in which he believes be expressed by Undershaft, the capitalist and munitions maker, and instead of letting the idealistic Major Barbara of the Salvation Army win over her father Undershaft to her spiritual values, he makes her eventually accept Undershaft's materialism and wealth as the best way of improving the condition of man. To startle his audience into thought, and also presumably to dramatize the socialist doctrine that economic conditions are of primary importance to society, Shaw unexpectedly and almost perversely makes what the audience would naturally consider good (the Salvation Army) into an ineffectual and positively harmful force, and what the audience would naturally consider bad (the manufacture of munitions) into the basis for new life, new hope, and new self-respect for mankind.

Though incongruity does indeed, then, seem to play a significant part in many aspects of comedy, a word of caution is in order. It is doubtful whether it, alone, can really serve as the basic definition of comedy, as is sometimes claimed. For one thing, in order to include all the different types of comedy, it would have to be stretched almost beyond recognition. For another, it does not necessarily distinguish comedy from other genres. Particularly in the case of tragedy, incongruities also seem to abound. For example, the partners are oddly matched in the meeting between the blind Tiresias who sees so much and the seeing Oedipus who sees so little. A character trait is markedly exaggerated in King Lear with his unreasonable vanity and wrath at the beginning of the play. And an extraordinary disproportion often exists between the flaw and the downfall of a tragic hero. Without denying that incongruity is a significant element in much of comedy, therefore, we had better regard it as only one of several characteristics. And we should also take into account the particular way in which the incongruity is treated—a way which presumably distinguishes comic from tragic incongruity.

The question that we are raising here is, fundamentally, that of the characteristic tone of comedy, and this is far from easy to define since it may cover a remarkably wide range. Comedy is sometimes described as a light and witty, or gay and humorous play, and indeed, both wit and humor seem to be important aspects of the typical comic tone. By wit, we mean an intellectual sharpness or brightness, the very word being related to knowledge or the intellect, as in the phrase "use your wits" or "keep your wits about you." It also often still has some of the overtone of its eighteenth-century meaning, the perception of similarities, in contrast to judgment, the perception of differences, and it may have the further overtone of a clever surprise twist. Usually, wit manifests itself in the very phrasing. A good example is the way in which Congreve's Mirabell describes the activity of the ladies who meet regularly on certain evenings "like a coroner's inquest, to sit upon the murdered reputations of the week." This delightful allusion to the common activity of gossip conveys, in an extraordinarily concentrated way, the gusto and officiousness of the participants (since they are like an inquest), the regularity with which they perform their task (dealing as they are with the reputations of only "the week"), the helplessness and number of their victims (since their reputations are described as "murdered," and since the plural form of "reputation" has been carefully inserted), and finally, the fact that they are not the first to engage in the scandalmongering in each case (for they are only performing the "inquest" on a reputation that has already been "murdered"). All the chief elements of wit are present here: the perception of the similarity between a party of gossiping women and an inquest; the fact that the comparison is at once surprising and, on closer scrutiny, justified; and the very brevity of the phrasing which is, in Polonius' words, "the soul of wit." Often, especially in Restoration comedy, the wit takes the form of **repartee**, the swift and duel-like exchange of clever remarks, and it may also include the so-called **double-entendre,** an obvious kind of ambiguity whereby something other is meant than what is expressed. Again *The Way of the World* offers a striking example. When Witwoud makes known the imminent arrival of "that fool, my brother" with a flood of ill-chosen similes, Mirabell cannot resist protesting, "A fool, and your brother, Witwoud!" His sarcasm is lost on Witwoud, who immediately replies: "Ay, ay, my half-brother. My half-brother he is, no nearer upon honour." Continuing the banter, Mirabell quickly retorts: "Then 'tis possible he may be but half a fool." This last statement is a *double-entendre;* it seems to suggest that the half not related to Witwoud is the fool, but actually means that the half that the two have in common is the foolish one, and thereby subtly but firmly calls Witwoud the very thing he is, but least wishes to be.

As for **humor,** it is a broader and still less easily definable term than *wit.* To begin with, it referred to the four chief bodily fluids—blood, phlegm, yellow bile or choler, and black bile or melancholy—and by extension to the kind of temperament dominated by each of these fluids— the sanguine, phlegmatic, choleric, and melancholic. Ben Jonson created the characters of his comedies by letting some one weakness or foible greatly predominate, and through this so-called **comedy of humors** the term took on the meaning of oddity or eccentricity. Nowadays it is used much more loosely, to describe a rather gentle, warm, and genial attitude of laughing at and with the world. It tends to be complacent rather than critical, accepting life even when it sees its shortcomings. Furthermore, it lacks the elegance of phrasing, the epigrammatic quality, that seems to be characteristic of wit. The glimpse that Dylan Thomas gives of his Polly Garter in the garden with her new baby exemplifies not wit but humor. She says:

> Nothing grows in our garden, only washing. And babies. And where's their fathers live, my love? Over the hills and far away. You're looking up at me now. I know what you're thinking, you poor little milky creature. You're thinking, you're no better than you should be, Polly, and that's good enough for me. Oh, isn't life a terrible thing, thank God? [1]

Polly sees her somewhat sordid environment and her own unconventional ways very clearly, but accepts them smilingly as part of a life that is, after all, good and fruitful. Unlike wit, furthermore, humor is not always intentional. The amusing misuse of words which we call **malapropism** in honor of Mrs. Malaprop, one of the minor figures in Sheridan's *Rivals,* is

[1] Copyright 1954 by New Directions. Reprinted by permission of New Directions.

an example of unconscious humor. Wit and humor are not, however, mutually exclusive. The brilliant scene in *Henry IV, Part I,* in which Falstaff describes his supposed bravery during the Gad's Hill robbery to Prince Hal, who has just witnessed his cowardice, is witty in much of the phrasing, unintentionally humorous from the point of view of Falstaff, who is misled into vastly embellishing his accomplishments, and intentionally and more fundamentally humorous in its acceptance of Falstaff's boastfulness as part of a lovable though roguish creature who embodies gusto and the love of life.

Wit and humor belong to the lighter sides of comedy. And yet we cannot restrict the tone of comedy to these, for the genre also includes, we should bear in mind, satire of manners or of character that can be very bitter indeed. The indignities to which Malvolio of *Twelfth Night* is subjected when Sir Toby Belch and his companions lock him into a dark cubbyhole and declare him mad are much too brutal to be considered either witty or humorous, and so, in a different way, are the scenes between Fainall and Mrs. Marwood in *The Way of the World* in which their masks fall for a moment and their weaknesses are devastatingly revealed. There is, moreover, a special type of comedy popular in the eighteenth century and known as **sentimental comedy** or, even more expressively, as **comédie larmoyante** (tearful comedy), which aimed at being high-minded and at arousing the emotions of sadness and pity, rather than at keeping the audience in gales of laughter. Steele's *Conscious Lovers* is one of the few examples of this type still read today; it is full of noble speeches in which the young hero extols filial duty and opposes the fashion of dueling, and the only wit was introduced as an afterthought, in the form of two amusing servants.

If we apply what we have said about the range of tone associated with comedy to the question of incongruity we discussed earlier, we shall have to acknowledge that any treatment, from the light and amusing to the sharp and bitter, can be included in the genre, and that only really painful incongruities would be excluded as belonging to the realm of tragedy. Drawing a more general conclusion, we can also see that comedy is not to be identified with or limited to purely *funny* plays.

Apart from the consideration of the plot, characters, and tone of comedy, one of the ways of approaching or defining the genre which we should notice at least briefly is, as in the case of tragedy, to describe it in terms of the audience's experience. In simplest form, comedy is sometimes defined merely as the ludicrous, that which arouses laughter or at least a smile, and fascinating theories have then been proposed to account for the phenomenon of laughter. At one extreme is the idea, going back to Hobbes, that laughter is "a kind of sudden glory" that comes from recognizing, usually through some sort of surprise, one's own superiority over another. This is the traditional way of accounting for our response to someone's slipping on a banana peel and similar farcical situations. At the other extreme is the idea derived from Kant that laughter is the response to some sort of tension followed by an anticlimax, or that it comes when the audience's expectations are frustrated. A great many jokes depend on this kind of response, and so does a good deal of witty dialogue. For example, when Dylan Thomas' Mr. Waldo dreams of all the women who are lining up to marry him, and the Preacher has asked the traditional question "Will you take this woman . . . ," we laugh when the phrase is completed with the unexpected anticlimax "to be your awful wedded wife"—an anticlimax which also, incidentally, reveals Mr. Waldo's worst unconscious fears on the subject of women.

In many periods, furthermore, the view that comedy is essentially that which arouses laughter had a strongly didactic or moral concomitant; it was thought that by arousing laughter at the follies and weaknesses of mankind, comedy in all its various forms would teach the audience to avoid similar follies. Satire, Swift maintained, attacks only those foibles and vices that mankind can mend, and in Pope's words, it "heals with morals what it hurts with wit." Another and more modern view, however, is that far from taking what we see to heart and improving ourselves accordingly, we remain thoroughly detached, and that the very effect of comedy depends on this detachment. It is often argued that the so-called "psychical distance" is necessary if we are to laugh rather than to feel painfully disturbed when we see how one character in a farce throws a pie into another's face, or when, in social comedy, the foppishness or pretentiousness or witlessness of a character is mercilessly ridiculed. George Meredith vividly describes this detached frame of mind in his famous "Essay on Comedy." Though he is restricting the term *comedy* to the witty and sophisticated form of high comedy, it is significant that he finds the characteristic and proper response to this form to be neither a strong identification with the characters nor a boisterous laugh at their expense, but rather the most civilized kind of intellectual smile. The same kind of detachment is suggested in his brilliant description of the Comic Spirit, which hovers over the best comedy, as an almost godlike, Olympian creature, looking "humanely malign" (that is, at once benevolently and critically) at all the manifold idiocies of man and greeting them with "volleys of silvery laughter."

Meredith's description of the Comic Spirit raises another interesting question related to the genre: whether there is a counterpart to what is known as the tragic vision or tragic view of life—some sort of **comic vision** or comic view of life. Curiously enough, the comic vision seems not to have been defined as clearly as the tragic vision. Nonetheless, it is possible to suggest at least tentatively what sort of ideas are expressed or implied in comic works. For Meredith, as we have seen, the comic spirit is an almost godlike detachment, a smiling and sardonic acceptance of the absurdities of man. It recalls Puck's comment in *A Midsummer Night's Dream*: "What fools these mortals be!" But the comic vision can also be described as a sense of proportion, a capacity for not taking others or, for that matter, oneself too seriously; in short, all that we understand by the common phrase "a sense of humor." This is the attitude that shines through Polly Garter's speech in the garden in Thomas' *Under Milk Wood,* and particularly in her delightfully paradoxical exclamation: "Oh, isn't life a terrible thing, thank God?" It has been suggested, furthermore, that the comic vision is ultimately concerned less with the problems of the individual than with those of society, and that it is characteristic of comedy that at the end, when the fops, fools, and fortune hunters are bested and the lovers reunited, the good of society is maintained. Finally, and perhaps most profoundly, this view of life has been said to consist of some sort of affirmation of life, whether joyous or only grudging—a conviction that whatever the difficulties, they will eventually be solved and life will remain good. This feeling that all problems will eventually be resolved into a happy ending is epitomized in *The Tempest,* for what governs and colors all the plotting, all the intrigue, and even the apparent death of Ferdinand's father, the King of Naples, is Prospero's word to Miranda near the beginning of the play, when she is aghast at the shipwreck: "There's no harm done." It is this sense of "no harm" that seems to be one of the chief characteristics of the comic vision, and that distinguishes it from the tragic vision with its awareness that human problems cannot always be solved and that even if the evil in the world is in one way or another destroyed, much that is good may be wasted along with it.

Though the various ways of describing comedy which we have just reviewed are usually presented separately, they are not, we should recognize, mutually exclusive, any more than are the various ways of describing tragedy. The happy ending; the focus on characters embodying the unheroic sides of man and their choice to represent a series of deviations from a norm; the exploitation of incongruities; and some kind of general affirmation that life is good—each of these is best considered not as the sole distinctive feature of comedy but as one of several facets of the genre.

In the course of time, a great many distinctive conventions have come to be associated with comedy. There are certain figures which recur frequently enough so that they have come to be regarded as the stock characters of comedy. The two pairs of young lovers, the duped husband, the flighty wife, the husband-hunting widow, the peculiar elderly aunt, the foundling, the witty servant, the rustic oaf—we recognize these immediately. Some stock characters have a long history. The braggart soldier, for example, was popular in the classical Roman comedy and in the kind of improvised play developed in Italy in the sixteenth century that was known as *commedia dell'arte*. The type reaches a high point in Shakespeare's Falstaff. Two other popular stock figures also come from the *commedia dell'arte*: Harlequin (Arlecchino), the bright and lively clown with his colorful patched coat, and Punch (Pulcinella), the more dim-witted clown who is Harlequin's butt and companion. The fop and the ill-mannered fool from the country are the stock figures of Restoration and eighteenth-century comedy; Irishmen with heavy brogues and Scotsmen with indistinct burrs are age-old favorites, and likely to appear in modern American as well as English plays.

Together with these characters, certain incidents and devices seem to occur with such frequency and predictability that they have become the **stock situations** and **stock devices** of comedy. There is the **eternal triangle**, which is exploited in nineteenth-century French bedroom farces and the modern drawing-room comedies of Noel Coward. Equally popular are the basic situations of fortune hunting, and of the conflict between parents who favor a sensible marriage for money and position and their children who yearn to marry for love. **Disguise** is one of the favorite devices of romantic comedy; usually it is the heroine who disguises herself as a boy, as do Shakespeare's Rosalind and Viola, but sometimes the young man disguises himself as a music master or doctor or similarly plausible professional in order to gain admittance to his beloved. Disguise is also used in farcical scenes, for instance when Waitwell in *The Way of the World* pretends to be the rich and marriageable Sir Rowland and woos the elderly Lady Wishfort, or when the young hero in *Charley's Aunt* dresses as an eminently respectable old lady and becomes the chaperone for a group of young girls. Another standard device is **mistaken identity**, which may or may not be the result of disguise. Goldsmith uses this delightfully in *She Stoops to Conquer*, in which the young hero, Marlow, believes he has arrived at an inn when he is actually in the house of Mr. Hardcastle, his father's old friend and his future father-in-law. Not only does he mistake Hardcastle for an officious innkeeper, but he is also misled into taking the charming heroine, Kate, for a common barmaid. Finally, there are all sorts of "props," stage properties or tangible objects, which are frequently used to further the comic plot. These range from letters that fall into the wrong hands to well- or ill-timed telegrams, and from jewels that are mislaid or found to mysterious swords or articles of dress that eventually reveal the true identity and parentage of one or another of the characters.

When these conventional characters, incidents, and devices are poorly handled, we are aware only that they have been used often before.

We are all familiar with the abuses of comic conventions, the ringing of the telephone or doorbell that disrupts the clandestine meeting of lovers at the wrong or right moment, or the implausible discovery of the strawberry mark that resolves a seemingly insoluble tangle of misunderstandings. But we should recognize that when they are well used, we accept the same conventions quite freely, and see them as part of the artificiality we in any case tend to associate with comedy. Oscar Wilde's *The Importance of Being Earnest* is perhaps the supreme example of the gleeful exploitation of all imaginable stock characters, stock situations, and stock devices. Wilde shamelessly introduces the standard two pairs of lovers: Algy and Jack, two young-men-about-town, and two girls who complement each other, the sophisticated Gwendolen who lives in town and the slightly more innocent Cecily who lives in the country. The intrigue is based partly on mistaken identity, since Algy pretends that his name is Ernest when he lives in town and that he has a loose-living brother called Ernest when he lives in the country, and partly on disguise, since Jack unexpectedly arrives in the country pretending that he is Algy's profligate brother Ernest. The minor characters are all easily identifiable stock types, from Lady Bracknell, a splendid and outrageously farcical version of the comic aunt, to Miss Prism, the high-minded but scatterbrained elderly governess who is Lady Bracknell's counterpart, to Dr. Chasuble, the pedantic clergyman, who is eventually and somewhat implausibly paired off with Miss Prism. All this and much more confusion is resolved when Algy, a foundling, is identified as being, indeed, Jack's long-lost brother, and by a happy coincidence christened Ernest to boot. His identity is established through the "prop" of a portmanteau in which he was left in a railroad station as a baby. The play ends with the embrace of all available couples, each one in turn uttering the phrase: "At last!" This staggering survey of comic conventions is amusing, quite apart from the witty dialogue which accompanies it, precisely because it is too complete to be taken seriously. In another sense, however, it also contributes to a meaningful theme at which Wilde is delicately hinting: the desirability of the frivolous way of life, as an antidote to Victorian solemnity. The very title is a frivolous paradox, for though it seems to be affirming the importance of earnestness, it is to be interpreted only literally as the importance, for one of the lovers, of bearing the name of Ernest.

The comic conventions can, of course, also be extended or even played against. George Bernard Shaw delights in breaking with the comic conventions by the simple expedient of reversing them. Instead of having the young men pursue the young women, he amusingly makes the women pursue the men in *Man and Superman*. In *Major Barbara* it is not a foundling who must prove his identity before he can win his goal but a man who must prove that he is a foundling; nor is his goal the usual one of winning the hand of the heroine but rather the taking over of the munitions works. To be sure, both these reversals suggest some of Shaw's more serious ideas—that the woman is the dominant partner in the love-relationship because a universal Life Force or creative instinct is expressing itself through her, and that the most efficient men are likely to be the ones unhampered by family and other conventional social ties. But they are also intrinsically amusing, and what makes them so is our familiarity with the kinds of conventions that are being broken or reversed.

We have been considering tragedy and comedy as two separate and sharply contrasting genres. And yet we should bear in mind that it is not always possible to draw a sharp dividing line between the two. This is not just a matter of there being comic elements in certain tragedies, for the comic relief in Elizabethan tragedies does not prevent these from being clearly tragic. Nor is it a matter of the mingling of tragic and comic elements in tragicomedy, which, as we saw, is really a separate genre, a sensational play that is neither tragedy nor comedy. But there are certain plays which can be interpreted as either tragedy or comedy, so that there seems to be a middle ground where the two are almost indistinguishable. The outstanding example of this kind of play is Chekhov's *Cherry Orchard*. With its impression of a whole society coming to an end as the estate passes out of the hands of a family, with its sense of many lives that are wasted, and with the brooding melancholy that hangs over much of its action, the work has a distinct affinity to tragedy. But with its choice of characters to show the weaknesses and absurdities of man and to illustrate innumerable deviations from a social and a moral norm, with its gently ironic tone, witty dialogue, and sweetly plaintive music in the background, it has an equal affinity to comedy. This kind of play reminds us once again that tragedy and comedy, like the other genres, are fluid groupings, and that they are only two of the many possible interpretations which a writer can give of life.

Periods, Movements, and Schools

The classification by genres is not, in any case, the only way of grouping works of literature. Another way which has preoccupied many scholars and literary historians ranges works by periods, movements, or schools. We all tend to think along these lines to some extent, when we speak of the Renaissance or Elizabethan as opposed to medieval literature, or of romanticism as opposed to classicism, or of realism, naturalism, expressionism, and the like. College courses are usually organized by periods and sometimes also by movements; that is, by general tendencies or trends (English romanticism, German realism). Since works of one period often have a great many characteristics in common, and may indeed differ markedly from works of the preceding or following period, it is often possible to give a fairly full description of each group.

Let us consider, for the moment, two such familiar terms as *classicism* and *romanticism*. They are associated with a certain period: especially when they are opposed to each other, the former apparently refers to the eighteenth, the latter to the early nineteenth century. Strictly speaking, however, **classicism** has to do with the arts of ancient Greece or Rome, and we should use the term **neoclassicism** (new classicism) for those of the eighteenth century. But it is no simple matter to fix the dates for these periods with any accuracy. If we concentrate on England, we might argue that neoclassicism begins not in the eighteenth but in the last quarter of the seventeenth century, with Dryden, and that it extends not to the end of the eighteenth century but only to its last quarter, to Dr. Johnson. Incidentally, Dryden, Addison, Steele, Swift, and Pope also thought of themselves, by another oblique reference to the ancients, as **Augustans,** and so their period has come to be known as the Augustan, in honor of the emperor Augustus under whom the Roman arts flourished. In France, the neoclassical period includes most of the seventeenth as well as much of the eighteenth century, extending from Corneille and Racine to Voltaire. The German counterpart would seem to be the era of Lessing in the mid-eighteenth century, even though the term *classicism* (*die Klassik*) is usually applied to the later works of Goethe and Schiller in the early nineteenth century.

As for **romanticism,** it is usually thought to begin, in England, with the publication of Wordsworth and Coleridge's *Lyrical Ballads* in 1798, and the Preface appended to this collection in 1800 is often regarded as the first great manifesto or public declaration of intention for the group. English romanticism is commonly held to be over by about 1830, when several of the major poets—Bryon, Keats, and Shelley —were dead, and when Wordsworth and Coleridge were no longer writing major poetry. Sometimes 1832 is mentioned as the terminal date, and the passing of the Reform Bill in that year is taken to usher in the Victorian period with its social and political preoccupations. German romanticism, dominated by such figures as the Schlegels, Novalis, E. T. A. Hoffmann, Brentano, von Arnim, and Tieck, is roughly contemporaneous with the English, though it also coincides, confusingly enough, with the so-called classicism of Goethe and Schiller. The French also begins about 1800, but goes on much longer, as Alfred de Vigny and Victor Hugo continued to produce major works.

When the term *romanticism* is used not just for the early nineteenth century period but for a whole movement, it covers a much wider area. It can, for example, be applied to the English writers working in the second half of the eighteenth century, such as Young, Macpherson, Chatterton, and even Gray and Goldsmith, all of whom are sometimes called the **pre-romantics**. The term can also be used to cover Rousseau, and the whole turbulent German movement of Storm and Stress (**Sturm und Drang**) to which the young Schiller and Goethe contributed from the seventeen-seventies on. Furthermore, in some of its aspects, as we shall see, romanticism can be said to continue down to the present. Unlike the career of an individual writer, then, a period or movement may not be clearly demarcated, and it may have a somewhat different history in different countries.

When considered as distinctive movements, neoclassicism and romanticism can be shown to have quite definite and special characteristics in their literary theory and practice. The former, as its name suggests, has strong ties with the classicism of the ancients. It values order, proportion, balance, symmetry—all that, in the visual arts, is epitomized in a Greek or Roman temple. Not only does it cultivate the closed form, in which beginning and end are clearly defined, but it also emphasizes polish, refinement, and the kind of simplicity and clarity which come when art hides art. As Pope says in his *Essay on Criticism,*

> True ease in writing comes from art, not chance,
> As those move easiest who have learned to dance.

This is a point of view which considers writing a craft, and literature something to be consciously shaped and reshaped, polished and repolished. The qualities of form and craftsmanship are vividly illustrated in *Gulliver's Travels,* with its four complementary parts, and in *The Rape of the Lock,* with its five equal cantos, beginning with the preparations for the seizure of Belinda's curl, presenting in the middle the climax of the actual snipping, and ending with the final disposition of the lock in heaven. The same qualities are illustrated in small in Pope's heroic or closed couplet, with its parallelism, balance, and antithesis.

Neoclassicism is furthermore characterized by a strong sense of tradition, so much so that conscious attempts were made to emulate and imitate the ancients. The epics of Homer and Virgil, together with classical tragedy, were the genres most admired. The unities and decorum were observed rather strictly, not merely in veneration for the ancients but on the theory that these writers had found the most effective and pleasing devices. Pope says:

> Those rules of old discovered, not devised,
> Are nature still, but nature methodized.

Oddly enough, however, the genre most successfully cultivated in neo-classic literature is neither the epic nor tragedy but social comedy and satire, and it is significant that so typical a work as *The Rape of the Lock* is a satiric mock-epic.

Hand in hand with the sense of tradition goes a firm belief that there is a fundamental uniformity of experience and that human nature remains essentially unchanged. This belief manifests itself in the focus on the typical and representative, either on man in general, as in Pope's *Essay on Man,* or on man in society, as in social comedy and satire. On the other hand, the interest in these latter genres reveals that the neoclassic writers also had a keen sense of man's absurdities, of the many ways in which he can deviate from the norm.

In almost every respect, the literary theory and practice of romanticism is the direct opposite of the neoclassic. Its keynote is experimentation and rebelliousness. What is valued is diversity, fluidity, a loose open form to which there is no sharply defined end. The architectural shape admired by the romantics, the very opposite of the Greek temple, is the Gothic cathedral with its soaring lines and its often unfinished towers. The prime example in literature is Goethe's *Faust,* with its vast scope, loosely episodic structure, free experimenting with innumerable older and newer devices and conventions, and an ending which manages to suggest continued aspiration and upward movement. It is significant that Goethe worked on this drama or dramatic poem, whose very genre is a matter of doubt, for more than sixty years, and that he did not hesitate to leave parts of it fragmentary or not quite consistent with the rest. What interested him was less the finished product than the very process of creation. The same willingness to leave works in fragmentary form can be seen in Wordsworth's *Excursion,* Coleridge's "Kubla Khan" and "Christabel," and Keats' *Hyperion.* This kind of writing is considered the product not so much of the careful craftsman as of the inspired original genius, a godlike figure spontaneously creating worlds of his own.

In romanticism, traditions and conventions, especially those associated with classical and neoclassic art, are consciously rejected. Although there is an interest in the past, it is in the medieval or Gothic, the very period that the neoclassic writers considered crude and unattractive. The Elizabethans in general and Shakespeare in particular are admired, mainly for their ambitious scope and for their disregard of the classical rules. When Greece is important, as it is in the poetry of Byron and Shelley, it is a symbol of liberty or of Platonic idealism, not of a controlled and unified art. The genres held in the highest esteem and most frequently adopted are the various forms of lyric poetry: the ode, the sonnet, the ballad, and the short songlike poem known as lyric.

What interests the romantic writers is not the typical and universal but rather the particular and individual. There is a correspondingly wide and varied range of subjects or themes, all of them strikingly different from those typical of neoclassicism. Personal emotions are explored; hence the popularity of the lyric, the genre best adapted to this kind of theme. And since the emotions most familiar to the poet are usually his own, much of the writing from Rousseau to Wordsworth to Alfred de Musset is autobiographical and subjective. Often the poet feels himself an exile, an outcast from society. Or he is fascinated by characters who are in one way or another aloof, isolated from society: the titanic Faustian man whose aspirations are boundless, or the demonic, "possessed" man, a moody rebel sometimes called, for obvious reasons, the Byronic hero. But the child in his innocence and the peasant close to nature also become important themes. And so, on the other hand, do the supernatural, the strange, and the exotic, which are exploited to the full in Coleridge's "Christabel," Keats' "Lamia," and many of the German fairy tales (*Märchen*) developed as a special literary type by E. T. A. Hoffmann, Tieck, and others. It is in this atmosphere, in which strange and emotionally compelling subjects are cultivated, that the possibilities of symbolism are explored—that highly complex and suggestive form whereby multiple meanings are presented and the particular, in its own way, once more takes on a certain universality. This is the aspect of romanticism that still, of course, exerts a profound influence on modern writing.

Behind these literary interests of neoclassicism and romanticism there is, in each case, a special intellectual climate as well as a distinctive set of values. Neoclassicism extols reason, so much so that the period is sometimes called the **Age of Reason** or the **Enlightenment**. This emphasis on reason manifests itself in two ways: on the one hand, in the cultivation of philosophical and scientific inquiry under the influence of such eminent figures as Newton, Locke, and Hume; on the other hand, especially in literature, in a belief in straightforward practical judgment, what we call good sense or common sense, rather than in any rigorous formal logic or ratiocination. It is generally thought that man is either, as Hobbes maintained, basically selfish, rapacious, and aggressive, or, as Locke suggested, initially a *tabula rasa,* a blank tablet which comes to be marked by all the varying impressions that crowd in through the senses. In either case, a conscious cultivation of good sense seems desirable. So does a life within a stable society, preferably in the city, where men can be held in check. The ancient virtue of moderation is valued, along with good manners, sophistication, articulateness, wit—all that comes under the heading of urbanity. This very term, incidentally, well describes the neoclassic ideal of behavior, since it suggests both the polished, courteous, and affable manners and, by its very root (Latin *urbs,* "city"), the emphasis on town life. The comedies of the period, we may recall, feature the stock figure of the unmannerly fool from the country. As for the universe in which man lives, it is held to be a stable, ordered hierarchy; in fact, writers such as Pope and Addison still accept the Renaissance notion of a **chain of being**, a scale on which everything from the lowest animals to the angels has its assigned place and which is not to be disturbed without disastrous results. Or it is thought of as a machine, originally created by God but running now according to fixed and recognizable natural laws.

The romantic view of life contrasts strikingly to all this. Romantic writers extol not reason in one form or another but the emotions. Man is thought to be basically good, and at his best when allowed spontaneously to follow the dictates of his feelings. Not just the emotions but the whole non-rational side of man is valued. Wordsworth believes in a "wise passiveness" whereby man can let nature speak to him; other romantics are fascinated by the imagination and by dreams, both of which they regard as great sources of truth. The modern preoccupations with the subconscious or, in the case of D. H. Lawrence and William Faulkner, with the instinctual life are a direct outgrowth of romanticism.

The idea that man is basically good, popularized by Rousseau and fundamental to much romantic thought, has several ramifications. It accounts for the belief that man should live close to nature, that he is likely to be morally at his best in the country and corrupted by the city. This, in turn, leads to an interest in the peasant at home and in the so-called noble savage abroad, the American Indian or the Laplander. Both the peasant and the savage can be taken to represent the simple and unspoilt aspects of man. The idealizing of early man is known as **primitivism**, and it has borne fruit in at least one important respect, namely in the recording and collecting of different kinds of folk literature, especially ballads and fairy tales. In England, this work was undertaken by Bishop Percy in the latter half of the eighteenth century; in Germany, slightly later, by the brothers Grimm.

As for the romantic view of the universe, this varies considerably from writer to writer and again suggests the dominant individualism of the movement. Generally speaking, we can say that it tends to be unorthodox, and to see the universe not as a static and clearly defined chain of being or a machine but as a dynamic, evolving, and constantly changing organism. Nature and God are seen in mystical terms. Wordsworth in his early years accepts the pantheistic doctrine that God and nature are one; Keats and Shelley in varying ways hold the Platonic view that the sensuous aspects of nature and human life at once reflect and lead up to the Absolutes of the True, the Good, and the Beautiful. The German romantics and Baudelaire, a self-styled romantic, are fascinated by the idea of a great system of correspondences, whereby all the facets of the universe mirror each other. In all these theories, man's task is thought to be to attune himself to the rest of the universe—not to reason about it but to feel and respond to it. All these theories, furthermore, constitute an atmosphere that is particularly favorable to symbolism, for they suggest that even the smallest concrete detail, a flower or a bird, has a far deeper though not always fully definable meaning in the total context.

Neoclassicism and *romanticism,* then, are large and loose terms, referring to movements that have both a common literary theory and practice, and a more or less coherent world view. Other movements are somewhat more restricted. **Realism,** for example, is primarily a matter of technique. It aims at giving an authentic picture of ordinary life, usually by showing typical people of the middle and lower classes engaged in ordinary pursuits, and by recording their activities in great and concrete detail. In the novels of the eighteenth and nineteenth centuries, particularly those of Defoe and Balzac and Howells, great emphasis is given to seemingly inconsequential people, who are portrayed in a rigorously unidealized way, and to such externals as the sights and sounds of common life. We are so accustomed to the technique that we now tend to take it for granted, especially in the novel, but when Tolstoy's contemporaries read in *War and Peace* about Pierre's suddenly becoming conscious of the creaking of Princess Hélène's corset, many were startled and dismayed by the intimate realistic detail. When attention is paid not only to externals but also to the intricate workings of the mind, as it is in the subtle and detailed characterizations of Henry James, the term **psychological realism** is used.

An extreme and special type of realism is **naturalism,** which tries, in the words of its chief exponent Emile Zola, to take a "slice of life" (**tranche de vie**) and subject it to dispassionate, almost scientific analysis. Its aim is an almost photographic and phonographic representation of sights and sounds. Usually this technique is coupled with a specific philosophical view, the deterministic one whereby man is seen as a victim of forces and circumstances which he can neither escape nor control. In Zola's great novel series about the Rougon-Macquart family or Gerhart Hauptmann's well-known play *The Weavers,* dramatizing the plight of the poverty-stricken workmen, it is heredity and environment that shape the lives of the characters. So intent are the naturalists on showing life "as it really is," and not some idealized or heroic version of it, that they tend to focus on the seamiest and most sordid side. In actual fact, and in spite of their avowed aim of being wholly objective, they are selecting and interpreting their material quite as much as any other writers.

Whereas realism and naturalism try to present life objectively, another modern movement, **expressionism,** aims at presenting moods and emotions as immediately and startlingly as possible. Its exponents, who include the German Ernst Toller and the American Eugene O'Neill, are fascinated by dreamlike effects, and they do not shun outrageous distortions and other shock effects. In *The Great God Brown,* which is also a symbolic play touching on the archetypal themes of rebirth or regeneration by becoming one with the cycle of fertility, O'Neill makes his chief characters wear masks to distinguish their real selves from their social faces, and in the second part of the play he lets one of his main figures, Brown, assume the mask and then, progressively, the personality of the other main figure, the tormented Dion Anthony. When Brown's supposed death is announced, only his mask is carried on stage, though the bearers pretend that they are carrying a body, and the audience is expected to assume that the bearers believe they have the body. As this manipulation of the masks suggests, the expressionists tend to rely greatly on visual effects, on the very staging, and their technique has a direct relationship to expressionism in art, which became popular especially in Germany in the second decade of this century.

The study of literary periods and movements is important, we might say, because it makes us aware of the fact that poems, dramas, or novels are seldom written in isolation. They may well have something in common with other works written during the same period, either an intellectual climate or a clearly defined technique or both. We shall understand Wordsworth's *Prelude,* the long autobiographical poem in which he traces as faithfully as he can the growth of his own mind and imagination, much better if we recognize that it belongs to a very different movement from that of *The Rape of the Lock,* and *The Great God Brown* much better if we recognize that it does not try to present a realistic view of life. And yet, if we are critical readers rather than literary historians, we shall want to focus attention less on the periods and movements *per se* than on the individual works that make up the movements. We shall want to avoid making the works fit the movements and, even more, praising or condemning them out of hand simply because they are romantic rather than neoclassic, or vice versa. In other words, we shall be interested in periods and movements, the characteristics of which are in any case not always easy to define, primarily for the way they illuminate a given poem, play, or novel.

Traditional Motifs and Conventions

Certain literary conventions are associated with neither genres nor movements. They are, rather, traditional and recurring themes, also known as **motifs.** One of these is known as the **ubi sunt** motif, meaning "where are they?" The term is derived from the opening of a number of medieval Latin lyrics, each one lamenting the passage of time or of youth.

François Villon's "Mais où sont les neiges d'antan?", translated by Dante Gabriel Rossetti as "Where are the snows of yesteryear?", is perhaps the most famous example, and Charles Lamb's poem beginning "Where are they gone, the old familiar faces?" is also written in this tradition. Another such motif is known as **carpe diem,** based on a quotation from Horace meaning "seize the day"; it suggests that life is short and time is fleeting and that one had therefore better make the most of the moment. It is charmingly expressed by Herrick not only in his well-known lyric "Gather ye rosebuds while ye may" but also in the last stanza of the more elaborate "Corinna's Going A-Maying." Having urged Corinna to get up and go out into the fields on this beautiful May morning, the speaker reminds her that

> We shall grow old apace, and die
> Before we know our liberty,
> Our life is short, and our days run
> As fast away as does the sun.

He concludes:

> Then while time serves, and we are but decaying,
> Come, my Corinna, come, let's go a-Maying.

A number of other recurring themes or motifs have to do with love. Although this would seem to be a subject on which each poet would wish to write from personal experience, it is often treated in a highly conventional way, particularly in medieval and Renaissance literature. One of the great conventions is that of **Platonic love.** In his *Symposium,* Plato has the wise Diotima describe what has come to be known as the "ladder of love," a series of steps whereby the lover may proceed from the love of physical beauty in a single person to the love of all physical beauty, from there to love of the beauty of the soul, and eventually to the contemplation of the Idea of Beauty, one of the great Absolutes in which Plato believed. This notion came down to the Renaissance through Plotinus and the Neoplatonists in such a way as to suggest not that the lower stages should be left behind as the lover progresses, but that his love of physical beauty will lead him to feel the beauty of the soul and indirectly also the ultimate, eternal, absolute Beauty. In this version, Platonic love is frequently expressed in the Elizabethan sonnet cycles, notably in Sidney's *Astrophel and Stella* and Spenser's *Amoretti.* The latter writes eloquently:

> The sovereign beauty which I do admire,
> Witness the world how worthy to be praised;
> The light whereof hath kindled heavenly fire
> In my frail spirit, by her from baseness raised;
> That being now with her huge brightness dazed,
> Base thing I can no more endure to view.

Not only is the lover shown to be ennobled by his love, but physical beauty is frequently interpreted as a sign of the beauty of the soul. In the first of Spenser's *Four Hymns,* which are, significantly, written in praise of Beauty, Love, Heavenly Love, and Heavenly Beauty, the poet maintains that "all that fair is, is by nature good." Much of the characterization in *The Faerie Queene,* in which the virtuous Una is beautiful and the wicked Duessa only seems to be so and is eventually revealed as a hideous old hag, is influenced by this Platonic notion. In romantic poetry, too, the motif of Platonic love makes itself felt. When Shelley describes his beloved in glowing terms in his "Epipsychidion,"

> See where she stands! a mortal shape indued
> With love and life and light and deity,
> And motion which may change but cannot die;
> An image of some bright Eternity,

he is giving the theme a particularly intense expression.

During the Middle Ages, a special convention known as **courtly love** arose in Provence and strongly influenced Dante, Chaucer, and many other writers. It is not entirely clear to what extent this is merely a literary motif and to what extent it was also based on social fact. The convention assumes that the lover is a devoted servant of his mistress, almost as if he were her feudal vassal. The mistress is never his wife, so that the element of possible adultery is strong. C. S. Lewis, who gives a vivid description of this so-called *Frauendienst* (service to the lady) in his *Allegory of Love,* suggests that its four chief characteristics are Humility, Courtesy, Adultery, and the Religion of Love. The last refers to an elaborate ritual prescribed for approaching the mistress and doing her bidding. The convention dominates such works as *The Romance of the Rose,* which is also an allegory, and Chaucer's *Troilus and Criseyde,* especially the early sections in which Troilus is trying to win his beloved. It also has echoes in religious poetry, in the lyrics devoted to the Virgin Mary. As C. S. Lewis points out, our modern Western assumption that in social situations the woman naturally takes precedence, not at all shared by the peoples of the Far East, is a direct outgrowth of this particular tradition.

The **Petrarchan convention** is a later version of the ideal of courtly love, and it still has some of the overtones of Platonic love. Named after Petrarch, who expressed his love for Laura in a famous sonnet cycle, it is characterized not only by rather artificial diction, with many puns and antitheses, but also by the recurring situation of a plaintive or pleading lover who is either lamenting the hard-heartedness of his mistress or urging her to relent. The situation recurs, as we have observed, in many pastoral lyrics. To express his devotion, the lover may give an extensive catalogue of his mistress' features, likening her eyes to the sun, her cheeks, lips, and teeth to the appropriate precious stones or jewels. To express his own plight, the lover may use the image of a storm-tossed ship, or of being scorched or chilled by his beloved, or of being wounded by Cupid's arrows. Sidney neatly summarizes many of the Petrarchan images or conceits, the extravagant analogies which often play with antitheses, when he says that most lovers speak "Of living deaths, dear wounds, fair storms, and freezing fires." So widely adopted were the courtly love and the Petrarchan conventions, which are often indistinguishable in later poems, that they lent themselves all too well to parody. The endless cataloguing of the mistress' features is delightfully ridiculed in Shakespeare's mockingly defiant "My mistress' eyes are nothing like the sun," and the lover's plaintive state in Sir John Suckling's "Why so pale and wan, fond lover," which ends on an unexpectedly forceful note:

> If of herself she will not love,
> Nothing can make her.
> The devil take her!

Some of these conventional lines can be considered romantic, not in the special sense of having to do with literary romanticism, but in a popular sense of the term. They display, that is, a consistent idealizing of the mistress and of the plight of the lover. But since they also include the element of adultery or illicit love, it is better to distinguish the courtly and Petrarchan from the later convention or motif of **romantic love**, the aim or end of which is marriage. This is the motif that runs through much of modern fiction, in which boy meets girl and, after a series of obstacles, manages to marry her. It governs romantic comedy, too; in *As You Like It* or *Twelfth Night* or *She Stoops to Conquer* or *The Importance of Being Earnest* there is a wholesale and not always plausible pairing-off of the marriageable partners at the end.

We have seen enough of literary conventions to recognize that the use of one of the various motifs we have just considered is not at all the sign of an inferior or merely derivative piece of literature. For the writer, it is a way of aligning himself with a definite tradition, and also of showing how subtly and well he can work within a rather clearly defined area. As in the case of the other literary conventions, then, we shall be interested not so much in the fact that Herrick has chosen the *carpe diem* theme or that Sidney uses Petrarchan conceits as with what they do with these traditional motifs in the course of the poems.

Use of Literary Models and Allusions

At times writers make use not of generally known and widely used themes or motifs but of specific works by earlier writers. They may take over the characters or the basic situations, as Virgil does in his *Aeneid* when he bases some of the characters and episodes on those of Homer's *Iliad* and *Odyssey,* and as Dante does in the *Divine Comedy* when he pays tribute to Virgil by making him the guide and companion of his main character on the journey through the inferno and purgatory. Sometimes the use of earlier material is less obvious, and the reader needs special knowledge to recognize it. For instance, in *Absalom and Achitophel* Dryden endows Achitophel with a brilliant persuasiveness, a diabolic turn of mind, and a certain Latinate trick of phrasing, all of which makes him subtly similar to Milton's Satan. Dryden thereby magnifies Achitophel, the allegorical representation of the Earl of Shaftesbury, and emphasizes the danger to the state and to Charles II which he believes Shaftesbury to represent.

When a writer takes over the very phrases of an earlier work, which are supposed to recall their context to the reader's mind, the technique is called **literary allusion.** Virgil uses it, along with the taking over of characters and episodes, as a tribute to Homer, and the writing from the Renaissance to the eighteenth century is full of classical "tags," phrases that were certainly familiar to contemporary readers brought up on the classics, although they may have to be explained to readers of our own time. When Milton says that Lycidas himself knew how to sing, to "build the lofty rhyme," he is echoing a phrase of Horace's *Epistles,* and when Thomson describes the coming of the winter storms in his *Seasons,* he is consciously and directly taking over many of the details and phrases from Virgil's *Georgics.* It hardly needs mentioning that poets of all ages have felt free to use mythological and Biblical allusions, usually to emphasize or intensify their theme.

Whereas the older poets tend to allude to earlier works as a means of relating their subject to a long and glorious tradition, modern writers often do so for the very opposite effect. Joyce's *Ulysses* is patterned on the *Odyssey,* and many of the characters and incidents are parallels to those in Homer's epic. But Joyce is suggesting the ironic contrast between the heroic figures of the past and their singularly unheroic counterparts in modern Dublin. Leopold Bloom, with his passion for fried kidneys, his unsatisfactory relationship with his wife and mild flirtation with a secretary, and his inchoate benevolence toward young Stephen Dedalus, is a far cry from the manly Ulysses; Molly Bloom, with her sensuousness, her lover, and her passionate yea-saying to life, is an almost comic contrast to the faithful and rather shadowy Penelope. The very fact that Mr. Bloom and Stephen, the modern versions of Ulysses and his son Telemachus, are not related at all, and actually follow each other around Dublin for most of the day without meeting, represents a contrast to the firm familial and social bonds of the past, and suggests, among other things, the atomistic quality and lack of communication many writers find typical of modern society. In *The Waste Land* T. S. Eliot introduces a series of subtle allusions to the whole body of Western literature, from Virgil to Shakespeare to Baudelaire, to create a similar ironic contrast. His intensely neurotic modern lady brushes her hair in a chair reminiscent of Cleopatra's dazzling throne, under a ceiling that recalls the splendid one in Dido's palace, but the allusions to Shakespeare and Virgil serve only to emphasize how incapable she is of the strong and passionate involvement which distinguished the earlier heroines. The picnickers on the banks of the Thames are called "nymphs," and the section describing them is punctuated by the refrain "Sweet Thames, run softly till I end my song." But the allusion to Spenser's *Prothalamion,* coupled as it is with the fact that the so-called nymphs are gone and have left behind them only assorted rubbish, from sandwich wrappings to cigarette butts, serves to suggest merely the ugliness and sterility of the modern counterparts to Spenser's wedding party. Even though Joyce and Eliot allude to earlier works primarily in order to emphasize the differences between modern life and that of the past, their very use of allusions suggests that they, as writers, still have a strong and vital sense of tradition.

As we review the ways in which genres, conventions, and allusions are used in works of literature, we can hardly help acknowledging how often, and in how many different ways, these function. We shall want to avoid being prescriptive in our approach, or declaring some conventions more desirable than others, and we shall want to avoid paying so much attention to the conventions that we lose sight of the individual poem, play, or story. Still, we can be aware of the great sense of tradition felt by most writers, whether they are working within the established conventions or breaking with them. T. S. Eliot, in a famous essay entitled "Tradition and the Individual Talent," makes a strong plea to writers and critics alike to be conscious of the intellectual climate of Europe, past and present. It is this consciousness that we, as critical readers, will also want to cultivate.

CHAPTER FOUR

Frames of Reference

In considering the traditional terms in which literature can be analyzed and the conventions that help to determine literary form, we have had to recall that the objects of criticism are specific works: a poem, a story, or a play. Technical knowledge and a sense of literary history are important to the critical reader mainly as they help him to understand and judge these individual works. It will be necessary still to keep this in mind as we proceed now to consider the relevance of terms and concepts that are not strictly literary—of economic rather than metrical analysis, for instance, and political history rather than literary history. Literary works are never purely literary, as music is purely musical. A poem may be described as an elegiac Petrarchan sonnet in the pastoral tradition, using metaphysical conceits, but it has also to be about something—about, say, the death of a certain man who lived in a certain time and place and had specific beliefs. And so we cannot avoid using the language of history or religion or philosophy, the words used to describe men and times and beliefs. We can, to be sure, avoid taking the poem merely as a piece of biographical and historical information or merely as a religious commentary. We can try to grasp the total structure of the work. The historical and social meanings that contribute to this structure, we can recognize, do not wholly determine it or fully explain its meaning. Nevertheless, these meanings help to define the work of art, and so a sense of the larger context they represent may be necessary.

Certain modern critics are especially interested in these historical and social meanings. Lionel Trilling, for example, writes as a critic not only of literature but also of society. He belongs to the tradition of Matthew Arnold, the great nineteenth-century essayist who preached the doctrine of culture, of the civilizing effect derived from wide and critical reading. Like Trilling, other writers for the less academic journals of opinion are likely to stress both the ways in which literary art reflects social values and the ways in which it judges them. Leslie Fiedler, who relies a good deal on political and psychological analysis, emphasizes the importance of "connecting" all parts of experience in the criticism of literature. The danger of this emphasis is that it may force connections where no very clear ones exist, imposing the critic's current interest—in the psychological ideas of Jung or the rites of Eskimos or the theology of Kierkegaard—upon everything he reads. Still, the value of it is that it can oblige the reader to see how theory and experience are inseparable, to understand that literature is a part of life.

Biography

One of the most obvious frames of reference for a piece of writing is the life of its author. Critics and scholars of literature have often used biographical information, if only as a means of introducing critical considerations. Dr. Johnson's *Lives of the Poets,* for example, combine factual material with judicious comments on the poets' art, the biography often preceding the criticism. More recent critics have gone further in using biography as a means of dealing with the body of a writer's work, tending to explain the work in terms appropriate to an outline of the life. Sir Harold Nicolson's study of Tennyson, for instance, divides the poet's life and art into periods, analyzing and judging the events and the poetry of each period in turn. Such a method can be useful if subtly managed, as it is in this study—and, to cite another example, in Newton Arvin's critical biography of Melville. The biography illuminates those settings that play so important a part in Melville's stories of sailors and the ocean, by reference to logs and journals of sea voyages; it also shows the specific relevance of Melville's reading to his lyric and symbolic fiction, interpreting it with all these clues at hand. The result is a critical study using the outlines of biography but focusing attention on certain stories, and especially on Melville's greatest novel, *Moby-Dick.*

The interest of some biographical information is often evident even for the work of writers like Shakespeare of whom full-scale biographies can hardly be written because full knowledge is lacking. And whether or not we agree that a biographical study is a good method of organizing criticism of Milton, for example—a figure for whom quantities of biographical evidence are available—we can see that certain facts are significant. The opening lines of "Lycidas,"

> Yet once more, O ye laurels, and once more
> Ye myrtles brown, with ivy never-sear,
> I come to pluck your berries harsh and crude,

are somewhat puzzling unless we know that the phrase "once more," beginning a poem that is so much concerned with the poet's own literary career, is a reminder of his having written a Latin elegy shortly before attempting this one. The "I" of the poem is aware of his youth, aware that this is an early effort, but also that it is not at all a tentative first effort.

No critical question has been more often debated in our time than that of the relationship between criticism and biography. C. S. Lewis and E. M. W. Tillyard have carried on a lively discussion of the problem in a series of open letters published under the title of *The Personal Heresy;* the same question is touched upon in essays by W. K. Wimsatt and Monroe Beardsley ("The Intentional Fallacy") and by Leslie Fiedler ("Archetype and Signature"). Most readers, however, would probably agree without so much debate that there are several ways in which knowledge of an artist's life can be useful for an understanding of his writing. First, it may serve to underline elements and motifs already apparent in the work. The sensitive reader who knows nothing of Milton's life might well be struck by the poet's recurring visions of brilliant light, but the knowledge of Milton's blindness could make him more sensitive to that impression. And this example suggests a second, more important point. In certain passages Milton alludes to his blindness, as Spenser sometimes alludes to his personal dissatisfactions. When the writer's life is thus brought into his art, there is some necessity to understand it, just as there is when other topical or historical references occur. Milton's allusions are usually clear enough and explain what we have to know; but Spenser's oblique comments on his own ambition and frustrations may require some reading of footnotes. When biographical information is lacking, such allusions can be puzzling, or can even go unrecognized. We cannot be sure that new facts about Shakespeare's life would not lead us to find in his sonnets some richness we now miss—for instance, verbal complexities such as half-hidden allusions to names and places. If we lacked the knowledge of even Shakespeare's first name and knew him only as W. Shakespeare, we might possibly overlook such plays upon *will* : *Will* as this in his sonnet 135:

> Whoever hath her wish, thou hast thy *Will,*
> And *Will* to boot, and *Will* in overplus.

One danger, however, in literary biography is that it may substitute the criticism of a life for the criticism of a work. Lives of writers often have intrinsic interest—although the biography of a great artist can sometimes, too, be surprisingly dull—and may be recounted without any attempt at literary criticism. But when the judgment of a man's private affairs is extended into a judgment of his art, the result is likely to be a distortion. Shelley has been damned as a poet because of his bad behavior as a husband. For just this reason Matthew Arnold (who, incidentally, insisted that no biography of himself be written) regretted the publicizing of Shelley's life. A less clear-cut example is provided by the varying reactions to Milton, who has been admired by extreme Protestants for his religious and political views, and for the same reasons has been disliked by loyal Anglicans. Even so subtle a critic as T. S. Eliot seems to have been swayed in his attitude toward Milton's poetry by an antagonism to his religion and politics.

Nowadays most readers would agree that good literature is not necessarily written by good men. The contrasting view, that the great poet or artist must be a neurotic and perhaps a socially irresponsible person, now also seems extremely dubious. It is evident that Sir Thomas Malory, Christopher Marlowe, the Earl of Rochester, and Lord Byron led disreputable lives: Marlowe apparently died in a tavern brawl, Malory finished the *Morte d'Arthur* in prison, Rochester wrote pornography that perhaps reflects his debauched and drunken life, and Byron was guilty of adulterous affairs if not of incest. It is also true that Geoffrey Chaucer and Charles Lamb were respected civil servants, George Herbert and Gerard Manley Hopkins were admirable clergymen, and in our own time Wallace Stevens was a successful executive in an insurance company. Neither licentiousness nor respectability seems to guarantee or to work against literary genius.

Even so, the possibility of confusing our opinion of the writer with what should be our opinion of his writing has made both modern poets and modern critics uneasy. This uneasiness is largely due, no doubt, to the excesses in which Romantic theories resulted: the theory, especially, that great art can best be defined as the expression of a great and very special personality, so that the personal qualities of the artist must be of profound and constant interest. As if to deny this view, some writers have been inclined to avoid any personal revelation in their work, to keep it as impersonal as they can. Even the forms of their names that writers use may suggest this inclination. In his later career, William Butler Yeats was known merely as W. B. Yeats; and other prominent poets of the mid-twentieth century, T. S. Eliot and W. H. Auden, also avoid using their first names, Thomas and Wystan. The comparable reaction by critics against a Romantic substitution of personal interest in the writer for interest in his writing has led sometimes to the extreme position of denying that biography can ever have any relevance to literary criticism.

If we reject this last view and agree that the biography of the writer may provide a convenient vehicle for and complement to criticism, and, more important, that biographical facts are sometimes helpful to a reader, and even occasionally indispensable, we have finally to consider another, related question. Readers often assume that the best way to explain the meaning of a work is to understand as best we can, from letters, papers, and so on, what the author intended by it. Goethe's celebrated dictum that criticism asks what a writer intends, whether he achieves his aim, and if it was worth achieving, is taken to show the importance of getting, so to speak, into the writer's mind. But the difficulties here are several. First, it is impossible for us to know the personal intentions of many great writers. Second, as depth psychology suggests, a man may be aware of one motive but in reality may act, or write, from deeper and more mixed motives. Even when a writer is conscious of a single social purpose, like the intention to make effective propaganda, he can work better and more artfully than he knows; and the single purpose, the single meaning, will not be enough to explain the quality of his novel or his play. Virgil's *Aeneid* is not only a patriotic celebration of Augustan Rome; Tolstoy's *War and Peace* amounts to much more than a large-scale attack upon an heroic interpretation of human history. The assumption that a writer's conscious intention constitutes the meaning of his work has been called by Wimsatt and Beardsley the **intentional fallacy.**

It is not necessary, then, to insist literally that every writer makes the best interpretation of his own writing, or that the only or invariably the best means of understanding a poem is to understand all the external experiences and conscious thoughts of the poet. This is, in fact, at least as extreme and doubtful a position as the opposite one which insists that all such biographical suggestions and pieces of information are useless for critical reading.

Social and Political History

Related to the problem of biography is another question, that of how social and political history can be important for criticism. Often the reader cannot afford to ignore the historical context of what he reads, a context that may be relevant in any of several ways. First, it is helpful to know something of the subject matter in order to explain the allusions and even the meaning of a work. The historical significance of, say, place-names can change rapidly enough for us to lose what to a contemporary of the author is an obvious meaning. For those who remember political events of 1938, the name of the city Munich still suggests at once the act of appeasement: specifically, the appeasement of an aggressive Hitler by a timid British government. But many students today have no such association for the name and would fail to recognize its implications in a story. Such allusions to names and places are inevitable in literature, and the older a work is, the more we are likely to need some aid from history. In Dante's *Divine Comedy,* which is filled with references to people, places, and events, the necessity for historical information is quite evident. Editions of the poem usually include a great many footnotes, largely for this reason. Certain periods in English literature, too, have produced numbers of works in which topical references are crucial: for example, the period from 1660, the date when the English monarchy was restored with the coronation of Charles II, to 1688, the time of the so-called Glorious Revolution, when James II was deposed and replaced on the English throne by William and Mary. Dryden's *Astraea Redux, Absalom and Achitophel, The Medal,* and other partisan and satirical poems of this era require some knowledge on the reader's part of the political and religious controversies they deal with, for this is an age in which literature and politics are closely allied.

Second, knowledge of the social temper and the political state in a period may qualify our sense of the tone if not of the whole meaning of a play or story. It needs no arguing that political allegory requires such knowledge. But even when an author is neither strictly allusive nor allegorical, it can be helpful. When Swift's Gulliver describes the king of Lilliput, we miss much of the point if we fail to understand that his portrait is a neat inversion of King George I. Swift's readers thought of "the King" as someone awkward and dull, who could speak no English and would interest himself in virtually none of his subjects' problems. Gulliver characterizes the King of Lilliput as a graceful man, intelligent, urbane, and articulate, in every point precisely unlike George of England. The ironic implications are unmistakable if we remember the historical context, including the facts that Swift identified himself with the Tory party and that King George was notoriously a partisan of the Whigs.

The importance of an historical sense for reading literature from earlier periods can hardly be exaggerated, even when the relevance of the knowledge is less specific than in these examples. Indeed, a very large body of scholarship has been concerned primarily with providing historical background, of greater or lesser value, for the reader. Sometimes that background is generally rather than specifically useful. The political situation of Elizabethan England figures in Shakespeare's history plays as it does in Spenser's allegory; the social unrest of the Victorian era enters into Tennyson's dramatic verse as it does into the novels of Thomas Hardy. And, with or without footnotes and scholarly guides, the reader who has at least some sense of these historical settings will probably grasp more of what he reads.

Quite often, to be sure, a literary work that draws largely on history can provide its own information. We may learn as much about the Napoleonic wars in Russia from reading *War and Peace* as we could learn about the historical setting of Tolstoy's masterpiece by reading histories of the times. Or, to cite a very different example, the favorable interpretation of St. Thomas à Becket in T. S. Eliot's *Murder in the Cathedral* can stand on its own merits unaltered by the documents which describe that complicated historical figure. Still, in the second case, by understanding the problem of interpretation that Eliot deals with in his poetic tragedy, we should at least arrive at a fuller appreciation of his particular achievement.

Keeping in mind the value of historical knowledge both for specific understanding of allusions and overtones and for understanding of tone, of implicit attitudes and feelings, we have nevertheless to recognize the danger of confusing one sort of inquiry with another—of judging literature as if it were history. Certain great historical works, such as Gibbon's *Decline and Fall of the Roman Empire* and Carlyle's more lyrical *French Revolution,* have earned the right to be called literature in one sense, and perhaps are better literature than history, because of their brilliant design and style. In contrast, there are historical novels that display enough grasp of facts and movements to be more admired as interpretations of history than as literature. But in all cases we have to distinguish the kinds of values we are passing upon: the historian's values of accuracy and conceptual order, or the literary values of richness and imaginative coherence.

Another, and an equally dubious, assertion of the relevance of history to criticism is the theory that a poem or play or story should be judged according to its reception in its own time. This belief assumes that because critical standards have changed, it is only fair to evaluate a piece of literature as its contemporary audience would. According to such a relativist view, medieval tales that we now find tediously prolix would be at least on a par with the fiction of Henry James. Literary criticism, furthermore, would consist largely of trying to establish earlier popularity ratings.

A final, and again highly questionable, way in which criticism can be related to history is that assumed by scholars who have given most attention to those literary works which have most influenced events, or works that are most clearly in the "main stream" of intellectual history. In fact, such an inferior but influential novel as *Uncle Tom's Cabin* is of historical interest but not for that reason of literary value. And even less evidently mediocre writing, if it has exerted significant influence on social history or on literary history, can be overpraised as literature, according to this **historic estimate**, as Matthew Arnold calls it. Arnold adds that it is not a truly critical estimate.

History and literary criticism, then, are necessarily related subjects, but they are distinct. This is true of political history, and it is true of the "history of ideas." Scholars and critics concerned with the social and intellectual context of literature sometimes point out, rightly, that no work exists in a vacuum. On the other hand, each work exists in a particular form, often a fictional form, that stands out from its background. We must beware, then, of reading such a poem as Chaucer's *Troilus and*

Criseyde either as a work *sui generis,* unrelated to late medieval concepts
of courtly love and divine love, or as a direct statement of attitude toward
chivalry and religion, simply representing "the" late medieval point of
view. Making the first error, we fail to understand what the poem is
about. Making the second, we distort and simplify its sense, and we
almost certainly distort and simplify history as well.

Psychology

Another discipline that has been related to literature and to criticism is psychology. Many writers, from the time of Ben Jonson and the
comedy of humors to the modern period with the psychological drama
of Eugene O'Neill, have consciously drawn upon various theories of
human motivation. Jonson's characters, we have seen, may be virtual
embodiments of the four elements, blood, phlegm, choler, and bile, that
were once supposed to determine personality. And in O'Neill's *Mourning
Becomes Electra,* a dramatic trilogy, the title and the action both suggest
the Freudian idea of an "Electra complex," the daughter's attachment
to her father and jealous hatred of her mother. Just as the old idea of the
four humors and the modern ideas about unconscious sexual urges and
frustrations have influenced schools and periods of literature, so in the
English Romantic poetry of the late eighteenth and early nineteenth centuries the theories of associationist psychology, especially as they are
stated by David Hartley, play an important role. Wordsworth's poetry, in
particular, draws from this source: Hartleian psychology inspires, at least
in part, the idea in *The Prelude* that complex attitudes and ethical pre-
dispositions arise gradually from the child's early associations of events
with people and objects. In one famous passage Wordsworth recalls the
boyhood experience of taking a boat without permission and of floating
in it until a mountain peak loomed suddenly over him, filling him with
awe and uneasiness. Such experiences, he adds, can affect the moral
development, associating forbidden action with fear, just as the infant's
associating the gratification of his desires with his mother can affect his
emotional development.

It may be that a complete knowledge of the humors, of Freudian
ideas, or of associationist theory is not necessary to understand most of
Jonson, O'Neill, Wordsworth, or other writers who are influenced by
these conceptions. But there are certainly characters and passages that will
be clearer if we have some background of such knowledge. Even in reading Shakespeare this is true. Jaques in *As You Like It,* for instance, may
seem to be a pointlessly flat and unreal character unless we recognize
him as a comic version of an extreme type in the comedy of humors, the
melancholic who is dominated by black bile.

The more problematic means of relating psychology to literature is that undertaken not by poets or playwrights but by critics. In our time no critic seriously and consistently applies the theory of the humors, even though we still speak of being in a bad humor and still describe people as sanguine, phlegmatic, choleric, or melancholy. The associationist psychology, too, although we accept some of its assertions, is unlikely now to be called upon as a systematic means of explaining character development. But the language and the ideas of Freudian, Jungian, Adlerian, and other modern psychological schools are available and may be useful to modern interpreters of literature. For if we take any of these methods of analysis as having some general validity, we may find it valid as a way of understanding the people in a story or play—and perhaps also of interpreting literary symbolism.

Thus the fiction of Edgar Allan Poe, who wrote before these psychologies were formulated, can be analyzed in terms Freud has used, so that some readers will recognize the presence of sexual symbols and hidden motives—like the desire for death—in the settings, action, and language of his fantastic tales. Furthermore, a psychological interpretation of writing may go along with a psychological interpretation of the writer; this approach, then, is specifically related to the biographical. An example of the psychoanalytical—that is to say, Freudian—analysis which is biographical as well as literary is the study of Poe by Marie Bonaparte. In this critical work, the symbols that express the artist's controlling attitudes and interests are emphasized, along with the motives of fictional characters.

Somewhat less clearly biographical in its emphasis is William Empson's reading of *Alice in Wonderland* and *Alice through the Looking Glass.* The first *Alice* is regarded, in this analysis, as representing the child's attitude toward coming into the world and growing up both physically and socially. The tears that Alice sheds and in which, after being reduced in size, she must swim, suggest the fluid in which an infant exists before birth—as the womblike waters of the ocean do, in such myths as that of Venus rising from the sea. Out of this fluid appear the various animals who race with her, as well as Alice. The child's attitude toward growing up, losing her childhood directness, learning all the rules—often arbitrary rules—of adult life, and facing also the loss of her sexual innocence, is one of uncertainty, sometimes of fear. The Queen of Hearts, according to this reading, is a symbol of animal passion as well as of adult authority, and she is often a frightening figure. In fact, at the end of *Alice in Wonderland,* as if to suggest the girl's hesitation about growing into a woman, Alice rejects the whole experience, including the final trial of the knave of hearts for stealing sweets from the queen, as nothing more than a fantasy, a dream.

Stories that are fantastic, in many ways dreamlike, such as Poe's tales and *Alice in Wonderland,* lend themselves more readily to Freudian interpretation than strictly realistic stories do. The strangeness of the dream or the dreamlike narrative invites an explanation, and much of the work of psychological analysts has in any case been directed precisely toward the elucidation of fantasy and dream.

In general, critics have been inclined to apply modern psychological ideas to the motives of characters in modern stories more often than to those of people in earlier works. Presumably this is true because we feel that the writer for whose times these ideas are current may well be representing them in his characterization, even unconsciously. Thus there is less danger of our imposing a psychological significance quite arbitrarily. Not that Shakespeare had to be aware of the "Oedipus complex"—the incestuous attraction of a son to his mother, his hostility toward his father, and his consequent sense of guilt and fear—in order to represent its effect in *Hamlet.* But we are likely to feel that this aspect of Hamlet is at most subtly present, a largely hidden and highly ambiguous motive. We may speak of it then with caution as one means of explaining the violence of Hamlet's emotions, especially in his reference to his mother and his scenes with her. With the stories of D. H. Lawrence, however, we need not be so cautious. Even though Lawrence has denied being influenced by Freud or agreeing with him, such a story as "The Prussian Officer" deals so directly and plainly with the kind of frustrated homo-erotic urge which that psychology describes, perverted into neurosis and fatal violence, that a sophisticated reader can hardly avoid interpreting the tale this way, in Freudian language. The conception of a character like that of the officer who beats and taunts his handsome orderly to the point of danger, a character turned to cruelty and the lust for self-de-struction by his denial of deeply felt passions, invites such language.

No doubt the term *Freudian* is applied loosely in critical usage as it is in common usage. We often label a remark by that word when we mean only that it has implications of which the speaker is unconscious. The idea of the "Freudian slip," the error in speech that reveals a sub-conscious intention, is related to the idea that any gesture can be sym-bolic, can signify by its literal nature more than it seems to intend. Literary symbolism assumes, of course, just that. In fact, Freud himself insists that his ideas are anticipated in imaginative form by writers of fiction and poetry. Even so, the impact on modern writers of Freud's conceptions, his new way of putting insights into the human psyche, has been profound and widespread. As Frederick Hoffman shows in his study of *Freudianism and the Literary Mind,* it has directly affected Joyce, Kafka, Mann, and a number of English and American writers. The relevance of psychology to the criticism of these writers, then, is hardly deniable. Nor can we deny the universal modern influence of Freud's new emphasis on the contrast between conscious and hidden intentions, or his emphasis on sexual motivations even in childhood.

Not all recent psychological methods of interpreting literature, however, are strictly Freudian. The criticism of F. L. Lucas, contained in his *Literature and Psychology,* displays the influence of Wilhelm Stekel in its treatment of Shakespearean drama and Romantic poetry— and in its hostility to surrealism. Other critics have been especially impressed by the theories of Carl Jung; and, although they may not take literally his notion of a racial unconscious or racial memory, they have found the idea useful, if modified, to explain certain kinds of literary symbolism. These critics may not, that is, believe that every man actually has a deep intuited memory of the great experiences his ancestors underwent, but they would agree that the dimly recalled and partly transmitted needs and actions of the ancient past have still some power, some meaning, in the minds of modern men. And this sort of group memory or "communal unconscious" can be called upon to interpret those recurring themes and **archetypal patterns** that typify the long history of a culture. One of these, for instance, dealt with in Maud Bodkin's *Archetypal Patterns in Poetry,* is the experience of suffering, virtual death, and rebirth; this pattern, Miss Bodkin shows, is exemplified in various works, including Coleridge's *Ancient Mariner.* Another motif is the experience of conflict between generations, often between father and son, represented in *Oedipus* and other tragedies. Indeed, those who emphasize the ritual aspect of tragedy, as suggesting the symbolic sacrifice that assures health and fertility, are likely to draw on Jung's theory or to assert something like it in explaining how a modern audience can react to classical drama.

Once more, as with the use of other disciplines, there are certain difficulties and dangers in the psychological interpretation of literature. First, one may be tempted to read a work as simply a psychological document revealing the peculiarities of its author. The cheapest sensational novel may to the well-trained reader suggest as much about the personality of the novelist as the subtle fiction of, say, Edith Wharton reveals about the peculiar traits of its author. But there is no comparison to be made otherwise between such works. Clearly, it is important to distinguish the possible clinical interest of a writer's production from its literary value.

Second, we may be tempted to make a psychological interpretation do more than it properly can. We are often in danger of reducing the complex art of a writer to a single meaning or a series of meanings that fit neatly into a preconceived theory; but trying to make novels or poems into mere illustrations of psychological theory is an especially present danger. Even with a work to which this analysis is appropriate, such as one of Lawrence's stories, or one of Sherwood Anderson's tales of loneliness, frustration, and violence, the rich and unique quality of the writing and the complication of style and theme should make for something more than the meaning of a case history illustrating Freud's ideas. And if we think only of the psychological significance of a play like *Hamlet,* we must stress exclusively the relations between a central character and others—his mother, father, stepfather, fiancée, friends, and so on— failing to do justice to the philosophical reflections in the drama, the embodiment of political ideas, the religious elements, or even the mixture of sharp comic irony with the controlling tragic tone.

Sociology and Economics

In considering the relations of sociology and economics to literature and to criticism, we have to distinguish once more between the two kinds of relevance: first, the writer's drawing upon principles from these disciplines in his art; and second, the critic's use of the ideas and the language of the sociologist or economist for interpreting literary art.

The embodiment of systematic ideas about society is evident in literary works of the past as well as in modern novels of "social consciousness." For instance, Bernard Mandeville's *Fable of the Bees,* an early eighteenth-century allegorical poem to which the author appended a series of essays on society, derives its doctrine, that social good results from individual vices, in part from the views of the seventeenth-century writer Thomas Hobbes on the origin and nature of the state. For Hobbes, and for Mandeville, the motive of social action is egoism. This belief is elaborated on by Hobbes in his *Leviathan,* where the body politic is seen as completely subject to the power of its sovereign, represented metaphorically in the title of this treatise as a whale or great sea monster; and by Mandeville in the *Fable,* where the body politic is represented as a beehive. Some knowledge both of the political circumstances of these writers—Hobbes' work was published during the dictatorship of Oliver Cromwell, and Mandeville's in the reign of Queen Anne—and of the skeptical traditions they draw upon concerning human nature and the social value of tranquillity, will make their production seem less strange, if not less repugnant to our beliefs in progress and democracy.

Such writers as these preach doctrines about society in its political and economic aspects; other less doctrinaire writers seem rather to assume and embody ideas that we have to recognize. The importance of maintaining a legitimate ruler and a fixed line of succession to power is evident, for example, in *Hamlet,* in *Macbeth,* and elsewhere in Shakespeare, although these assumptions are not often stated. A similar conservative attitude toward the necessity of an imposed order, a class hierarchy, and a loyal population is more clearly indicated in the Tory satires of both Dryden and Pope. And the more liberal temper of the nineteenth century is embodied in the lyrics of Byron glorifying freedom, even when there is no explicit attack upon the idea of absolute legitimate monarchy.

More strictly sociological, rather than political, theories—theories about the structure of societies in groups or classes—are relatively modern, and have had less obvious influence on poets and novelists. The sober analysis of such matters has even seemed to some writers to impinge upon the traditional domain of fiction; it is often said that the great continuing subject of the English novel, from Richardson's *Pamela,* in the eighteenth century, about the attempted seduction of a servant-girl by a nobleman and their ultimate marriage, to Kingsley Amis' *Lucky Jim,* a recent novel about the comic struggle of a teacher to improve his position or escape his provincial background, is just the distinction and the relation between social classes.

The related subject of economic theory has perhaps a more obvious relevance. This is true especially because of the impact of Marxist ideas on intellectuals, including writers, in the second and third decades of the twentieth century. In England, Auden and more especially Stephen Spender were close as young poets to the Communist position on the necessary reconstruction of society. And yet, even with these writers— and certainly in the work of the American novelist Theodore Dreiser, whose sympathy with communism appears to include fairly little technical grasp of the economic ideas involved—we are struck much less by the influence of economic analysis than by the impact of social ideals of equality, plenty, and common social purpose, ideals that are not necessarily tied to any specific theories about the means of production and the causes for class warfare.

Undoubtedly, however, the general concern in America, particularly in the 1930s, with the social and the economic well-being of people in a democracy, found expression in Marxism as well as in liberal-to-radical doctrines of reform. And undoubtedly these various doctrines have their echoes and parallels in literature. Not only the work of Dreiser and the stories of Howard Fast but such novels as *The Jungle* by Upton Sinclair reveal a powerful sense that the environment of the slum with its poverty and exploitation of human beings as "wage slaves," inevitably produces a warfare between the man subjected to such forces and his economic masters. The Marxist theory of economic determinism may be implicit in, and at least is not alien to, this sense. John Steinbeck's earlier writing, too, and especially *The Grapes of Wrath,* about the desperate struggle of a displaced farm family from Oklahoma to stay alive and retain dignity in spite of exploitation, poverty, and humiliation, will seem clearer to us now if we remember both the circumstances and the emphasis on various kinds of economic reform (New Deal, Socialist, and Communist) that these produced.

When we turn to the critics, to ask about their use of ideas from sociology and economics, we find ourselves less limited to the literature of the recent past. There is as yet no large body of literary criticism that draws from the vocabulary and the techniques of sociology, but we have often to distinguish classes and groups and their modes of behavior in the novels of Jane Austen—and even in the comedies of Bernard Shaw. Sometimes, in commenting on these matters, the sociological critic will appear to be less critic than sociologist, using literary material to exemplify changes in the structure and the temper of society. This is in part, at least, the aim of Leo Lowenthal in his study of *Literature and the Image of Man,* where he deals with the shifting conceptions of man's place in society that are displayed in the work of such writers as Cervantes, Shakespeare, Racine, and Goethe. But if he writes primarily as a sociologist, Lowenthal suggests interesting facts about Shakespeare's *Tempest;* we may question his assertion that Prospero's development in the play represents a Renaissance, secular process of self-discovery and self-assertion, and yet agree that this tragicomedy has to do with the contrast between rational authority—that of Prospero—and the irrational will that would turn society into a jungle of intrigue and betrayal—the wills of Antonio the usurper and, especially, of the half-human Caliban.

An even more ambitious recent study, Raymond Williams' *Culture and Society 1780–1950,* adduces evidence of changing attitudes toward politics, class, and art from poets, prophets, novelists, and literary critics. This work provides only a general context for any particular piece of literature, rather than bringing the terms of social analysis to bear in an extended literary analysis; but for such novelists as Dickens and George Eliot, and for such essayists as Mill and Arnold, the context is most valuable.

Criticism of literature on grounds of economic theory has been, if it is not now, rather familiar. The Marxist school of criticism has contributed at least an emphasis on the social and economic implications of fiction, and has, thus, very largely qualified our way of reading certain sorts of literature. A Marxist interpretation of Dickens, for example, would stress the pictures that show grim aspects of industrialized society and would indicate in them the effects of laissez-faire capitalism. To some extent, at least, this emphasis is fair to the intention of the work, especially of such a novel as *Hard Times,* for Dickens writes from a personal awareness of the evils inherent in an uncontrolled industrial society, writes in fact under the influence of Thomas Carlyle's preaching against laissez-faire economic theory.

But the tendency of genuinely Marxist criticism is to annex literature to an economic and social movement, so that not only Dickens but also such a personal and mystical writer as William Blake can be given a special relevance to socialism, because he speaks out against child labor and the tyranny of stultifying conventions. The Marxist critic may be led to find foreshadowings and versions of the class struggle in any warfare against established order, from the *Prometheus Bound* of Aeschylus to the *Prometheus Unbound* of Shelley. And he may try to establish a reading of literary history on dogmatic grounds, as Christopher Caudwell does in a chapter entitled "English Poets: The Decline of Capitalism." Caudwell argues that Tennyson's vision of a ruthless Nature is in reality the vision of a ruthless economic system; and he describes the development of styles and movements in the terms used by Marx and Engels, so that the nineteenth-century reaction against moralizing expressed in the phrase "art for art's sake" becomes an example of "commodity-fetishism."

The difficulty with a social-economic criticism such as this is, once again, that it may reduce a piece of literature to a one-dimensional document, and that the language of a particular sort of analysis may very soon be forced into explaining more than it can fairly explain, for the sake of neat consistency with a systematic view of the world. Given Shakespeare's apparent bias against the masses of people, a Marxist critic would seem to be forced either to reject Shakespeare or to misread him. And with Shelley, Blake—even with Dickens—the danger of distortion by a strictly doctrinaire method of explication, whatever the doctrine, is very great.

Anthropology and Religion

Another matter of interest to recent criticism is the relationship between literature on the one hand and, on the other, anthropology and religion. It is apparent that just as a vast number of literary works refer to contemporary social and political questions, so a large number of the poems, plays, and even stories that we read deal more or less explicitly with religious ideas and sentiments. Some acquaintance with the basic beliefs of Christianity is important, quite clearly, for a reading of Chaucer, John Donne, Gerard Manley Hopkins, or T. S. Eliot. But more than that, glancing allusions to and subtle assumptions of religious practice and belief occur in literary works where they are not so clear. As Louis Martz has shown in a study of seventeenth-century poetry, certain devices in the devotional verse of this period are drawn directly from the techniques for meditation—on the nativity, the passion of Christ, and so on—taught by religious writers such as St. Ignatius Loyola. This new knowledge explains some of the images, clarifies the meaning, and gives a new dimension to the reading of metaphysical poetry.

Not all writers who refer to religious systems accept, like Dante, the ordered belief which their work reflects. James Joyce in *A Portrait of the Artist as a Young Man* and again in *Ulysses* uses the teachings of the Jesuits, and especially the theology of St. Thomas Aquinas, showing its intellectual fascination but at last rejecting it. T. S. Eliot uses the symbols of primitive religions, especially of fertility cults, in his poem *The Waste Land,* only as a means of showing the spiritual emptiness and infertility of his world. He is not preaching the tribal cult or the oriental religions to which he also refers, but we must have some conception of these references to grasp the sense of this complex work—as Eliot himself suggests by appending footnotes, some of them probably jokes but some serious, to his poem.

Eliot is not the only recent writer to use, with a degree of conscious intention, the anthropological knowledge of folk rites and primitive religion. In the stories of William Faulkner, for example, there sometimes occur what seem to be folk motifs and ideas. This element is especially prominent in his story "The Old People," where the relations between the lives of men and the life of the wilderness suggest a magical parallel between animal and vegetable vitalities—and most strikingly when one of the characters, part-Indian and part-Negro in his heritage, hails the great deer he hunts as the incarnation of his own ancestor. Here the conception of *totem* seems unmistakably to be a part of the theme: the idea that a kind of animal has an intimate relationship with a clan of people.

We may suppose that Faulkner is aware, as we can become aware by some knowledge of anthropology, of how his characters and their actions reproduce a primitive religious or a magical feeling. We cannot be entirely certain about the directness of such relationships between art and the folklore in much earlier works. Even so, it can be argued that the figure of the Green Knight who challenges and tests the hero in the fourteenth-century alliterative poem *Gawain and the Green Knight* embodies in part an ancient image of the god of vegetation, of fertility, who demands trial and sacrifice as a part of the ritual which propitiates him. Details in the poem tend to bear out this idea that behind its story is a vaguely magical feeling about denial preceding richness, or chastity being enforced before the fruitfulness—of men and lands—is possible. So Gawain, under the orders of the mysterious knight, is obliged to control himself in spite of sexual temptations and to follow seemingly meaningless rules and prohibitions even to the point of apparent death. He has to do all this in order to succeed and at last escape his danger— almost as if he himself came back to life, in the way the mythical embodiments of vegetation die in winter and come back to life in spring. If we argue these parallels, however, it must be realized that we are suggesting overtones of the story, perhaps far distant meanings in some ancient folk source, rather than the full significance of the work of art which is the fourteenth-century version. To identify such folk and mythical sources, by the way, the most useful reference work is Stith Thompson's *Motif-Index of Folk Literature.*

Now, too, we are touching upon the second aspect of this matter, the question of how far criticism can legitimately go in using anthropological and religious ideas to interpret literature. Another example we might have cited that suggests the direct association of chastity and fruitfulness, of ritual order and fertility, is provided by Shakespeare's *Tempest,* when Prospero, the magician in the play, follows his laying down of rules for the young lovers' conduct, including trials and labors for the suitor Ferdinand, with a masque that conjures up the goddess of bounty, Ceres, and promises Miranda and Ferdinand a fruitful union. Here, again, fertility is to be achieved by disciplining natural impulses. But this is only one more part of the tragicomedy; and if Prospero can be interpreted as a figure from Renaissance society or as the controlling power in a version of magical myth, another reading can be made, a Christian interpretation, according to which he is the embodiment of divine justice. This reading of *The Tempest* as a religious drama suggests a very different meaning in the play from that secular individualism emphasized in Leo Lowenthal's sociological commentary. In the religious view, Prospero is not so much a self-made man of his times as a godlike figure who causes but controls the tempests of the world, both natural ones like the storm at the beginning of the play, and moral ones like the contending passions of ambition and lust that bring disorder to the social world. From the point of view of all the other characters, life is a series of discords and storms, and at least potentially tragic. From the higher point of view of Prospero, as from the ultimate heavenly point of view in the *Divine Comedy,* life is an ordered whole in which storms and disorders play a role, but only a partial one, and it is at last, precisely, a divine comedy.

For this interpretation, and for the various religious interpretations of symbolic tales, we have to apply familiar conceptions to the work of writers who may not have been wholly conscious of such meanings but who were nevertheless aware of the symbolic possibilities, say, of Christian thought. Sometimes, to be sure, the religious interpretation applies only to parts of a work; and, although certain critics may be inclined to exaggerate, to see Christlike figures almost everywhere and to view almost every garden in literature as a version of Eden, it seems defensible to find such overtones in some pastoral figures and some gardens. Certainly the traditional Biblical associations with shepherds, gardens, solemn feasts (the last supper, the communion), and sacrificial suffering permit the critic as well as the author to sense—and to demonstrate—echoes of religious myth and ritual in literature.

As these last remarks should indicate, however, there is again a danger with either the anthropological or the religious interpretation, a danger of our ignoring the complex whole to stress only the single meaning—and perhaps, too, with symbolic works especially, of trying to find the special meanings in every possible, or impossible, place.

In fact, there are literary works to which a number of the disciplines we have treated so far may be applied. So we have observed that *The Tempest* can be interpreted from the sociological or the anthropological or the strictly religious point of view. Clearly, with this play, the sociological reading would be contradicted by the religious reading. Some works, however, cannot be finally explained by reference to any single set of meanings. Franz Kafka's fantastic novel *The Castle,* for example, tells of a man called K who waits interminably in a village below the great castle to make some communication with the Count whom he never sees or can directly address. There is considerable evidence to suggest that Kafka's feeling of alienation from the higher authority, expressed here, derives from his relations, at once intense and frustrating, with his father—and the writer himself seems to be aware of this fact. Not only is biographical information relevant, then, but a psychological reading of this and Kafka's other stories inevitably presents itself: they deal with the child's resentment, sense of guilt, and frustrated longing, in being cut off from the father's love. At the same time, the Count in the novel can be understood not only as a father-figure but also as God the Father; Kafka's language often invites this religious interpretation. Symbolically, then, the story is partly about man's feeling of isolation from God, his spiritual longing and despair, even his uncertainty about the existence of a divine authority. But to take only one of these meanings and to ignore the others would be to oversimplify the story. To take all the overtones of meaning into account is, on the other hand, the aim of careful and sensitive reading.

Philosophy

Next, we might consider the way in which philosophy is important both to the work of literature that accepts or draws upon systematic philosophical ideas and to the critical reading that applies philosophical formulations.

In some of the earliest philosophers whose work we know, the distinction between philosophy and literature is by no means clear. Plato's

Symposium is a work of fiction as well as a discourse on love. It begins with a narrator's telling his listener what he in turn has heard about from a third person, the tale of a drinking party that occurred years earlier. And after all this placing of distance between the narrator and his subject, there is a further use of artistic indirection within the story. When Socrates takes his turn in the discussion of love, and sums the subject up in a climactic philosophical statement, he attributes his ideas to another person, the wise old woman Diotima. With Socratic irony, he presents himself as being ignorant and uncertain about the truth until it was revealed by this oracle. Even after the philosophy of love is stated, Plato's tale goes on, as all the party except Socrates get drunk. The language of the speakers is metaphorical, almost poetic sometimes, and the method of the whole dialogue is dramatic, with its interchanges that reveal both philosophical clashes and personal jealousies or flirtations.

Later writers, however, have come to distinguish more and more between formal philosophy and art, and to draw upon the systematic thought they have inherited rather than to create new philosophies in poetry or fiction. (Even modern philosophers, such as Jean-Paul Sartre, who are also artists, tend to illustrate their formal philosophies in their fiction rather than combining the two.) Thus Spenser in his sonnets clearly refers to the Platonic idea, outlined in the *Symposium,* that love can ascend from taking a beautiful person for its object to achieve a larger philosophical knowledge of beauty and goodness as its ideal objects. And the Romantic poets of the nineteenth century, Wordsworth, Coleridge, and Keats, who thought of themselves as embodying the "philosophic mind," had also to be aware of the difference between formal and poetic philosophy, the latter drawing on the former and giving an imaginative, metaphorical version of the ideas which philosophers would phrase in technical language.

Undoubtedly, shifts in the interests and ideas of philosophers from age to age have in part affected, as they have in part reflected, changes in imagination and in literary taste. Medieval scholasticism, reaching its apogee with Aquinas, is echoed not only in the *Divine Comedy* with its vision of a great mystic order, the earthly elements of which are rationally explicable, but also more faintly in the work of Chaucer, with its sense of order comprehending disorder. One could argue, too, from philosophical passages in Shakespeare, that his drama exemplifies a tension, sometimes a delicate balance, between the medieval and scholastic assurance of rationality in the governance of the world, and the Renaissance skepticism about these matters that finds its philosophic voice in the classical humanists, as it finds its clearest literary expression in Montaigne and Francis Bacon. Humanism, the emphasis upon secular and human values, especially that emphasis given by the teachers and writers of the late fifteenth and early sixteenth centuries in England and Western Europe, has its influence in the literary revival of classical ideas, along with classical forms: the ideas of the Stoics, for instance, who would make calm and fortitude the greatest virtues, rather than Christian meekness and charity, may be embodied in the noble characters of Shakespeare's plays as in those of Marlowe and other Elizabethans. And, to cite another period, the ideas of the German transcendentalists who developed and built upon the philosophy of Kant are distinctly related to those expressed in the English Romantic poets of the nineteenth century. The philosophical distinction between *subjective* and *objective* realities, for instance, and the emphasis upon the way in which the human mind conditions and in a sense creates experience, are reflected in Wordsworth's metaphorical assertion of both the intuitive and the creative powers of the poet's mind.

Often, of course, the philosophical attitudes expressed by poets are "in the air" of their times, and often the ideas are altered as they enter into a literary context. Nevertheless, there are evidently certain ideas and groups of ideas from which poets, novelists, and playwrights draw, and which, if we become aware of them, can sharpen our understanding of what many poems, novels, and plays are about.

When the critic applies to literature a philosophical attitude, and uses the language of a philosophy not clearly drawn upon by the author, again there may be both advantages and difficulties. If we accept a certain view of man and the world as valid, then it should have validity when used to characterize an artist's representation of man and the world— just as psychological theories, if they are true for men, can be relevant to art. In fact, however, only certain brands and schools of philosophy give much evidence of interest in the substance, as distinct from the theory, of literature.

Since the beginning of the twentieth century the philosophical ideas of Henri Bergson have proved to be useful for critics, as well as being influential on such writers as Thomas Mann and Virginia Woolf; Bergson's emphasis upon time, especially upon duration rather than idea as the ultimate reality, has suggested the critical analysis of time in literature: both conceptions of time and technical uses of time in narrative. We compare, for instance, the sense in Homer's *Iliad* of an heroic age fixed in the past with Virgil's sense of the heroic past as leading into and being implied in the present, or again with Dante's simultaneous feeling for the minute-by-minute elapsing of historical time and the eternal reality above time. Or we may notice that whereas the traditional novel selects periods and scenes that are significant over a period of months or years, such works as Joyce's *Ulysses* and Virginia Woolf's *Mrs. Dalloway* take a span of only hours in which they show the development of characters. Again, to use a more specifically Bergsonian mode of analysis, we can observe the vital importance of evolution in time, and of the memory that defines the razor's edge of the present as it creates the reality of the immediate future by recollecting the flow of the past, in Proust's *A la Recherche du Temps Perdu, Remembrance of Things Past* (but literally "in search of lost time"). And we can see how Faulkner suggests this process by a breaking up of time sequence, so that the distant past obtrudes into the present just as the effect and memory of what has been is always present in what is becoming.

Another recent philosophical movement that has had direct influence on literary critics is **existentialism**, in its several varieties—in the thought of Kierkegaard (a nineteenth-century Danish writer) and the religious existentialists, and that of Sartre and the atheistic existentialists. The starting point which these men have in common is the belief that "existence precedes essence." Indeed, except for this belief and the suspicion it implies of traditional philosophy, the various existentialists have little common doctrine. It has been suggested that the whole movement is not a philosophy but a way of thinking about philosophical questions. The assertion that existence precedes essence means in effect that man does not have an essential nature which he has to recognize but rather that every man exists in his own right and can find or make his own realities. "Know yourself," the ancient philosophical dictum, becomes, then, "Create yourself—and your world." Not that existentialists deny the contingencies of time and space or the limits of human possibility, but they make a distinct and extreme assertion of the moral freedom of the individual to act, to produce meanings and values. It is evident how this philosophical temper applies to the work of existentialist artists, like Sartre himself, and to some of the writing of Albert Camus. But it can also be a means of interpreting earlier literature. The existentialist critic might, for example, argue that Cervantes' *Don Quixote* is a demonstration of the extent to which a man is able to create his own reality from the external order he finds. The irony of the book, from this point of view, would be that the apparently sane characters and the narrator himself suppose that Don Quixote is a madman, failing to grasp the facts; but that he is by force of his action imposing his imagined values upon them all until the literal world of things fades into triviality. In this sense, he is an extreme and comic version of the existentialist hero.

From such examples, it should be evident what limitations the several philosophical methods impose. Some works can be dealt with suggestively, no doubt, by using the conceptions of Bergson and those of existentialism; some, no doubt, are much less susceptible to these kinds of analysis.

Other Disciplines: Art, Music, and Science

Among the other disciplines related to literature are art and archeology, music, and the natural sciences. All of these areas have fascinated poets and playwrights, novelists and essayists, as well as literary critics.

It is not surprising that writers should be concerned with the work of fellow artists. Often, indeed, men have combined talents required in the several arts: Michelangelo was not only painter and designer but also the author of sonnets; in English literature of the mid-nineteenth century, the "Pre-Raphaelite" Dante Gabriel Rossetti was equally celebrated as poet and painter—some of his paintings illustrate his poems—while his contemporary William Morris complemented poetic achievement with skill in designing fabrics, wallpapers, books, and even stained glass. In this same period of close relationships between art and literature, Robert Browning displays particular interest in painting and painters with his poetic monologues, especially in such Renaissance Italian painters as Lippo Lippi and Andrea del Sarto. Browning has expressed his attitude toward art, including the art of poetry, through the speeches of these men and of musicians, for he believes that the arts are one in their giving voice or vision to man's imperfect but continual aspiration.

The comparing of the arts in theoretical statement is sometimes referred to by the term *paragone* or *paragon* (the Italian for "touchstone"): in particular, that term is applied to the debates of ancient and Renaissance artists about the superiority of their media, of painting as opposed, say, to sculpture. But more recent critics and artists, like Browning, have often tried as well to define what the arts have in common. Critics have even attempted to describe the styles that literature and painting share. Wylie Sypher does just this in several ambitious studies: his *Rococo to Cubism in Art and Literature* asserts that the fiction of André Gide is cubist in style, taking a word from the vocabulary of the art historian. Such special terms as this and *baroque* or *impressionistic* when applied to literature can be, at least, suggestive critical metaphors.

Another suggestive and interesting use of the visual arts to describe a literary work—in this instance, a classical work—is Cedric Whitman's comparison, in his book on Homer, of the *Iliad* to the geometrically ornamented pottery of ancient Greece. According to Whitman, the over-all design of that epic can be called geometrical because of the precise and elaborate balances in the plot. Here it is the material of archeology, the study of art and other objects from the ancient past, upon which the literary scholar draws.

A less debatable, less impressionistic way in which the scholar draws on art to illuminate literature is shown by the explications of poetry on the basis of iconography. **Iconography** means literally "description by images" (*eikon* is the Greek word for "image"); it is the use of pictures or emblems to signify persons and ideas, to tell stories and embody beliefs. The four writers of the Christian gospels, Matthew, Mark, Luke, and John, are represented iconographically by four figures: Matthew by a man, Mark by a lion, Luke by a bull, and John by an eagle. The people who worshipped in and lived near medieval churches were taught their religion by familiar emblems of Biblical history and theological ideas in the images of sculpture and stained glass, images which we may now admire but often fail to understand without the scholar's aid. In medieval literature the same images may be used. Thus, when Chaucer's Franklin, in *The Canterbury Tales,* describes Janus sitting by the fire, the details in his description correspond to those in conventional pictures representing the month of January, the season in this part of Chaucer's tale. Nor is this method limited to medieval literature. Rosemond Tuve's study of the seventeenth-century poet George Herbert shows how a number of images in Herbert's poetry can be understood by reference to the earlier iconography of stained glass, carvings, paintings, and illumination. Christ is described by Herbert as a miraculous bunch of grapes; his associations with that image would include pictures of the cross as a kind of wine press, of the wine in the eucharist as the blood of the grape, and of Mary as the fruitful vine. These pictures are relevant to "The Bunch of Grapes" and to other poems as well.

Using a source neither medieval nor obscure, George Meredith suggests in his novel *The Egoist* an ironic version of the story "told" by the widely known willow pattern chinaware, a Chinese tale of love and adventure. The version is ironic because, in Meredith's work, what might be a love story involves egoism and empty convention, not true love, and because his heroine is trying not to escape with her devoted lover, but rather to escape *from* her self-centered fiancé. The first of many clues to this elaborate inversion of the familiar picture-tale of the willow pattern is the very name of Meredith's egoist, Sir Willoughby Patterne.

Even more striking and consistent than an interest in visual art is the fascination of writers, and especially of poets, with the art of music. There is reason to believe that all of our earliest poetry, including the epic and the first versions of tragedy, had a musical form, so that poetry and music were not until later times distinguished one from the other. Whether or not the *Iliad* was composed as a geometrical poem, it was undoubtedly composed as a poem to be chanted or sung in some way. One scholar, John Pope, has worked out an essentially musical system of notation for the rhythm of another epic, the old English *Beowulf,* to indicate how it was chanted. Evidently, too, many of the technical terms in Greek poetry, including those that describe parts of the tragedy, derive from the combination of dancing and singing which was inseparable from the literary form.

In the manuscripts of much later poems—as late as the thirteenth and fourteenth centuries—music is often included with the words, so that the lyric nature of the verse is particularly apparent. Now, of course, we speak of musical *accompaniment* for lyrics, and we seldom have poets who create the musical settings for their own words. But the first poets were almost certainly at the same time musicians. Metaphorical references to singing or playing an instrument to mean the composing of poetry are still, as they have been for centuries, quite familiar. The embodiment of poetry is Orpheus, the embodiment also of music; and the symbol of poetry is not a pen or a typewriter but a lyre.

No period in English literature provides more examples of the close relations between music and poetry than the sixteenth and seventeenth centuries. In this period Milton alludes learnedly to the earthly music of the poet as it echoes the music of the spheres (in his Nativity hymn); and Dryden produces his tributes to the lyric muse in the "Song for St. Cecilia's Day" and "Alexander's Feast," both written for a London musical society to celebrate the feast day of the patroness of music. As John Hollander has shown in *The Untuning of the Sky,* a knowledge of both musical theory and musical practice in the Renaissance permits a fuller reading of these poems than is otherwise possible, for they amount to more than imitations of sound-effects or appropriate lyrics for song.

Hollander reveals, furthermore, that technical musical terms enter into the poetry of this and earlier periods—terms that we may easily fail to recognize. John Donne, for instance, in the "Second Anniversary," refers to "breaking," the rapid elaborations on a melodic line, when he uses the phrase "broken and soft notes"; and other lines in other poems require just such explication.

Of the nineteenth-century poets, Browning repeatedly tried to imitate musical rhythms and to evoke musical moods: in "A Toccata of Galuppi's," "Abt Vogler," and the *Parleying* with Charles Avison. Each of these, like a long passage in *Saul* on the harp-playing of David, shows the poet's interest in how musical harmony reflects and creates a sense of larger harmony in the whole world. Behind Browning's practice, then, as behind that of Dryden and Milton, lies a theory of what music means. A modern poet who suggests something of this same interest is Wallace Stevens. There is a shifting of tempo in the four parts of Stevens' "Peter Quince at the Clavier" that echoes the changes in a four-part musical form, perhaps the form of a clavier sonata. The first section is fast, the second slow and deliberate, the third lively and rapid as a *scherzo,* and the fourth again fast, repeating the original theme. This theme, along with the title of the poem and frequent figures of speech, reinforces our impression of a musical echo, for it is the statement of how emotion can be like a melody, whether a poignant or a sadly beautiful music.

It is not only the poet who can draw on musical sources for analogy, for inspiration, and for subject matter. In his novel *Doctor Faustus,* Thomas Mann uses elaborate musical descriptions as part of his story about a modern composer. The drama as well, even that which is divorced from the musical form of early tragedy, may display musical parallels. We think of the duet, quartet, or sextet as a musical form, one that occurs often in Italian opera. But just as lyric poetry can use the refrain and other repetitive devices of musical form, the drama can use operatic devices. In his surrealistic comedy *The Rhinoceros,* Eugene Ionesco allows his characters to speak in virtual imitation of a quartet, with several of them repeating a single refrain in unison, although the meaning of the words differs according to the speaker. So two contrasting conversations going on at once before us are arbitrarily and formally—as it were, musically—related to each other.

All of these echoes, imitations, parallels, and relationships can fairly be pointed out by a scholar and critic of literature. The critic may also feel justified in using musical metaphors, calling a novel symphonic or a play operatic. While we remember that these terms are metaphors, are meant to suggest something of its quality rather than to define a work technically, we have also to remember that one of the most ancient genres of poetry has become a term that is only metaphorical, but remains useful. A highly *lyric* poem, one that is rhythmic and composed of striking sounds, is not quite literally a piece of music; but it is still in some ways close to music.

In our time we are likely to associate literature more often with the other arts, such as painting and music, than with the natural sciences. Here again, however, the separation of the literary from the other areas of human interest has increased since earlier days. It was possible for Lucretius to write his philosophical treatise *Of the Nature of Things* (*De Rerum Natura*), expounding the theory of atoms, in verse form; we can hardly imagine a modern philosopher or scientist presenting his speculations in this way. But the very word *science,* we have to remind ourselves, means simply "knowledge." Men of letters as well as men of the laboratory, novelists as much as nuclear physicists, are interested in knowledge of the world. The modern scientist and novelist C. P. Snow has argued that "two cultures" exist in our world, the literary and the scientific, and that a truly cultivated man today must have some knowledge of both. In his novels he tries to include the two areas.

We must often be concerned with relationships between scientific thought and literature, especially in the Renaissance and through the eighteenth century. Marjorie Nicolson, in a series of essays and books, has shown how great an impact scientific developments had in these periods on the imagery, the language, even the imaginative conceptions

of epic, lyric, and satire. The telescope of astronomers Tycho Brahe and
Kepler enlarged as well as intrigued the imaginations of Donne and of
Milton; the microscope provided a subject and then, with the greatly magnified figures of Swift's *Gulliver's Travels,* a method for satirists to use.
Miss Nicolson demonstrates also, in her *Newton Demands the Muse,*
the pervasive influence of Newtonian optics, physical theories of vision
and light, upon English writers of the eighteenth century: descriptions of
colors as prismatic, reflections on the way men see and the quality of
light, even the metaphysical speculations in this age of "enlightenment"
owe much to the formulations of the great scientist. Here, for example,
is a passage from Pope's *Essay on Criticism:*

> False Eloquence, like the prismatic glass,
> Its gaudy colours spreads on every place;
> The face of Nature we no more survey,
> All glares alike, without distinction gay:
> But true expression, like th'unchanging Sun,
> Clears, and improves whate'er it shines upon,
> It gilds all objects, but it alters none.

It is only with Blake and the Romantic movement, at the end of the
eighteenth century, that poets shift from merely cautioning against man's
excessive pride in his science to condemning those investigations which
reduce nature to analyzable elements. For Blake, Newton is a diabolical
figure; for Keats his "cold philosophy" is the destroyer of color and of
beauty.

And yet, even to writers of the early nineteenth century the science
of the times can have importance. Ironically, as Miss Nicolson observes,
when Shelley pays tribute to Keats in his elegy "Adonais," his most memorable image is probably suggested by Newton's prism that breaks light
into its various colors:

> Life like a dome of many-coloured glass
> Stains the white radiance of Eternity,
> Until death tramples it to fragments.

Even more ironically, Wordsworth rejects the methods of the biologist,
who would "peep and botanize/Upon his mother's grave," and yet his
idea of the world is an idea drawn from biology, the conception of an
organism characterized by growth and interrelationship of all parts. This
idea is specifically formulated and applied to art in Coleridge's theory of
"organic form."

The writers in the latter part of the nineteenth century are yet
more likely to be aware of scientific thought. Tennyson's *In Memoriam,*
for instance, is filled with the evolutionary notions so much in the air of

mid-Victorian England; and it was published some nine years before Darwin's *Origin of Species.* After Darwin produced his thesis, the influence of scientific theories on all of literature was profound, and often profoundly disturbing.

Affected perhaps by both Romantic hostility to scientific analysis and Victorian uneasiness about the implications of Darwin, modern writers have ranged in their reactions to science from rejecting completely to embracing plaintively what they take to be the scientific ideas of their times. In *The Heel of Elohim,* a study of science and values in recent American poetry, Hyatt Waggoner shows how T. S. Eliot makes technical analytical language reveal the sterility of the modern world which he rejects; while, in contrast, Robinson Jeffers uses dry terms of natural description to evoke the scientific data which are for him the only reality—going so far as to suggest the meaninglessness of poetry, of human values, even of conscious life. To some extent, however, the reaction of these poets is a reaction less to the work of scientists than to what Waggoner calls "scientism," the exalting of the laboratory method and datum into a whole philosophy or dogma. In particular, the writers of the early decades in the twentieth century were shaken by the now widely challenged view of human life called **behaviorism,** a view that belongs to the least clearly scientific of the scientific disciplines, psychology. The behaviorist reduction of human activity to sheer physical and chemical properties, all subject to prediction, is not primarily the work of physicists or chemists.

Some specific and more recent scientific ideas, finally, have no doubt had their positive if indirect effects on literature, as the astronomy of the seventeenth century had on writers of that time. It may be that certain novelists' interests in distorting and apparently fusing time and space, and even a sense of how truth is relative to an observer's point of view, reflect imaginatively complex ideas in modern physics: the idea of a time-space *continuum,* identifying time and space as one, and the more comprehensive idea of relativity, that the motion of any object can be observed only in relation to the observer's own motion. It would be difficult, however, to go further than this vague general statement. We can hardly prove the influence of Einstein on the way one of Faulkner's characters thinks or the method of showing multiple points of view used in novels by Lawrence Durrell. If he borrows the language of physics or of chemistry to indicate qualities in current literature, the critic has to do so with some modesty and some care.

We can, in fact, conclude as we began by recalling that all critical uses of extra-literary disciplines—biography, history, psychology, economics, anthropology, religion, philosophy, and other relevant fields of knowledge such as art history and archeology, music, and science—are justified not in the abstract but to the extent that they illuminate particular literary works. That all of these sources of knowledge can sometimes be useful we have now observed. And we may also fairly conclude, from these observations, that the reader of literature who has some breadth of experience in these subjects, who has achieved some of that culture which is the aim of a general education, is very likely as a result to be a more perceptive and thus a more critical reader.

CHAPTER FIVE

The Judgment of Literature

All the time that we are analyzing a poem, play, or novel, or considering the literary traditions to which it belongs, or gathering the biographical, historical, and other information about it that may be relevant, we are, of course, in one way or another passing judgment on it. Our decision to go on reading or, on the other hand, to put the book down, in itself implies some kind of judgment. As we read, we are probably also thinking that the work is very good, or very bad, or just indifferent, or that it is not merely good but positively great. We may even find ourselves revising our judgment several times as we proceed. Naturally, the more we know about a work, the better we shall be able to judge it, and it is, presumably, our ultimate aim as critical readers to give as full and fair an evaluation as we can.

This kind of evaluation is also our most difficult task. For on what are we to base our judgment? There seem to be so many different ways of evaluating literature, and there is considerable disagreement among critics past and present about what criteria or principles of judgment to adopt. Almost invariably, too, the choice of criteria depends on one's basic conception of literature. As a matter of fact, many of the time-honored ways of judging a work are a direct result of one of the three traditional ways of looking at literature that we considered in our opening chapter. We might therefore begin by reviewing, at least briefly, the chief criteria of this kind that have been proposed, and by considering the relative merits and limitations of each.

Imitation: The Criterion of Truth

We often hear a play, story, or novel praised because "everything seems so real" or because it is "so true to life" or because it is "so profoundly true." Alternatively, we hear one or the other of these criticized because "life isn't like that." Behind these statements is the view that literature is basically a mimetic art, an imitation of life in the sense of being either a copy or a representation or perhaps a freer recreation of human experiences. In each case, we are judging whatever is represented in a work by comparing it with certain aspects of life as we know it, and we are adopting some sort of criterion of truth.

But the truth, as we well know, has many faces, and in the three commonplace statements just quoted, rather different kinds of truth are implied. When we say that everything seems real or *true to life,* we are usually concerned with how the characters and the action or plot are presented. We are inclined to praise the Christmas dinner scene in Joyce's *A Portrait of the Artist* because we recognize it as a brilliant and amusing representation of those fatal dinner parties that occur in every family, which begin with a general show of good feelings and end in a blazing quarrel. Or we may delight in the glimpse that Chaucer gives of the Wife of Bath in the Prologue to *The Canterbury Tales,* when he mentions that she is furious if anyone else tries to make the offering in church before her, because we see this mingling of charity (her eagerness to make an offering) and of vanity (her pique if she is not allowed to be the first) as a very human trait. Or, again, we may appreciate the kind of ending that Henry James provides for many of his novels, especially for *The Portrait of a Lady,* whereby most of the minor characters are left as they are, without either dying or being married off to a suitable spouse, because we find this closer to our own experience than an arbitrary distribution of rewards and punishments and a neat tying up of all the threads. Conversely, we may condemn the triumphant marriage of the secretary to the head of the firm or the complete and unexpected repentance of the villain in a supposedly realistic play or novel, because we know this kind of ending to be a gross oversimplification of life as it is.

Though this criterion of truth to our own experience of life is one of the commonest ways of judging literature, it has, as we can easily see on second thought, a very limited application. As a matter of fact, it is applicable mainly to realistic works, or naturalistic ones which aim at giving a faithful representation of ordinary life. But what about the many obvious exaggerations and distortions that abound in literature? Even novels that are as universally praised as those of Charles Dickens owe much of their strength to the magnificent comic caricatures, based on the blatant exaggeration of one or two character traits, and they are full of thrilling melodramatic scenes. Quite as far removed from ordinary life as we know it are whole literary genres, such as the chivalric romance with its thoroughly implausible giants, dragons, and other monsters, not to mention the indefatigable knights who have nothing better to do than to pursue them; or the pastoral, with its eternally warm-hearted shepherds and cold-hearted shepherdesses, living an idyllic life devoted almost exclusively to love and poetry. In any case, we have seen enough of the many conventions or artificial contrivances on which much of literature depends to recognize that it cannot be judged simply by whether it is true to our daily experience.

But, of course, one can argue that **truth to life** need not be restricted to our ordinary experiences. We saw, earlier in our discussion, that the very term *life* can mean not only the varied and particular experiences of daily living (as in the exclamation "What an eventful life he leads!") but also human life in its broader and more enduring aspects ("Well, that's life!"). And so the truth we seek in a piece of literature may be some sort of ideal truth, a truth to life not as it is, but as it ought to be. Clearly, the conversations in the comedies of Congreve, Wilde, and Shaw are infinitely more witty—more pointed, more concise, and more elegantly phrased—than even the wittiest conversations we have ever heard or carried on in our own life, and we admire them precisely because they are better. Clearly, poetic justice, whereby rewards and punishments are distributed according to just deserts, is not a characteristic of real life, in which the unscrupulous may flourish at the expense of good and warm-hearted people; yet we usually enjoy seeing some sort of poetic justice worked out at the end of a comedy, knowing how rare it is in life. Clearly, too, the events which lead to someone's downfall seldom confine themselves to twenty-four hours and a single place, and yet we appreciate the thrilling concentration that is achieved when the unities of time and place are observed in a classical tragedy. For that matter, there are few if any tragic heroes in life; no man, so the saying goes, is a hero to his valet. Nevertheless, we are impressed by the way in which Sophocles or Shakespeare elevates a figure such as Oedipus or Lear, making us feel the extraordinary greatness as well as the weakness of these figures. The very genres that seem completely implausible when judged by realistic standards become acceptable when seen in terms of this other kind of truth. The chivalric romance can be recognized as an idealized version of life, concentrating on love and adventure; the pastoral, as another idealized version, focusing on a state of simplicity and innocence.

In all of these examples, life "as it ought to be" can be understood in the sense of life as we might desire it: adorned by clever conversations, governed by the laws of justice, filled with events that have at least a concentrated intensity, and lived by paragons of heroism, dignity, or virtuous simplicity. But the word *ought* can be ambiguous, as the word *ideal* often is; and the literature that represents ideal characters and actions, or life as it ought to be, may show not the desirable—"the ideal" or "idealized" in our usual sense of the phrase—but the typical and essential, "the ideal" in a philosophical sense.

This criterion of truth to life as it is not in its literal details but in its essence has a long history, going back to Aristotle with his idea that literature should imitate events that are "probable" or likely to happen rather than "possible," actually happening but only as unique and unexpected occurrences. Aristotle goes so far as to prefer "probable impossibilities" (events that have never happened but might well occur) to "improbable possibilities" (events that have happened once, but so freakishly that no one would expect them to occur again). Later critics, especially in the Renaissance, seventeenth and eighteenth centuries, use the term **verisimilitude** for what *seems* to be true in a poem, play, or novel, in contrast to what is literally or historically true but not quite believable. This principle has many applications, most strikingly to the portrayal of characters. It was held, from Horace on, that young lovers should be made to behave with the impetuosity and ardor of young lovers; old men, with the querulousness and nostalgia of old men. In other words, though the playwright or novelist might know an old Mr. X who once behaved as if he were young Romeo, or a young lover who once behaved as if he were approaching senility, he should refrain from presenting these very special cases in his work. Interpreted narrowly, this criterion might well lead to the approval mainly of very conventional stock characters and the disapproval of the best kind of individualizing touches. But when interpreted in a wider sense, it calls primarily for a certain consistency of characterization: the villain is not to repent all at once, contrary to all expectations; the supposedly inarticulate farm hand should not, suddenly, be made to write a letter to his girl friend in which he shows an extensive knowledge of the Petrarchan conventions.

Widely accepted as was the criterion of truth to an ideal, it is, in its own way, almost as limited as the criterion of truth to ordinary life. If we accept "the ideal" in its usual positive sense of the desirable or idealized, we must, in fact, exclude the truth to life as it actually is. We shall have to reject the many realistic and naturalistic plays or novels that dwell on the seamy sides and, like Gerhart Hauptmann's play *The Weavers,* show good but downtrodden people confronted with horrifying injustices. We shall also have to reject a good deal of modern poetry, from Baudelaire to T. S. Eliot, which explores the ugly as well as the beautiful sides of human existence. It is significant that the eighteenth-century critics who adopted this criterion of truth called for the imitation not of nature in general but only of "beautiful nature" and that they strongly disapproved of anything coarse or ugly in the genres they considered elevated, in tragedy or the epic (although coarse details were thought permissible in the lower genres such as satire). They quite failed to recognize what could be gained from the sort of comic relief for which Shakespeare is famous, but which they thought unworthy of his tragic subjects. And in the same way, they failed to understand the sharpness and concentration of meaning that Shakespeare achieved by introducing puns and other examples of what they considered low and unworthy language into *Hamlet* and *King Lear*.

If, on the other hand, we demand that literature represent the ideal in the sense of the typical or essential, rather than the desirable, we cut ourselves off from the kind of literature that is circumstantial and detailed, that communicates the sense of characters in literal places rather than types in typical settings. Although Dr. Johnson, following this criterion, insists that the business of the poet is to give a generalized view of the world and not to number the streaks of the tulip, many poets, particularly the romantics, are in fact celebrated for the skill with which they describe subtle distinctions in the shapes and colors of unique forms.

There is, however, still another way of interpreting the criterion of truth. This is the broadest conception, the hardest to put into words, but perhaps also the most meaningful. We may call it the criterion of symbolic truth. By it, literature is judged not as a good copy of the ordinary life we know nor as the representation of some ideal, but as a great parable or paradigm of life in any one of its manifold aspects. No matter how distorted, or untypical, or unidealized the plot and characters of a work may be, they should give us, we might say, the impression of having caught some of the basic rhythm of existence. We get this impression, for example, in the very pairing of the characters in Cervantes' *Don Quixote*. As the half-mad would-be knight and his simple-minded companion Sancho Panza go from adventure to adventure, endlessly discussing each one before and after it happens, we become aware of the fact that Cervantes is really presenting, in an infinitely varied and inventive fashion, two of the dominant sides of human nature—roughly, the idealistic and the practical. Similarly, as Faust and Mephistopheles carry on their brilliant exchanges of opinion in *Faust*, we recognize that Goethe is representing two other but equally basic sides of man's nature, on the one hand the creative, affirmative, and aspiring, and on the other the destructive, skeptical, and nihilistic. It is when we are confronted with such characters that we are likely to say, not that they are "true to life," but that they are, rather, in a very different sense, "profoundly true."

Not only the choice of characters but also the way in which the plot is developed may give us such an impression of symbolic truth. As Tolstoy fills in his vast canvas in *War and Peace*, following the life-stories of a great many different and highly individualized characters who live through the exciting alternation of war and temporary peace that constitutes the Napoleonic era, we come to feel that he is also conveying the very basic rhythm of everyone's life: adolescence and young love, false steps and disappointments in private and public life, a great crisis, and eventually the attainment of a very moderate happiness and peace of mind that comes with maturity and middle age. Perhaps we can also account for the effectiveness of certain kinds of plots, such as those based on a voyage or journey (the *Odyssey, Tom Jones, Huckleberry Finn,* or *Heart of Darkness*) or those based on the search for a father (the *Odyssey* again, or Joyce's *A Portrait of the Artist* and *Ulysses*), because these are, as we have seen, the archetypal patterns which express some of our most personal but also most universal experiences.

The idea of symbolic truth may, furthermore, enable us to give a more profound reason for approving of such genres as the chivalric romance and the pastoral than the argument that they present an idealized view of life. We may feel that they suggest, ultimately, quite fundamental and valid sides of human experience—man's yearning to lead a life of heroism and adventure or, in the case of the pastoral, his longing to turn to an uncomplicated, innocent, idyllic life, either as an escape or as a new perspective from which to view his own more complicated society.

Just as the principle of symbolic truth makes us approve of a literary work that is, we feel, "profoundly true," so, conversely, it makes us critical of those works that lack this ultimate relevance and validity. Most of the detective stories and Westerns that are popular today are indisputably exciting and hold our interest to the end. Many Broadway comedies are amusing and visually delightful. But they leave us dissatisfied in the long run, because there is little of interest except the actual story. They have no meaning in larger human terms, and it is precisely this further meaning that we find and value in greater works of literature.

At times, it is not the presentation of human experience through the characters and the plot that is judged by some principle of truth, but the presentation of ideas. This would seem to be a simpler kind of judgment: surely we can make up our mind whether we consider the ideas of a poem, play, or story tenable or untenable. In actual fact, it is again a very difficult judgment to make, partly because there is often no easy way of deciding whether the ideas are right or wrong, and partly because we may be influenced, whether we know it or not, by personal prejudices. We may find ourselves approving of those works that reflect our own political or religious convictions, and disapproving of others that are written from a very different point of view. In other words, the judgment of ideas is intimately related to the whole question of our personal beliefs.

To clarify matters, we should bear in mind that there are actually two quite different types of ideas in literature—those presented by the various characters in the course of a poem, play, or story, and those that constitute the ultimate theme or meaning of the whole work—and that these present two rather different problems. When the ideas are expressed by certain characters within a work, we must be careful not to take them purely at face value. It is possible that an obviously wrong-headed point of view has been introduced, either in order to let the weaknesses of a character speak for themselves, as they do when Shakespeare's Richard III reveals his villainous plans in a soliloquy, or in order to create a contrast to the views held by other, more sensible characters. Immediately after the catastrophic snipping of Belinda's hair in *The Rape of the Lock,* for example, her friend Thalestris makes a heated speech in which she warns that incessant gossip will ensue, that Belinda has incurred a shameful loss of honor, and that she will never be able to hold up her head in public again. But this is obviously a very limited view of the situation. It is in direct contrast to Clarissa's subsequent advice that Belinda should take her loss in a spirit of good sense and good humor, recognizing that she has cultivated her beauty in the first place not for its own sake but in order to attract a husband and thereby fulfil her proper function as wife and mother. We may disapprove of Thalestris' ideas because we find them superficial, but we can see how good her speech is artistically as soon as we see it as a foil to Clarissa's advice, and also as one of several comic deviations from the norm of good sense, good manners, and good humor which Clarissa obviously represents in the poem. It is also possible, to take another case, that certain characters are made to express ideas that are not obviously wrong but somehow one-sided and only partly tenable. This is certainly true of *Don Quixote* or of *Faust.* Neither the idealism of Don Quixote nor the realism of Sancho Panza, neither the aspirations of Faust nor the cynicism of Mephistopheles, represents the whole truth as Cervantes and Goethe see it, and we shall be misinterpreting both works if we take the views of any one of the characters in isolation.

How, then, are we to evaluate these ideas? As the last examples suggest, they can be considered only in their context and in relation to the whole. Determined as they are by the dramatic necessity of the piece or by the character who expresses them, they can hardly be judged as if they were presented in and for themselves. In short, our concern can be only with how well they are presented. Thalestris' speech in *The Rape of the Lock* is, we can recognize, a little masterpiece of harebrained and conventional reasoning. She immediately paints the rather trivial snipping of the hair in the blackest possible colors, predicts the direst consequences for Belinda, and wholly fails to recognize that her view of honor is very narrow indeed, since she equates it not with any ethical values but only with what other people will say, with reputation in its lowest form:

> Methinks already I your tears survey,
> Already hear the horrid things they say,
> Already see you a degraded toast,
> And all your honour in a whisper lost!

Throughout her speech, it is clear that Pope actually holds a very different view of the situation, the one he later expresses through Clarissa, and the discrepancy between what Thalestris is saying and what Pope is thinking creates a delightful ironic effect. In any case, then, Thalestris' speech is rather more complicated than any "idea" that it expresses.

When we turn from this rather simple example to the plays or novels in which ideas, as such, play a much more prominent part, we can see again that these can be judged not by what they are but by how skillfully they are presented. Thomas Mann's *Magic Mountain* is a classic case in point. Through a series of brilliant conversations in which the Italian Settembrini sets forth his position of Western humanism and the Eastern European Naphta develops his authoritarian view of life, as well as through the extensive lectures in which the Polish Dr. Krokowski explicates the Freudian theory of love and death, Mann dramatizes the leading intellectual currents of Europe in the early twentieth century. He is interested in these partly for their own sake, but chiefly for their effect on his central character, Hans Castorp, the young German who is reaching maturity by coming into contact with these diverse philosophies of life. As we look more closely, we find that Mann has, on the one hand, chosen just that character for each leading idea who can most plausibly and vividly express it, and that he is, on the other hand, tacitly commenting on or qualifying each idea by associating it with its particular spokesman. Settembrini, with his encyclopedic mind, love of stimulating talk, and background of Italian liberalism, is the perfect representative of the humanistic view of life; but his weakness of endlessly talking and never actually doing anything also suggests Mann's implied criticism that there is a certain ineffectuality in the liberal position. The Jesuit Naphta, with his fascinating intensity and intellectual ruthlessness, is a striking representative of what we might call intellectual totalitarianism; his sinister persuasiveness and ruthlessness also, on the other hand, suggest Mann's view that this authoritarianism constitutes a real threat to Europe. The ideas, then, are an integral and dramatic part of the novel. They make up the dialogue and play an important part in the characterization. It is in these terms that they—and, in fact, all ideas of this sort that are expressed by the characters within a work—should be judged. What we should finally consider is how vividly, dramatically, and subtly they are presented, and perhaps also how consistent they are with the characters who express them.

When we come to evaluate the ideas that are implied or expressed in a poem, play, or story as a whole—that is, the central theme or meaning—we are confronted by many more difficulties. In the first place, it may be far from easy to define just what *is* the central idea, in the sense of a philosophical statement; and in trying to define it, we run the danger of reducing the literary work to an abstract statement, a paraphrase, which does not do justice to the complexities and nuances of the original. Lyrical poetry in general and the lyrics of the romantic period in particular suffer under this approach, for the exploration of certain moods and feelings is likely to seem thin indeed when rephrased in terms of "ideas," or else they may sound cumbersome and heavy-handed. It is just as flat and unsatisfactory to say that Wordsworth's "I wandered lonely as a cloud" records the poet's experience and later recollection of a moment of beauty, as it is to say that the poem dramatizes the contrast between Nature, embodied in the daffodils, and Man, embodied in the speaker, and that the contrast is resolved in the speaker's mind at the end. Neither of these statements gives us an adequate basis for judging the poem. Moreover, as the many different interpretations of Shakespeare's plays suggest, it is, if anything, still more difficult to express the chief ideas of a great and complex tragedy than to sum up those of a little lyric.

Even if we can solve the problem of adequately describing the central idea of a piece of literature, we are, in the second place, confronted with the problem of how to judge that idea. The problem is complicated, as we have seen, by the fact that we may be misled into letting our personal standards and beliefs blind us to the value of the work as a whole. We can easily recognize how limited such personal judgments may be when we find an unreligious reader rejecting all of the *Divine Comedy* because it is based on a wholly Catholic point of view; or, alternatively, a Catholic reader rejecting Joyce's *A Portrait of the Artist* because it is bitterly critical of the Church; or, to take a more extreme example still, a Marxist deploring Shakespeare's blindness because he fails to give a prominent place and favorable treatment to the common people.

To avoid such limited and biased judgments, we shall, at least as a first step, want to evaluate the central ideas or themes in the same way as the ideas expressed by characters within a work, not so much by what they are as by how well—how fully, clearly, and subtly—they are represented. Whether we are Catholics or not, we can admire Dante for the extraordinarily clear and vivid expression he gives to the Catholic doctrine and dogma in every facet of the *Divine Comedy*. He brilliantly embodies the notions of sin, purgation, and salvation in the three realms of the inferno, purgatory, and paradise, in the experiences of the travelers through these regions, and in the many other figures drawn from public and private life, from history and legend. We can appreciate the poet's splendid way of suggesting the basic conception of an orderly and hierarchic universe by the very construction of his work, the symmetrical division into three parts of thirty-three cantos each, with one extra canto bringing the number to the fullness of one hundred. And we can be impressed by the tribute Dante pays to Christian values, not only through all that his chief character learns, but also through the recurrence, in the very structure and verse form, of the number three, symbolic as it is of the Trinity. Whether or not we accept the so-called optimistic view of life expressed in the *Essay on Man,* we can appreciate the concise and witty way in which Pope uses all the potentialities of the couplet to explain his theodicy, his view that everything in the universe has a purpose, although man may be too limited to understand it. And more profoundly, we can value the impression Pope manages to convey of a powerful mind that surveys the "mighty maze" of the universe, returning to the far from optimistic conclusion that man has no recourse other than to accept his place on the scale or chain of being, to "submit" and to "hope humbly." Whether or not, finally, we share or approve of Joyce's violent antipathy to the Jesuits who dominated his own childhood, we can recognize how cleverly this negative feeling has been insinuated in *A Portrait of the Artist as a Young Man,* even in the opening chapter, when little Stephen is ostensibly accepting all the teachings of the Jesuits, but when he is already subconsciously associating them with a horrid kind of wetness, coldness, dampness, whiteness—and dead rats in a ditch. We can also feel how well this anti-Catholic bias is made to fit in with Stephen's basic development, his ultimate rejection of all the forces of religion, patriotism, and family life which might prevent him from being a free and independent, though isolated, artist.

And yet, once we have evaluated its artistic effectiveness, we shall probably, as a final step, want to pass some kind of judgment on the truth of the central idea or meaning of a work, turning to some criterion of general truth or validity. Certain ideas are, we might argue, less one-sided in their view of life, more generally valid, than others. This is not to say that there is any simple rule for identifying some ideas or themes as automatically true and acceptable, others as untrue and untenable. We should bear in mind that we are not examining ideas in the abstract, but the total meaning that shines through and is determined by all the aspects of a poem, play, or story. Just how to decide on this ultimate truth and validity is so complex a subject that we shall be approaching it repeatedly in the course of this chapter, and we shall want to discuss it again later on.

Effect: The Criteria of Pleasure and Instruction

Whereas the various criteria of truth are related to the traditional view of literature as a form of imitation and tend to judge a work by comparing it with certain aspects of life outside the work, another important group of criteria is related to the so-called pragmatic or affective theories which interpret and evaluate literature by its effect on the reader or spectator. We all tend to judge a play, novel, or poem by the degree of pleasure it gives us, and to associate pleasure with intensity. We speak enthusiastically of "an exciting evening in the theater," "a thrilling adventure story," and "a deeply moving lyric." On the other hand, we dislike a dull play or novel, and to express our disapproval we may say that it "leaves me cold."

Naturally, we ought not to try to discount our personal reactions. They are, in a sense, the chief guide we have for judging literature, since no absolute or infallible criteria seem to exist. Besides, if we actively dislike a novel, we simply do not go on reading it, and if a play bores us enough, we fall asleep. But most of us have had the experience of reading a novel, especially a love story or a mystery, with breathless attention, knowing all the while that it is not really good; or of reading some very complex and demanding piece of literature which we know to be good, without really enjoying the effort of attention. There is, then, a question of whether pleasure and intensity are the best criteria, especially when these are taken as the only ones. W. K. Wimsatt and Monroe C. Beardsley have recently argued that this judging by our emotional reactions can be called the **affective fallacy**. We should bear in mind that if we are looking for unadulterated pleasure, we may well rule out a great deal of literature, from the elegy to realistic and naturalistic novels to much of modern poetry, which is sad, painful, or positively unpleasant. And if we are looking for intensity, for a thrilling experience, we may find ourselves admiring sentimentality, the indulging in emotions for their own sake, or melodrama, the exploiting of sensational and violent material. In short, we are likely to prefer strong to subtle effects. In that case, however, literature offers no real competition to other forms of experience. As Edmund Burke pointed out in the eighteenth century, a public execution is likely to empty even the best theaters of the neighborhood. Putting this whole matter more flippantly, we might even argue that for an immediate and intense pleasure, a good story rarely surpasses a good Sunday dinner.

Two other criteria that are frequently mentioned, either separately or together, are **novelty** and **familiarity**. The former refers to a certain freshness, an element of surprise, a sense that we are presented with something we have never read or seen before. The latter refers to the pleasing recognition of something already known, the kind of experience we have when we see that Sidney, in his sonnets, is working out all possible variations of the Petrarchan convention, or that Herrick, at the end of "Corinna's Going A-Maying," is giving yet another charming statement of the *carpe diem* theme. There is, certainly, no denying that both novelty and familiarity can give us great pleasure, or that a combination of the two can also be very effective. For instance, we may enjoy recognizing that Shaw has taken over some of the stock characters of comedy, such as the foundling, and we may also be pleased by the fact that he has surprisingly reversed the convention in *Major Barbara* by making someone prove not who his parents are but that he *is* a foundling. We may enjoy recognizing both that Goethe, at the end of *Faust,* is using the old form of the morality play, and that he does so for the unusual purpose of saving and bringing to heaven the kind of hero whom any medieval morality would have sent straight to hell. Nevertheless, neither criterion is wholly satisfactory. The desire for the completely new and different can easily lead us to call for the merely odd and eccentric, for what, from the poet's point of view, would be called originality at any price. The desire for familiarity, on the other hand, may lead us to place undue emphasis on the conventional, to shy away from the new and experimental. More fundamentally, as our examples from *Major Barbara* and *Faust* suggest, both criteria tend to draw our attention chiefly to the separate parts of a piece of literature. We may find ourselves admiring a surprise twist in the plot, because of its novelty, or a stock figure or stock situation, in the name of familiarity. These criteria do not, in other words, make us take into account the work as a whole.

Closely related to the liking for familiarity is the demand, frequently made in our own time, that a work should have easy and immediate **intelligibility.** Many readers have complained that modern poets such as Ezra Pound, T. S. Eliot, and Wallace Stevens are "willfully obscure," and by **obscurity** (from Latin *obscurus,* meaning "covered over" or "dark") they mean a hiding of meaning, a lack of clarity, something close to incomprehensibility. As a matter of fact, however, the demand for immediate intelligibility is not at all new. From Dryden to Dr. Johnson, the metaphysical poets of the seventeenth century were thought to be extremely and unnecessarily difficult. John Donne's love poetry, with its elaborate conceits and allusions to scientific and philosophical material, was criticized by Dryden in these terms: "He affects the metaphysics, and perplexes the minds of the fair sex with nice speculations of philosophy, when he should engage their hearts, and entertain them with the softnesses of love." In contrast, the poetry of Denham and Waller, hardly read today, was praised for being "sweet" and "easy" and "flowing," for combining clarity with grace.

Without denying the attractiveness of a clear, direct, easy, and graceful presentation, especially as found in some of the Elizabethan songs or the lyrics of Dryden and Wordsworth, we would, surely, not want to cut ourselves off from the great body of literature that has greater surface difficulty. We would be rejecting not only the metaphysical poets and much of modern poetry, but also a good deal of prose, from the baroque involutions of Sir Thomas Browne to modern experiments with stream-of-consciousness in the novels, say, of Virginia Woolf or James

Joyce. More than that, however, as Randall Jarrell has pointed out in his *Poetry and the Age,* we would be condemning a great deal of the most admired poetry of all times. With its characteristic use of subtle connotations, multiple meanings, allusions, and the echoing of the sense by the sound, it is by its very nature "difficult" and requires a considerable effort of attention. George Herbert's religious lyrics "Virtue" and "Discipline," for example, are deceptively smooth and simple; a closer look reveals a wealth of complicated themes, allusions, and wordplay. Milton's "Lycidas," Keats' odes, Browning's "Childe Roland" and "Rabbi Ben Ezra" —all acknowledged classics—require very full analysis before they are understood. It is not so much the ease or difficulty with which we grasp the meaning of these poems that should determine our judgment, we might say, as what that meaning actually is and how well it is expressed.

Pleasure and intensity, novelty and familiarity, easy intelligibility —all these are related to the kind of pragmatic or affective theories which hold that literature should, primarily, delight. There is, however, as we saw earlier, a theory that it should teach as well, that it should, to use Horace's terms, be not only delightful (*dulce*) but also useful (*utile*). And so a poem, play, or novel is sometimes judged by whether it provides moral or intellectual improvement. This **didactic view** of literature (from the Greek word meaning "teach") was widely held from the Renaissance to the eighteenth century and into the nineteenth. For instance, the catharsis the audience supposedly experiences when watching a tragedy was valued for its moral effect, and the display of man's foibles and follies in comedy and satire was considered a means, as we have observed, of laughing the audience out of similar weaknesses.

The didactic view raises the difficult question of how, if at all, literature can offer instruction. Speaking very broadly, we can perhaps say that by reading about the experiences of other people and, more important, by coming into contact with the ideas and the vision of life of many great writers, we can broaden our intellectual horizons and refine our sensibility, our general perceptiveness. Perhaps, in this very general way, we can also strengthen our moral sense, although this is a matter of psychology on which there is very little evidence. But evaluating a work by whether or not it provides improvement is something else again. For surely this is neither the primary aim nor the function of literature. Simply on the basis of common sense, we can argue that if it is intellectual betterment that is wanted, it can be gained much more quickly and reliably from other sources, such as a sound historical study or a good philosophical treatise. Similarly, if a moral effect is desired, one can hardly do better than to read one of the great moral philosophers or to listen to a good sermon.

Other objections are more telling still. If we really judge literature by whether it provides intellectual improvement, we shall presumably place the highest value on philosophical poems such as Lucretius' *Of the Nature of Things* or Pope's *Essay on Man,* or a novel of ideas such as Thomas Mann's *Magic Mountain.* We may also find ourselves taking the ideas out of their context and judging them in and for themselves, in a way which, we have just seen, hardly does justice to the work of art of which they are only a part. Or, if we judge literature by its moral effect, we may well be led to value most highly the so-called didactic poetry that clearly sets out to teach some moral truth. Though much of great literature can, in a sense, be called didactic—for instance, Spenser's *Faerie Queene* with its moral allegory or Milton's *Paradise Lost* with its attempt to "justify the ways of God to man"—so can much writing that is mediocre or positively bad, such as the kind of poetry we call "inspirational verse." Besides, Spenser and Milton, we might argue, are great for other reasons than their didactic intent.

Without denying that philosophical poems, novels of ideas, and didactic pieces in general can be very good indeed, we would not, in any case, want to limit ourselves to these. There are a great many other works, notably the epics of Homer and the tragedies of Shakespeare, which we are likely to value highly, but which are so complex that it is difficult if not impossible to say what it is they teach, either intellectually or morally. To try to formulate such teachings would, in fact, be limiting their meaning unduly. The famous moralistic reading of the *Iliad* current in the seventeenth and eighteenth centuries, whereby the poem was interpreted as teaching the leaders of great nations not to quarrel among themselves, hardly does justice to what Homer has achieved. *Othello* cannot be reduced to any simple lesson that husbands should refrain from being jealous of their wives, or *King Lear* to the lesson that kings should not subdivide their realms. Furthermore, even if a play or novel has some sort of moral, that may not be the reason for admiring it. The roguish hero of nearly all picaresque novels repents at the end, but what we are likely to admire is much less his final pious decision than his previous escapades and the rich variety of human experiences that are presented while he makes his way in the world. Finally, certain great works, when considered from an ethical point of view, actually seem thoroughly immoral. Shakespeare's *Antony and Cleopatra* appears to extol adultery, since Antony leaves Octavia soon after marrying her to return to Cleopatra, and eventually the play seems to glorify suicide, when Cleopatra poisons herself with the asps in order to be reunited with Antony. And are we to condemn, out of hand, the various nineteenth-century writers, from De Quincey to Baudelaire, who celebrated intoxication, the taking of narcotics, and the cultivation of perverse passions, partly as a means of exploring the subconscious and partly as a romantic revolt against conventionality? If we do so—in fact, if we adopt a strictly moral principle of judgment altogether—we are likely to judge a piece of literature primarily for its subject matter instead of considering it as an artistic whole.

Occasionally, the opinion is expressed that literature should not only provide intellectual or moral improvement but should go a step further and be an incitement to action. It is sometimes argued that a play or novel should dramatize certain problems, usually social or political ones, so vividly that we feel impelled to go out and do something constructive to alleviate the existing conditions. High-minded as it sounds, this point of view has the disadvantage of making us value the kind of literature that actually, from other vantage points, has great limitations: the play or novel with a "message," or, to use a more negative term, **propaganda,** the kind of writing that propagates or popularizes a particular idea with which it tries to indoctrinate the public. This kind of writing is likely to be very much time-bound, for the burning issues of one period may have given way to new and different ones in the next. Now that slavery has been abolished, few of us read Harriet Beecher Stowe's *Uncle Tom's Cabin* with breathless attention, nor do we feel strongly about the dismal picture of poverty in nineteenth-century England which Dickens paints in *Hard Times.* Furthermore, in this kind of writing, the end is likely to justify the means, and so gross overstatement, oversimplification of the issues, and other far from subtle devices may be used to wring the audience's heart. Mrs. Stowe did not shun sentimentality or melodrama when she described Eliza crossing the ice or Simon Legree going to work with his whip.

All this is not to deny that a few works which are generally acknowledged to be very good indeed were originally conceived as propaganda. To cite a classic example, Swift's "A Modest Proposal," that masterpiece of ironic understatement with its tongue-in-cheek suggestion that infants be slaughtered and sold as food in order to overcome the problems of overpopulation, poverty, famine, and the like, was written to draw attention to the terrible social and economic conditions in eighteenth-century Ireland. But it is admired nowadays for quite different reasons, and has therefore managed to transcend its initial aims. On the whole, it seems fair to say that what makes for good propaganda is not at all what makes for good literature, for this is usually much more complex, with no unmistakable message and often without the strong assault on one's emotions. It hardly seems fair, then, to judge a work by whether it makes us take some positive action, any more than it is fair to judge a landscape painting by whether it makes us want to buy the property it depicts.

Expression: The Criteria of Originality and Sincerity

A third group of criteria is related to the so-called expressive theories, which tend to interpret literature as the product of the poet. One of the most widely accepted is the principle of **originality**. We say, with obvious approval, that Wordsworth's *Prelude* or Goethe's *Faust* is a remarkably original work, and we tend to consider originality as the mark of genius. On the other hand, we say with obvious disapproval that a certain play or novel is utterly hackneyed or trite (both words mean "worn-out by overuse"), or that it is derivative, or, quite flatly, that it is completely uninspired and unoriginal.

It is, however, often far from easy to tell just what *originality* means when applied to literature. Usually, one thinks of it as referring to the creation of something entirely fresh and novel; the very word is related to *origin*. As a term of praise, it came into vogue quite late, with the pre-romantics of the late eighteenth century and the romantics of the nineteenth, the very people, we should recall, who admired genius, inspiration, and spontaneity more than craftsmanship and "the labor of the file." For them, Homer and Shakespeare were the greatest original geniuses of all time, and they loved the vitality and imaginative daring with which these two created their all-embracing canvases. Critics from Herder on felt that both poets owed their strength to the fact that they were unhampered by a knowledge of the classical "rules" and of literary conventions: Homer, because he lived before they were devised; Shakespeare, because he ignored some and was unfamiliar with others. So great was the admiration for the original genius that the romantic critics conceived the image of the poet in general and Shakespeare in particular as a godlike creator, using "the word" to bring into being a whole new world or microcosm in each of his works.

Before the romantics, however, originality was not really a term of approbation. To call someone "an original," up to the eighteenth century, was to call him an oddity, an eccentric, and usually an uncouth one at that. The dominant view of literature, as we have seen, was that it is a form of imitation, and frequently this idea of imitation was interpreted much more narrowly than as a recreation of life; it meant following the model of earlier writers, either in subject matter or in form or in both. Writers took a positive pride in working within the established genres and conventions. Pope, for example, wrote nothing that did not fit squarely into one of the established literary types. It hardly seems fair to condemn this great body of literature for being unoriginal. Moreover, if we look more closely at the work of Homer and Shakespeare, we find that they, too, seem to have drawn on earlier works. It is now believed that Homer was influenced by previously existing *lays* (short narrative poems sung by bards) and that he may have taken over the sections in the *Iliad* in which he gives an extensive catalogue of the Greek and Trojan armies from an earlier source. It is well known that Shakespeare derived nearly all his plots from earlier plays and stories, and that he was familiar with all kinds of literary conventions: the Petrarchan, which he uses in his sonnets, for instance, and the pastoral, which he introduces, in a minor way, into his comedies from *As You Like It* to *The Winter's Tale*. Then, too, even as typically romantic a work as Goethe's *Faust* makes extensive use of existing literary material. For the story of his Faust, Goethe turned both to a sixteenth-century German collection that recorded the deeds and reputation of the actual Dr. Faustus, a combination scholar, alchemist, and quack who appeared at various German carnivals, and to Marlowe's *Doctor Faustus*. In his great dramatic poem, Goethe also makes full use of innumerable well-established genres, from the bourgeois tragedy to the ballad to the masque to allegory to the final morality play, when the angels and the devils fight for the soul of Faust. Even here, then, there can be no question of the completely new and different.

All this is not to say that there is no such thing as originality. In one sense, every work is unique and original, since there is no other quite like it. In a broader and, for us, a more meaningful sense, there is an unmistakable vitality, a freshness of approach, what we might call a certain individuality, which is the mark of great writers and which is obviously admirable. It is this fact that makes us able to speak of the Homeric, or the Shakespearean, or the Miltonic, or the Dickensian, thinking of each writer as having a special and distinctive way of looking at the world, a special and distinctive "voice." What we should, however, bear in mind is that this kind of originality does not necessarily imply the creation of something completely new and different. It may make itself felt in the reworking of older material, as it does in the case of Shakespeare and Goethe, or in the subtlety and refinement of expressing "what oft was thought, but ne'er so well expressed," as it does in the case of Pope, or in the imaginative use of whatever literary traditions and conventions have been adopted. It is, however, true that we tend to consider a more extensive breaking away from older forms and the accepted literary conventions more original than the subtlest working within the framework of these forms and conventions. We find *Faust,* with its extraordinary reworking of the Faustus legend and the imaginative use of the very loose, open form into which the various traditional genres have been incorporated, more original than any of Pope's little masterpieces. In other words, originality is likely to be a matter of degree.

If we accept this very broad interpretation of originality, we can use the principle to rule out the kind of literature that is merely conventional and derivative: the wooden exchanges between yet another shepherd and his shepherdess in the minor verse of the seventeenth and eighteenth centuries; the running in and out of the wrong bedroom in the popular French farces of the nineteenth century; the inevitable chase after the villain that has become the stock finale of the modern Western and detective story. On the other hand, we can recognize that originality, far from being an assurance of success, may be as little desirable as frigid conventionality. The frantic search for novelty can easily lead, as we have seen, to an overvaluing of the merely odd or eccentric, as it does in the case of the dadaists, a small group of writers and painters during and after World War I, who experimented with utterly meaningless sounds, words, and phrases in the hope of exploring the unconscious and symbolic (their very name is derived from the infantile sound *da-da-da*). This flirtation with meaninglessness, however revolutionary and original, is bound to have a rather limited significance. On the whole, then, we must conclude that originality is both a relatively new and a relatively unreliable principle for judging literature.

Even more unreliable is another criterion that is associated with the view of literature as the product of the poet, that of sincerity. There is no question that we admire straightforwardness, trustworthiness, and integrity in real life, and that we disapprove of hypocrisy, flattery, crocodile tears, double-dealing, and deceit. In literature, we may well disapprove of obvious insincerity, the hollow flattery one finds in the grossly overstated praise for a patron in the commendatory verses of seventeenth- and eighteenth-century poets who were dependent on the favor of a noble lord. But how far beyond this rather simple judgment will the principle of sincerity take us? Are we to judge a love lyric by whether the poet was really in love, an elegy by whether he actually felt the loss of the dead? Few of us would agree with Dr. Johnson's disapproval of "Lycidas": "It is not to be considered as the effusion of real passion; for passion runs not after remote allusions and obscure opinions. Passion plucks no berries from myrtle and ivy, nor calls upon Arethuse and Mincius, nor tells of 'rough satyrs and fauns with cloven heel.' Where there is leisure for fiction there is little grief." In other words, Dr. Johnson holds that the elaborate pastoral conventions and the numerous mythological allusions are a sign of insincerity, and that this insincerity, in turn, is a weakness in the poem.

It is, in actual fact, far from clear whether we can really tell when a writer is being sincere, when he is baring his innermost feelings. The dramatist, epic poet, or novelist is presenting the feelings and beliefs of a number of characters, none of which is necessarily identical with his own. Keats rightly drew attention, in his letters, to the "chameleon" quality of certain great poets, notably of Shakespeare, who are able to present convincingly the most widely different points of view in their various characters, and of a certain **negative capability** whereby these poets may accept and embody quite different ideas in various works. Even in the different types of lyrics, the speaker, as we have observed, is only the poet in a certain mood—in or out of love, joyful about the wedding, mournful about the death of someone or other. We should, surely, be judging these poems much less by whether the poet was really in love, or overjoyed, or heartbroken, than by how successfully these various moods are expressed within each poem.

Far from being a sign of great literature, sincerity may, as a matter of fact, be a sign of the very opposite. Countless verses are written every day by ordinary people to express their deepest feelings and strongest moral, political, or religious convictions. We are all familiar with the kind of verse in which the writer has poured out his feelings for his sweetheart or mother, for nature or his country. However well-meant, this verse usually lacks the richness of theme and the mastery of technique we associate with poetry (and here we are using our terms to imply a value judgment, "mere verse" as opposed to "poetry"). As a matter of fact, modern poets and critics have suggested that the very opposite of sincerity may be the sign of good poetry. They point out that the writer of love poetry is usually not at all in love, and that most elegies are written not immediately after the sad event or not about a personal friend, but some time later, and often, as in "Lycidas," about someone not really close to the poet. In these cases, the poet has a certain detachment from his material, and instead of indulging in his emotions, he can concentrate on his craft. This kind of argument is, perhaps, only a reversal of the one that makes sincerity a valuable asset. The emphasis, in both cases, is on the psychology of the poet, on how he feels about his subject; and about this it is really impossible to generalize. And yet, in another sense, a significant point is involved. Quite often, sincerity makes itself felt in the straightforward, affirmative statement of the particular belief the writer holds, or in very strongly stated feelings, which may border on sentimentality and naiveté. On the other hand, a certain detachment, especially if it takes the form of irony, is likely to produce a more inclusive point of view or greater thematic complexity.

Structure: The Criteria of Complexity, Coherence, and Economy

We have questioned the complete validity of several familiar and traditional ways of judging literature. In fact, of course, all of us are likely to refer casually and perhaps unconsciously to these grounds of judgment when we talk and write about stories, plays, or poems. Even in the work of critics who would not subscribe to the theories that literature should be judged finally by its truth to everyday life, or its novelty, or its sincerity, or its probable moral effect on the reader, it is possible to find phrases that imply each of these criteria: "The characters in this novel are all unbelievably rich, clever, and beautiful"; "Here is the newest, most absolutely original experiment in poetry for many years"; "Moral fervor, a direct and honest sense of human values, shines through every page"; "In sum, it is a profoundly evil book, subtly designed to appeal to those very prejudices and hatreds that it seems to deprecate." But most critics and teachers of literature today, even if they use such phrases, tend in theory at least to defend another criterion, one that recognizes the value of a work in what might be called its intrinsic characteristics.

By **intrinsic** characteristics are mean those self-evident qualities of a literary work that we have discussed in Chapter Two, the qualities that submit to analysis: plot, characterization, setting, symbol, style, and tone. The so-called **extrinsic** elements would include those considered under "Frames of Reference": the biographical and historical allusions, psychological, religious, or philosophical ideas, and so on. Clearly, this distinction cannot always be hard and fast; for example, the setting of a novel may be an historical one. But the aim of critics who tend to stress the intrinsic qualities that any careful reader can observe is to focus attention on the work itself rather than its background, and to pass judgment on the essential nature of the work, not on the personality or intention of the writer, or the possible effect on the reader. This is the aim, in fact, of what John Crowe Ransom calls **ontological criticism,** referring to the philosophical term *ontology,* a study of the nature of being. Sometimes this kind of analysis seems to be meant, too, when people refer to the **New Criticism,** although that is a rather vague and uncertain phrase.

Such terms as *intrinsic* and *ontological* suggest the desire of many modern critics, then, to distinguish the literary object, the poem or novel itself, from other objects of attention: the world outside it which in some way it imitates or represents; the writer who produced it; and the reader who reacts to it. According to this view that emphasizes the quality of each piece of writing in itself, the truth or falsehood of its ideas is not essential, and there are no more or less good subjects for literature. There are no "poetic" subjects, for instance, as earlier critics insist when they point out that adventures of peasants are inappropriate for an epic and that vulgar and ugly things do not belong in lyric poetry. The more modern critics might well reply that they cannot separate the subject from the form of a work, because these words are only two ways of describing one reality. Certainly most critics now would reject Addison's argument that the description of Heaven in *Paradise Lost* is finer than that of Hell because the more beautiful subject is intrinsically better. Similarly, for these critics of the work itself, the life and the feelings of the poet, novelist, or playwright have at most a very limited relevance to criticism. And, for them, the impact of a work on various readers provides no index of its value. The insistence upon criticism that attends to the mode of being of a literary work, and not to its sources or effects, has led to a sharply reduced concern in our time for literary biography and literary history. It has led also to a method of studying poems as individual entities, even ignoring the names and periods of their authors.

In contrast to terms that point toward extrinsic values, toward something that exists outside the pages of a book—such words as *true, sincere,* and *moving*—are the terms of ontological criticism that describe desirable intrinsic qualities of literature: for example, *complex, coherent, tight.* Each of these words requires, however, some explanation.

Complexity, first of all, can be of several kinds. We have already seen how so-called "round characters" in fiction, those displaying complicated personalities so that not all their actions are predictable, seem ordinarily to be more interesting than the "flat characters" of allegory or farce comedy. Shakespeare's Hamlet, with his alternating moods of noble dedication and uncertainty, of tender feelings and fierce anger, is a character very much more complex than, say Dickens' consistently sweet and virtuous heroine of *Bleak House,* Esther Summerson. We must remember, however, that the interactions of complex and simplified figures can be a means of giving meaningful complication to the structure of the story, as it is in Melville's *Billy Budd.*

Another kind of complexity is provided by details of imagery and setting. In such details *Bleak House* is rich, for it contrasts minutely realized city slums with scenes of opulence, the grimmest aspects of English life with some of the brightest. Perhaps the best possible example of a great work that is rich in symbolic and local detail is the *Divine Comedy,* with its cosmic panorama that includes the lowest brutes of men and the greatest saints, the pettiest descriptions of gesture or speech and the ultimate glorious vision of a universal order.

More difficult to define, but perhaps more important, is complexity of tone. The expression of a mixed or qualified attitude, rather than simple approval, condemnation, or disinterest, utter delight or utter despair, has seemed to modern critics to mark the greatest literary works. This is to say in part that actions and characters are not presented morally as perfectly black and white. But the preference for a subtle complex tone implies as well that the best work recognizes how complicated human life is when we consider it fairly: it is hardly ever all good and beautiful or all bad and ugly. The literary tone that some readers find especially appealing, and one that may be subtly present in almost all very great literature, is irony. At least in one modern sense of that term, as we have seen, irony means a refusal of complete commitment to any simple view of experience, a sense instead that life is filled with contradictions and that all truths are partial, all values imperfect, to be qualified by other truths and values. The ironic tone, then, is that which most distinctly expresses a feeling of complexity in the subject. Even in the *Divine Comedy,* although it is a clear affirmation of faith, there are elements of such irony. The pilgrim who at last achieves a vision of the whole of creation is often bumbling and obtuse, and as he addresses questions and comments to Virgil, or later to Beatrice, we are aware of both his human dignity and his human foolishness. Not only is the poem filled with such complications, as when the gates of Hell proclaim that eternal punishment is ordained by eternal love; but a subtly ironic tone is also now and again evident in the very voice of the narrator, especially when he describes sinners like Paolo and Francesca or Brunetto Latini, sinners who are being punished in the Inferno but who are still in some way sympathetic, even impressive figures. When Brunetto Latini is described as running as if in a race, and seeming to be victorious, we know that his exertion is in fact the form of punishment assigned him; and yet the words suggest surprisingly not only the suffering of a man in hell but also the triumph of a highly talented man. The language and its rhythm help to produce this tone, along with the imagery.

A final kind of complexity, one that might be said to embrace the others, is that of theme. The greatness of Shakespeare's tragedies derives in part from their thematic fullness, so that no one statement of meaning can be adequate to them. *Hamlet* is about an obsession with injustice, the perversion of family relationships (wife and husband, brother and brother, mother and son), the social disorder that results from usurpation; and while all of these are related, each carries larger implications which are moral, psychological, and political. The *Divine Comedy,* of course, is designed to be read as embodying a number of themes— ethical, social, and religious—as they are worked out in the pilgrimage toward an ultimate vision of the good, the just, and the true. To take examples from a less great and more recent poet, Matthew Arnold has written verse that now seems meager because of its thematic simplicity, as well as richer symbolic poetry that suggests more complex meanings. The first kind is represented by a sonnet which begins, "In harmony with nature?" and argues that there are two distinct realms of existence, the human or moral, and the natural or physical, that must always be in contrast with each other. The richer kind of poem is exemplified by "The Forsaken Merman," a dramatic monologue spoken by the sea-creature as he stands on the shore looking landward, calling to the human bride who has deserted both him and their mermaid children, in order to rejoin her people at Easter time. This poem suggests again the theme of a contrast between the human and the natural order—the land with its towns and churches opposed to the sea with its freedom, its vivid forms and colors—but it does not do so simply and flatly. In fantasy, man and nature, or the human wife and the merman, have been temporarily joined, "in harmony." But, more than this, the poem implies other related themes: the bleakness of a purely dutiful life and the appeal of amoral spontaneity; the bitterness of love, the loneliness of those who love, in a world of uncertainty, of flux. Partly because it is not explicitly limited to spelling out a theme, "The Forsaken Merman" is very much richer in theme than the sonnet.

The criterion of **coherence** is sometimes mentioned along with that of complexity, for it is not only the complicated work but the complicated whole work that we recognize as valuable. Mere aimless complication cannot be considered a virtue. Dante's masterpiece is one of the world's great works of literature largely because it unifies such a richly detailed variety of people, places, experiences, and ideas in the allegorical structure of one man's journey from earth through hell and purgatory to the highest heaven, a journey that moves in spirals but always upon the axis of a single straight line. In fact, the term *complexity* as applied to the *Divine Comedy* or any other work might be taken always to imply some sort of coherence or unity. Otherwise, we would speak rather of confusion. The story that wholly lacks coherence because it deals with a variety of unrelated characters and events, or characters and events related to each other in only the most superficial way, will not be so much complex as full of incident. At best, such a work, joining episodes by some arbitrary device, will be a series of tales: this is the loose structure of certain movies, for example, like the one which represents the various effects on the lives of people chosen at random from a telephone directory to inherit large sums of money from an eccentric millionaire.

Nevertheless, the term may be useful to emphasize a point—as we may usefully distinguish between true complexity and meaningless pouring out of words and details, by referring to tightness or **economy**. This criterion applies both to the style of a writer, in which every word should be necessary to express the full meaning, and to the large structure of his work. Of bad lines in verse—

> O Beauty is, yes beauty is all truth, and all the truth
> That must be known on earth below is This and This alone—

we can often say that they are wordy: that phrases ("and this alone") and words ("below") are unnecessary. Not that repetition for effect is to be condemned; but the best writing avoids the ineffectual looseness of which these lines are guilty. Compare with them the original lines by Keats:

> Beauty is truth, truth beauty,—that is all
> Ye know on earth, and all ye need to know.

In larger details, too, a work can be marred by prolixity, as some of Dickens' novels are, and as the long epistolary novels of Samuel Richardson, in the eighteenth century, certainly are. Probably no modern reader of *Pamela* has not felt that the story was dragged out much too long for its importance.

Other Critical Terms

Complexity, coherence, and economy are not unusual or uniquely modern criteria for judging literature. But the list of terms can be lengthened, for recent critics have used a variety of special words to express value judgments. One of the most familiar of these is *tension,* a term we have already noted, and one that Robert Penn Warren explains and illustrates in his essay on "Pure and Impure Poetry." Another, perhaps more debatable as a valuative word, is *paradox;* Cleanth Brooks has insisted that all great literature is in some sense paradoxical, and he uses this word in a rather large and special sense as one of praise.

Both of these terms, and others, can be useful and fair if their meanings are clear and if they are carefully applied. **Tension** suggests the internal energy, the presence of contrasts and qualifications, that we associate with valuable art, in contradistinction to the monotonous simplicity of an inferior poem or tale. It is often associated, furthermore, with the **resolution** or balancing that gives a sense of finality or of wholeness to a work. The dramatic tension of such a Shakespearean tragedy as *Hamlet* is resolved in the deaths of all the leading characters, clearing the stage, as it were, for a new and harmonious order. Tension between a negative sense of the mortality and decay of the sick rose and a positive vision of its almost animate vitality and richness is held in balance by the simple unifying form of Blake's poem. **Paradox**, as Brooks employs it, means the expressing of a simultaneous sense of different, even opposing, ideas, facts, or qualities, that is implied at least by all great sustained pieces of literature. In this sense. it is paradoxical that Achilles in the *Iliad* should be recognized as being at once a nearly godlike leader of men and a foolish spoiled child; if he were only one thing or the other, the epic would lose its meaning and its greatness.

These terms and others can easily become jargon, impressive sounding but without a very definite special meaning to justify them in place of more familiar words. It is often clearer to speak of contrast rather than tension, of complicated characters and language rather than paradox, or of various implications in a story rather than "levels of meaning," to use another recently fashionable phrase. Nevertheless, all such parts of the critic's vocabulary pose, as they should, the question of judgment, and they imply answers to the question. Perhaps the most extreme of those critics whom Ransom would call ontological—those writers sometimes grouped as the New Critics—have exaggerated their claims for the poem or novel as an independent structure, too often ignoring the importance of history and of literary history to the words in a work and to its tone. But the tendency of the so-called New Criticism has been, at least, to direct attention to the problem of evaluation, the ultimate critical problem. As a result, historical, biographical, and sociological treatments of literature today are much less likely to substitute the judgment of a time, a man, or a society for the judgment of literature. Furthermore, with the increased interest in theories of value that has resulted from the work of such diverse critical writers as I. A. Richards, T. S. Eliot, Ransom, Brooks, R. P. Warren, Tate, René Wellek, and Austin Warren, the educated reader today is not likely to be satisfied with a simply casual impression of the nature and value of literary works. He will wish to examine the grounds of his judgment.

Any abstract terms can, of course, be vaguely used or misused; the reader who expresses his approval of a poem by saying merely that it is filled with tension and paradox, or that it displays complexity, economy, and coherence, may be making a hardly more firm, explicit judgment than the reader who praises the same poem by saying that it gave him intense pleasure. The end of critical reading is conscious judgment, and these and other words that apply to the structure of a work are meaningfully used only if they sum up specific unique qualities of which the reader is conscious. There are, furthermore, no special universally recognized critical phrases for evaluating intrinsic qualities. We might speak of variety or richness instead of complexity, of unity or wholeness instead of coherence. Still, some terms have to be used, and so we may as well exemplify the method of judging literature according to its intrinsic characteristics by appealing again to such evaluative words as *complex, coherent,* and *economical.*

Evaluation of Two Poems

To illustrate this method, we can consider two poems, both dealing with love and both using the traditional image of the rose as the symbol of fleeting youth, beauty, and love. The first is Robert Herrick's "To the Virgins, to Make Much of Time."

Gather ye rosebuds while ye may,
  Old Time is still a-flying:
And this same flower that smiles to-day
  To-morrow will be dying.

The glorious lamp of heaven, the sun,
  The higher he's a-getting,
The sooner will his race be run,
  And nearer he's to setting.

That age is best which is the first,
  When youth and blood are warmer;
But being spent, the worse, and worst
  Times still succeed the former.

Then be not coy, but use your time,
  And while ye may, go marry:
For having lost but once your prime,
  Ye may for ever tarry.

These lines may appear simple enough. The imagery of rosebuds and the lamp of heaven, along with the theme of *carpe diem,* "seize the day," are perfectly conventional. And yet in using these images and this theme, Herrick displays art and produces something more than a repetition of an old idea. The metrical scheme of the poem is extremely light and lyrical, with the movement of song or dance. The normally iambic tetrameter and iambic trimeter lines succeed each other, the short lines providing further variety by the addition of a final unaccented syllable that results in a feminine ending. Along with this easy and gay-sounding rhythm goes the light and almost flippant diction: "Old Time" describes the conventional personification of time, but it also has a hearty and familiar sound, as when one speaks of "old So-and-so"; and terms like *a-flying* and *a-getting* sound less than perfectly formal (whereas Herrick could have written, "Old Time is ever flying" and "The higher he is getting"). This is a lively song, then, about the subject of dying, an almost gaily spoken sermon in lyric form on the profoundly serious subjects of youth and age, love and death. In other words, the manner contrasts with the matter so that these lines have a half-mocking, half-serious effect.

In small details, too, the poet's complicating art is evident: "The worse, and worst/ Times" seems to repeat but actually varies a sound, to contrast the present with the future; and the following of *to-day* at the end of one line by *to-morrow* at the beginning of the next is another artful device for emphasis. Not only the tone and these details, furthermore, but the logical and grammatical structures of the lyric give evidence of complication within an order. The first and last stanzas are primarily in the imperative voice—"Gather ye rosebuds," "be not coy"—while the sentences that compose the two central stanzas are statements illustrating the point of these commands. The first illustration, however, is that of the ephemeral flower, in the first stanza, and the others are variations on a theme: the sun rises only to sink, creatures grow only to lose their youth and warmth, and all is *dying, setting.*

We might even argue that all of these artful devices and complexities find their culmination, and that the tone is at last summed up, in a paradoxical ending. The moral of the poem appears until the end to be simply that no one stays young or lives forever; but the speaker's conclusion is that if you fail to enjoy youth, you may tarry, wait, "for ever." Here the meaning is not that you may wait literally forever, but all your life, without fulfillment. The fact that man can seize life only as he gradually dies is the lesson which the virgins have to learn from roses and sun: the fact that they can use, can enjoy their time instead of waiting life out passively. Like the bud that smiles, the sun that runs his race, and the warmth that spends itself, they should act, smile, run, and spend their lives, not waste them: they should marry. To be living, then, is to be dying—this is the paradox—but it is better to die in a lively way than to languish and neither live nor die with much intensity.

Commenting on all these complexities, on the contrast between subject and manner, the variety of poetic devices, and the complicated, even paradoxical ending, we imply also the coherence of this poem, with its unified tone, at once deftly light and serious. Virtually every detail in these lines, of both imagery and diction, is directly relevant to the subject of passing time that robs life of spent or unspent beauty and vigor: the rosebud and the sun are thus related; and nouns and adverbs that refer to time recur insistently. All the emphatic rhyme words in the short lines of the first two stanzas are in the progressive form that embodies knowledge of temporal process—*flying, dying, getting, setting.* Even within stanzas there are special echoing arrangements of words. In the second stanza each of the series of comparatives comes as the second word, and the third and fourth syllable, in a series of three lines: *higher, sooner, nearer.* In the third stanza these are replaced by superlatives: the *best* is *first;* then the earlier series is recalled in the comparatives *warmer* and *worse,* with the climax coming in the *worst.* Finally, the last word of the poem, *tarry,* if our interpretation is accurate, bears a negative importance (do not tarry, the speaker says, but spend your life or it will be spent); and it is related to all the other words, the verbs of movement and change, the adverbs of temporal qualification, and the comparative adjectives, that carry the theme of time.

The lyric embodies complexity, then, and coherence—and, in its brisk rapid movement, an unmistakable economy in words, phrases, and images. This somewhat elaborate analysis suggests clearly enough a judgment of Herrick's short poem as having some value. Not that it is a perfect poem. If its imagery, for instance, were more vivid and particular, it might be a richer lyric still.

The second poem is Thomas Hood's "Time of Roses."

> It was not in the Winter
> Our loving lot was cast;
> It was the time of roses—
> We pluck'd them as we pass'd!
>
> That churlish season never frown'd
> On early lovers yet:
> O no—the world was newly crown'd
> With flowers when first we met!
>
> 'Twas twilight, and I bade you go,
> But still you held me fast;
> It was the time of roses—
> We pluck'd them as we pass'd!

At first reading one could suppose that this is a subtler poem than Herrick's. Whereas Herrick explains his metaphors and makes flat statements—roses die, the lamp of heaven is the sun, youth is better than age—Hood implies metaphorical significance. The time of roses is youth, of course, and plucking roses means experiencing the joys of youth, but the point is nowhere explicitly made. On the other hand, the meaning is plain enough so that there is hardly a difference of difficulty involved; and, indeed, it might be argued that if roses and the winter are to be given such a familiar meaning without their becoming literal and particular, the meaning can better be stated flatly in the manner of a partly ironic sermon than implied in a quite obvious way. One can take the curse off a cliché by using it half-flippantly rather than sincerely. Or, to put it another way, the flower in Blake's "The Sick Rose" is more than a stereotype because it is related to a worm and is described as having curious qualities; the flowers in Herrick's verse do not invite a stock response because they are spoken of in a rather odd and airy voice; but Hood's roses are simply conventional and seem to ask for a simple conventional reaction.

If we look for artful complications in this second lyric, we notice that the original reference to winter is echoed in the first part of the second stanza, but without a sense of contrast, and that the last line of the first stanza is repeated as the last line of the poem, but with no variation and in fact with no apparent enlarging or changing of its significance provided by the lines that intervene. More to the point, however, than these repetitions that offer little complexity, is the rhetorical use of negatives: "It was not in the Winter" but in "the time of roses." The implication justifying this otherwise gratuitous device may be that as the lover speaks, it *is* winter, not the time of roses: that he is now aging but still recalls the transient joys of youth.

As for the diction and rhythm of these lines, they are apparently more of a single quality than Herrick's are. There is, for instance, no use here of the feminine endings (*dying, setting*) that are often associated with light verse; and the consequent difference in the movements of the short lines in these two poems is considerable. "Ye may for ever tarry" sounds unlike "Ye may for ever stay," and "We pluck'd them as we pass'd" unlike "We pluck'd them as we journeyed." Hood's lines, then, seem to lack the slight variation of rhythm that Herrick's have.

Finally, if we ask about both the logical development of the whole, or the nature of its coherence, and the economy of it, we have to observe not only that the second stanza adds little to the sense of the first, but also that the necessity of certain words and phrases—such as "O no"— can be questioned. The third stanza, to be sure, provides the image of twilight, which may perhaps be related to that of winter by its suggestion of time passing away; and a final contrast between the lover's need to go and desire to stay. These are appropriate details, certainly, in a poem recalling past experience and, probably, dead love. But one cannot find a very striking climax or culmination in these lines, even though they are for the most part quite coherent. The means of coherence is rather plain and easy; the end of this lyric is, precisely, a repetition and not a turn that complicates the sense of the whole.

Such comments indicate that Hood's poem reads as a simpler work than Herrick's. The difference can perhaps be summed up finally as one of tone. An opposition between the rather light and lively style and the serious or even morbid subject, suggesting that the joy of living is intensified by the knowledge of dying, produces Herrick's very slightly ironic tone as he addresses the virgins. In Hood's work, however, the tone is simpler, as the idea involves a less mixed view of experience. Not that it can be described as absolutely simple: the very use of roses and the phrase "We pluck'd them as we pass'd" imply a bittersweet memory of love and youth. But this sense is not much developed, nor does the lyric voice give any suggestion of a feeling more complicated than nostalgia. On the grounds of intrinsic complexity, tightness, and wholeness, then, we should probably place the poem by Herrick higher than that by Hood.

The more complex of these two lyrics is not one of the very greatest works of literature, and the simpler is not a hopelessly incompetent piece of doggerel. Critical judgments like the ones we have just attempted, based upon analysis of structure, are likely to be relative in the sense that they describe a work as better or worse rather than as absolutely good or absolutely bad. We have also to recognize the importance of scope in making comparisons; distinguishing between good and great literature, we observe that almost no lyric can have the richness of an epic, and so we will not compare Herrick's good poem with Milton's great *Paradise Lost*. Obviously, judgments are much more difficult when the works contrasted are vastly different in kind and subject, unlike our two superficially similar short poems. How are we to compare, even, such a cryptic story as Kafka's "Metamorphosis," describing the transformation of a man into a giant cockroach, with such a literal tale as Sherwood Anderson's autobiographical "Death in the Woods," dealing with the death of an old woman on her way home from shopping? It quickly becomes evident that the judgment of complexity and coherence demands the appreciation of many different sorts of inner complication and many possible modes of achieving wholeness.

The Act of Judgment: A Last Word

Yet another problem that our exercise has not posed is one already raised by considering another criterion. Suppose that a more complex and economical lyric, play, or novel distorts literal and psychological reality and insists on trivial, false, or evil ideas: is it nevertheless a better piece of art than the truer and more humanly admirable work?

At this point we may have to admit that in certain instances the criterion of intrinsic quality of structure has to be combined with the criterion of general truth or validity. However it imitates or represents human experience, a literary work can be expected not to distort and thus to misrepresent reality. If, for instance, a story that clearly sets out to be, and mostly is, realistic, glamorizes and thus falsifies the life a group of college students live, in the manner of motion pictures about college days, we can criticize its falsity. A more difficult example would be that of the novel that plainly glorifies totalitarian ideas, justifying an exploitation of people in the interests of one class, race, or group that is represented as being consistently superior. Very often—indeed, almost always—such works would be judged harshly on more formal grounds in any case, for they are likely to be oversimple in structure, bland or sentimental in tone. But it may be, too, that we shall have to keep in mind this negative qualification to even the most rigorously "intrinsic" mode of criticism: that inconsistency with our experience of the world as it is and with men as they are cannot be redeemed by purely internal artistic consistency. Not, of course, that extremely unreal or distorted versions of life are to be condemned, for literature deals in psychological and symbolic truths as well as literal truth. But there would seem to be occasions when a reader can fairly say of a work that it is, taken on its own terms, false.

Criticism, finally, like literature itself, tends always to be impure. When we read and judge, we cannot wholly escape from our prejudices, our limitations of understanding and taste. Just as a literary work refers to topical and ephemeral things, so the reading of it involves knowledge, assumptions, and experiences of the reader that may be partly but only partly relevant. Nevertheless, as an ideal, we can accept the proposition —at least, most critics do in our own time—that once a piece of writing is recognized as having enough validity and enough art to make it worth our attention, it can best be examined and evaluated on its own merits as a whole and complex verbal structure. The more aware we are of what the work involves, the more experience we have of reading, the clearer our sense of the structure should be. The pleasure of understanding and of judging with awareness belongs, then, to the critical reader.

An Anthology of Critical Essays

This anthology of essays is planned not as an historical sampling, nor as a collection of the world's best criticism. All of the critics represented here are modern, and their essays have been chosen to illustrate the methods and interests already discussed in the text.

The essays have been grouped by sections parallel with those in the first part of this book. There are, however, no sections in the anthology corresponding to Chapter One, on definition, or to Chapter Three, on genres and conventions. Essays on the definition of literature are for the most part too long for inclusion here. But we recommend that the reader become acquainted with Suzanne Langer's work on esthetics, especially *Feeling and Form;* M. H. Abrams' study of literary theory, *The Mirror and the Lamp,* more particularly the first chapter of that book; and above all, the most useful and most influential statement of literary theory, the *Poetics* of Aristotle. As for genres and conventions, the chapter on that subject in our text goes into detailed analysis, so that further examples— which are in any case not easily abstracted from larger works of criticism —do not seem necessary here.

Even though they are intended to be illustrative rather than completely representative, these essays should indicate the wide variety of theories and methods in present-day critical writing—writing of which, we hope, the reader may want to have some further experience.

Structure and Context

E. M. FORSTER

People

We now turn from transplantation to acclimatization. We have discussed whether people could be taken out of life and put into a book, and conversely whether they could come out of books and sit down in this room. The answer suggested was in the negative and led to a more vital question: can we, in daily life, understand each other? Today our problems are more academic. We are concerned with the characters in their relation to other aspects of the novel; to a plot, a moral, their fellow characters, atmosphere, etc. They will have to adapt themselves to other requirements of their creator.

It follows that we shall no longer expect them to coincide as a whole with daily life, only to parallel it. When we say that a character in Jane Austen, Miss Bates for instance, is "so like life" we mean that each bit of her coincides with a bit of life, but that she as a whole only parallels the chatty spinster we met at tea. Miss Bates is bound by a hundred threads to Highbury. We cannot tear her away without bringing her mother too, and Jane Fairfax and Frank Churchill, and the whole of Box Hill; whereas we could tear Moll Flanders away, at least for the purposes of experiment. A Jane Austen novel is more complicated than a Defoe, because the characters are inter-dependent, and there is the additional complication of a plot. The plot in *Emma* is not prominent and Miss Bates contributes little. Still it is there, she is connected with the principals, and the result is a closely woven fabric from which nothing can be removed. Miss Bates and Emma herself are like bushes in a shrubbery—not isolated trees like Moll—and any one who has tried to thin out a shrubbery knows how wretched the bushes look if they are transplanted elsewhere, and how wretched is the look of the bushes that remain. In most books the characters cannot spread themselves. They must exercise a mutual restraint.

The novelist, we are beginning to see, has a very mixed lot of ingredients to handle. There is the story, with its time-sequence of "and then . . . and then . . ."; there are ninepins about whom he might tell the story, and tell a rattling good one, but no, he prefers to tell his story about human beings; he takes over the life by values as well as the life in time. The characters arrive when evoked, but full of the spirit of mutiny. For they have these numerous parallels with people like ourselves, they try to live their own lives and are consequently often engaged in treason against the main scheme of the book. They "run away," they "get out of hand": they are creations inside a creation, and often inharmonious towards it; if they are given complete freedom they kick the book to pieces, and if they are kept too sternly in check, they revenge themselves by dying, and destroy it by intestinal decay.

These trials beset the dramatist also, and he has yet another set of ingredients to cope with—the actors and actresses—and they appear to side sometimes with the characters they represent, sometimes with the play as a whole, and more often to be the mortal enemies of both. The weight they throw is incalculable, and how any work of art survives their arrival I do not understand. Concerned with a lower form of art, we need not worry—but, in passing, is it not extraordinary that plays on the stage are often better than they are in the study, and that the introduction of a bunch of rather ambitious and nervous men and women should add anything to our understanding of Shakespeare and Tchekov?

No, the novelist has difficulties enough, and today we shall examine two of his devices for solving them—instinctive devices, for his methods when working are seldom the same as the methods we use when examining his work. The first device is the use of different kinds of characters. The second is connected with the point of view.

1. We may divide characters into flat and round.

Flat characters were called "humours" in the seventeenth century, and are sometimes called types, and sometimes caricatures. In their purest form, they are constructed round a single idea or quality: when there is more than one factor in them, we get the beginning of the curve towards the round. The really flat character can be expressed in one sentence such as "I never will desert Mr. Micawber." There is Mrs. Micawber—she says she won't desert Mr. Micawber, she doesn't, and there she is. Or: "I must conceal, even by subterfuges, the poverty of my master's house." There is Caleb Balderstone in *The Bride of Lammer-moor*. He does not use the actual phrase, but it completely describes him; he has no existence outside it, no pleasures, none of the private lusts and aches that must complicate the most consistent of servitors. Whatever he does, wherever he goes, whatever lies he tells or plates he breaks, it is to conceal the poverty of his master's house. It is not his idée fixe, because there is nothing in him into which the idea can be fixed. He is the idea, and such life as he possesses radiates from its edges and from the scintillations it strikes when other elements in the novel impinge. Or take Proust. There are numerous flat characters in Proust, such as the Princess of Parma, or Legrandin. Each can be expressed in a single sentence, the Princess's sentence being, "I must be particularly careful to be kind." She does nothing except to be particularly careful, and those of the other characters who are more complex than herself easily see through the kindness, since it is only a by-product of the carefulness.

One great advantage of flat characters is that they are easily recognized whenever they come in—recognized by the reader's emotional eye, not by the visual eye, which merely notes the recurrence of a proper name. In Russian novels, where they so seldom occur, they would be a decided help. It is a convenience for an author when he can strike with his full force at once, and flat characters are very useful to him, since they never need reintroducing, never run away, have not to be watched for development, and provide their own atmosphere—little luminous disks of a pre-arranged size, pushed hither and thither like counters across the void or between the stars; most satisfactory.

A second advantage is that they are easily remembered by the reader afterwards. They remain in his mind as unalterable for the reason that they were not changed by circumstances; they moved through circumstances, which gives them in retrospect a comforting quality, and preserves them when the book that produced them may decay. The Countess in *Evan Harrington* furnishes a good little example here. Let us compare our memories of her with our memories of Becky Sharp. We do not remember what the Countess did or what she passed through. What is clear is her figure and the formula that surrounds it, namely, "Proud as we are of dear papa, we must conceal his memory." All her rich humour proceeds from this. She is a flat character. Becky is round. She, too, is on the make, but she cannot be summed up in a single phrase, and we remember her in connection with the great scenes through which she passed and as modified by those scenes—that is to say, we do not remember her so easily because she waxes and wanes and has facets like a human being. All of us, even the sophisticated, yearn for permanence, and to the unsophisticated permanence is the chief excuse for a work of art. We all want books to endure, to be refuges, and their inhabitants to be always the same, and flat characters tend to justify themselves on this account.

All the same, critics who have their eyes fixed severely upon daily life—as were our eyes last week—have very little patience with such renderings of human nature. Queen Victoria, they argue, cannot be summed up in a single sentence, so what excuse remains for Mrs. Micawber? One of our foremost writers, Mr. Norman Douglas, is a critic of this type, and the passage from him which I will quote puts the case against flat characters in a forcible fashion. The passage occurs in an open letter to D. H. Lawrence, with whom he is quarrelling: a doughty pair of combatants, the hardness of whose hitting makes the rest of us feel like a lot of ladies up in a pavilion. He complains that Lawrence, in a biography, has falsified the picture by employing "the novelist's touch," and he goes on to define what this is:

> It consists, I should say, in a failure to realize the complexities of the ordinary human mind; it selects for literary purposes two or three facets of a man or woman, generally the most spectacular, and therefore useful ingredients of their character and disregards all the others. Whatever fails to fit in with these specially chosen traits is eliminated—must be eliminated, for otherwise the description would not hold water. Such and such are the data: everything incompatible with those data has to go by the board. It follows that the novelist's touch argues, often logically, from a wrong premise: it takes what it likes and leaves the rest. The facts may be correct as far as they go but there are too few of them: what the author says may be true and yet by no means the truth. That is the novelist's touch. It falsifies life.

Well, the novelist's touch as thus defined is, of course, bad in biography, for no human being is simple. But in a novel it has its place: a novel that is at all complex often requires flat people as well as round, and the outcome of their collisions parallels life more accurately than Mr. Douglas implies. The case of Dickens is significant. Dickens' people are nearly all flat (Pip and David Copperfield attempt roundness, but so diffidently that they seem more like bubbles than solids). Nearly every one can be summed up in a sentence, and yet there is this wonderful feeling of human depth. Probably the immense vitality of Dickens causes his characters to vibrate a little, so that they borrow his life and appear to lead one of their own. It is a conjuring trick; at any moment we may look at Mr. Pickwick edgeways and find him no thicker than a gramophone record. But we never get the sideway view. Mr. Pickwick is far too adroit and well trained. He always has the air of weighing something, and when he is put into the cupboard of the young ladies' school he seems as heavy as Falstaff in the buck-basket at Windsor. Part of the genius of Dickens is that he does use types and caricatures, people whom we recognize the instant they re-enter, and yet achieves effects that are not mechanical and a vision of humanity that is not shallow. Those who dislike Dickens have an excellent case. He ought to be bad. He is actually one of our big writers, and his immense success with types suggests that there may be more in flatness than the severer critics admit.

Or take H. G. Wells. With the possible exceptions of Kipps and the aunt in *Tono Bungay,* all Wells' characters are as flat as a photograph. But the photographs are agitated with such vigour that we forget their complexities lie on the surface and would disappear if it was scratched or curled up. A Wells character cannot indeed be summed up in a single phrase; he is tethered much more to observation, he does not create types. Nevertheless his people seldom pulsate by their own strength. It is the deft and powerful hands of their maker that shake them and trick the reader into a sense of depth. Good but imperfect novelists, like Wells and Dickens, are very clever at transmitting force. The part of their novel that is alive galvanizes the part that is not, and causes the characters to jump about and speak in a convincing way. They are quite different from the perfect novelist who touches all his material directly, who seems to pass the creative finger down every sentence and into every word. Richardson, Defoe, Jane Austen, are perfect in this particular way; their work may not be great but their hands are always upon it; there is not the tiny interval between the touching of the button and the sound of the bell which occurs in novels where the characters are not under direct control.

For we must admit that flat people are not in themselves as big achievements as round ones, and also that they are best when they are comic. A serious or tragic flat character is apt to be a bore. Each time he enters crying "Revenge!" or "My heart bleeds for humanity!" or whatever his formula is, our hearts sink. One of the romances of a popular contemporary writer is constructed round a Sussex farmer who says, "I'll plough up that bit of gorse." There is the farmer, there is the gorse; he says he'll plough it up, he does plough it up, but it is not like saying "I'll never desert Mr. Micawber," because we are so bored by his consistency that we do not care whether he succeeds with the gorse or fails. If his formula was analysed and connected up with the rest of the human outfit, we should not be bored any longer, the formula would cease to be the man and become an obsession in the man; that is to say he would have turned from a flat farmer into a round one. It is only round people who are fit to perform tragically for any length of time and can move us to any feelings except humour and appropriateness.

So now let us desert these two-dimensional people, and by way of transition to the round, let us go to *Mansfield Park,* and look at Lady

Bertram, sitting on her sofa with pug. Pug is flat, like most animals in fiction. He is once represented as straying into a rose-bed in a cardboard kind of way, but that is all, and during most of the book his mistress seems to be cut out of the same simple material as her dog. Lady Bertram's formula is, "I am kindly, but must not be fatigued," and she functions out of it. But at the end there is a catastrophe. Her two daughters come to grief—to the worst grief known to Miss Austen's universe, far worse than the Napoleonic wars. Julia elopes; Maria, who is unhappily married, runs off with a lover. What is Lady Bertram's reaction? The sentence describing it is significant: "Lady Bertram did not think deeply, but, guided by Sir Thomas, she thought justly on all important points, and she saw therefore in all its enormity, what had happened, and neither endeavoured herself, nor required Fanny to advise her, to think little of guilt and infamy." These are strong words, and they used to worry me because I thought Jane Austen's moral sense was getting out of hand. She may, and of course does, deprecate guilt and infamy herself, and she duly causes all possible distress in the minds of Edmund and Fanny, but has she any right to agitate calm, consistent Lady Bertram? Is not it like giving pug three faces and setting him to guard the gates of Hell? Ought not her ladyship to remain on the sofa saying, "This is a dreadful and sadly exhausting business about Julia and Maria, but where is Fanny gone? I have dropped another stitch"?

I used to think this, through misunderstanding Jane Austen's method—exactly as Scott misunderstood it when he congratulated her for painting on a square of ivory. She is a miniaturist, but never two-dimensional. All her characters are round, or capable of rotundity. Even Miss Bates has a mind, even Elizabeth Eliot a heart, and Lady Bertram's moral fervour ceases to vex us when we realize this: the disk has suddenly extended and become a little globe. When the novel is closed, Lady Bertram goes back to the flat, it is true; the dominant impression she leaves can be summed up in a formula. But that is not how Jane Austen conceived her, and the freshness of her reappearances are due to this. Why do the characters in Jane Austen give us a slightly new pleasure each time they come in, as opposed to the merely repetitive pleasure that is caused by a character in Dickens? Why do they combine so well in a conversation, and draw one another out without seeming to do so, and never perform? The answer to this question can be put in several ways: that, unlike Dickens, she was a real artist, that she never stooped to caricature, etc. But the best reply is that her characters though smaller than his are more highly organized. They function all round, and even if her plot made greater demands on them than it does, they would still be adequate. Suppose that Louisa Musgrove had broken her neck on the Cobb. The description of her death would have been feeble and ladylike—physical violence is quite beyond Miss Austen's powers—but the survivors would have reacted properly as soon as the corpse was carried away, they would have brought into view new sides of their character, and though *Persuasion* would have been spoiled as a book, we should know more than we do about Captain Wentworth and Anne. All the Jane Austen characters are ready for an extended life, for a life which the scheme of her books seldom requires them to lead, and that is why they lead their actual lives so satisfactorily. Let us return to Lady Bertram and the crucial sentence. See how subtly it modulates from her formula into an area where the formula does not work. "Lady Bertram did not think deeply." Exactly: as per formula. "But guided by Sir Thomas she thought justly on all important points." Sir Thomas' guidance, which is part of the formula, remains, but it pushes her ladyship towards an independent and undesired morality. "She saw therefore in all its enormity what had happened." This is the moral fortissimo—very strong but carefully introduced. And then follows a most artful decrescendo, by means of negatives. "She neither endeavoured herself, nor required Fanny to advise her, to think little of guilt or infamy." The formula is reappearing, because as a rule she does try to minimize trouble, and does require Fanny to advise her how to do this; indeed Fanny has done nothing else for the last ten years. The words, though they are negatived, remind us of this, her normal state is again in view, and she has in a single sentence been inflated into a round character and collapsed back into a flat one. How Jane Austen can write! In a few words she has extended Lady Bertram, and by so doing she has increased the probability of the elopements of Maria and Julia. I say probability because the elopements belong to the domain of violent physical action, and here, as already indicated, Jane Austen is feeble and ladylike. Except in her school-girl novels, she cannot stage a crash. Everything violent has to take place "off"—Louisa's accident and Marianne Dashwood's putrid throat are the nearest exceptions—and consequently all the comments on the elopement must be sincere and convincing, otherwise we should doubt whether it occurred. Lady Bertram helps us to believe that her daughters have run away, and they have to run away, or there would be no apotheosis for Fanny. It is a little point, and a little sentence, yet it shows us how delicately a great novelist can modulate into the round.

All through her works we find these characters, apparently so simple and flat, never needing reintroduction and yet never out of their depth—Henry Tilney, Mr. Woodhouse, Charlotte Lucas. She may label her characters "Sense," "Pride," "Sensibility," "Prejudice," but they are not tethered to those qualities.

As for the round characters proper, they have already been defined by implication and no more need be said. All I need do is to give some examples of people in books who seem to me round so that the definition can be tested afterwards:

All the principal characters in *War and Peace,* all the Dostoevsky characters, and some of the Proust—for example, the old family servant, the Duchess of Guermantes, M. de Charlus, and Saint Loup; Madame Bovary—who, like Moll Flanders, has her book to herself, and can expand and secrete unchecked; some people in Thackeray—for instance, Becky and Beatrix; some in Fielding—Parson Adams, Tom Jones; and some in Charlotte Brontë, most particularly Lucy Snowe. (And many more—this is not a catalogue.) The test of a round character is whether it is capable of surprising in a convincing way. If it never surprises, it is flat. If it does not convince, it is a flat pretending to be round. It has the incalculability of life about it—life within the pages of a book. And by using it sometimes alone, more often in combination with the other kind, the novelist achieves his task of acclimatization and harmonizes the human race with the other aspects of his work.

II.   Now for the second device: the point of view from which the story may be told.

To some critics this is the fundamental device of novel-writing. "The whole intricate question of method, in the craft of fiction," says Mr. Percy Lubbock, "I take to be governed by the question of the *point of view*—the question of the relation in which the narrator stands to the story." And his book *The Craft of Fiction* examines various points of view with genius and insight. The novelist, he says, can either describe the characters from outside, as an impartial or partial onlooker; or he can assume omniscience and describe them from within; or he can place himself in the position of one of them and affect to be in the dark as to the motives of the rest; or there are certain intermediate attitudes.

Those who follow him will lay a sure foundation for the aesthetics of fiction—a foundation which I cannot for a moment promise. This is a ramshackly survey and for me the "whole intricate question of method" resolves itself not into formulae but into the power of the writer to bounce the reader into accepting what he says—a power which Mr. Lubbock admits and admires, but locates at the edge of the problem instead of at the centre. I should put it plumb in the centre. Look how Dickens bounces us in *Bleak House.* Chapter I of *Bleak House* is omniscient. Dickens takes us into the Court of Chancery and rapidly explains all the people there. In Chapter II he is partially omniscient. We still use his eyes, but for some unexplained reason they begin to grow weak: he can explain Sir Leicester Dedlock to us, part of Lady Dedlock but not all, and nothing of Mr. Tulkinghorn. In Chapter III he is even more reprehensible: he goes straight across into the dramatic method and inhabits a young lady, Esther Summerson. "I have a great deal of difficulty in beginning to write my portion of these pages, for I know I am not clever," pipes up Esther, and continues in this strain with consistency and competence, so long as she is allowed to hold the pen. At any moment the author of her being may snatch it from her, and run about taking notes himself, leaving her seated goodness knows where, and employed we do not care how. Logically, *Bleak House* is all to pieces, but Dickens bounces us, so that we do not mind the shiftings of the view point.

Critics are more apt to object than readers. Zealous for the novel's eminence, they are a little too apt to look out for problems that shall be peculiar to it, and differentiate it from the drama; they feel it ought to have its own technical troubles before it can be accepted as an independent art; and since the problem of a point of view certainly is peculiar to the novel they have rather over-stressed it. I do not myself think it is so important as a proper mixture of characters—a problem which the dramatist is up against also. And the novelist must bounce us; that is imperative.

Let us glance at two other examples of a shifting view point.

The eminent French writer, André Gide, has published a novel called *Les Faux Monnayeurs*[1]—for all its modernity, this novel of Gide's has one aspect in common with *Bleak House:* it is all to pieces logically. Sometimes the author is omniscient: he explains everything, he stands back, "il juge ses personnages"; at other times his omniscience is partial; yet again he is dramatic, and causes the story to be told through the diary of one of the characters. There is the same absence of view point, but whereas in Dickens it was instinctive, in Gide it is sophisticated; he expatiates too much about the jolts. The novelist who betrays too much interest in his own method can never be more than interesting; he has given up the creation of character and summoned us to help analyse his own mind, and a heavy drop in the emotional thermometer results. *Les Faux Monnayeurs* is among the more interesting of recent works: not among the vital: and greatly as we shall have to admire it as a fabric we cannot praise it unrestrictedly now.

For our second example we must again glance at *War and Peace*. Here the result is vital: we are bounced up and down Russia—omniscient, semi-omniscient, dramatized here or there as the moment dictates—and at the end we have accepted it all. Mr. Lubbock does not, it is true: great as he finds the book, he would find it greater if it had a view point; he feels Tolstoy has not pulled his full weight. I feel that the rules of the game of writing are not like this. A novelist can shift

[1] Translated by Dorothy Bussy as *The Counterfeiters* (Knopf).

his view point if it comes off, and it came off with Dickens and Tolstoy. Indeed this power to expand and contract perception (of which the shifting view point is a symptom), this right to intermittent knowledge: — I find it one of the great advantages of the novel-form, and it has a parallel in our perception of life. We are stupider at some times than others; we can enter into people's minds occasionally but not always, because our own minds get tired; and this intermittence lends in the long run variety and colour to the experiences we receive. A quantity of novelists, English novelists especially, have behaved like this to the people in their books: played fast and loose with them, and I cannot see why they should be censured.

They must be censured if we catch them at it at the time. That is quite true, and out of it arises another question: may the writer take the reader into his confidence about his characters? Answer has already been indicated: better not. It is dangerous, it generally leads to a drop in the temperature, to intellectual and emotional laxity, and worse still to facetiousness, and to a friendly invitation to see how the figures hook up behind. "Doesn't A look nice—she always was my favourite." "Let's think of why B does that—perhaps there's more in him than meets the eye—yes, see—he has a heart of gold—having given you this peep at it I'll pop it back—I don't think he's noticed." "And C—he always was the mystery man." Intimacy is gained but at the expense of illusion and nobility. It is like standing a man a drink so that he may not criticize your opinions. With all respect to Fielding and Thackeray it is devastating, it is bar-parlour chattiness, and nothing has been more harmful to the novels of the past. To take your reader into your confidence about the universe is a different thing. It is not dangerous for a novelist to draw back from his characters, as Hardy and Conrad do, and to generalize about the conditions under which he thinks life is carried on. It is confidences about the individual people that do harm, and beckon the reader away from the people to an examination of the novelist's mind. Not much is ever found in it at such a moment, for it is never in the creative state: the mere process of saying, "Come along, let's have a chat," has cooled it down.

Our comments on human beings must now come to an end. They may take fuller shape when we come to discuss the plot.

NEWTON ARVIN

Counterfeit Presentments

Everyone knows—we owe the knowledge to a hundred travelers and anthropologists—how intensely the "primitive man" feels on the subject of having his portrait painted or his picture taken—and how alarmingly he sometimes acts. Is it possible that such feelings survive in our civilized psyche in some unconfessed and deeply buried guise? The history of western portrait-painting since the early Renaissance would hardly suggest such a thought, and just as little would the prosperous history of the portrait photographer since the days of Daguerre and Draper. Sir James Frazer tells us that the Tepehuanes of Mexico were once panic-stricken by the prospect of having a camera turned on them, and that, when at last they agreed to pose, it was with the conviction that death or some other great evil would follow. And indeed he alleges that even in western Scotland, in the nineteenth century, there were persons who refused to have their likenesses taken in the fear that such pictures might ruin their luck or their health. Is the distance between ourselves—contemporaries of Steichen and Weston—and the Tepehuanes or the western Scots so great as we commonly imagine?

Perhaps it is, but if so it is not because we are not, in our own manner, obsessed with the idea of the portrait. The almost mysterious formulas which prescribe, in any given age, the recurrence of favorite words or images in titles, betray this fact. Everyone, surely, has observed how often the very word "portrait" or some word like it has echoed and re-echoed through the titles of our recent literature. To go, for the moment, no further backward, it has been a favorite ever since, in the early eighties, Henry James published *The Portrait of a Lady.* Walter Pater was close on James's heels, in 1887, with *Imaginary Portraits,* and then very quickly came Oscar Wilde with *The Portrait of Mr. W. H.* and of course *The Picture of Dorian Gray.* Since Wilde's time we have had a novel by Ford Madox Ford entitled simply *The Portrait,* the *Portrait of the Artist as a Young Man,* Mr. Eliot's poem ("Portrait of a Lady"), a poem of Ezra Pound's ("Portrait d'une femme"), Mr. Dylan Thomas's *Portrait of the Artist as a Young Dog*—and who can say how many other "portraits" and "pictures" in the titles of lesser writers than these? Does not all this suggest a singular preoccupation on our part with the "counterfeit presentment"?

Reprinted from the *Partisan Review,* XV (June, 1948), 673–680, by permission of the author.

For of course the titles tell by no means all the story or indeed the more interesting part of it. What is far more striking than these verbal echoes is the active, the essential, the "symbolic" role that pictures of all kinds, and portraits especially, have played in the fiction of the last century or so. The portrait that is not merely dimly evoked by a title but that, on the contrary, hangs on the wall in a frame, or is being painted by an artist on an easel, and makes its existence felt, sometimes decisively, in the tale—this is the portrait that solicits our attention here. How frequently it has figured in fiction or drama we rarely pause to reflect. A fairly recent instance for the stage, within the memory of all but the youngest theater-goers, is of course John Balderston's play of the twenties, *Berkeley Square;* and the notion for this piece, as most readers remember, was derived from a late and unfinished novel of Henry James's, *The Sense of the Past.*

No writer ever made use of this emblem more richly, more delicately, or with a finer witchery of interfused "reality" and uncanniness. Readers of James's fragmentary novel will remember the young American, a twentieth-century Man of Feeling, with a deeply imaginative "sense of the past," who falls heir to an ancestral townhouse in London and who finds there the singular portrait of a youth of George the Fourth's period—singular because the face of the young man is *turned away* from the puzzled onlooker. The thought forces itself on Ralph Pendrel that, when unobserved, the portrayed figure is quite capable of turning about and facing outward, in the familiar fashion; and indeed, as it eventuates, the youth in the picture proves to be capable of stepping bodily out of the frame itself, helping himself to a lighted candle, and coming to meet Ralph Pendrel as he returns, with his own taper, to the room in which the portrait hangs. The young man of 1820 turns out to have a passion of curiosity about the future which matches Ralph's own passion for the past, and the two inevitably make an exchange of epochs. In doing so, as James's notes indicate, they were only to confirm the disquieting premonitions which had visited the painter of the portrait himself.

Did ever a portrait behave so, so oddly and also so impressively, in literature before? The answer is, yes, again and again. Portraits had been behaving in this manner in European and American fiction for the better part of two centuries before James set to work on his never-to-be-completed novel. Like so many motives in literature, James's mysteriously animated portrait comes at the end of a long series, not at its beginning. A glance at a few of this ancestral portrait's own ancestors will only fortify our respect for James's art, and perhaps have a curious interest of its own.

The subject is only one aspect of a much more inclusive one, the appearance of works of art generally in literature. That is a subject which has almost literally no beginning and is not likely to have a very early end. If one cast one's net only wide enough to take in written and not oral literature, one would doubtless have to begin with the shield of Achilles in the *Iliad,* once so familiar to at least a few schoolboys; one would not be able to pass over the pictured scenes from the Trojan War, painted on the temple walls of Carthage, which move Aeneas so deeply in the first book of the *Aeneid* (*et mentem mortalia tangunt*); and so one would work one's way gradually down to our own time and to the Botticellis and the Vermeers of which Proust made such beautiful use in *Remembrance of Things Past.* It would be a question of taking in not only pictures but statues as well, statues which also come to life, like the statue in Mérimée's famous *conte, La Vénus d'Ille*—the "source" of which can be tracked down through all the winding corridors of literary history to the dusky regions of folklore.

The same thing is true even when we limit ourselves to the narrower subject of portraits; in any collection of fairy-stories or folk-tales, one is bound to stumble sooner or later on this motif—on the notion that an individual's image can, under certain circumstances, come to life, and behave in any one of various uncanny ways which suggest a magical identification with the individual himself. The portraits of the Virgin or of various saints which, in medieval folklore, are represented as weeping or bleeding or leaving their shrines, belong unmistakably to the primordial line of which I am speaking; they are an obvious example of what folklorists call Magic Objects, and it is only because they represent individual human beings that they interest us here so much more than the bleeding branches or the speaking reeds which belong to the same broad category.

In any case, we can hardly set out on a treasure hunt through oral and written literature for painted likenesses. I am broaching only the smaller question of portraits and their use in the fiction of the last century or two. Just when these particular works of art first made their appearance, I do not know and will not undertake to say; let us assume for convenience that at least a very early example of the Romantic Portrait is that grim likeness of Prince Manfred's grandfather which, in Horace Walpole's stagey little novel, *The Castle of Otranto,* steps down out of its frame and, to Manfred's consternation, stalks with a melancholy air out of the apartment in which it has been hanging. Whether it is really the very first of our modern line or not, Walpole's picture did surely indicate that the ancient emblem was about to take on a new life; the "Gothic" portrait had arrived on the scene, and a peculiarly modern quality of feeling, a peculiarly modern nuance of the poetic, the complex, the equivocal, was about to attach itself to the old motif.

It very soon became evident that Gothic or Romantic writers were going to find the portrait a device quite as irresistible to them as music or musical instruments. Mrs. Radcliffe's novels abound in mysterious miniatures which end by revealing unsuspected identities; there is a beautiful and sinister portrait in the famous shocker, *The Monk,* by M. G. Lewis, which becomes an emblem of sensual and demoniac beauty; and perhaps the most memorable of them all is the terrible picture with the frightening eyes which young John Melmoth, in Maturin's *Melmoth the Wanderer,* finds hanging in his uncle's closet and burns to ashes after his uncle's death.

No one of these portraits behaves in quite what could be called a frankly magical manner; there were plenty that did—though sometimes to the effect merely of charm or comedy, as in Gautier's witty story, *Omphale,* in which the picture of a lovely eighteenth-century marchioness comes to life for the amorous benefit of a young Parisian of a later epoch. Nor does the preternatural power reside always in the painted image itself; it is sometimes a question rather of super-normal insight or divination on the part of the artist. What must be a rather early embodiment of this long-lived theme is one of E. T. A. Hoffmann's tales, *Doge und Dogaressa:* what happens here is that a nineteenth-century painter represents in a painting two genuinely historical personages, Marino Faliero and his young bride, and quite without consciously intending to do so, imparts to the young Dogaressa's countenance an expression which is subtly premonitory of the fate that, unbeknown to the artist, did in fact befall her. The painting has revealed much more of the truth than the painter himself, in any literal sense, could have "known."

Portraits which take on a magical animation, portraits which speak of an otherwise unsuspected reality—these are two of the kinds of portraits which adorn the walls of Romantic fiction; a third is the portrait which mysteriously exercises a baleful and even a fatal influence either on the painter himself or on the sitter or on some third personage who falls under its spell. There can be few more intense expressions of this theme than a story of Gogol's called simply "The Portrait," a story in which a young painter's career is ravaged and wrecked by the mere possession of a portrait—for its subject, an evil old money-lender, is a symbol of low ambition and worldly avarice.

How often the emblem may appear in the minor Russian writers I cannot say; it was certainly a favorite with our own Gothic and romantic writers in America. Everyone will recall the young painter in Poe's tale, "The Oval Portrait," who, in a "dark high turret-chamber where the light dripped upon the pale canvas only from overhead," paints a portrait of his young and lovely bride, which, stroke by stroke as he paints it, steals from the girl a portion of her vitality, so that at the moment when it is finished, she herself expires, having imparted to the picture the substance of her life. Like the picture of Dorian Gray—the most celebrated of all these works of art—this portrait of Poe's is a kind of inverse example of what folklorists call the Life-Token, the magic object which is vitally identified with an individual, so that it flourishes with his health and withers with his illness and dies with his death; which may even *bring on* his death if it is blighted or cut down.

The American writer for whom, even more than for James, the portrait was to be highly characteristic, was Hawthorne; but Melville, too, rather unexpectedly, turns up with a very curious example in *Pierre*. There is a likeness in Hawthorne's tale, "The Prophetic Pictures," which, in the style of Hoffmann's, anticipates more of the tragic future than even the painter himself could rationally have foreseen; and in "Edward Randolph's Portrait" the picture of the wicked governor is "rumored" to have "started from the wall, and spoken face to face" with one of his successors at a crisis in the colony's history. Most familiarly of all, in *The House of the Seven Gables,* the grim old seventeenth-century portrait of Colonel Pyncheon, hanging on the wall of the room in which he died, "seemed to symbolize an evil influence, and so darkly to mingle the shadow of [its] presence with the sunshine of the passing hour, that no good thoughts or purposes could ever spring up and blossom there." In *Pierre* the so-called "chair portrait," a likeness of Pierre's father as a youth, "seems to say" a whole series of things to Pierre as he sits gazing at it in the little room where, at his mother's insistence, he has hung it out of the way; there "seems" to lurk "some mystical intelligence and vitality" in it; and when Pierre sets fire to it—disenchanted as he is about his father—it stares tormentedly at him in beseeching horror. It is an all but literally animated portrait, and it plays a conspicuous role in this somewhat Radcliffean novel.

Such are a few of the most striking and memorable likenesses among the many in which modern fiction, from Horace Walpole to Henry James, has abounded. The chances are, I suspect, that with the revival of something like the Gothic manner in our fiction, the old symbol will reappear, from time to time, in a fresh and unhackneyed embodiment. Meanwhile, one cannot help wondering why it has recurred so frequently as it has already done, and just what the secret is not only of its curious beauty but of its troublous, equivocal effect upon the fancy. For certainly, in the hands of a genuinely imaginative writer, a portrait that behaves as if it were a living man or woman ceases to be a mere pleasing work of the pictorial art; it troubles us with a sense that the ordinary limits of conscious and rational experience have been well overpassed; that some deeper and darker levels of existence have been penetrated, and their mysterious waters stirred.

Naturally, as I need not say, every appearance of an emblem like this, in serious writing, is in a certain sense unique, and no ingenious interpretation will fit every case like a glove. The chances are, nevertheless, that a common strand, however slight it may be, will run through and unite a hundred appearances of such an obsessive symbol as this has proved to be; and here, I believe, we have a clue to that common strand in Freud's remarkable essay on "The Uncanny." The point of this essay is that the word "uncanny" does not apply to all frightening things whatever, but only to the kind of things that not only frighten us but carry us back to something long known to us, something once familiar but "forgotten" with the lapse of time, buried below the drifting accumulations of later experience, or actually repressed by an inner censor which cannot allow them to obtrude into consciousness directly. Infantile wishes and fears are among these forgotten things, but so, too, according to Freud, are all those primitive beliefs, superstitions, and terrors which civilized men imagine themselves long since to have surmounted, but which lurk nevertheless in the obscure recesses of the psyche; beliefs which, though they may never emerge into the conscious daylight, are always with us, and can always be evoked, however disguised, by the imagery of a poem or a tale.

If Freud is right, then the uncanniness of the animated portrait is an admirable case in point. For certainly no primitive conviction could be deeper-rooted or more widespread than the "superstition" that lies in ambush just below the rich and dusky literary surface we have been examining. It is the superstition I began by alluding to. Primitive people, almost universally, are said to believe that every individual has a soul, but that this soul is by no means an impalpable and, as we should say, spiritual entity; it is a very palpable and substantial thing, a tiny man within a man, which resembles the individual himself in everything but its size, and in sleep or trance or illness, and of course in death, can take its leave of the body. This is the Separable Soul of anthropological lore, and belief in it accounts for a thousand fears of which primitive man is a victim; for of course if the soul can detach itself from the body, or be malignantly detached from it, the direst results may follow. It may fail to get back into the body when the man awakes; it may fall into the hands of enemies; it may sicken and die. And all these dangers are multiplied and intensified by the equally well-established "fact" that a man's shadow, his reflection, his effigy, or portrait may all be identified with his soul—separable from him in the same way and exposed to all the same risks and terrors.

No wonder primitive men attempt to defend their shadows against being trodden on or struck; no wonder they avoid gazing at their own reflections in pools and mirrors; no wonder they threaten and sometimes assault the civilized visitors who try to paint their portraits or take their pictures with cameras. And perhaps it is not surprising that vestiges of these beliefs have survived among the peasantry of Europe and in remote corners of America even into our own time. Nor is it odd that the Gothic, the Romantic imagination, which re-evoked and (so to say) transliterated so much of the imagery of folklore, should have found itself peculiarly captivated by the symbol of the portrait—the symbol that fused in one whole the beauty and the grace of the civilized aesthetic and the darkness, the fearfulness, the primordial anxieties of an immemorial conviction. We literate moderns have no conscious belief whatever in a Separable Soul; most of us do not even know that our forebears once had such a belief; but the notion is by no means so far behind us as we should like to suppose. It joins hands, moreover, with an awareness which each of us does have in some degree or other, the awareness that our individuality is very far from being the simple unity it superficially appears to be, that just below the surface we are divided, confused, multifarious, and discordant, and that we do indeed have other selves, if not separable selves, besides the self in whose name we legally function. The uncanny ambiguousness of being an individual—the sense of this is a sense which, on the irrational level, primitive man and modern man share between them, and for both of them it is a perplexity and a source of pain. Of this perilous dualism or multiplicity the romantic portrait is an admirable symbol.

MAYNARD MACK
:
:
:   The World of *Hamlet*
:

My subject is the world of *Hamlet.* I do not of course mean Denmark, except as Denmark is given a body by the play; and I do not mean Elizabethan England, though this is necessarily close behind the scenes. I mean simply the imaginative environment that the play asks us to enter when we read it or go to see it.

Great plays, as we know, do present us with something that can be called a world, a microcosm—a world like our own in being made of people, actions, situations, thoughts, feelings, and much more, but unlike our own in being perfectly, or almost perfectly, significant and coherent. In a play's world, each part implies the other parts, and each lives, each means, with the life and meaning of the rest.

From *The Yale Review,* XLI (1952), 502–523. Copyright 1952 by the Yale University Press. Reprinted by permission of the author and the publisher.

This is the reason, as we also know, that the worlds of great plays greatly differ. Othello in Hamlet's position, we sometimes say, would have no problem; but what we are really saying is that Othello in Hamlet's position would not exist. The conception we have of Othello is a function of the characters who help define him, Desdemona, honest Iago, Cassio, and the rest; of his history of travel and war; of a great storm that divides his ship from Cassio's, and a handkerchief; of a quiet night in Venice broken by cries about an old black ram; of a quiet night in Cyprus broken by swordplay; of a quiet bedroom where a woman goes to bed in her wedding sheets and a man comes in with a light to put out the light; and above all, of a language, a language with many voices in it, gentle, rasping, querulous, or foul, but all counterpointing the one great voice:

> Put up your bright swords, for the dew will rust
>   them.

>   O thou weed
> Who are so lovely fair and smell'st so sweet
> That the sense aches at thee. . . .

>   Yet I'll not shed her blood
> Nor scar that whiter skin of hers than snow,
> And smooth as monumental alabaster.

>   I pray you in your letters,
> When you shall these unlucky deeds relate,
> Speak of me as I am; nothing extenuate,
> Nor set down aught in malice; then must you speak
> Of one that lov'd not wisely but too well;
> Of one not easily jealous, but being wrought
> Perplex'd in th' extreme; of one whose hand,
> Like the base Indian, threw a pearl away
> Richer than all his tribe . . .

Without his particular world of voices, persons, events, the world that both expresses and contains him, Othello is unimaginable. And so, I think, are Antony, King Lear, Macbeth—and Hamlet. We come back then to Hamlet's world, of all the tragic worlds that Shakespeare made, easily the most various and brilliant, the most elusive. It is with no thought of doing justice to it that I have singled out three of its attributes for comment. I know too well, if I may echo a sentiment of Mr. E. M. W. Tillyard's, that no one is likely to accept another man's reading of *Hamlet,* that anyone who tries to throw light on one part of the play usually throws the rest into deeper shadow, and that what I have to say leaves out many problems—to mention only one, the knotty problem of the text. All I would say in defense of the materials I have chosen is that they

and gets some strange advice about his daughter: "Conception is a bless-
ing, but as your daughter may conceive, friend, look to 't." Rosencrantz
and Guildenstern investigate and get the strange confidence that "Man
delights not me; no, nor woman neither." Ophelia is "loosed" to Hamlet
(Polonius's vulgar word), while Polonius and the king hide behind the
arras; and what they hear is a strange indictment of human nature, and
a riddling threat: "Those that are married already, all but one, shall live."

On the other hand, from Hamlet's point of view, there is Ophelia.
Kneeling here at her prayers, she seems the image of innocence and
devotion. Yet she is of the sex for whom he has already found the name
Frailty, and she is also, as he seems either madly or sanely to divine, a
decoy in a trick. The famous cry "Get thee to a nunnery" shows the
anguish of his uncertainty. If Ophelia is what she seems, this dirty-
minded world of murder, incest, lust, adultery, is no place for her. Were
she "as chaste as ice, as pure as snow," she could not escape its calumny.
And if she is not what she seems, then a nunnery in its other sense of
brothel is relevant to her. In the scene that follows he treats her as if
she were indeed an inmate of a brothel.

Likewise, from Hamlet's point of view, there is the enigma of the
king. If the ghost is *only* an appearance, then possibly the king's appearance is reality. He must try it further. By means of a second and different kind of "apparition," the play within the play, he does so. But then,
immediately after, he stumbles on the king at prayer. This appearance
has a relish of salvation in it. If the king dies now, his soul may yet be
saved. Yet actually, as we know, the king's efforts to come to terms with
heaven have been unavailing: his words fly up, his thoughts remain below. If Hamlet means the conventional revenger's reasons that he gives
for sparing Claudius, it was the perfect moment not to spare him—when
the sinner was acknowledging his guilt, yet unrepentant. The perfect
moment, but it was hidden, like so much else in the play, behind an
arras.

There are two arrases in his mother's room. Hamlet thrusts his
sword through one of them. Now at last he has got to the heart of the
evil, or so he thinks. But now it is the wrong man; now he himself is a
murderer. The other arras he stabs through with his words—like daggers, says the queen. He makes her shrink under the contrast he points
between her present husband and his father. But as the play now stands
(matters are somewhat clearer in the bad Quarto), it is hard to be sure
how far the queen grasps the fact that her second husband is the murderer of her first. And it is hard to say what may be signified by her inability to see the ghost, who now for the last time appears. In one sense
at least, the ghost is the supreme reality, representative of a hidden ultimate power, in Bradley's terms—witnessing from beyond the grave

seem to me interesting, close to the root of the matter even if we continue
to differ about what the root of the matter is, and explanatory, in a
modest way, of this play's peculiar hold on everyone's imagination, its
almost mythic status, one might say, as a paradigm of the life of man.

The first attribute that impresses us, I think, is mysteriousness.
We often hear it said, perhaps with truth, that every great work of art
has a mystery at the heart; but the mystery of *Hamlet* is something else.
We feel its presence in the numberless explanations that have been
brought forward for Hamlet's delay, his madness, his ghost, his treatment of Polonius, or Ophelia, or his mother; and in the controversies
that still go on about whether the play is "undoubtedly a failure" (Mr.
Eliot's phrase) or one of the greatest artistic triumphs; whether, if it is a
triumph, it belongs to the highest order of tragedy; whether, if it is such
a tragedy, its hero is to be taken as a man of exquisite moral sensibility
(Bradley's view) or an egomaniac (Madariaga's view).

Doubtless there have been more of these controversies and explanations than the play requires; for in Hamlet, to paraphrase a remark
of Falstaff's, we have a character who is not only mad in himself but a
cause that madness is in the rest of us. Still, the very existence of so
many theories and counter-theories, many of them formulated by sober
heads, gives food for thought. *Hamlet* seems to lie closer to the illogical
logic of life than Shakespeare's other tragedies. And while the causes of
this situation may be sought by saying that Shakespeare revised the play
so often that eventually the motivations were smudged over, or that the
original old play has been here or there imperfectly digested, or that the
problems of Hamlet lay so close to Shakespeare's heart that he could not
quite distance them in the formal terms of art, we have still as critics to
deal with effects, not causes. If I may quote again from Mr. Tillyard,
the play's very lack of a rigorous type of causal logic seems to be a part
of its point.

Moreover, the matter goes deeper than this. Hamlet's world is pre-
eminently in the interrogative mood. It reverberates with questions, anguished, meditative, alarmed. There are questions in this play which, to
an extent probably unparalleled in any other, mark the phases and even
the nuances of the action, helping to establish its peculiar baffled tone.
There are other questions whose interrogations, innocent at first glance,
are subsequently seen to have reached beyond their contexts and to point
toward some pervasive inscrutability in Hamlet's world as a whole. Such
is that tense series of challenges with which the tragedy begins: Bernardo's of Francisco, "Who's there?" Francisco's of Horatio and Marcellus, "Who is there?" Horatio's of the ghost: "What art thou . . . ?" And
then there are the famous questions. In them the interrogations seem to
point not only beyond the context but beyond the play, out of Hamlet's

predicaments into everyone's: "What a piece of work is a man! . . .
And yet to me what is this quintessence of dust?" "To be or not to be,
that is the question." "Get thee to a nunnery. Why wouldst thou be a
breeder of sinners?" "I am very proud, revengeful, ambitious, with more
offences at my beck than I have thoughts to put them in, imagination
to give them shape, or time to act them in. What should such fellows as
I do crawling between earth and heaven?" "Dost thou think Alexander
look'd o' this fashion i' th' earth? . . . And smelt so?"

Further, Hamlet's world is a world of riddles. The hero's own
language is often riddling, as the critics have pointed out. When he puns,
his puns have receding depths in them, like the one which constitutes
his first speech: "A little more than kin, and less than kind." His utter-
ances in madness, even if wild and whirling, are simultaneously, as
Polonius discovers, pregnant: "Do you know me, my lord?" "Excellent
well. You are a fishmonger." Even the madness itself is riddling: How
much is real? How much is feigned? What does it mean? Sane or mad,
Hamlet's mind plays restlessly about his world, turning up one riddle
upon another. The riddle of character, for example, and how it is that in
a man "whose virtues else are pure as grace," some vicious mole of nature,
some dram of eale, can "all the noble substance oft adulter." Or the
riddle of the player's art, and how a man can so project himself into a
fiction, a dream of passion, that he can weep for Hecuba. Or the riddle
of action: how we may think too little—"What to ourselves in passion
we propose," says the player-king, "The passion ending, doth the purpose
lose"; and again, how we may think too much:

> Thus conscience does make cowards of us all,
> And thus the native hue of resolution
> Is sicklied o'er with the pale cast of thought . . .

There are also more immediate riddles. His mother—how could
she "on this fair mountain leave to feed, And batten on this moor?" The
ghost—which may be a devil, for "the de'il hath power T' assume a pleasing shape." Ophelia—what does her behavior to him mean? Surprising
her in her closet, he falls to such perusal of her face as he would draw
it. Even the king at his prayers is a riddle. Will a revenge that takes him
in the purging of his soul be vengeance, or hire and salary? As for himself, Hamlet realizes, he is the greatest riddle of all—a mystery, he warns
Rosencrantz and Guildenstern, from which he will not have the heart
plucked out. He cannot tell why he has of late lost all his mirth, forgone
all custom of exercises. Still less can he tell why he delays:

> I do not know
> Why yet I live to say, "This thing's to do,"
> Sith I have cause and will and strength and means
> To do 't.

Thus the mysteriousness of Hamlet's world is of a piece.
simply a matter of missing motivations, to be expunged if only
find the perfect clue. It is built in. It is evidently an importan
what the play wishes to say to us. And it is certainly an elen
the play thrusts upon us from the opening word. Everyone, I
calls the mysteriousness of that first scene. The cold middle of
on the castle platform, the muffled sentries, the uneasy atmos
apprehension, the challenges leaping out of the dark, the quest
follow the challenges, feeling out the darkness, searching for i
for relations, for assurance. "Bernardo?" "Have you had quiet
"Who hath reliev'd you?" "What, is Horatio there?" "What,
thing appear'd again tonight?" "Looks 'a not like the king?" "H
Horatio! . . . Is not this something more than fantasy?" "Wh
you on 't?" "Is is not like the king?" "Why this same strict and
servant watch . . . ?" "Shall I strike at it with my partisan?"
consent we shall acquaint [young Hamlet] with it?"

We need not be surprised that critics and playgoers ali
been tempted to see in this an evocation not simply of Hamlet
but of their own. Man in his aspect of bafflement, moving in
on a rampart between two worlds, unable to reject, or quite acc
one that, when he faces it, "to-shakes" his disposition with thou
yond the reaches of his soul—comforting himself with hints and
We hear these hints and guesses whispering through the darknes
several watchers speak. "At least, the whisper goes so," says one.
it be no other but e'en so," says another. "I have heard" that
crowing of the cock "Th' extravagant and erring spirit hies To
fine," says a third. "Some say" at Christmas time "this bird of da
sings all night, "And then, they say, no spirit dare stir abroad." "
I heard," says the first, "and do in part believe it." However we
to take the scene, it is clear that it creates a world where uncer
are of the essence.

Meantime, such is Shakespeare's economy, a second attri
Hamlet's world has been put before us. This is the problematic na
reality and the relation of reality to appearance. The play begi
an appearance, an "apparition," to use Marcellus's term—the gho
the ghost is somehow real, indeed the vehicle of realities. Thro
revelation the glittering surface of Claudius's court is pierced, and
let comes to know, and we do, that the king is not only hateful
but the murderer of his father, that his mother is guilty of adul
well as incest. Yet there is a dilemma in the revelation. For possi
apparition *is* an apparition, a devil who has assumed his father's

This dilemma, once established, recurs on every hand. Fr
court's point of view, there is Hamlet's madness. Polonius inves

against this hollow world. Yet the man who is capable of seeing through to this reality, the queen thinks is mad. "To whom do you speak this?" she cries to her son. "Do you see nothing there?" he asks, incredulous. And she replies: "Nothing at all; yet all that is I see." Here certainly we have the imperturbable self-confidence of the worldly world, its layers on layers of habituation, so that when the reality is before its very eyes it cannot detect its presence.

Like mystery, this problem of reality is central to the play and written deep into its idiom. Shakespeare's favorite terms in *Hamlet* are words of ordinary usage that pose the question of appearances in a fundamental form. "Apparition" I have already mentioned. Another term is "seems." When we say, as Ophelia says of Hamlet leaving her closet, "He seem'd to find his way without his eyes," we mean one thing. When we say, as Hamlet says to his mother in the first court scene, "Seems, Madam! . . . I know not 'seems,'" we mean another. And when we say, as Hamlet says to Horatio before the play within the play, "And after, we will both our judgments join In censure of his seeming," we mean both at once. The ambiguities of "seem" coil and uncoil throughout this play, and over against them is set the idea of "seeing." So Hamlet challenges the king in his triumphant letter announcing his return to Denmark: "Tomorrow shall I beg leave to see your kingly eyes." Yet "seeing" itself can be ambiguous, as we recognize from Hamlet's uncertainty about the ghost; or from that statement of his mother's already quoted: "Nothing at all; yet all that is I see."

Another term of like importance is "assume." What we assume may be what we are not: "The de'il hath power T' assume a pleasing shape." But it may be what we are: "If it assume my noble father's person, I'll speak to it." And it may be what we are not yet, but would become; thus Hamlet advises his mother, "Assume a virtue, if you have it not." The perplexity in the word points to a real perplexity in Hamlet's and our own experience. We assume our habits—and habits are like costumes, as the word implies: "My father in his habit as he liv'd!" Yet these habits become ourselves in time:

> That monster, custom, who all sense doth eat
> Of habits evil, is angel yet in this,
> That to the use of actions fair and good
> He likewise gives a frock or livery
> That aptly is put on.

Two other terms I wish to instance are "put on" and "shape." The shape of something is the form under which we are accustomed to apprehend it: "Do you see yonder cloud that's almost in shape of a camel?" But a shape may also be a disguise—even, in Shakespeare's

time, an actor's costume or an actor's role. This is the meaning when
the king says to Laertes as they lay the plot against Hamlet's life:
"Weigh what convenience both of time and means May fit us to our
shape." "Put on" supplies an analogous ambiguity. Shakespeare's mind
seems to worry this phrase in the play much as Hamlet's mind worries
the problem of acting in a world of surfaces, or the king's mind worries
the meaning of Hamlet's transformation. Hamlet has put an antic disposition on, that the king knows. But what does "put on" mean? A mask,
or a frock or livery—our "habit"? The king is left guessing, and so
are we.

What is found in the play's key terms is also found in its imagery.
Miss Spurgeon has called attention to a pattern of disease images in
Hamlet, to which I shall return. But the play has other patterns equally
striking. One of these, as my earlier quotations hint, is based on clothes.
In the world of surfaces to which Shakespeare exposes us in *Hamlet,*
clothes are naturally a factor of importance. "The apparel oft proclaims
the man," Polonius assures Laertes, cataloguing maxims in the young
man's ear as he is about to leave for Paris. Oft, but not always. And so
he sends his man Reynaldo to look into Laertes's life there—even, if need
be, to put a false dress of accusation upon his son ("What forgeries you
please"), the better by indirections to find directions out. On the same
grounds, he takes Hamlet's vows to Ophelia as false apparel. They are
bawds, he tells her—or if we do not like Theobald's emendation, they
are bonds—in masquerade, "Not of that dye which their investments
show, But mere implorators of unholy suits."

This breach between the outer and the inner stirs no special emotion in Polonius, because he is always either behind an arras or prying
into one, but it shakes Hamlet to the core. Here so recently was his
mother in her widow's weeds, the tears still flushing in her gallèd eyes;
yet now, within a month, a little month, before even her funeral shoes
are old, she has married with his uncle. Her mourning was all clothes.
Not so his own, he bitterly replies, when she asks him to cast his "nighted
color off." " 'Tis not alone my inky cloak, good mother"—and not alone,
he adds, the sighs, the tears, the dejected havior of the visage—"that can
denote me truly."

> These indeed seem,
> For they are actions that a man might play;
> But I have that within which passes show;
> These but the trappings and the suits of woe.

What we must not overlook here is Hamlet's visible attire, giving
the verbal imagery a theatrical extension. Hamlet's apparel now is his
inky cloak, mark of his grief for his father, mark also of his character

as a man of melancholy, mark possibly too of his being one in whom appearance and reality are attuned. Later, in his madness, with his mind disordered, he will wear his costume in a corresponding disarray, the disarray that Ophelia describes so vividly to Polonius and that producers of the play rarely give sufficient heed to:

> Lord Hamlet with his doublet all unbrac'd,
> No hat upon his head; his stockings foul'd,
> Ungarter'd, and down-gyved to his ankle.

Here the only question will be, as with the madness itself, how much is studied, how much is real. Still later, by a third costume, the simple traveler's garb in which we find him new come from shipboard, Shakespeare will show us that we have a third aspect of the man.

A second pattern of imagery springs from terms of painting: the paints, the colorings, the varnishes that may either conceal or, as in the painter's art, reveal. Art in Claudius conceals. "The harlot's cheek," he tells us in his one aside,

> beautied with plastering art,
> Is not more ugly to the thing that helps it
> Than is my deed to my most painted word.

Art in Ophelia, loosed to Hamlet in the episode already noticed to which this speech of the king's is prelude, is more complex. She looks so beautiful—"the celestial, and my soul's idol, the most beautified Ophelia," Hamlet has called her in his love letter. But now, what does beautified mean? Perfected with all the innocent beauties of a lovely woman? Or "beautied" like the harlot's cheek? "I have heard of your paintings too, well enough. God hath given you one face, and you make yourselves another."

Yet art, differently used, may serve the truth. By using an "image" (his own word) of a murder done in Vienna, Hamlet cuts through to the king's guilt, holds "as 'twere, the mirror up to nature," shows "virtue her own feature, scorn her own image, and the very age and body of the time"—which is out of joint—"his form and pressure." Something similar he does again in his mother's bedroom, painting for her in words "the rank sweat of an enseamed bed," making her recoil in horror from his "counterfeit presentment of two brothers," and holding, if we may trust a stage tradition, his father's picture beside his uncle's. Here again the verbal imagery is realized visually on the stage.

The most pervasive of Shakespeare's image patterns in this play, however, is the pattern evolved around the three words, "show," "act," "play." "Show" seems to be Shakespeare's unifying image in *Hamlet*. Through it he pulls together and exhibits in a single focus much of the diverse material in his play. The ideas of seeming, assuming, and putting on; the images of clothing, painting, mirroring; the episode of the dumb show and the play within the play; the characters of Polonius, Laertes, Ophelia, Claudius, Gertrude, Rosencrantz and Guildenstern, Hamlet himself—all these at one time or another, and usually more than once, are drawn into the range of implications flung round the play by "show."

"Act," on the other hand, I take to be the play's radical metaphor. It distils the various perplexities about the character of reality into a residual perplexity about the character of an act. What, this play asks again and again, is an act? What is its relation to the inner act, the intent? "If I drown myself wittingly," says the clown in the graveyard, "it argues an act, and an act hath three branches; it is to act, to do, to perform." Or again, the play asks, how does action relate to passion, that "laps'd in time and passion" I can let "go by Th' important acting of your dread command"; and to thought, which can so sickly o'er the native hue of resolution that

> enterprises of great pitch and moment
> With this regard their currents turn awry
> And lose the name of action;

and to words, which are not acts, and so we dare not be content to unpack our hearts with them, and yet are acts of a sort, for we may speak daggers though we use none. Or still again, how does an act (a deed) relate to an act (a pretense)? For an action may be nothing but pretense. So Polonius, readying Ophelia for the interview with Hamlet, "with pious action," as he phrases it, "sugar[s] o'er The devil himself." Or it may not be a pretense, yet not what it appears. So Hamlet spares the king, finding him in an act that has some "relish of salvation in 't." Or it may be a pretense that is also the first foothold of a new reality, as when we assume a virtue though we have it not. Or it may be a pretense that is actually a mirroring of reality, like the play within the play, or the tragedy of *Hamlet*.

To this network of implications, the third term, "play," adds an additional dimension. "Play" is a more precise term, in Elizabethan parlance at least, for all the elements in *Hamlet* that pertain to the art of the theater; and it extends their field of reference till we see that every major personage in the tragedy is a player in some sense, and every major episode a play. The court plays, Hamlet plays, the players play, Rosencrantz and Guildenstern try to play on Hamlet, though they cannot play on his recorders—here we have an extension to a musical sense. And the final duel, by a further extension, becomes itself a play, in which everyone but Claudius and Laertes plays his role in ignorance: "The queen desires you to show some gentle entertainment to Laertes

before you fall to play." "I . . . will this brother's wager frankly play."
"Give him the cup."—"I'll play this bout first."

The full extension of this theme is best evidenced in the play within
the play itself. Here, in the bodily presence of these traveling players,
bringing with them the latest playhouse gossip out of London, we have
suddenly a situation that tends to dissolve the normal barriers between the
fictive and the real. For here on the stage before us is a play of false
appearances in which an actor called the player-king is playing. But
there is also on the stage Claudius, another player-king, who is a spectator of this player. And there is on the stage, besides, a prince who is a
spectator of both these player-kings and who plays with great intensity
a player's role himself. And around these kings and that prince is a
group of courtly spectators—Gertrude, Rosencrantz, Guildenstern, Polonius, and the rest—and they, as we have come to know, are players
too. And lastly there are ourselves, an audience watching all these audiences who are also players. Where, it may suddenly occur to us to ask,
does the playing end? Which *are* the guilty creatures sitting at a play?
When is an act not an "act"?

The mysteriousness of Hamlet's world, while it pervades the tragedy,
finds its point of greatest dramatic concentration in the first act, and its
symbol in the first scene. The problems of appearance and reality also
pervade the play as a whole, but come to a climax in Acts II and III, and
possibly their best symbol is in the play within the play. Our third attribute, though again it is one that crops out everywhere, reaches its full
development in Acts IV and V. It is not easy to find an appropriate name
for this attribute, but perhaps "mortality" will serve, if we remember
to mean by mortality the heartache and the thousand natural shocks
that flesh is heir to, not simply death.

The powerful sense of mortality in *Hamlet* is conveyed to us, I
think, in three ways. First, there is the play's continuous emphasis on
human weakness, the instability of human purpose, the subjection of
humanity to fortune—all that we might call the aspect of failure in man.
Hamlet opens this theme in Act I, when he describes how from a single
blemish, perhaps not even the victim's fault, a man's whole character
may take corruption. Claudius dwells on it again, to an extent that goes
far beyond the needs of the occasion, while engaged in seducing Laertes
to step behind the arras of a seemer's world and dispose of Hamlet by
a trick. Time qualifies everything, Claudius says, including love, including purpose. As for love—it has a "plurisy" in it and dies of its own
too much. As for purpose:

> That we would do,
> We should do when we would, for this "would" changes,
> And hath abatements and delays as many

> As there are tongues, are hands, are accidents;
> And then this "should" is like a spendthrift's sigh,
> That hurts by easing.

The player-king, in his long speeches to his queen in the play within the play, sets the matter in a still darker light. She means these protestations of undying love, he knows, but our purposes depend on our memory, and our memory fades fast. Or else, he suggests, we propose something to ourselves in a condition of strong feeling, but then the feeling goes, and with it the resolve. Or else our fortunes change, he adds, and with these our loves: "The great man down, you mark his favorite flies." The subjection of human aims to fortune is a reiterated theme in *Hamlet,* as subsequently in *Lear.* Fortune is the harlot goddess in whose secret parts men like Rosencrantz and Guildenstern live and thrive; the strumpet who threw down Troy and Hecuba and Priam; the outrageous foe whose slings and arrows a man of principle must suffer, or seek release in suicide. Horatio suffers them with composure: he is one of the blessed few

> Whose blood and judgment are so well co-mingled
> That they are not a pipe for fortune's finger
> To sound what stop she please.

For Hamlet the task is of greater difficulty.

Next, and intimately related to this matter of infirmity, is the emphasis on infection—the ulcer, the hidden abscess,

> th' imposthume of much wealth and peace
> That inward breaks and shows no cause without
> Why the man dies.

Miss Spurgeon, who was the first to call attention to this aspect of the play, has well remarked that so far as Shakespeare's pictorial imagination is concerned, the problem in *Hamlet* is not a problem of the will and reason, "of a mind too philosophical or a nature temperamentally unfitted to act quickly," nor even a problem of an individual at all. Rather, it is a condition—"a condition for which the individual himself is apparently not responsible, any more than the sick man is to blame for the infection which strikes and devours him, but which, nevertheless, in its course and development, impartially and relentlessly, annihilates him and others, innocent and guilty alike." "That," she adds, "is the tragedy of *Hamlet,* as it is perhaps the chief tragic mystery of life." This is a perceptive comment, for it reminds us that Hamlet's situation is mainly not of his own manufacture, as are the situations of Shakespeare's other tragic heroes. He has inherited it; he is "born to set it right."

We must not, however, neglect to add to this what another student of Shakespeare's imagery has noticed—that the infection in Denmark is presented alternatively as poison. Here, of course, responsibility is implied, for the poisoner of the play is Claudius. The juice he pours into the ear of the elder Hamlet is a combined poison and disease, a "leperous distilment" that curds "the thin and wholesome blood." From this fatal center, unwholesomeness spreads out till there is something rotten in all Denmark. Hamlet tells us that his "wit's diseased," the queen speaks of her "sick soul," the king is troubled by "the hectic" in his blood, Laertes meditates revenge to warm "the sickness in my heart," the people of the kingdom grow "muddied, Thick, and unwholesome in their thoughts"; and even Ophelia's madness is said to be "the poison of deep grief." In the end, all save Ophelia die of that poison in a literal as well as figurative sense.

But the chief form in which the theme of mortality reaches us, it seems to me, is as a profound consciousness of loss. Hamlet's father expresses something of the kind when he tells Hamlet how his "most seeming-virtuous queen," betraying a love which

> was of that dignity
> That it went hand in hand even with the vow
> I made to her in marriage,

had chosen to

> decline
> Upon a wretch whose natural gifts were poor
> To those of mine.

"O Hamlet, what a falling off was there!" Ophelia expresses it again, on hearing Hamlet's denunciation of love and woman in the nunnery scene, which she takes to be the product of a disordered brain:

> O what a noble mind is here o'erthrown.
> The courtier's, soldier's, scholar's, eye, tongue, sword;
> The expectancy and rose of the fair state,
> The glass of fashion and the mould of form,
> Th' observ'd of all observers, quite, quite down!

The passage invites us to remember that we have never actually seen such a Hamlet—that his mother's marriage has brought a falling off in him before we meet him. And then there is that further falling off, if I may call it so, when Ophelia too goes mad: "Divided from herself and her fair judgment, Without the which we are pictures, or mere beasts."

Time was, the play keeps reminding us, when Denmark was a different place. That was before Hamlet's mother took off "the rose From the fair forehead of an innocent love" and set a blister there. Hamlet then was still "Th' expectancy and rose of the fair state"; Ophelia, the "rose of May." For Denmark was a garden then, when his father ruled. There had been something heroic about his father—a king who met the threats to Denmark in open battle, fought with Norway, smote the sledded Polacks on the ice, slew the elder Fortinbras in an honorable trial of strength. There had been something godlike about his father too:

> Hyperion's curls, the front of Jove himself,
> An eye like Mars . . . ,
> A station like the herald Mercury.

But, the ghost reveals, a serpent was in the garden, and "the serpent that did sting thy father's life Now wears his crown." The martial virtues are put by now. The threats to Denmark are attended to by policy, by agents working deviously for and through an uncle. The moral virtues are put by too. Hyperion's throne is occupied by a "vice of kings," "a king of shreds and patches"; Hyperion's bed, by a satyr, a paddock, a bat, a gib, a bloat king with reechy kisses. The garden is unweeded now, and "grows to seed; things rank and gross in nature Possess it merely." Even in himself he feels the taint, the taint of being his mother's son; and that other taint, from an earlier garden, of which he admonishes Ophelia: "Our virtue cannot so inoculate our old stock but we shall relish of it." "Why wouldst thou be a breeder of sinners?" "What should such fellows as I do crawling between earth and heaven?"

"Hamlet is painfully aware," says Professor Tillyard, "of the baffling human predicament between the angels and the beasts, between the glory of having been made in God's image and the incrimination of being descended from fallen Adam." To this we may add, I think, that Hamlet is more than aware of it; he exemplifies it; and it is for this reason that his problem appeals to us so powerfully as an image of our own.

Hamlet's problem, in its crudest form, is simply the problem of the avenger: he must carry out the injunction of the ghost and kill the king. But this problem, as I ventured to suggest at the outset, is presented in terms of a certain kind of world. The ghost's injunction to act becomes so inextricably bound up for Hamlet with the character of the world in which the action must be taken—its mysteriousness, its baffling appearances, its deep consciousness of infection, frailty, and loss—that he cannot come to terms with either without coming to terms with both.

When we first see him in the play, he is clearly a very young man, sensitive and idealistic, suffering the first shock of growing up. He has taken the garden at face value, we might say, supposing mankind to be only a little lower than the angels. Now, in his mother's hasty and incestuous marriage, he discovers evidence of something else, something bestial —though even a beast, he thinks, would have mourned longer. Then comes the revelation of the ghost, bringing a second shock. Not so much because he now knows that his serpent-uncle killed his father; his prophetic soul had almost suspected this. Not entirely, even, because he knows now how far below the angels humanity has fallen in his mother, and how lust—these were the ghost's words—

> though to a radiant angel link'd
> Will sate itself in a celestial bed,
> And prey on garbage.

Rather, because he now sees everywhere, but especially in his own nature, the general taint, taking from life its meaning, from woman her integrity, from the will its strength, turning reason into madness. "Why wouldst thou be a breeder of sinners?" "What should such fellows as I do crawling between earth and heaven?" Hamlet is not the first young man to have felt the heavy and the weary weight of all this unintelligible world; and, like the others, he must come to terms with it.

The ghost's injunction to revenge unfolds a different facet of his problem. The young man growing up is not to be allowed simply to endure a rotten world, he must also act in it. Yet how to begin, among so many enigmatic surfaces? Even Claudius, whom he now knows to be the core of the ulcer, has a plausible exterior. And around Claudius, swathing the evil out of sight, he encounters all those other exteriors, as we have seen. Some of them already deeply infected beneath, like his mother. Some noble, but marked for infection, like Laertes. Some not particularly corrupt but infinitely corruptible, like Rosencrantz and Guildenstern; some mostly weak and foolish like Polonius and Osric. Some, like Ophelia, innocent, yet in their innocence still serving to "skin and film the ulcerous place."

And this is not all. The act required of him, though retributive justice, is one that necessarily involves the doer in the general guilt. Not only because it involves a killing, but because to get at the world of seeming one sometimes has to use its weapons. He himself, before he finishes, has become a player, has put an antic disposition on, has killed a man—the wrong man—has helped drive Ophelia mad, and has sent two friends of his youth to death, mining below their mines, and hoisting the engineer with his own petard. He had never meant to dirty himself with these things, but from the moment of the ghost's challenge to act, this dirtying was inevitable. It is the condition of living at all in such a world. To quote Polonius, who knew that world so well, men become "a little soil'd i' th' working." Here is another matter with which Hamlet has to come to terms.

Human infirmity—all that we have discussed with reference to instability, infection, loss—supplies the problem with its third phase.

Hamlet has not only to accept the mystery of man's condition between the angels and the brutes, and not only to act in a perplexing and soiling world. He has also to act within the human limits—"with shabby equipment always deteriorating," if I may adapt some phrases from Mr. Eliot's *East Coker,*

> In the general mess of imprecision of feeling,
> Undisciplined squads of emotion.

Hamlet is aware of that fine poise of body and mind, feeling and thought, that suits the action to the word, the word to the action; that acquires and begets a temperance in the very torrent, tempest, and whirlwind of passion; but he cannot at first achieve it in himself. He vacillates between undisciplined squads of emotion and thinking too precisely on the event. He learns to his cost how easily action can be lost in "acting," and loses it there for a time himself. But these again are only the terms of every man's life. As Anatole France reminds us in a now famous apostrophe to Hamlet: "What one of us thinks without contradiction and acts without incoherence? What one of us is not mad? What one of us does not say with a mixture of pity, comradeship, admiration, and horror, Goodnight, sweet Prince!"

In the last act of the play (or so it seems to me, for I know there can be differences on this point), Hamlet accepts his world and we discover a different man. Shakespeare does not outline for us the process of acceptance any more than he had done with Romeo or was to do with Othello. But he leads us strongly to expect an altered Hamlet, and then, in my opinion, provides him. We must recall that at this point Hamlet has been absent from the stage during several scenes, and that such absences in Shakespearean tragedy usually warn us to be on the watch for a new phase in the development of the character. It is so when we leave King Lear in Gloucester's farmhouse and find him again in Dover Fields. It is so when we leave Macbeth at the witches' cave and rejoin him at Dunsinane, hearing of the armies that beset it. Furthermore, and this is an important matter in the theater—especially important in a play in which the symbolism of clothing has figured largely—Hamlet now *looks* different. He is wearing a different dress—probably, as Granville-Barker thinks, his "sea gown scarf'd" about him, but in any case no longer the disordered costume of his antic disposition. The effect is not entirely dissimilar to that in *Lear,* when the old King wakes out of his madness to find fresh garments on him.

Still more important, Hamlet displays a considerable change of mood. This is not a matter of the way we take the passage about defying augury, as Mr. Tillyard among others seems to think. It is a matter of Hamlet's whole deportment, in which I feel we may legitimately see the deportment of a man who has been "illuminated" in the tragic sense. Bradley's term for it is fatalism, but if this is what we wish to call it, we must at least acknowledge that it is fatalism of a very distinctive kind—a kind that Shakespeare has been willing to touch with the associations of the saying in St. Matthew about the fall of a sparrow, and with Hamlet's recognition that a divinity shapes our ends. The point is not that Hamlet has suddenly become religious; he has been religious all through the play. The point is that he has now learned, and accepted, the boundaries in which human action, human judgment, are enclosed.

Till his return from the voyage he had been trying to act beyond these, had been encroaching on the role of providence, if I may exaggerate to make a vital point. He had been too quick to take the burden of the whole world and its condition upon his limited and finite self. Faced with a task of sufficient difficulty in its own right, he had dilated it into a cosmic problem—as indeed every task is, but if we think about this too precisely we cannot act at all. The whole time is out of joint, he feels, and in his young man's egocentricity he will set it right. Hence he misjudges Ophelia, seeing in her only a breeder of sinners. Hence he misjudges himself, seeing himself a vermin crawling between earth and heaven. Hence he takes it upon himself to be his mother's conscience, though the ghost has warned that this is no fit task for him, and returns to repeat the warning: "Leave her to heaven, And to those thorns that in her bosom lodge." Even with the king, Hamlet has sought to play at God. *He* it must be who decides the issue of Claudius's salvation, saving him for a more damnable occasion. Now, he has learned that there are limits to the before and after that human reason comprehends. Rashness, even, is sometimes good. Through rashness he has saved his life from the commission for his death, "and prais'd be rashness for it." This happy circumstance and the unexpected arrival of the pirate ship make it plain that the roles of life are not entirely self-assigned. "There is a divinity that shapes our ends, Rough-hew them how we will." Hamlet is ready now for what may happen, seeking neither to foreknow it nor avoid it. "If it be now, 'tis not to come; if it be not to come, it will be now; if it be not now, yet it will come: the readiness is all."

The crucial evidence of Hamlet's new frame of mind is the graveyard scene. Here, in its ultimate symbol, he confronts, recognizes, and accepts the condition of being man. It is not simply that he now accepts death, though Shakespeare shows him accepting it in ever more poignant forms: first, in the imagined persons of the politician, the courtier, and the lawyer, who laid their little schemes "to circumvent God," as Hamlet puts it, but now lie here; then in Yorick, whom he knew and played with as a child; and then in Ophelia. This last death tears from him a final cry of passion, but the striking contrast between his behavior and Laertes's reveals how deeply he has changed.

Still, it is not the fact of death that invests this scene with its peculiar power. It is instead the haunting mystery of life itself that Hamlet's speeches point to, holding in its inscrutable folds those other mysteries that he has wrestled with so long. These he now knows for what they are, and lays them by. The mystery of evil is present here—for this is after all the universal graveyard, where, as the clown says humorously, he holds up Adam's profession; where the scheming politician, the hollow courtier, the tricky lawyer, the emperor and the clown and the beautiful young maiden all come together in an emblem of the world; where even, Hamlet murmurs, one might expect to stumble on "Cain's jawbone, that did the first murther." The mystery of reality is here too—for death puts the question, "What is real?" in its irreducible form, and in the end uncovers all appearances: "Is this the fine of his fines and the recovery of his recoveries, to have his fine pate full of fine dirt?" "Now get you to my lady's chamber, and tell her, let her paint an inch thick, to this favor she must come." Or if we need more evidence of this mystery, there is the anger of Laertes at the lack of ceremonial trappings, and indeed the ambiguous character of Ophelia's own death. "Is she to be buried in Christian burial when she wilfully seeks her own salvation?" asks the gravedigger. And last of all, but most pervasive of all, there is the mystery of human limitation. The grotesque nature of man's little joys, his big ambitions. The fact that the man who used to bear us on his back is now a skull that smells; that the noble dust of Alexander somewhere plugs a bunghole; that "Imperial Caesar, dead and turn'd to clay, Might stop a hole to keep the wind away." Above all, the fact that a pit of clay is "meet" for such a guest as man, as the gravedigger tells us in his song, and yet that, despite all frailties and limitations, "That skull had a tongue in it and could sing once."

After the graveyard and what it indicates has come to pass in him, we know that Hamlet is ready for the final contest of mighty opposites. He accepts the world as it is, the world as a duel, in which, whether we know it or not, evil holds the poisoned rapier and the poisoned chalice waits; and in which, if we win at all, it costs not less than everything. I think we understand by the close of Shakespeare's *Hamlet* why it is that unlike the other tragic heroes he is given a soldier's rites upon the stage. For as William Butler Yeats once said, "Why should we honor those who die on the field of battle? A man may show as reckless a courage in entering into the abyss of himself."

RICHARD HARTER FOGLE

The Imaginal Design of Shelley's "Ode to the West Wind"

Such an exposition as I am about to attempt requires some justification, especially when the poem to be expounded is almost universally known, widely recognized as a masterpiece, and reprinted in hundreds of anthologies of English poetry. Only a few years ago this enterprise would have been reckoned quite unnecessary. Today, however, the situation is somewhat changed. The gentle—or ungentle—art of explication is enjoying a still-increasing vogue, while at the same time our most influential explicators have been categorically, and to me unwarrantably, hostile to Shelley. John Crowe Ransom considers him merely feeble, Allen Tate indicts him for confusion of metaphor—a terrible charge in contemporary criticism, despite the immortal evidence of the "To be or not to be" soliloquy—and Cleanth Brooks in *Modern Poetry and the Tradition* consigns him to limbo posthaste as "a very unsatisfactory poet," sentimental and guilty of "poor craftsmanship." Those, on the other hand, who know Shelley best have generally been too much occupied with learning still more about him to heed the attackers, who are frequently, as in the instances I have cited, critics of unquestionable influence and power. A detailed defense, as this is intended to be, of a lyric generally accepted as representative of Shelley at his best, should therefore fill a genuine need.

The general standards employed here, I am confident, would be approved even by Shelley's most uncompromising disapprovers, being, in fact, their own; although it might be remarked that they used to belong to Samuel Taylor Coleridge. Broadly, I assume that a good poem should impose an imaginative unity upon diverse materials; that it should provide a complex human problem with a satisfactory solution; that through the medium of artistic form it should give coherence to the intellectual, emotional, and sensuous experience of the poet.

My method, however, is unlike theirs in being deliberately tentative, eclectic, and impure. Undoubtedly the poem itself is the important issue, but despite much contemporary opinion it should not be isolated from the mind of the poet, his environment, his artistic theories, and the body of his poetry. To do so, in my opinion, is to deprive the poem of its legitimate background, leaving only general criteria which can too

Reprinted from *ELH*, XV (1948), 219–226, by permission of the publisher, The Johns Hopkins Press, Baltimore, Maryland.

easily be manipulated to serve the prejudices of the critic. It is interesting, by the way, that those who are austerest in approaching Romantic poetry are often less abstemious in other situations. Professor Cleanth Brooks, for example, advances upon Shelley equipped only with his standards and his bare fists. He has, however, given us excellent expositions of the esoteric background of Eliot's *Wasteland,* and of the eccentric historico-cosmogony of Yeats, with no apparent feeling that these are irrelevant.

No explication, fortunately, can entirely account for a poem. One may dilute, expand, and appreciate, but full explanation is impossible. Interpretation, I believe, must be tentative, and frankly metaphorical. Some method must obviously be found, and some standard of judgment applied, but no method or standard dare claim unique validity. I shall attempt to define what I see in the poem in its own particularity, rather than, as has become the predominant practice, what I do not see. My standards, save in the general sense, which has earlier been specified, derive from the poem itself, and I introduce whatever material seems calculated to advance understanding and appreciation of it. In order to speak fully of the imagery, which is perhaps most vital, I am regretfully compelled to omit consideration of the stanzaic, rhetorical, syntactical, and sound patterns, although these are well worthy of thorough study. Finally, my immediate purpose is to demonstrate that the "Ode to the West Wind" is a lyric of great complexity and consummate artistic design.

On the most elementary level, the poem deals in the first three stanzas with the action of the West Wind upon the leaf, the cloud, and the wave. Through this action Shelley steps progressively toward an imaginative examination of the possibility of identifying himself with the wind, and what it stands for. These first three stanzas are, at any rate on the surface, objective descriptions of natural phenomena. In stanza iv the identification is suggested, tentatively and provisionally, through Nature, in terms which bind the natural pattern of leaf-cloud-wave firmly to the emerging personality of the poet:

> If I were a dead leaf thou mightest bear;
> If I were a swift cloud to fly with thee;
> A wave to pant beneath thy power . . .

and culminates in stanza v—"Be thou, Spirit fierce, My spirit! Be thou me, impetuous one!"

This identification represents, so to speak, the unity which the poem is to win from variety. The individual is to be merged with the general; Shelley is to become the instrument through which speaks the universal voice. The medium by which this unity is imaginatively achieved is the nature-imagery of the three beginning stanzas—the action upon and the interrelationship of the West Wind with the leaf, the cloud, and the wave.

The stress, or structure, or problem of the "Ode" may also be defined as the "death and regeneration" contrast, which has been discussed by I. J. Kapstein, Newman Ivey White, and others. For the West Wind is both destroyer and preserver; it shatters established structures that new ones may be built from their ruins; it scatters the withered leaves, but in order to "quicken a new birth." This contrast, like the individual–general contrast earlier mentioned, needs and gets a poetic reconciliation, a unification concretely and emotionally satisfying.

This theme is partially developed in stanza i, in which the wind scatters and disperses the forms of Nature, but preserves its order and continuity by spreading the "winged seeds" where at the propitious time they may issue forth anew. Stanza i, we may add, has a dual function of design. It introduces the contrast of death and rebirth, Autumn and Spring, but it also serves to introduce the leaf-image of the leaf-cloud-wave pattern. Here we must notice a difficulty in our terms. Reference to the "death and regeneration" theme is likely to be misleading unless we point out that the West Wind of Autumn, while both destroyer and preserver, is not also regenerator. The difference is more than a technicality, for it will fundamentally affect our notion of what Shelley is writing about, what he claims for the Wind and for his own poetry.

It is left for another West Wind, the Zephyrus or Favonius of Lucretius and Virgil, "thine azure sister of the Spring," to blow "Her clarion o'er the dreaming earth," and recall to life the dead who do but sleep. The West Wind of Autumn is a power of destruction, which nevertheless preserves whatever of the existing order is vital and promising. Fruition, however, is left to another power, kindred but still distinct. Shelley, in fact, is more modest, even amidst affirmation, than would appear at a glance. Indeed, it might be pointed out that not merely here but even in the earlier and less mature *Revolt of Islam* (IX. xxi–xxix) the same personal modesty tempers revolutionary confidence and hope.

Predominant, then, is the expression of a dynamic force, the tremendous power of revolutionary change. In stanza ii the wind is both architect and wrecker of "the approaching storm," whose "congregated might of vapors" will give vent to the bursting forth of "Black rain, and fire, and hail." The mingled menace, power, and beauty of the clouds, agents of the unseen wind, are symbolized in complex personifications: *"Angels* of rain and lightning," and the *"Bright hair* uplifted from the head of some *fierce Maenad."* Images of height and motion artfully contribute to the attraction—and repulsion—aroused by the scene: "the *steep* sky's *commotion"* (a richly synthetic term); "even from the dim verge of the horizon to the Zenith's height": along with the motor and kinesthetic force of "Loose clouds . . . *shed"*; *"Shook* from the tangled boughs . . ."; "Black rain . . . will burst." The scene is full of movement and force, applied to the solid structure of the "vaulted dome" of the sky. The suggestion that the change may be beneficent and fruitful is subtly implied by the linking of the clouds to the "decaying leaves" of stanza i, carried further in the *"tangled boughs* of Heaven and Ocean," with their connotations of cyclical and reciprocal interfertilization.

In stanza ii Shelley has viewed the revolutionary process complexly, as at once beautiful and terrible, fruitful and destructive; and he has reconciled these opposites, has unified and given them form, by the widely inclusive picture of wind, storm, and sky, simultaneously visible and harmoniously interrelated. In stanza iii another difficulty is to be met and conquered.

Change and reform, in their iconoclastic vigor, destroy good as well as evil, for in the fabric of society the two are inextricably interwoven. The exquisite calm of the blue Mediterranean must be rudely shattered, although it frames in its motionless and idealizing medium ("the wave's intenser day") the loveliest forms of the past. The mellow patina of the centuries has its own attractions. We must also consider that the scene is Baiae, with its mingled associations of social splendor, amenity, and injustice. These "old palaces and towers," spiritualized by their medium (itself an emblem of the perspective of Time), and softened by their clothing of Time and Nature, are almost overpowering to sensibility; "so sweet the sense faints picturing them."

If it is suspected that I am over-reading these lines, I would refer the doubter to Shelley's *Philosophical View of Reform,* in which he takes account in explicit and abstract prose of the problem here expressed poetically and imaginally. "Tyranny," he remarks among other things, "entrenches itself within the existing interests of the best and most refined citizens of a nation and says 'If you dare trample upon these, be free.'" Or note the subtly blended delight and reprehension projected in the "Lines Written Among the Euganean Hills," as the poet looks down at the "Column, tower, and dome, and spire" of beautiful and dishonored Venice. Or examine in *Adonais* the atmosphere of lovely, decadent Rome,

> . . . at once the Paradise,
> The grave, the city, and the wilderness.

Shelley has, in my opinion, harmonized and reconciled the discordances and difficulties of the theme: not by proposing a complete solution, indeed—the only possible solution is to let the West Wind have its way—but by understanding, accepting, and realizing the dilemma in art.

In order fully to comprehend the complexity which Shelley resolves, the weight of intellect and emotion which the poem must carry, it is well to consider more thoroughly the central symbol of the West Wind. In the context of the "Ode" it stands for the spirit of revolution, or for revolutionary change; and we have seen that, like Moses, it opens the way to the promised land, without itself being permitted to enter. Its qualities, however, betray its relationship with more universal and more gracious meanings. An unseen, irresistible power, it is a single door which opens upon the central unity of all things, the very fulcrum of Shelley's thought. It is an aspect of the master concept of his most significant poetry.

The West Wind is an absolute and hidden power which informs all things, while it is perceptible and to be imaged only in its effects, like "the one Life within us and abroad" of Coleridge, or Wordsworth's

> . . . motion and a spirit, that impels
> All thinking things, all objects of all thought,
> And rolls through all things.

In the poetry of Shelley it is akin to the secret fire which inwardly illumines "the visioned maid" of *Alastor*. It is related to the "awful shadow" of Intellectual Beauty, which "floats though unseen among us"; and to the "imageless, deep truth" of *Prometheus Unbound*. In *Adonais* it becomes the Eternal, the "burning fountain" whither shall return the creative genius of Keats:

> . . . that sustaining Love
> Which through the web of being blindly wove
> By man and beast and earth and air and sea,
> Burns bright or dim, as each are mirrors of
> The fire for which all thirst.

In another guise, it is the skylark, the symbol of the poet, unseen, but inundating the sky with "profuse strains of unpremeditated art." Again, it has affinities with the unaccountable power of poetic inspiration as it is described in the *Defence of Poetry:* "the mind in creation is as a fading coal, which some invisible influence, like an inconstant wind, awakens to transitory brightness." The symbolism of the West Wind, in short, opens out into far-reaching associations, rich and deep in their freight of intellect and emotion.

Likewise rich in its imaginative ramifications is Shelley's development of the "death and regeneration" theme, into which is woven the myths of the seasons; of Christ, his resurrection, and of Judgment Day; and the imagery of the pastoral; all so skillfully harmonized that the shift from one to another is almost imperceptible. The leaves and the "winged seeds" will play their part in the great cyclical rebirth of Spring, and the image of the seeds leads us also into the Christian resurrection of Easter. They "lie cold and low" until awakened by the gentle wind of Spring, which suggests both the resurrection and Judgment Day as she blows "her clarion o'er the dreaming earth." The pastoral enters also, blended with the wind, "Driving sweet buds like *flocks* to *feed* in air," linked to the Christian by the shepherd-sheep image, and merging once more with the rebirth of Spring and Nature, as the wind fills "With living hues and odors plain and hill." It may not perhaps be too fanciful to suggest yet another enriching association, harmonizing with the seasonal and religious myth alike: the West Wind is both Siva and Vishnu of the Hindu triad, destroyer and preserver together. Only Brahma, the creator, it is not.

Consequently, when in stanza iv Shelley turns to the subjective and individual, his problem is given meaning and reference not merely by his attempted self-identification with the West Wind, but also by his relation of the individual to the ideological, cultural, religious, and natural wholes. By using the symbol of the West Wind, and by describing its effects upon leaf, cloud, and wave, he has realized and objectified the revolutionary ideal in Nature; and by introducing the seasonal, religious, and pastoral myths he has softened and humanized a conception in itself perhaps a little rigorous. Then, in culmination, the personal binds the two aspects of the theme together. From the nature imagery of leaf-cloud-wave arises the prayer to be united with the wind: a union which will provide the means for the only sort of regeneration which Shelley—I should say modestly—deemed personally possible. That is, filled with an inspiration not of his own making or owning, his thoughts should be driven "Like withered leaves to quicken a new birth"; his words should be scattered among mankind.

There has arisen of late years a strange disposition to deny a place to the subjective in poetry. This view I confess I do not fully understand; it would appear to lead to a hopeless confusion of the genres. An objective lyric seems to me as much a contradiction in terms as an actionless narrative, or a plotless drama. For those who are dismayed by the entrance of the poet upon the scene, however, it may be pointed out that in the "Ode to the West Wind" the personal element is an integral part of the design, as presumably could be established of any good lyric. The "Ode" is about self-abnegation, the absorption of the individual Ego into a larger unity. It is, I think, then, more than a mere play on words to demand that there should be the imaginative realization of a self to be abnegated and absorbed. If the offering is to have significance, let it be prized by the giver.

The lines "I fall upon the thorns of life . . ." and "A heavy weight of hours has chained and bowed/One too like thee," which some have found objectionable, are obviously part of the imaginal design. The West Wind is free and uncontrollable. Shelley calls for a like though a lesser freedom—not egotistically, but through the power of self-dedication to a cause—to become the fitting instrument and medium of a voice, the trumpet of a prophecy not his own. That he introduces his own emotions, his sufferings, frailties, forebodings—serves to intensify the stress and increase the voltage of the poetic argument, to broaden its scope. Poems should end in reconciliation, but a unity too easily won is lacking in value. The personal stanzas of the "Ode to the West Wind" round out the expression of a problem that is felt and real. This reconciliation, to conclude, has as its materials the stress between the individual and the general, the actual and the ideal, each given its "ample room and verge enough." The resolvent is hope—hope tempered with humility—hope firm-based in the revolutionary idealism symbolized by the West Wind, and in the immemorial logic of seasonal, religious, and pastoral Myth.

CLEANTH BROOKS

Wit and High Seriousness

Critics like Johnson and Wordsworth are inclined, as we have seen, to suspect the good faith of poets who indulge in witty comparisons. Wordsworth, thinking of poetry as a spontaneous overflow of powerful emotions, naturally distrusted the lack of spontaneity in the poets of wit. There seemed to be no overflow at all—merely an ingenious ladling out. The witty poets impressed him as lacking what Arnold was later to term "high seriousness." The phrase has become prescriptive. As the authors of a recent textbook put it: "There is plenty of room in verse for frivolity, light humour, the tongue-in-cheek attitude, but great poetry, absolute poetry, will tolerate none of these insincerities."

The necessity for high seriousness is the principle usually appealed to in order to discredit the radical poetry of the moderns, and it has a particular convenience. The critic is allowed to compliment the poets on their cleverness while at the same time denying that they are true poets at all.

Arnold's position, of course, represents no real advance over that

Reprinted, by permission, from *Modern Poetry and the Tradition,* Chapel Hill, N. C.: The University of North Carolina Press, 1939.

of the Romantic critics. Arnold too believed in a poetic subject matter—that it was "an advantage to a poet to deal with a beautiful world." He dealt with such in his own poetry. He believed in poetic diction; indeed, he makes the diction of a poem one of the most important elements by which the poet's high seriousness is revealed.

But even in his making the violation of this special subject matter and diction a mark of insincerity, Arnold is foreshadowed by earlier critics. If Arnold states that high seriousness "comes from absolute sincerity," one remembers Coleridge's objection to the play of wit because it implied "a leisure and self-possession . . . incompatible with the steady fervour of a mind possessed and filled with the grandeur of its subject." Arnold's high seriousness amounts to little more than this "steady fervour."

Leisure and self-possession are attributes of the critical intellect, and the poet for both Coleridge and Arnold is possessed.[1] The divine madman must not testify against the reality of his frenzy.

There is a sense, of course, in which Arnold and his predecessors are right. Trifling may indicate a lack of deep feeling; and where the poet enters into a compact with his reader to be direct, and to mean literally what he says, such trifling is best disposed of by saying that the poet is insincere. For Arnold, the poet necessarily enters into such a compact. But the play of the intellect and the play of wit are not incompatible with the poet's seriousness, nor with his sincerity in implying to the reader that he means to be taken seriously. To see this, one need only consider the poets themselves. But one must ask a reader brought up in the tradition of the last century to lay aside his prejudices for the moment in considering them.

The Elizabethan and Jacobean poets will be instructive. The Elizabethans wrote a great deal of witty verse, particularly in their sonnet sequences, some of it good, some bad, but in any case verse which was meant to be read as a sort of courtly *vers de société*. John Lyly's "Cupid and Campaspe Played" will represent very well this sort of verse at its best.

> Cupid and my Campaspe played
> At cards for kisses; Cupid paid;
> He stakes his quiver, bow, and arrows,
> His mother's doves, and team of sparrows;
> Loses them too; then, down he throws
> The coral of his lip, the rose

[1] This idea probably derives ultimately from Plato. See the long passage in the *Ion* which begins: "For all good poets . . . compose their beautiful poems not as works of art, but because they are inspired and possessed. And as the Corybantian revellers when they dance are not in their right mind, so the lyric poets are not in their right mind when they are composing their beautiful strains. . . ."

> Growing on's cheek (but none knows how);
> With these, the crystal of his brow,
> And then the dimple of his chin:
> All these did my Campaspe win.
> At last, he set her both his eyes;
> She won, and Cupid blind did rise.
>   O Love! has she done this to thee?
>   What shall (alas!) become of me?

This is not love poetry of the type of Burns's "O my luve is like a red, red rose," and critics like Sir Sidney Lee have badly confounded matters by judging this kind of verse as an attempt at such poetry. At its best this witty poetry is arch, adroit, and graceful. The figures which it employs are often enough instruments of fancy, merely in Coleridge's use of the term "fancy." But we shall find among the Elizabethans, and to a greater extent among the poets of the seventeenth century who followed them, witty poets who use the effect of frivolous ingenuity as a means to a serious intensity. It is important to distinguish between mere *vers de société* and this other poetry with its more profound repercussions. The line of division between the two types is vague, and the poets of the period are continually crossing over it with confidence that their readers are on the alert to follow them. There are many poems, for instance, which begin frankly with a tone of *vers de société* only to deepen into something more serious. It is most important to notice that the increasing seriousness, when it occurs, is *not* accompanied by a correspondent lessening of the play of wit. Habington's "To Roses in the Bosom of Castara" begins, as the title would suggest, by striking the note of conscious and artful gallantry appropriate to an occasional poem of exaggerated compliment:

> Yee blushing Virgins happy are
> In the chaste Nunn'ry of her brests,
> For hee'd prophane so chaste a faire
> Who ere should call them *Cupids* nests.
>
> Transplanted thus how bright yee grow;
> How rich a perfume doe yee yeeld?
> In some close gardens, Cowslips so
> Are sweeter than i' th' open field.
>
> In those white cloysters live secure
> From the rude blasts of wanton breath,
> Each houre more innocent and pure,
> Till you shall wither into death.

But with the last stanza the poem has surely modulated into something else:

> Then that which living gave you roome,
> Your glorious sepulchere shall be,
> There wants no marble for a tombe,
> Whose brest hath marble beene to me.

A still more serious tone is achieved in Carew's "Ask Me No More":

> Ask me no more where *Jove* bestowes,
> When *June* is past, the fading rose:
> For in your beauties orient deep,
> These Flowers as in their causes sleep.
>
> Ask me no more whither doe stray
> The golden Atomes of the day:
> For in pure love heaven did prepare
> Those powders to enrich your hair.
>
> Ask me no more whither doth hast
> The Nightingale, when *May* is past:
> For in your sweet dividing throat
> She winters, and keeps warm her note.
>
> Ask me no more where those starres light,
> That downwards fall in dead of night:
> For in your eyes they sit, and there,
> Fixed, become as in their sphere.
>
> Ask me no more if East or West,
> The Phoenix builds her spicy nest:
> For unto you at last she flyes,
> And in your fragrant bosome dies.

Here, certainly, are all the appurtenances of wit. There is the clever ingenuity (e.g., the falling stars find in the spheres of her eyes their proper spheres, and thus become fixed stars with a permanent place in the universe, etc.); there is the exaggerated compliment; there is the witty verbal ingenuity ("orient" is used to suggest the gorgeous splendour of the east, and the east associated with the day-spring, and the orient where the phoenix was fabled to live); there is even the tag of scholastic philosophy, "These Flowers as in their causes sleep." Yet the poem does give a definite effect of seriousness—not in spite of the wit, but by means of the wit. Without the calculated, yet graceful ingenuity, the poem would be merely a trifle of glib hyperbole. The poet's sincerity is not to be measured by whether he believes that the nightingale really inhabits his mistress's throat any more than it is to be measured by his literal belief in the existence of the phoenix. The test of his sincerity is to be measured by the integrity of tone which the poem achieves, and this in turn, as the poem indicates, may be achieved by ingenuity as well as simplicity—by a sense of consciously artificial statement as well as by a sense of natural statement.

The case of John Hoskins' "Absence" is somewhat more complex. The poem begins with the lover's statement that absence cannot estrange him from his mistress:

> Absence heare my protestation
>> Against thy strengthe
>> Distance and lengthe,
> Doe what thou canst for alteration:
>> For harts of truest mettall
>> Absence doth joyne, and time doth settle.

> Who loves a Mistris of right quality,
>> His mind hath founde
>> Affections grounde
> Beyond time, place, and all mortality:
>> To harts that cannot vary
>> Absence is present, time doth tary:

> My Sences want their outward motion
>> Which now within
>> Reason doth win,
> Redoubled by her secret notion:
>> Like rich men that take pleasure
>> In hidinge more than handling treasure.

But in the course of the poem, the simple defiance of the power of absence is ingeniously developed into an argument for the positive advantages of being absent:

> By absence this good means I gaine
>> That I can catch her
>> Where none can watch her
> In some close corner of my braine:
>> There I embrace and kiss her,
>> And so enjoye her, and so misse her.

A superficial view might dismiss the poem as merely a pleasant sophistry. But closer reading will show that the development of the wit has succeeded in endowing the poem with a sense of personal tenderness and sincerity lacking in the more abstract opening stanzas. The ability to be tender and, at the same time, alert and aware intellectually is a complex attitude, a mature attitude, but not necessarily a self-contradictory attitude. Only a sentimentalist will feel it to be so. Moreover, the tenderness is achieved, not in spite of the wit, but through it. One has only to remem-

ber that with later poets "close corner of my braine" would probably
have become vulgarized to "depth of my heart" in order to appreciate its
importance here in dictating the particular delicacy of tone achieved.

That the use of wit to intensify seriousness was frequently conscious on the poet's part is very clearly illustrated in Donne's "Valediction: of My Name, in the Window." After arguing that his name engraved in the glass of his mistress's window will serve to remind her of
him during his absence, and after a series of brilliant analogies developed
from the image of the engraved name, the poet in the last stanza apparently dismisses all that he has said as merely idle speculation:

> But glasse, and lines must be,
> No meanes our firme substantiall love to keepe;
> Neere death inflects this lethargie,
> And this I murmure in my sleep;

The fancies in which he has indulged are merely the images of a sort of
delirium—they are a mere babbling induced by approaching death. He
now seems to be on the point of repudiating them in favour of a completely final word. But with the last lines

> Impute this idle talke, to that I goe,
> For dying men talke often so—

we are suddenly back on the same level with the material of the earlier
stanzas. The "death" is the parting which he must endure, and far from
making a retraction of the play of wit, the retraction is itself caught up
into the pattern of wit.

But the effect of the repudiation-of-the-repudiation, is not to end
the poem on a note of mere flippancy. On the contrary the effect is to
justify the poet's use of wit, here an adequate—and in this experience,
at least, an inevitable—instrument. We may describe the effect somewhat clumsily as follows: the poet is conscious of the fantastic nature
of his development of the original conceit, but having indicated his awareness of this, can only brazen out the fantasy; or, he would tell his mistress what he wishes to tell her in sober statement, not in "idle talk," if
he could, but, having considered the possibility, he can, after all, make
use of no better instrument than his original metaphorical language. The
poem, then, may be said to carry within itself an ironical justification of
the method which it employs.

Here one may pause to reflect that all the examples so far considered
represent poems in which there is a considerable development of the
poet's attitude, and definite, even violent, shifts in the tone of the poem.
To cite one more instance of this, Marvell's "To his Coy Mistress" represents at least two powerful shifts of tone, and a development of the poet's
attitude from the frank playfulness of the opening lines into a passionately

serious, though controlled, apprehension of the meaning of death. We have said that Arnold's high seriousness is little more than Coleridge's "steady fervour of a mind . . . filled with the grandeur of its subject." The damaging bias of this view ought now to be thoroughly apparent. Identification of depth of sincerity with a steady fervour leaves out of account the possibility of dramatic *development* of the fervour. It is significant that Arnold attempts to realise in his own poetry a sort of magnificent monotone. Granting that it is one of the ways to write poetry, it does not exhaust the ways, nor does it indicate necessarily the best way.

Thus far we have considered only love poems. The same considerations, however, apply to the religious poetry of the metaphysical poets. This poetry will present an even more striking indictment of the belief that wit and sincerity are antithetical, for surely religious poetry imposes the most stringent requirements of sincerity. Indeed, on the assumption that wit is inevitably bound up with an attitude of levity, we should expect the metaphysical poets to lay aside their witty devices when they undertake religious poetry. But this is precisely what they do not do. Unless we are prepared to count the pious rector of Bemerton and the Dean of St. Paul's cynics, we must allow that they at least felt that wit might be employed appropriately in their most solemn poems.

To grant this is not to prove, of course, that their witty religious poems are successful in transmitting a sense of their seriousness to us as readers. Here again, one must ultimately rest his judgment on the poems themselves. To take a rather well-known example, consider Donne's "Batter My Heart, Three-Personed God," which, after a series of bold figures, ends as follows:

> . . . for I
> Except you enthrall mee, never shall be free,
> Nor ever chaste, except you ravish me.

The application of the sexual figure to the idea of spiritual chastity is audacious, but most unprejudiced readers will experience here the charm and surprise of great poetry. Notice also that in this case the question of the poet's seriousness—whatever else may be questioned—does not arise. The same generalisation may be made with regard to Herbert and Crashaw. Their failures are many and notorious. The reader who knows nothing else of metaphysical poetry is familiar with the absurdity of Crashaw's "walking baths" and his pillow "stuffed with down of angel's wing." But even cases of admitted failure do not call in question the poet's personal sincerity; and the successes, it is important to notice, are not achieved by the poet's abandoning his characteristic method in favour of unintellectual simplicity.

Most destructive of all to the proposition that wit can never be united with seriousness is the case of poetry in which the pun, that most frivolous of the instruments of wit, contributes to serious effects. Donne's poem, "To Christ," has been much admired by critics of all schools, largely, one suggests, because of its supposed simplicity and freedom from conceits. But many critics have failed to notice the puns in the third and fifth lines of the following stanza:

> I have a sinne of feare, that when I have spunne
> My last thred, I shall perish on the shore;
> But sweare by thy selfe, that at my death, thy Sonne
> Shall shine as he shines now, and heretofore;
> And, having done that, Thou haste done,
> I feare noe more.

The second of the two is quite startling; but "Thou haste done" would have been recognized as a play on the poet's name by an age which recognized a similar play in Shakespeare's one hundred and thirty-fifth sonnet. The pun does not disfigure the poem; and it allows the poet to say "Thou hast finished" and "Thou hast me" in what is literally the same breath.

F. C. Prescott has pointed out an even more striking example of the pun in *Romeo and Juliet*. He shows that the verb "to die" was used in the seventeenth century with the meaning "to experience the consummation of the sexual act," and suggests that there is a shade of this meaning latent in

> *Juliet.* Yea, noise?—then I'll be brief.—O happy dagger! (*Snatching Romeo's dagger*)
> This is thy sheath; (*Stabs herself*) there rust, and let me die. (*Falls on Romeo's body and dies.*)

Prescott points out that the mature and thoughtful reader "will remember Shakespeare's constant word-play—sometimes coarse, sometimes poetical—in this tragedy and throughout. He will note that Romeo puns in his dying speech ('Oh, here will I set up my everlasting rest') and indeed falls with this same word 'die' as his last ('Thus with a kiss I die'). The wordplay here ceases to be mere pun or witticism and becomes highly poetical, adding greatly to the dramatic effect, though it is perhaps a little more in the Elizabethan taste than ours. Indeed the whole tragedy of love and death is summed up in this last word and corresponding last action of each of the two lovers."

Prescott's observation that Shakespeare's pun "is perhaps a little more in the Elizabethan taste than ours" deserves a further comment, for it raises the whole problem with which the present book concerns itself. The historical considerations which Prescott introduces are really irrelevant here. If the word-play is once effective and justified, then it is always justified—regardless of the period in which the play was produced. To justify it by saying that it is "in the Elizabethan taste" is gratuitous and misleading.

Some of the functions performed by devices of wit have already been indicated by the examples cited above: we have noticed the use of wit for precision (as in Donne's compass conceit or in Marvell's comparison of the lovers to parallel lines), and for concentration (as in Shakespeare's pun just referred to). One might make a very good case for breaking over the conventional boundaries of the "poetic" for the sake of an increased psychological subtlety or for dramatic concentration of effect. But the most general and most important function of wit is that which must be termed—for want of a more accurate phrase—the ironical function.

This function too has already been dealt with by implication. It may well bear some elaboration. As long as figurative language is regarded as inessential to poetic communication—as long as one's test for good metaphor is the fact that it "both illustrates and ennobles" the subject— the immensely important function of metaphor in qualifying the poet's attitude will be slighted. To repeat what was said in the previous chapter: To "illustrate and ennoble" implies that what the poet says may be said without benefit of metaphor and that the real excuse for using metaphor is that the metaphor decorates the idea and states it more clearly. But we have argued that the poet's attitude is a highly important element of *what* is communicated; and figurative language is continually used to indicate shadings of attitude. The phrase, "to illustrate and ennoble," itself indicates some sort of realisation of this function. But it allows room only for the attitude of approbation. There is no recognition of the need on occasion for an ironical function—for imagery which will do other than ennoble. It may be argued that the orthodox criticism does, however, allow room for derogatory imagery *in its proper place*—in lampoon, satire, and comedy—and that none would be quicker than Dr. Johnson himself to allow for such use of figurative language. The point is well taken. But lampoon, satire, and comedy are by implication less serious forms. Orthodox criticism hardly allows a place in *serious* poetry for ironical imagery. Most important of all, by rigorously segregating the approbative and satirical attitudes it has obscured the fact that very many, and, indeed, nearly all mature attitudes represent some sort of mingling of the approbative and the satirical. Frequently, the more complex attitudes are expressed, and necessarily expressed, in varying degrees of irony: bitter, playful, whimsical, tragic, self-inclusive, etc. To illustrate what is meant, consider the following stanzas from Yeats's "All Souls' Night":

> Horton's the first I call. He loved strange thought
> And knew that sweet extremity of pride
> That's called platonic love,
> And that to such a pitch of passion wrought
> Nothing could bring him, when his lady died,
> Anodyne for his love.
> Words were but wasted breath;
> One dear hope had he:
> The inclemency
> Of that or the next winter would be death.
>
> Two thoughts were so mixed up I could not tell
> Whether of her or God he thought the most,
> But think that his mind's eye,
> When upward turned, on one sole image fell;
> And that a slight companionable ghost
> Wild with divinity,
> Had so lit up the whole
> Immense miraculous house,
> The Bible promised us,
> It seemed a gold-fish swimming in a bowl.

The final comparison comes as a shock in this particular context. It is hardly a decorative image. But most readers who feel the shock will also sense the rightness of the figure in the total context of the poem.

It may be difficult to give specific reasons for the rightness, but speculation on the matter may touch upon such observations as these: The poet has a deep respect for his friend and means to stress his friend's passionate belief. At the same time, he does not identify himself with the belief. Horton's platonic love is after all a "sweet extremity of pride," partaking of fantastic exaggeration, though magnificent in its exaggeration. The primary shock in the comparison rests in the clash between "Immense miraculous house,/The Bible promised us" and the matter-of-fact domesticity of the goldfish bowl. But the comparison, shock and all, does justice to the various factors of the situation. If it is whimsical with a trace of irony, the whimsy grows legitimately out of what is, after all, only an accurate description of the friend's belief. The poet is aware of the element of magnificence in the belief, if at the same time aware of the fantastic element; and he has found means of letting the two elements work together in his picture of the crystal sphere of the heavens holding one golden and magnified image, "wild with divinity."

If this attempt to indicate how the poet uses his figure to qualify, to make reservations, to notice by implication "the other side" of the matter, seems too crude—if we have distorted Yeats's irony into an attitude of satire which is not intended—the commentary has at least this virtue: It indicates by its literal crudity that figurative language is the indispensable tool of the poet. There are nuances of attitude that can be given in no other way than by the aid of the qualification which the metaphor or simile produces.

The effect produced by Marvell's figure of the parallel lines may be cited here as another instance of this function. But one is not forced to rely on the metaphysical poets or on the moderns for illustration. One may find, to cite an instance from the Romantic poets, a very brilliant case of qualifying irony as used by Keats. Consider the transition from the seventh to the eighth stanza of the "Ode to a Nightingale":

> The same that oft-times hath
> Charmed magic casements, opening on the foam
> Of perilous seas, in faery lands forlorn.
>
> Forlorn! the very word is like a bell
> To toll me back from thee to my sole self—

In the first instance, "forlorn" is being used primarily in its archaic sense of "utterly lost." The faery lands are those of a past which is remote and far away. But the meaning of "forlorn" is definitely shifted as the poet repeats the word. In its meaning, "pitiable; left desolate," "forlorn" describes the poet's own state, and applies, as he suddenly realises in the poem, to his own case. The very adjective which is used to describe the world of the imagination which the bird symbolizes, ironically enough can be used to describe his own situation. The psychological effect is that of a man in a reverie suddenly stumbling, and being wrenched out of the reverie. The real world makes its demands; no matter how beautiful the realm of the imagination, one cannot free oneself from actuality and live in the imagination permanently. Indeed, the general theme of the poem may be described as that of the following paradox: the world of the imagination offers a release from the painful world of actuality, yet at the same time it renders the world of actuality more painful by contrast. Keats's repetition of "forlorn" is thus a concentrated instance of the theme of the whole poem. Recognition of the irony makes the poem not less, but more, serious.

The foregoing account of the various uses of wit will allow us to understand more clearly the real significance of the change in taste which occurred in the middle of the seventeenth century. For the really important effect of the change was to play down the importance of qualifying irony. That this is true we shall see by re-examining the critical revolution of this period. It was an aspect of the general codifying process of the mid-century, a process carried on with the best of intentions under the auspices of rationalism and the new science, and backed by the authority of Hobbes with his simplified picture of the mind. Primary emphasis was placed upon analysis and classification. There was a tendency to departmentalize the mind, separating into neat categories the emotional and the intellectual, the serious and the frivolous, the dignified and the mean, the "poetic" and the "nonpoetic." Moreover, not only was there a tendency towards distinction and separation but towards segregation as well. The tendency of the period toward "order" had, in literature, far more important effects than that of making the closed heroic couplet *de rigueur*. It tended to remove the conflict of opposites which is the very life of metaphysical poetry.

The effect was pervasive, but it expresses itself most clearly in the treatment of metaphor. Hobbes is willing, of course, to allow metaphor a place in poetry (as he is willing, indeed, to allow a place to poetry itself). But the function of metaphor is conceived of as unimportant. Metaphor is essentially linked with absurdity, even in common expressions: "For though it be lawful to say, for example, in common speech, *the way goeth, or leadeth hither, or thither, the proverb says this or that,* whereas ways cannot go, nor proverbs speak; Yet in reckoning, and seeking of truth, such speeches are not to be admitted." It is Hobbes's constant concern in the *Leviathan* to point out that in "all rigorous search of truth, judgment does all, except sometimes the understanding have need to be opened by some apt similitude. . . . [Hobbes's own metaphor here is obscure; presumably he means that metaphor may be used to stimulate the mind to come to serious grips with the problem.] But for metaphors, they are in this case utterly excluded. For seeing they openly profess deceit: to admit them into counsel, or reasoning, were manifest folly."

No one will object to Hobbes's attempt to remove the poetry from scientific discourse. But if metaphor is not to be used in such discourse, where is it properly used, and what function is it to perform? Hobbes makes a fourfold division of the uses of speech. One and two deal with scientific aspects, three with practical. Plainly poetry falls under the fourth use which is "to please and delight ourselves and others, by *playing with our words,* for *pleasure or ornament, innocently* [italics mine]." The function allowed metaphor is all too plain.

If we inspect Hobbes's literary criticism we shall find that metaphor never loses this taint of extravagance and unreliability. The extravagance must be curbed by judgment, particularly in more serious poetry.

What was apparently the Jacobean and Elizabethan view of the problem has received a powerful restatement in our own day in the view that the poet, the imaginative man, has his particular value in his superior power to reconcile the irrelevant or apparently warring elements of experience. As Eliot has put it, "When a poet's mind is perfectly equipped for its work, it is constantly amalgamating disparate experience; the ordinary man's experience is chaotic, irregular, fragmentary. The latter falls in love, or reads Spinoza, and these two experiences have nothing to do with each other, or with the noise of the typewriter or the smell of cooking; in the mind of the poet these experiences are always forming new wholes." Or to quote from another modern critic, Richards has contrasted the poet with the ordinary man thus: ". . . the ordinary man suppresses nine-tenths of his impulses, because he is incapable of managing them without confusion. He goes about in blinkers because what he would otherwise see would upset him."

The neo-classic poets were apparently far more modest in their ambitions than the Elizabethans. The weight of Hobbes, their foremost aesthetician, was definitely in favour of the ordinary man. For the imaginative act of fusing what in ordinary experience is inharmonious, the Hobbesian poet tended to substitute the rational act of sorting out the discordant and removing it from the context.

The critics of the period talk as if they were the first in English to insist on decorum. But obviously the Elizabethan and Jacobean poets had a decorum too; theirs, however, was an imaginative decorum as opposed to the essentially *logical* decorum of the Restoration. Hobbes and the members of the Royal Society were thinking primarily of expository prose, of course, when they thundered against the general unreliability of metaphor, for even the tamest metaphor involves some violation of science. But it is not easy for a writer to keep his right hand from knowing what his left hand is doing. In squeezing the poetry out of science, some of the poetry was squeezed out of poetry itself.

Confusion on the point was made all the easier by the didactic theory of poetry which the critics of the period had inherited from the Renaissance. A poem was conceived of as essentially a statement; the test of the statement's value, its truth; and the success of the poet, his success as an expositor. The poet of course differed from the scientist or moralist in that the truths which he had to impart were less sublunary, less urgently practical, and in that he might decorate his information with pleasing imagery and harmonious sound. But the implication was clear that the imagery and the metrics were to give an absolute pleasure in themselves. They do bear a relation to what is said in the poem: they may render it more agreeable to the reader by the capacity to give pleasure. But this is a very different conception of the function of imagery and metre from that which holds that they actually determine what is said by the poem. It is no accident that the neo-classic poets reprehend Donne, not only for his difficult imagery, but also for his rough verse.

When we conceive of the poet as primarily the expositor, the character of the imagery is predetermined. And here we come—to indicate how little the Romantic Revolt altered the essentially Hobbesian conception—upon the basis of Matthew Arnold's high seriousness. A serious expositor, one who endeavours to state "high poetic truth," will use clear illustrations and illustrations which dignify and heighten; he will not indulge in fanciful playfulness; he will not leave the reader in doubt as to what he means; his attitude will be relatively simple. Quite naturally, Arnold's high seriousness is a function of the poet's sincerity—for the poet is a teacher.

The first critical revolution in modern English poetry, then, may be described as a *simplification* of poetry—a simplification, not primarily of the ideas expressed, but rather a simplification of the poet's attitude towards his material. Dryden's famous stricture on Donne will illustrate. Dryden objected to Donne's love poems because he "perplexes the minds of the fair sex with nice speculations of philosophy, when he should engage their hearts, and entertain them with the softnesses of love." This is to state the fault as that of an inappropriate intellectual difficulty. But there is further the clear implication that, whereas there might be legitimate difficulty in a theological or political poem, there is surely no conceivable justification for difficulty in a love poem. Moreover, Dryden goes on to imply that if you persist with the difficulty, using it not ignorantly but with full consciousness, the fair sex might properly doubt whether you were serious about the love after all.

It is this same objection, basically, that is raised by such a poem as, to cite a modern example, John Crowe Ransom's brilliant "Captain Carpenter." Captain Carpenter resolutely engages in combat with the forces of hell, only to be regularly defeated, and to lose in combat various pieces of his anatomy until there is left only the tongue to shout defiance. The irony in the poem is anything but a matter of simple contrasts and adjustments. To notice specifically only two or three facets of the poet's attitude: there is abundant sense of the Captain's bluster:

> Captain Carpenter mounted up one day
> And rode straightway into a stranger rogue
> That looked unchristian but be that as it may
> The Captain did not wait upon prologue.

But there is also definitely the sense that Captain Carpenter has been betrayed. According to all the stories the Captain should win, but his enemies perversely refuse to abide by the conventional formulae:

> Their strokes and counters whistled in the wind
> I wish he had delivered half his blows
> But where she should have made off like a hind
> The bitch bit off his arms at the elbows.

The poet does not conceal Captain Carpenter's ridiculous bravado:

> I heard him asking in the grimmest tone
> If any enemy yet there was to fight?

Yet Captain Carpenter is allowed to have at least a suggestion of self-irony: he chivalrously warns his enemies that he is a dangerous man, but he is willing to entertain the possibility that they may win. In that case the victor

> has a pretty choice
> From an anatomy with little to lose
> Whether he cut my tongue and take my voice
> Or whether it be my round red heart he choose.

The irony of the poem as a whole is a rich and complex blending of pity and laughter in which the attitude of the reader, far from being simplified, is developed and complicated. It is important to notice that irony functions here not only to give precision to the poet's attitude, but also to give another dimension to the symbol. But the plain reader (as Laura Riding and Robert Graves put it) "wants to know definitely whether he is to laugh or cry over Captain Carpenter's story, and if he is not given a satisfactory clue he naturally doubts the sincerity of the poet, he becomes suspicious of his seriousness and leaves him alone."

This statement puts forcibly the contrast between the sincerity on which Arnold's high seriousness is based and the concept of sincerity which emerges from our discussion of irony. The two conceptions are almost diametrically opposed. Arnold's sincerity expresses itself as a vigilance which keeps out of the poem all those extraneous and distracting elements which might seem to contradict what the poet wishes to communicate to his audience. It is the sincerity of the conscientious expositor who makes his point, even at the price of suppressions and exclusions. Poetry which embodies such a conception of sincerity, when it is unsuccessful, has, as its characteristic vice, sentimentality. For sentimentality nearly always involves an over-simplification of the experience in question. The sentimentalist takes a short cut to intensity by removing all the elements of the experience which might conceivably militate against the intensity. Every poet, of course, makes a selection, but the sentimentalist, we feel, selects on too narrow a basis. To put the matter in terms of the poet's accuracy and fidelity to experience, the sentimental poet makes us feel that he is sacrificing the totality of his vision in favour of a particular interpretation. Hence the feeling on reading a sentimental poem that the intensity is the result of a trick.

The second conception of sincerity, on the other hand, reveals itself as an unwillingness to ignore the complexity of experience. The poet attempts to fuse the conflicting elements in a harmonious whole. And here one may suggest a definition of wit. Wit is not merely an acute perception of analogies; it is a lively awareness of the fact that the obvious attitude toward a given situation is not the only possible attitude. Because wit, for us, is still associated with levity, it may be well to state it in its most serious terms. The witty poet's glancing at other attitudes is not necessarily merely "play"—an attempt to puzzle us or to show off his acuteness of perception; it is possible to describe it as merely his refusal to blind himself to a multiplicity which exists.

One is even tempted to indulge in the following paradox: namely, that wit, far from being a playful aspect of the mind, is the most serious aspect, and that the only poetry which possesses high seriousness in the deepest sense is the poetry of wit. But some obvious reservations are to be made and some misapprehensions anticipated. We have defined wit in its most general terms. The wit of a Donne or of a Marvell is after all only one form, and an extreme form, which wit may take. There are obviously many fine poems, including some of Arnold's, which are not "witty" in the superficial sense at all. But if we are to understand the poetry of the Elizabethan and Jacobean periods we must discard the view that wit is to be associated with barren and shallow ingenuity.

Frames of Reference

W. K. WIMSATT, JR. • M. C. BEARDSLEY
The Intentional Fallacy

He owns with toil he wrote the following scenes;
But, if they're naught, ne'er spare him for his pains:
Damn him the more; have no commiseration
For dullness on mature deliberation.

WILLIAM CONGREVE
Prologue to *The Way of the World*

The claim of the author's "intention" upon the critic's judgment has been challenged in a number of recent discussions, notably in the debate entitled *The Personal Heresy*, between Professors Lewis and Tillyard, and at least implicitly in periodical essays like those in the "Symposiums" of 1940 in the *Southern* and *Kenyon Reviews*.[1] But it seems doubtful if this claim and most of its romantic corollaries are as yet subject to any widespread questioning. The present writers, in a short article entitled "Intention" for a *Dictionary* [2] of literary criticism, raised

Reprinted, by permission, from *The Verbal Icon: Studies in the Meaning of Poetry*, Lexington, Ky.: University of Kentucky Press, 1954.

[1] Cf. Louis Teeter, "Scholarship, and the Art of Criticism," *ELH*, V (Sept. 1938), 173–94; René Wellek, review of Geoffrey Tillotson's *Essays in Criticism and Research, Modern Philology*, XLI (May 1944), 262; G. Wilson Knight, *Shakespeare and Tolstoy*, English Association Pamphlet No. 88 (April 1934), p. 10; Bernard C. Heyl, *New Bearings in Esthetics and Art Criticism* (New Haven, 1943), pp. 66, 113, 149.
[2] *Dictionary of World Literature*, ed. Joseph T. Shipley (New York, 1942), pp. 326–339.

the issue but were unable to pursue its implications at any length. We argued that the design or intention of the author is neither available nor desirable as a standard for judging the success of a work of literary art, and it seems to us that this is a principle which goes deep into some differences in the history of critical attitudes. It is a principle which accepted or rejected points to the polar opposites of classical "imitation" and romantic expression. It entails many specific truths about inspiration, authenticity, biography, literary history and scholarship, and about some trends of contemporary poetry, especially its allusiveness. There is hardly a problem of literary criticism in which the critic's approach will not be qualified by his view of "intention."

"Intention," as we shall use the term, corresponds to *what he intended* in a formula which more or less explicitly has had wide acceptance. "In order to judge the poet's performance, we must know *what he intended*." Intention is design or plan in the author's mind. Intention has obvious affinities for the author's attitude toward his work, the way he felt, what made him write.

We begin our discussion with a series of propositions summarized and abstracted to a degree where they seem to us axiomatic, if not truistic.

1. A poem does not come into existence by accident. The words of a poem, as Professor Stoll has remarked, come out of a head, not out of a hat. Yet to insist on the designing intellect as a *cause* of a poem is not to grant the design or intention as a *standard*.

2. One must ask how a critic expects to get an answer to the question about intention. How is he to find out what the poet tried to do? If the poet succeeded in doing it, then the poem itself shows what he was trying to do. And if the poet did not succeed, then the poem is not adequate evidence, and the critic must go outside the poem—for evidence of an intention that did not become effective in the poem. "Only one *caveat* must be borne in mind," says an eminent intentionalist [3] in a moment when his theory repudiates itself; "the poet's aim must be judged at the moment of the creative act, that is to say, by the art of the poem itself."

3. Judging a poem is like judging a pudding or a machine. One demands that it work. It is only because an artifact works that we infer the intention of an artificer. "A poem should not mean but be." A poem can *be* only through its *meaning*—since its medium is words—yet it *is,* simply *is,* in the sense that we have no excuse for inquiring what part is intended or meant.[4] Poetry is a feat of style by which a complex of mean-

[3] J. E. Spingarn, "The New Criticism," in *Criticism and America* (New York, 1924), pp. 24–25.
[4] As critics and teachers constantly do. "We have here a deliberate blurring. . . ." "Should this be regarded as ironic or as unplanned?" ". . . is the

ing is handled all at once. Poetry succeeds because all or most of what is said or implied is relevant; what is irrelevant has been excluded, like lumps from pudding and "bugs" from machinery. In this respect poetry differs from practical messages, which are successful if and only if we correctly infer the intention. They are more abstract than poetry.

4. The meaning of a poem may certainly be a personal one, in the sense that a poem expresses a personality or state of soul rather than a physical object like an apple. But even a short lyric poem is dramatic, the response of a speaker (no matter how abstractly conceived) to a situation (no matter how universalized). We ought to impute the thoughts and attitudes of the poem immediately to the dramatic *speaker*, and if to the author at all, only by a biographical act of inference.

5. If there is any sense in which an author, by revision, has better achieved his original intention, it is only the very abstract, tautological, sense that he intended to write a better work and now has done it. (In this sense every author's intention is the same.) His former specific intention was not his intention. "He's the man we were in search of, that's true"; says Hardy's rustic constable, "and yet he's not the man we were in search of. For the man we were in search of was not the man we wanted." [5]

· · · · ·

"Is not a critic," asks Professor Stoll, ". . . a judge, who does not explore his own consciousness, but determines the author's meaning or intention, as if the poem were a will, a contract, or the constitution? The poem is not the critic's own." [6] He has diagnosed very accurately two forms of irresponsibility, one of which he prefers. Our view is yet different. The poem is not the critic's own and not the author's (it is detached from the author at birth and goes about the world beyond his power to intend about it or control it). The poem belongs to the public. It is embodied in language, the peculiar possession of the public, and it is about the human being, an object of public knowledge. What is said about the poem is subject to the same scrutiny as any statement in linguistics or in the general science of psychology or morals. Mr. Richards has aptly called the poem a *class*—"a class of experiences which do not

literal meaning intended . . . ?" ". . . a paradox of religious faith which is intended to exult. . . ." "It seems to me that Herbert intends. . . ." These examples are chosen from three pages of an issue of *The Explicator* (Fredericksburg, Va.), vol. II, no. 1 (Oct. 1943). Authors often judge their own works in the same way. See *This is My Best,* ed. Whit Burnett (New York, 1942), e.g., pp. 539–540.

[5] A close relative of the intentional fallacy is that of talking about "means" and "end" in poetry instead of "part" and "whole." We have treated this relation concisely in our dictionary article.

[6] E. E. Stoll, "The Tempest," *PMLA*, XLIV (Sept. 1932), 703.

differ in any character more than a certain amount . . . from a standard experience." And he adds, "We may take as this standard experience the relevant experience of the poet when contemplating the completed composition." Professor Wellek in a fine essay on the problem has preferred to call the poem "a system of norms," "extracted from every individual experience," and he objects to Mr. Richards' deference to the poet as reader. We side with Professor Wellek in not wishing to make the poet (outside the poem) an authority.

A critic of our *Dictionary* article, Mr. Ananda K. Coomaraswamy, has argued [7] that there are two kinds of enquiry about a work of art: (1) whether the artist achieved his intentions; (2) whether the work of art "ought ever to have been undertaken at all" and so "whether it is worth preserving." Number (2), Mr. Coomaraswamy maintains, is not "criticism of any work of art *qua* work of art," but is rather moral criticism; number (1) is artistic criticism. But we maintain that (2) need not be moral criticism: that there is another way of deciding whether works of art are worth preserving and whether, in a sense, they "ought" to have been undertaken, and this is the way of objective criticism of works of art as such, the way which enables us to distinguish between a skilful murder and a skilful poem. A skilful murder is an example which Mr. Coomaraswamy uses, and in his system the difference between the murder and the poem is simply a "moral" one, not an "artistic" one, since each if carried out according to plan is "artistically" successful. We maintain that (2) is an enquiry of more worth than (1), and since (2), and not (1), is capable of distinguishing poetry from murder, the name "artistic criticism" is properly given to (2).

II

It is not so much an empirical as an analytic judgment, not a historical statement, but a definition, to say that the intentional fallacy is a romantic one. When a rhetorician, presumably of the first century A.D., writes: "Sublimity is the echo of a great soul," or tells us that "Homer enters into the sublime actions of his heroes" and "shares the full inspiration of the combat," we shall not be surprised to find this rhetorician considered as a distant harbinger of romanticism and greeted in the warmest terms by so romantic a critic as Saintsbury. One may wish to argue whether Longinus should be called romantic,[8] but there can hardly be a doubt that in one important way he is.

[7] Ananda K. Coomaraswamy, "Intention," *The American Bookman*, I (Winter 1944), 41–48.
[8] For the relation of Longinus to modern romanticism, see R. S. Crane, review of Samuel Monk's *The Sublime, Philological Quarterly*, XV (April 1936), 165–66.

Goethe's three questions for "constructive criticism" are "What did the author set out to do? Was his plan reasonable and sensible, and how far did he succeed in carrying it out?" If one leaves out the middle question, one has in effect the system of Croce—the culmination and crowning philosophic expression of romanticism. The beautiful is the successful intuition—expression, and the ugly is the unsuccessful; the intuition or private part of art is *the* aesthetic fact, and the medium or public part is not the subject of aesthetic at all. Yet aesthetic reproduction takes place only "if all the other conditions remain equal."

> Oil-paintings grow dark, frescoes fade, statues lose noses . . . the text of a poem is corrupted by bad copyists or bad printing.

> The Madonna of Cimabue is still in the Church of Santa Maria Novella; but does she speak to the visitor of today as to the Florentines of the thirteenth century?

> *Historical interpretation* labours . . . to reintegrate in us the psychological conditions which have changed in the course of history. It . . . enables us to see a work of art (a physical object) as its *author saw it* in the moment of production.[9]

The first italics are Croce's, the second ours. The upshot of Croce's system is an ambiguous emphasis on history. With such passages as a point of departure a critic may write a close analysis of the meaning or "spirit" of a play of Shakespeare or Corneille—a process that involves close historical study but remains aesthetic criticism—or he may write sociology, biography, or other kinds of non-aesthetic history. The Crocean system seems to have given more of a boost to the latter way of writing.

"What has the poet tried to do," asks Spingarn in his 1910 Columbia Lecture from which we have already quoted, "and how has he fulfilled his intention?" The place to look for "insuperable" ugliness, says Bosanquet, in his third *Lecture* of 1914, is the "region of insincere and affected art." The seepage of the theory into a non-philosophic place may be seen in such a book as Marguerite Wilkinson's inspirational *New Voices,* about the poetry of 1919 to 1931—where symbols "as old as the ages . . . retain their strength and freshness" through "Realization." We close this section with two examples from quarters where one might least expect a taint of the Crocean. Mr. I. A. Richards' fourfold distinction of meaning into "sense," "feeling," "tone," "intention" has been

---

[9] It is true that Croce himself in his *Ariosto, Shakespeare and Corneille,* trans. Douglas Ainslie (London, 1920) Chapter VII, "The Practical Personality and the Poetical Personality," and in his *Defence of Poetry,* trans. E. F. Carritt (Oxford, 1933), p. 24, has delivered a telling attack on intentionalism, but the prevailing drift of such passages in the *Aesthetic* as we quote is in the opposite direction.

probably the most influential statement of intentionalism in the past fifteen years, though it contains a hint of self-repudiation: "This function [intention]," says Mr. Richards, "is not on all fours with the others." In an essay on "Three Types of Poetry" Mr. Allen Tate writes as follows:

> We must understand that the lines
>
>> Life like a dome of many-colored glass
>> Stains the white radiance of eternity
>
> are not poetry; they express the *frustrated will* trying to compete with science. The *will* asserts a rhetorical proposition about the whole of life, but the *imagination* has not seized upon the materials of the poem and made them into a whole. Shelley's simile is imposed upon the material from above; it does not grow out of the material.

The last sentence contains a promise of objective analysis which is not fulfilled. The reason why the essay relies so heavily throughout on the terms "will" and "imagination" is that Mr. Tate is accusing the romantic poets of a kind of insincerity (romanticism in reverse) and at the same time is trying to describe something mysterious and perhaps indescribable, an "imaginative whole of life," a "wholeness of vision at a particular moment of experience," something which "yields us the quality of the experience." If a poet had a toothache at the moment of conceiving a poem, that would be part of the experience, but Mr. Tate of course does not mean anything like that. He is thinking about some kind of "whole" which in this essay at least he does not describe, but which doubtless it is the prime need of criticism to describe—in terms that may be publicly tested.

III

> I went to the poets; tragic, dithyrambic, and all sorts. . . . I took them some of the most elaborate passages in their own writings, and asked what was the meaning of them. . . . Will you believe me? . . . there is hardly a person present who would not have talked better about their poetry than they did themselves. Then I knew that not by wisdom do poets write poetry, but by a sort of genius and inspiration.

That reiterated mistrust of the poets which we hear from Socrates may have been part of a rigorously ascetic view in which we hardly wish to participate, yet Plato's Socrates saw a truth about the poetic mind which the world no longer commonly sees—so much criticism, and that the most inspirational and most affectionately remembered, has proceeded from the poets themselves.

Certainly the poets have had something to say that the analyst and professor could not say; their message has been more exciting: that poetry should come as naturally as leaves to a tree, that poetry is the lava of the imagination, or that it is emotion recollected in tranquillity. But it is necessary that we realize the character and authority of such testimony. There is only a fine shade between those romantic expressions and a kind of earnest advice that authors often give. Thus Edward Young, Carlyle, Walter Pater:

> I know two golden rules from *ethics,* which are no less golden in *Composition* than in life. 1. *Know thyself;* 2dly, *Reverence thyself.*

> This is the grand secret for finding readers and retaining them: let him who would move and convince others, be first moved and convinced himself. Horace's rule, *Si vis me flere,* is applicable in a wider sense than the literal one. To every poet, to every writer, we might say: Be true, if you would be believed. Truth! there can be no merit, no craft at all, without that. And further, all beauty is in the long run only *fineness* of truth, or what we call expression, the finer accommodation of speech to that vision within.

And Housman's little handbook to the poetic mind yields the following illustration:

> Having drunk a pint of beer at luncheon—beer is a sedative to the brain, and my afternoons are the least intellectual portion of my life— I would go out for a walk of two or three hours. As I went along, thinking of nothing in particular, only looking at things around me and following the progress of the seasons, there would flow into my mind, with sudden and unaccountable emotion, sometimes a line or two of verse, sometimes a whole stanza at once. . . .

This is the logical terminus of the series already quoted. Here is a confession of how poems were written which would do as a definition of poetry just as well as "emotion recollected in tranquillity"—and which the young poet might equally well take to heart as a practical rule. Drink a pint of beer, relax, go walking, think on nothing in particular, look at things, surrender yourself to yourself, search for the truth in your own soul, listen to the sound of your own inside voice, discover and express the *vraie vérité.*

It is probably true that all this is excellent advice for poets. The young imagination fired by Wordsworth and Carlyle is probably closer to the verge of producing a poem than the mind of the student who has been sobered by Aristotle or Richards. The art of inspiring poets, or at least of inciting something like poetry in young persons, has probably gone further in our day than ever before. Books of creative writing such as those issued from the Lincoln School are interesting evidence of what a child can do if taught how to manage himself honestly.[10] All this, however, would appear to belong to an art separate from criticism, or to a discipline which one might call the psychology of composition, valid and useful, an individual and private culture, yoga, or system of self-development which the young poet would do well to notice, but different from the public science of evaluating poems.

Coleridge and Arnold were better critics than most poets have been, and if the critical tendency dried up the poetry in Arnold and perhaps in Coleridge, it is not inconsistent with our argument, which is that judgment of poems is different from the art of producing them. Coleridge has given us the classic "anodyne" story and tells what he can about the genesis of a poem, which he calls a "psychological curiosity," but his definitions of poetry and of the poetic quality "imagination" are to be found elsewhere and in quite other terms.

The day may arrive when the psychology of composition is unified with the science of objective evaluation, but so far they are separate. It would be convenient if the passwords of the intentional school, "sincerity," "fidelity," "spontaneity," "authenticity," "genuineness," "originality," could be equated with terms of analysis such as "integrity," "relevance," "unity," "function"; with "maturity," "subtlety," and "adequacy," and other more precise axiological terms—in short, if "expression" always meant aesthetic communication. But this is not so.

"Aesthetic" art, says Professor Curt Ducasse, an ingenious theorist of expression, is the conscious objectification of feelings, in which an intrinsic part is the critical moment. The artist corrects the objectification when it is not adequate, but this may mean that the earlier attempt was not successful in objectifying the self, or "it may also mean that it was a successful objectification of a self which, when it confronted us clearly, we disowned and repudiated in favor of another." [11] What is the standard by which we disown or accept the self? Professor Ducasse does not say. Whatever it may be, however, this standard is an element in the definition of art which will not reduce to terms of objectification. The evaluation of the work of art remains public; the work is measured against something outside the author.

IV

There is criticism of poetry and there is, as we have seen, author psychology, which when applied to the present or future takes the form

[10] See Hughes Mearns, *Creative Youth* (Garden City, 1925), esp. pp. 10, 27–29. The technique of inspiring poems keeps pace today with a parallel analysis of the process of inspiration in successful artists. See Rosamond E. M. Harding, *An Anatomy of Inspiration*, Cambridge, 1940; Julius Portnoy, *A Psychology of Art Creation*, Philadelphia, 1942.
[11] Curt Ducasse, *The Philosophy of Art* (New York, 1929), p. 116.

of inspirational promotion; but author psychology can be historical too, and then we have literary biography, a legitimate and attractive study in itself, one approach, as Mr. Tillyard would argue, to personality, the poem being only a parallel approach. Certainly it need not be with a derogatory purpose that one points out personal studies, as distinct from poetic studies, in the realm of literary scholarship. Yet there is danger of confusing personal and poetic studies; and there is the fault of writing the personal as if it were poetic.

There is a difference between internal and external evidence for the meaning of a poem. And the paradox is only verbal and superficial that what is (1) internal is also public: it is discovered through the semantics and syntax of a poem, through our habitual knowledge of the language, through grammars, dictionaries, and all the literature which is the source of dictionaries, in general through all that makes a language and culture; while what is (2) external is private or idiosyncratic; not a part of the work as a linguistic fact: it consists of revelations (in journals, for example, or letters or reported conversations) about how or why the poet wrote the poem—to what lady, while sitting on what lawn, or at the death of what friend or brother. There is (3) an intermediate kind of evidence about the character of the author or about private or semi-private meanings attached to words or topics by an author or by a coterie of which he is a member. The meaning of words is the history of words, and the biography of an author, his use of a word, and the associations which the word had for *him,* are part of the word's history and meaning.[12] But the three types of evidence, especially (2) and (3), shade into one another so subtly that it is not always easy to draw a line between examples, and hence arises the difficulty for criticism. The use of biographical evidence need not involve intentionalism, because while it may be evidence of what the author intended, it may also be evidence of the meaning of his words and the dramatic character of his utterance. On the other hand, it may not be all this. And a critic who is concerned with evidence of type (1) and moderately with that of type (3) will in the long run produce a different sort of comment from that of the critic who is concerned with type (2) and with (3) where it shades into (2).

The whole glittering parade of Professor Lowes' *Road to Xanadu,* for instance, runs along the border between types (2) and (3) or boldly traverses the romantic region of (2). " 'Kubla Khan,' " says Professor Lowes, "is the fabric of a vision, but every image that rose up in its weaving had passed that way before. And it would seem that there is

[12] And the history of words *after* a poem is written may contribute meanings which if relevant to the original pattern should not be ruled out by a scruple about intention. Cf. C. S. Lewis and E. M. W. Tillyard, *The Personal Heresy* (Oxford, 1939), p. 16; Teeter, *loc. cit.,* pp. 183, 192; review of Tillotson's *Essays, TLS,* XLI (April 1942), 174.

nothing haphazard or fortuitous in their return." This is not quite clear
—not even when Professor Lowes explains that there were clusters of
associations, like hooked atoms, which were drawn into complex relation
with other clusters in the deep well of Coleridge's memory, and which
then coalesced and issued forth as poems. If there was nothing "haphazard or fortuitous" in the way the images returned to the surface, that
may mean (1) that Coleridge could not produce what he did not have,
that he was limited in his creation by what he had read or otherwise
experienced, or (2) that having received certain clusters of associations,
he was bound to return them in just the way he did, and that the value
of the poem may be described in terms of the experiences on which he
had to draw. The latter pair of propositions (a sort of Hartleyan associa-
tionism which Coleridge himself repudiated in the *Biographia*) may not
be assented to. There were certainly other combinations, other poems,
worse or better, that might have been written by men who had read
Bartram and Purchas and Bruce and Milton. And this will be true. no
matter how many times we are able to add to the brilliant complex of
Coleridge's reading. In certain flourishes (such as the sentence we have
quoted) and in chapter headings like "The Shaping Spirit," "The Magical
Synthesis," "Imagination Creatrix," it may be that Professor Lowes pretends to say more about the actual poems than he does. There is a certain
deceptive variation in these fancy chapter titles; one expects to pass on
to a new stage in the argument, and one finds—more and more sources,
more about "the streamy nature of association." [13]

"Wohin der Weg?" quotes Professor Lowes for the motto of his
book. "Kein Weg! Ins Unbetretene." Precisely because the way is *un-
betreten,* we should say, it leads away from the poem. Bartram's *Travels*
contains a good deal of the history of certain words and romantic Flori-
dan conceptions that appear in "Kubla Khan." And a good deal of that
history has passed and was then passing into the very stuff of our language. Perhaps a person who has read Bartram appreciates the poem more
than one who has not. Or, by looking up the vocabulary of "Kubla Khan"
in the *Oxford English Dictionary,* or by reading some of the other books
there quoted, a person may know the poem better. But it would seem to
pertain little to the poem to know that *Coleridge* has read Bartram.
There is a gross body of life, of sensory and mental experience, which
lies behind and in some sense causes every poem, but can never be and
need not be known in the verbal and hence intellectual composition

[13] Chapters VIII, "The Pattern," and XVI, "The Known and Familiar Land-
scape," will be found of most help to the student of the poem.
  For an extreme example of intentionalistic criticism, see Kenneth
Burke's analysis of *The Ancient Mariner* in *The Philosophy of Literary Form*
(Louisiana State University Press, 1941), pp. 22–23, 93–102. Mr. Burke
must be credited with realizing very clearly what he is up to.

which is the poem. For all the objects of our manifold experience, especially for the intellectual objects, for every unity, there is an action of the mind which cuts off roots, melts away context—or indeed we should never have objects or ideas or anything to talk about.

It is probable that there is nothing in Professor Lowes' vast book which could detract from anyone's appreciation of either *The Ancient Mariner* or *Kubla Khan*. We next present a case where preoccupation with evidence of type (3) has gone so far as to distort a critic's view of a poem (yet a case not so obvious as those that abound in our critical journals).

In a well-known poem by John Donne appears the following quatrain:

> Moving of th' earth brings harmes and feares,
>   Men reckon what it did and meant,
> But trepidation of the spheares,
>   Though greater farre, is innocent.

A recent critic in an elaborate treatment of Donne's learning has written of this quatrain as follows:

> . . . he touches the emotional pulse of the situation by a skillful allusion to the new and the old astronomy. . . . Of the new astronomy, the "moving of the earth" is the most radical principle; of the old, the "trepidation of the spheres" is the motion of the greatest complexity. . . . As the poem is a valediction forbidding mourning, the poet must exhort his love to quietness and calm upon his departure; and for this purpose the figure based upon the latter motion (trepidation), long absorbed into the traditional astronomy, fittingly suggests the tension of the moment without arousing the "harmes and feares" implicit in the figure of the moving earth.[14]

The argument is plausible and rests on a well-substantiated thesis that Donne was deeply interested in the new astronomy and its repercussions in the theological realm. In various works Donne shows his familiarity with Kepler's *De Stella Nova,* with Galileo's *Siderius Nuncius,* with William Gilbert's *De Magnete,* and with Clavius's commentary on the *De Sphaera* of Sacrobosco. He refers to the new science in his Sermon at Paul's Cross and in a letter to Sir Henry Goodyer. In *The First Anniversary* he says the "new philosophy calls all in doubt." In the *Elegy on Prince Henry* he says that the "least moving of the center" makes "the world to shake."

It is difficult to answer argument like this, and impossible to an-

[14] Charles M. Coffin, *John Donne and the New Philosophy* (New York, 1927), pp. 97–98.

swer it with evidence of like nature. There is no reason why Donne might
not have written a stanza in which the two kinds of celestial motion
stood for two sorts of emotion at parting. And if we become full of astro-
nomical ideas and see Donne only against the background of the new science, we may believe that he did. But the text itself remains to be dealt
with, the analyzable vehicle of a complicated metaphor. And one may
observe: (1) that the movement of the earth according to the Coperni-
can theory is a celestial motion, smooth and regular, and while it might
cause religious or philosophic fears, it could not be associated with the
crudity and earthiness of the kind of commotion which the speaker in
the poem wishes to discourage; (2) that there is another moving of the
earth, an earthquake, which has just these qualities and is to be associated with the tear-floods and sigh-tempests of the second stanza of the
poem; (3) that "trepidation" is an appropriate opposite of earthquake,
because each is a shaking or vibratory motion; and "trepidation of the
spheres" is "greater far" than an earthquake, but not much greater (if
two such motions can be compared as to greatness) than the annual motion of the earth; (4) that reckoning what it "did and meant" shows
that the event has passed, like an earthquake, not like the incessant celestial movement of the earth. Perhaps a knowledge of Donne's interest in
the new science may add another shade of meaning, an overtone to the
stanza in question, though to say even this runs against the words. To
make the ego-centric and helio-centric antithesis the core of the metaphor is to disregard the English language, to prefer private evidence to
public, external to internal.

v

If the distinction between kinds of evidence has implications for
the historical critic, it has them no less for the contemporary poet and his
critic. Or, since every rule for a poet is but another side of a judgment
by a critic, and since the past is the realm of the scholar and critic, and
the future and present that of the poet and the critical leaders of taste,
we may say that the problems arising in literary scholarship from the
intentional fallacy are matched by others which arise in the world of progressive experiment.

The question of "allusiveness," for example, as acutely posed by
the poetry of Eliot, is certainly one where a false judgment is likely to
involve the intentional fallacy. The frequency and depth of literary allusion in the poetry of Eliot and others has driven so many in pursuit of
full meanings to the *Golden Bough* and the Elizabethan drama that it
has become a kind of commonplace to suppose that we do not know what
a poet means unless we have traced him in his reading—a supposition

redolent with intentional implications. The stand taken by Mr. F. O. Matthiessen is a sound one and partially forestalls the difficulty.

> If one reads these lines with an attentive ear and is sensitive to their sudden shifts in movement, the contrast between the actual Thames and the idealized vision of it during an age before it flowed through a megalopolis is sharply conveyed by that movement itself, whether or not one recognizes the refrain to be from Spenser.

Eliot's allusions work when we know them—and to a great extent even when we do not know them, through their suggestive power.

But sometimes we find allusions supported by notes, and it is a very nice question whether the notes function more as guides to send us where we may be educated, or more as indications in themselves about the character of the allusions. "Nearly everything of importance . . . that is apposite to an appreciation of 'The Waste Land,' " writes Mr. Matthiessen of Miss Weston's book, "has been incorporated into the structure of the poem itself, or into Eliot's Notes." And with such an admission it may begin to appear that it would not much matter if Eliot invented his sources (as Sir Walter Scott invented chapter epigraphs from "old plays" and "anonymous" authors, or as Coleridge wrote marginal glosses for *The Ancient Mariner*). Allusions to Dante, Webster, Marvell, or Baudelaire, doubtless gain something because these writers existed, but it is doubtful whether the same can be said for an allusion to an obscure Elizabethan:

> The sound of horns and motors, which shall bring
> Sweeney to Mrs. Porter in the spring.

"Cf. Day, *Parliament of Bees*": says Eliot,

> When of a sudden, listening, you shall hear,
> A noise of horns and hunting, which shall bring
> Actaeon to Diana in the spring,
> Where all shall see her naked skin. . . .

The irony is completed by the quotation itself; had Eliot, as is quite conceivable, composed these lines to furnish his own background, there would be no loss of validity. The conviction may grow as one reads Eliot's next note: "I do not know the origin of the ballad from which these lines are taken: it was reported to me from Sydney, Australia." The important word in this note—on Mrs. Porter and her daughter who washed their feet in soda water—is "ballad." And if one should feel from the lines themselves their "ballad" quality, there would be little need for the note. Ultimately, the inquiry must focus on the integrity of such notes as parts of the poem, for where they constitute special information about the meaning of phrases in the poem, they ought to be subject to

the same scrutiny as any of the other words in which it is written. Mr.
Matthiessen believes the notes were the price Eliot "had to pay in order
to avoid what he would have considered muffling the energy of his poem
by extended connecting links in the text itself." But it may be questioned
whether the notes and the need for them are not equally muffling. The
omission from poems of the explanatory stratum on which is built
the dramatic or poetic stuff is a dangerous responsibility. Mr. F. W.
Bateson has plausibly argued that Tennyson's "The Sailor Boy" would
be better if half the stanzas were omitted, and the best versions of ballads
like "Sir Patrick Spens" owe their power to the very audacity with
which the minstrel has taken for granted the story upon which he comments. What then if a poet finds he cannot take so much for granted in
a more recondite context and rather than write informatively, supplies
notes? It can be said in favor of this plan that at least the notes do not
pretend to be dramatic, as they would if written in verse. On the other
hand, the notes may look like unassimilated material lying loose beside
the poem, necessary for the meaning of the verbal symbol, but not in-
tegrated, so that the symbol stands incomplete.

We mean to suggest by the above analysis that whereas notes tend
to seem to justify themselves as external indexes to the author's *intention,* yet they ought to be judged like any other parts of a composition
(verbal arrangement special to a particular context), and when so judged
their reality as parts of the poem, or their imaginative integration with
the rest of the poem, may come into question. Mr. Matthiessen, for instance, sees that Eliot's titles for poems and his epigraphs are informative
apparatus, like the notes. But while he is worried by some of the notes
and thinks that Eliot "appears to be mocking himself for writing the note
at the same time that he wants to convey something by it," Mr. Matthiessen believes that the "device" of epigraphs "is not at all open to the objection of not being sufficiently structural." "The *intention,*" he says, "is
to enable the poet to secure a condensed expression in the poem itself."
"In each case the epigraph is *designed* to form an integral part of the
effect of the poem." And Eliot himself, in his notes, has justified his
poetic practice in terms of intention.

> The Hanged Man, a member of the traditional pack, fits my purpose
> in two ways: because he is associated in my mind with the Hanged God
> of Frazer, and because I associate him with the hooded figure in the
> passage of the disciples to Emmaus in Part V. . . . The man with
> Three Staves (an authentic member of the Tarot pack) I associate,
> quite arbitrarily, with the Fisher King himself.

And perhaps he is to be taken more seriously here, when off guard in a
note, than when in his Norton Lectures he comments on the difficulty

of saying what a poem means and adds playfully that he thinks of pre-fixing to a second edition of *Ash Wednesday* some lines from *Don Juan:*

> I don't pretend that I quite understand
> My own meaning when I would be *very* fine;
> But the fact is that I have nothing planned
> Unless it were to be a moment merry.

If Eliot and other contemporary poets have any characteristic fault, it may be in *planning* too much.[15]

Allusiveness in poetry is one of several critical issues by which we have illustrated the more abstract issue of intentionalism, but it may be for today the most important illustration. As a poetic practice allusive-ness would appear to be in some recent poems an extreme corollary of the romantic intentionalist assumption, and as a critical issue it challenges and brings to light in a special way the basic premise of intentionalism. The following instance from the poetry of Eliot may serve to epitomize the practical implications of what we have been saying. In Eliot's "Love Song of J. Alfred Prufrock," towards the end, occurs the line: "I have heard the mermaids singing, each to each," and this bears a certain re-semblance to a line in a Song by John Donne, "Teach me to heare Mer-maides singing," so that for the reader acquainted to a certain degree with Donne's poetry, the critical question arises: Is Eliot's line an allu-sion to Donne's? Is Prufrock thinking about Donne? Is Eliot thinking about Donne? We suggest that there are two radically different ways of looking for an answer to this question. There is (1) the way of poetic analysis and exegesis, which inquires whether it makes any sense if Eliot-Prufrock *is* thinking about Donne. In an earlier part of the poem, when Prufrock asks, "Would it have been worth while, . . . To have squeezed the universe into a ball," his words take half their sadness and irony from certain energetic and passionate lines of Marvell's "To His Coy Mistress." But the exegetical inquirer may wonder whether mermaids con-sidered as "strange sights" (to hear them is in Donne's poem analogous to getting with child a mandrake root) have much to do with Prufrock's mermaids, which seem to be symbols of romance and dynamism, and which incidentally have literary authentication, if they need it, in a line of a sonnet by Gérard de Nerval. This method of inquiry may lead to the conclusion that the given resemblance between Eliot and Donne is without significance and is better not thought of, or the method may have the disadvantage of providing no certain conclusion. Nevertheless, we

[15] In his critical writings Eliot has expressed the right view of author psy-chology (see *The Use of Poetry and the Use of Criticism*, Cambridge, 1933, p. 139 and "Tradition and the Individual Talent" in *Selected Essays*, New York, 1932), though his record is not entirely consistent (see *A Choice of Kipling's Verse*, London, 1941, pp. 10–11, 20–21).

submit that this is the true and objective way of criticism, as contrasted
to what the very uncertainty of exegesis might tempt a second kind of
critic to undertake: (2) the way of biographical or genetic inquiry, in
which, taking advantage of the fact that Eliot is still alive, and in the
spirit of a man who would settle a bet, the critic writes to Eliot and asks
what he meant, or if he had Donne in mind. We shall not here weigh
the probabilities—whether Eliot would answer that he meant nothing at
all, had nothing at all in mind—a sufficiently good answer to such a
question—or in an unguarded moment might furnish a clear and, within
its limit, irrefutable answer. Our point is that such an answer to such an
inquiry would have nothing to do with the poem "Prufrock"; it would
not be a critical inquiry. Critical inquiries, unlike bets, are not settled in
this way. Critical inquiries are not settled by consulting the oracle.

LESLIE A. FIEDLER

Archetype and Signature: A Study of the Relationship between Biography and Poetry

A central dogma of much recent criticism asserts that biographical
information is irrelevant to the understanding and evaluation of poems,
and that conversely, poems cannot legitimately be used as material for
biography. This double contention is part of a larger position which holds
that history is history and art is art, and that to talk about one in terms
of the other is to court disaster. Insofar as this position rests upon the
immortal platitude that it is good to know what one is talking about, it
is unexceptionable; insofar as it is a reaction based upon the procedures
of pre-Freudian critics, it is hopelessly outdated; and insofar as it depends upon the extreme nominalist definition of a work of art, held by
many "formalists" quite unawares, it is metaphysically reprehensible. It
has the further inconvenience of being quite unusable in the practical
sphere (all of its proponents, in proportion as they are sensitive critics,
immediately betray it when speaking of specific works, and particularly
of large bodies of work); and, as if that were not enough, it is in blatant
contradiction with the assumptions of most serious practising writers.

That the antibiographical position was once "useful," whatever its
truth, cannot be denied; it was even once, what is considerably rarer in
the field of criticism, amusing; but for a long time now it has been threat-

Reprinted, by permission, from *Sewanee Review*, LX (1952), 253–273.

ening to turn into one of those annoying clichés of the intellectually middle-aged, proffered with all the air of a stimulating heresy. The position was born in dual protest against an excess of Romantic criticism and one of "scientific scholarship." Romantic aesthetics appeared bent on dissolving the formally realized "objective" elements in works of art into "expression of personality"; while the "scholars," in revolt against Romantic subjectivity, seemed set on casting out all the more shifty questions of value and *gestalt* as "subjective," and concentrating on the kind of "facts" amenable to scientific verification. Needless to say, it was not the newer psychological sciences that the "scholars" had in mind, but such purer disciplines as physics and biology. It was at this point that it became fashionable to talk about literary study as "research," and graphs and tables began to appear in analyses of works of art.

Both the "scholarly" and the Romantic approaches struck the antibiographists as "reductive"—attempts to prove that the work of art was *nothing but* the personality of the Genius behind it, or the sum total of its genetic factors. In answer to both heresies of attack, the antibiographist offered what he came to call the "intrinsic" approach, which turned out, alas, to be another *nothing but* under its show of righteous indignation, namely, the contention that a poem was *nothing but* "words," and its analysis therefore properly *nothing but* a study of syntax and semantics. Any attempt to illuminate a poem by reference to its author's life came therefore to be regarded with horror, unless it confined itself to an examination of his "idiosyncratic use of words." This is not parody, but direct quotation.

By this time, a generation of critics have grown up, of whom I am one, to whom the contention that biographical material is irrelevant to the "essential experience" of a poem has been taught as basic doctrine. The word "experience" is important; it comes out of I. A. Richards at his most scientizing; and along with the "extrinsic-intrinsic" metaphor is a key to the antibiographist point of view. It must be understood for what the word "experience" is being substituted: as an "experience," a poem is no longer regarded as an "imitation," in any of the received senses of the word; nor even as an "expression" in the Crocean sense; and above all, not as a "communication." All three possible substitute terms imply a necessary inter-connectedness between the art object and some *other* area of experience—or at least an essentially intended pointing outward or inward toward some independently existent *otherness*. This is distasteful to the antibiographist, who shows the ordinary nominalist uneasiness at any suggestion that there are realities more comprehensive than particulars, to which words only refer.

An odd phenomenon is the support of a position to which Nominalism is logically necessary, by many confirmed anti-scientizers and realists;

they are betrayed into their ill-advised fellow-traveling, I think, by an excess of anti-Romanticism. It is no longer as fashionable as it once was to publicly anathematize Shelley and Swinburne, but the bias persists as a real force in current critical practise, and cuts off many, to whom the position would be temperamentally and metaphysically attractive, from Expressionism. What the modern sensibility finds particularly unsympathetic in some Romantic writing has been called, misleadingly I think, "the exploitation of personality"; it is rather a tendency toward the excessively "programmatic." Just as music and painting can be too "literary," so literature itself can be too "literary." In reaction against the programmatic, there are two possible paths, more deeply into and through the personalism of Romanticism to Expressionism, or outward and away toward the sort of "abstraction" achieved in cubist painting.

As a matter of fact, there has been at work all along in our period an underground, and probably harmful, analogy between poetry and the plastic arts. A poem, the feeling has been, should be as "palpable and mute" not merely as an actual fruit, but as the fruit become pure color and texture of Picasso or Matisse. As pictures have become frankly paint, so should poems be frankly words. "A poem should not mean but be." There is the slogan of the movement!

It is a rather nice phrase in the limited context of MacLeish's little poem, but a dangerous full-blown aesthetic position. The notion that a work of art is, or should be, absolutely self-contained, a discrete set of mutually inter-related references, needs only to be stated clearly to seem the *reductio ad absurdum* which it is. Yet this belief in the poem as a closed system, "cut-off" in ideal isolation, descends from the realm of theoretical criticism to practical criticism and class-room pedagogy (if not in practise, at least as an institutionalized hypocrisy) to become the *leit-motif* of the New Teacher: "Stay *inside* the poem!"

The narrative and dramatic poem, finally poetic drama itself, is assimilated to a formulation, even *apparently* applicable only to a lyric of the most absolute purity—and it becomes heretical to treat the work as anything but words, to ask those questions which attest our conviction that the work of art is "real"; that in the poem, the whole is greater than the sum of its parts; that certain created actions and characters exist, in some sense, *outside* of their formalizations. How long was Hamlet in Wittenberg? How many children did Lady Macbeth have? In what sense does Prospero speak for Shakespeare? What developing sensibility can be inferred from the Shakespearian corpus and be called (what *else?*) Shakespeare? We cannot ask these questions in the dewy innocence with which they were first posed; we re-state them on the second convolution, aware of all the arguments against them, and the more convinced that they are essential, and cannot be shelved any more than can those questions about the ends and origins of existence which have also been recently declared "unreal."

Closely associated with the Richardsian experiential-semantic approach in the total position of the antibiographist, is the psychological notion of the poem as an "objective correlative" or a complex of "objective correlatives" of the poet's emotional responses to the given world. Mr. Eliot's term is as elusive as it is appealing; but I am concerned here (Mr. Eliseo Vivas has elsewhere discussed from the "intrinsicist" point of view other of its difficulties) only with the adjective "objective" in one of its possible implications. Whatever its origins, Mr. Eliot seems to be asserting, a poem succeeds, as a poem, in so far as it is detached from the subjectivity of its maker. The poem is achieved by a process of objectification, and can be legitimately examined and understood only as an "object." This formulation leaves a somewhat second-best use for the biographical approach, as a way of explaining the particular badness of certain kinds of bad poems, e.g., Romantic verse and Shakespeare's *Hamlet.*

From this presumed insight follows the deprivation of the poet's right to explain his own poem, or at least the challenging of his claim to speak with final authority about his own work. Once realized, the argument runs, a successful poem is detached; and the author no longer has any property rights in what now belongs to the tradition rather than to him. If, benightedly, he protests against some critical analysis or interpretation which seems to him wrong on the basis of his special biographical knowledge, he reveals that either his poem is not truly "successful," or even worse, that he has never read "Tradition and the Individual Talent."

There are, in fact, two quite different contentions, one valid, one invalid, confused in most statements about the poet as commentator on his own work. First it is asserted (and with real truth) that a poem may contain more meanings than the maker is ever aware of; and second (this is false, of course) that nothing the poet can tell us about his own work is of any *decisive* importance, because the poet cannot help falling into the trap of talking about his "intentions." But the notion of "intention" implies the belief that there is a somehow pre-existent something against which the achieved work of art can be measured; and although this has been for all recorded time the point of view of the practising writer, every graduate student who has read Wimsatt and Beardsley on the Intentional Fallacy knows that we are all now to believe that there is no other poem except the poem of "words."

The fact that all recognized critics have consistently spoken of intention shows merely that in the unfortunate past the writer about literature has often (unfortunately!) spoken more like the poet than the scientific semanticist. This regrettable looseness of expression, it can only be hoped, will be amended in the future, now that we have been duly warned. It is difficult not to be tempted by analogy. Why, we want to ask, can we properly laugh at the visiting dignitary in the high hat when he slips on the steps to the platform, because of the disparity between the entrance he *intended* and the one he achieved; and still not speak of a bathetic disparity between what a poem obviously aims at and what it does? On what respectable grounds can it be maintained that a poem is all act and no potentiality?

It is difficult to understand the success of the antibiographist tendency in more respectable critical circles and in the schools, in light of its own internal contradictions. The explanation lies, I suppose, in its comparative newness, and in the failure of its opponents to arrive at any *coherent* theory of the relationship between the life of the poet and his work; so long as biographers are content merely to place side by side undigested biographical data and uninspired paraphrases of poems—linking them together mechanically or pseudo-genetically: "Wordsworth lived in the country and therefore wrote Nature poetry"; or even worse, so long as notes proving that Milton was born in one house rather than another continue to be printed in magazines devoted to the study of literature, people will be tempted into opposite though equal idiocies, which have at least not been for so long proved utterly bankrupt.

A recent phenomenon of some interest in this regard is the astonishing popularity of such texts as Thomas and Brown's class-room anthology called *Reading Poems*. The very title reveals the dogma behind the book; in a world of discrete, individual "experiences," of "close-reading" (a cant phrase of the antibiographist) as an ideal, one cannot even talk of so large an abstraction as poetry. It is only "poems" to which the student must be exposed, poems printed out of chronological order and without the names of the authors attached, lest the young reader be led astray by what (necessarily irrelevant) information he may have concerning the biography or social background of any of the poets. It is all something of a hoax, of course; the teacher realizes that the chances of any student knowing too much for his own good about such matters are slight indeed; and besides, there is an index in which the names of the poets are revealed, so that unless one is *very* virtuous, he can scarcely help looking them up. In addition, the good teacher is himself aware to begin with of the contexts, social and biographical, of a large number of the pieces. Frankly, that is why they make sense to him; and even when he admonishes the young to "stay *inside*" the poems, he is bootlegging from "outside" all kinds of rich relevancies, which he possesses because he is capable of *connecting*.

I cannot help feeling that the chief problem of teaching anything

in our atomized period lies precisely in the fact that the ordinary student
cannot or will not connect the few facts he knows, the slim insights he
has previously attained, the chance extensions of sensibility into which
he has been once or twice tempted, into a large enough context to make
sense of the world he inhabits, or the works of art he encounters. It is
because the old-line biographist fails to connect his facts with the works
they presumably illuminate, and not because he does connect them that
he is a poor critic. And the doctrinaire antibiographist, like the doctrinaire
biographist before him, secure in pride and ignorance of the newer psychologies, makes worse the endemic disease of our era—the failure to
connect. There is no "work itself," no independent formal entity which
is its own sole context; the poem is the sum total of many contexts, all of
which must be known to know it and evaluate it. "Only connect!" should
be the motto of all critics and teachers—and the connective link between
the poem on the page and most of its rewarding contexts is precisely—
biography.

The poet's life is the focusing glass through which pass the deter-
minants of the shape of his work: the tradition available to him, his understanding of "kinds," the impact of special experiences (travel, love etc.).
But the poet's life is more than a burning-glass; with his work, it makes
up his total meaning. I do not intend to say, of course, that some meanings of works of art, satisfactory and as far as they go sufficient, are not
available in the single work itself (only a really *bad* work depends for all
substantial meaning on a knowledge of the life-style of its author); but
a whole body of work will contain larger meanings, and, where it is available, a sense of the life of the writer will raise that meaning to a still
higher power. The latter two kinds of meaning fade into each other; for
as soon as two works by a single author are considered side by side, one
has begun to deal with biography, that is with an interconnectedness,
fully explicable only in terms of a personality, inferred or discovered.

One of the essential functions of the poet is the assertion and
creation of a personality, in a profounder sense than any non-artist can
attain. We ask of the poet a definition of man, at once particular and
abstract, stated and acted out. It is impossible to draw a line between the
work the poet writes and the work he lives, between the life he lives and
the life he writes. And the agile critic, therefore, must be prepared to
move constantly back and forth between life and poem, not in a pointless
circle, but in a meaningful spiraling toward the absolute point.

To pursue this matter further, we will have to abandon at this
point the nominalist notion of the poem as "words" or "only words." We
have the best of excuses; such terminology gets in the way of truth. We
will not, however, return to the older notions of the poem as a "document"
or the embodiment of an "idea," for these older views are, like the "in-

tricist" position, inimical to the concept of the "marvelous"; and they have the further difficulty of raising political and moral criteria of "truth" as relevant to works of art. To redeem the sense of what words are all the time pointing *to* and what cannot be adequately explained by syntactical analysis or semantics, I shall speak of the poem as *Archetype* and *Signature,* suggesting that the key to analysis is *symbolics;* and I shall not forget that the poet's life is also capable of being analyzed in those terms. We have been rather ridiculously over-emphasizing *medium* as a differentiating factor; I take it that we can now safely assume no one will confuse a life with a poem, and dwell on the elements common to the two, remembering that a pattern of social behavior can be quite as much a symbol as a word, chanted or spoken or printed. In deed as in word, the poet composes himself as maker and mask, in accordance with some contemporaneous *mythos* of the artist. And as we all know, in our day, it is even possible to be a writer without having written anything! When we talk therefore of the importance of the biography of the poet, we do not mean the importance of every trivial detail, but of all that goes into making his particular life-style, whether he concentrate on re-creating himself, like Shelley, in some obvious image of the Poet, or, like Wallace Stevens, in some witty anti-mask of the Poet. Who could contend that even the *faces* of Shelley and Stevens are not typical products of their quite different kinds of art!

The word Archetype is the more familiar of my terms; I use it instead of the word "myth," which I have employed in the past but which becomes increasingly ambiguous, to mean any of the immemorial patterns of response to the human situation in its most permanent aspects: death, love, the biological family, the relationship with the Unknown, etc., whether those patterns be considered to reside in the Jungian Collective Unconscious or the Platonic world of Ideas. The archetypal belongs to the infra- or meta-personal, to what Freudians call the Id or the Unconscious; that is, it belongs to the Community at its deepest, pre-conscious levels of acceptance.

I use Signature to mean the sum-total of individuating factors in a work, the sign of the Persona or Personality, through which an Archetype is rendered, and which itself tends to become a subject as well as a means of the poem. Literature, properly speaking, can be said to come into existence at the moment a Signature is imposed upon the Archetype. The purely archetypal, without signature-elements, is the Myth. Perhaps a pair of examples are in order (with thanks to Mr. C. S. Lewis). The story of Baldur the Beautiful and Shakespeare's *Tempest* deal with somewhat similar archetypal material of immersion and resurrection; but we recall the *Tempest* only in all its specificity: the diction, meter, patterns of imagery, the heard voice of Shakespeare (the Signature as

Means); as well as the scarcely motivated speech on pre-marital chastity, the breaking of the fictional frame by the unconventional religious *plaudite* (the Signature as Subject). Without these elements, the *Tempest* is simply not the *Tempest;* but Baldur can be retold in any diction, any style, just so long as faith is kept with the bare plot—and it is itself, for it is pure myth. Other examples are provided by certain children's stories, retold and re-illustrated without losing their essential identity, whether they be "folk" creations like *Cinderella,* or art-products, "captured" by the folk imagination, like Southey's *Three Bears.*

In our own time, we have seen the arts (first music, then painting, last of all literature) attempting to become "pure," or "abstract," that is to say, attempting to slough off all remnants of the Archetypal in a drive toward becoming unadulterated Signature. It should be noticed that the *theory* of abstract art is completely misleading in this regard, speaking as it does about pure forms, and mathematics, and the disavowal of personality. The abstract painter, for instance, does not, as he sometimes claims, really "paint paint," but signs his name. So-called abstract art is the ultimate expression of personality; so that the spectator says of a contemporary painting not what one would have said in the anonymous Middle Ages, "There's a *Tree of Jesse* or a *Crucifixion!*" or not even what is said of Renaissance art, "There's a Michel Angelo *Last Judgment* or a Raphael *Madonna!*" but quite simply, "There's a Mondrian or a Jackson Pollock!" Analogously, in literature we recognize a poem immediately as "a Marianne Moore" or "an Ezra Pound" long before we understand, if ever, any of its essential meanings.

The theory of "realism" or "naturalism" denies both the Archetype and the Signature, advocating, in its extreme forms, that art merely "describe nature or reality" in a neutral style based on the case report of the scientist. Art which really achieves such aims becomes, of course, something less than "poetry" as I have used the term here, turning into an "imitation" in the lowest Platonic sense, "thrice removed from the truth." Fortunately, the greatest "realists" consistently betray their principles, creating Archetypes and symbols willy-nilly, and setting them in a Signature distinguished by what James called "solidity of specification." The chief value of "realism" as a theory is that it helps create in the more sophisticated writer a kind of blessed stupidity in regard to what he is really doing, so that the archetypal material can well up into his work uninhibited by his intent; and in a complementary way, it makes acceptance of that archetypal material possible for an audience which thinks of itself as "science-minded" and inimical to the demonic and mythic. It constantly startles and pleases me to come across references to such creators of grotesque Archetypes as Dostoevski and Dickens and Faulkner as "realists."

A pair of *caveats* are necessary, before we proceed. The distinction between Archetype and Signature, it should be noted, does not correspond to the ancient dichotomy of Content and Form. Such "forms" as the structures of Greek Tragedy (cf. Gilbert Murray), New Comedy and Pastoral Elegy are themselves *versunkene* Archetypes, capable of being re-realized in the great work of art. (Elsewhere I have called these "structural myths.")

Nor does the present distinction cut quite the same way as that between "impersonal" (or even "non-personal") and "personal." For the Signature, which is rooted in the Ego and Super-ego, belongs, as the two-fold Freudian division implies, to the social collectivity as well as to the individual writer. The Signature is the joint product of "rules" and "conventions," of the expectations of a community, and the idiosyncratic responses of the individual poet, who adds a personal idiom or voice to a received style. The difference between the communal element in the Signature and that in the Archetype is that the former is *conscious,* that is, associated with the Super-ego rather than the Id. The relevant, archetypal metaphor for this situation would make the personal element the Son, the conscious-communal the Father, and the unconscious-communal the Mother (or the Sister, an image which occurs often as a symbolic euphemism for the Mother)—in the biological Trinity.

It is not irrelevant that the Romantic Movement, which combined a deliberate return to the Archetypal with a contempt for the conscious communal elements in the Signature, made one of the *leit-motifs* of the lives of its poets, as well as of their poems, the flight of the Sister from the threat of rape by the Father (Shelley's *Cenci,* for instance) and the complementary desperate love of Brother and Sister (anywhere from Chateaubriand and Wordsworth to Byron and Melville).

Even the most orthodox antibiographist is prepared to grant the importance of biographical information in the *understanding* of certain Ego elements in the Signature—this is what the intrinsicist calls "the study of an author's idiosyncratic use of words." But he would deny vehemently the possibility of using biographical material for the purposes of *evaluation.* Let us consider some examples. For instance, the line in one of John Donne's poems, "A Hymne to God the Father," which runs, "When thou hast done, thou hast not done . . ." would be incomprehensible in such a collection without authors' names as the Thomas.and Brown *Reading Poems.* Without the minimum biographical datum of the name of the poet, the reader could not realize that a pun was involved, and could consequently not even ask himself the evaluative question most important to the poem, namely, what is the value of the pun in a serious, even a religious, piece of verse? This is the simplest use of biography, referring us for only an instant outside of the poem, and letting us remain within it, once we have returned with the information. Similar examples are plentiful in Shakespeare's sonnets: the references to his own first name, for instance, or the troublesome phrase "all *hewes* in his controlling."

A second example which looks much like the first to a superficial glance, but which opens up in quite a different way, would be the verse "they'are but *Mummy* possest," from Donne's "Love's Alchemie." Let us consider whether we can sustain the contention that there is a pun on *Mummy,* whether deliberately planned or unconsciously fallen into. Can we read the line as having the two meanings: women, so fair in the desiring, turn out to be only dried-out corpses after the having; and women, once possessed, turn out to be substitutes for the Mother, who is the real end of our desiring? An analysis of the mere *word* does not take us very far; we discover that the *lallwort* "mummy" meaning mother is not recorded until 1830 in that precise spelling, but that there are attested uses of it in the form "mammy" (we remember, perhaps, that "mammy-apple" and "mummy-apple" are interchangeable forms meaning papaya) well back into Donne's period, and the related form *mome* goes back into Middle English. Inevitably, such evidence is inconclusive, establishing possibilities at best, and never really bearing on the question of probability, for which we must turn to life itself, to Donne's actual relations with his mother; and beyond that to the science of such relationships.

When we have discovered that John Donne did, indeed, live in an especially intimate relationship with his mother throughout her long life (she actually outlived her son); and when we have set the possible pun in a context of other literary uses of a mythic situation in which the long-desired possessed turns at the moment of possession into a shriveled hag who is also a mother (Rider Haggard's *She,* Hilton's *Lost Horizon,* and, most explicitly, Flaubert's *Education Sentimentale*), we realize that our original contention is highly probable, that the pun embodies a traditional version of what the psychologists have taught us to call the Oedipus Archetype. It should be noticed in passing, that the archetypal critic is delivered from the bondage of time, speaking of "confluences" rather than "influences," and finding the explication of a given work in things written later as well as earlier than the original piece. Following the lead opened up by *"Mummy* possest," we can move still further toward an understanding of Donne, continuing to shuttle between life and work with our new clue, and examining, for instance, Donne's ambivalent relations to the greater Mother, the Roman Church, which his actual mother represented not only metaphorically, but in her own allegiance and descent. This sort of analysis which at once unifies and opens up (one could do something equally provocative and rich, for instance, with the fact that in two of Melville's tales, ships symbolic of innocence are called *The Jolly Bachelor* and *The Bachelor's Delight*) is condemned in some quarters as "failing to stay close to the actual meaning of the work itself"—as if the work were a penny peep-show to which one must screw his eye, instead of a focus opening on an inexhaustible totality.

The "intrinsicist" is completely unnerved by any reference to the role of the Archetype in literature, fearing such references as strategies to restore the criterion of the "marvelous" to respectable currency as a standard of literary excellence; for not only is the notion of the "marvelous" pre-scientific, but it is annoyingly immune to "close analysis." Certainly, the contemplation of the Archetype pushes the critic beyond semantics, and beyond the kind of analysis that considers it has done all when it assures us (once again!) that the parts and whole of a poem cohere. The critic in pursuit of the Archetype finds himself involved in anthropology and depth-psychology (not because these are New Gospels, but because they provide useful tools); and if he is not too embarrassed in such company to look about him, he discovers that he has come upon a way of binding together our fractured world, of uniting literature and non-literature *without the reduction of the poem.*

It is sometimes objected that though the archetypal critic can move convincingly between worlds ordinarily cut off from each other, he sacrifices for this privilege the ability to distinguish the essential qualities of literary works, and especially that of evaluating them. Far from being irrelevant to evaluation, the consideration of the archetypal content of works of art is essential to it! One of the earlier critics of Dante says somewhere that poetry, as distinguished from rhetoric (which treats of the credible as credible), treats of the "marvelous" as credible. Much contemporary criticism has cut itself off from this insight, that is, from the realization of what poetry on its deepest levels *is*. It is just as ridiculous to attempt the evaluation of a work of art in *purely* formal terms (considering only the Signature as Means), as it would be to evaluate it *purely* in terms of the "marvelous," or the Archetypal. The question, for instance, of whether *Mona Lisa* is just a *bourgeoise* or whether she "as Leda, was the Mother of Helen of Troy, and, as St. Anne, was the mother of Mary" is just as vital to a final estimate of the picture's worth as any matter of control of the medium or handling of light and shadow.

The Romantics seem to have realized this, and to have reached in their distinction between Fancy and Imagination for rubrics to distinguish between the poetic method that touches the Archetypal deeply and that which merely skirts it. Even the Arnoldian description of Pope as "a classic of our prose," right or wrong, was feeling toward a similar standard of discrimination. It is typical and ironic, that Arnold in a moralizing age should have felt obliged to call the demonic power of evoking the Archetype "High Seriousness." Certainly, the complete abandonment of any such criterion by the intrinsicist leaves him baffled before certain strong mythopoeic talents like Dickens or Stevenson; and it is the same lack in his system which prevents his understanding of the complementary relationship of the life and work of the poet.

II

The Archetype which makes literature itself possible in the first instance is the Archetype of the Poet. At the moment when myth is uncertainly becoming literature, that is, reaching tentatively toward a Signature, the poet is conceived of passively, as a mere vehicle. It is the Muse who is mythically bodied forth, the unconscious, collective source of the Archetypes, imagined as more than human, and, of course, *female*. The Poet is still conceived more as Persona than Personality; the few characteristics with which he is endowed are borrowed from the prophet: he is a blind old man, impotent in his own right. That blindness (impotence as power, what Keats much later would call "negative capability") is the earliest version of the blessing-curse, without which the popular mind cannot conceive of the poet. His flaw is, in the early stages, at once the result and the pre-condition of his submitting himself to the dark powers of inspiration for the sake of the whole people.

But very soon, the poet begins to assume a more individualized life-style, the lived Signature imposed on the Archetype, and we have no longer the featureless poet born in seven cities, his face a Mask through which a voice not his is heard, but Aeschylus, the Athenian citizen-poet; Sophocles, the spoiled darling of fate; or Euripides, the crowd-contemner in his Grotto. The mass-mind, dimly resentful as the *Vates* becomes *Poeta,* the Seer a Maker, the Persona a Personality, composes a new Archetype, an image to punish the poet for detaching himself from the collective Id—and the Poet, amused and baffled, accepts and elaborates the new image. The legend asserts that Euripides (the first completely self-conscious alienated artist?) died torn to pieces by dogs, or even more to the point, by *women.* And behind the late, personalized application looms the more ancient *mythos* of the ritually dismembered Orpheus, ripped by the Maenads when he had withdrawn for lonely contemplation. The older myth suggests that a sacrifice is involved as well as a punishment—the casting-out and rending of the poet being re-interpreted as a death suffered for the group, by one who has dared make the first forays out of collectivity toward personality, and has endured the consequent revenge of the group as devotees of the unconscious.

In light of this, it is no longer possible to think of the *poète maudit* as an unfortunate invention of the Romantics, or of the Alienated Artist as a by-product of mass-communications. These are re-inventions, as our archetypal history repeats itself under the influence of the breakdown of Christianity. Our newer names name only recent exacerbations of a situation as old as literature itself, which in turn is co-eval with the rise of personality. Only the conventional stigmata of the poet as Scape-Hero have changed with time: the Blind Man becomes the disreputable Player, the Atheist, the Incestuous lover, the Homosexual, or (especially in America) the Drunkard; though, indeed, none of the older versions ever die, even the Homer-*typus* reasserting itself in Milton and James Joyce. Perhaps in recent times, the poet has come to collaborate somewhat more enthusiastically in his own defamation and destruction, whether by drowning or tuberculosis or dissipation—or by a token suicide in the work (cf. Werther). And he helps ever more consciously to compose himself and his fellow poets—Byron, for instance, the poet *par excellence* of the mid-Nineteenth Century, being the joint product of Byron and Goethe—and, though most of us forget, Harriet Beecher Stowe! Some dramatic version of the poet seems necessary to every age and the people do not care whether the poet creates himself in his life or work or both. One thinks right now of F. Scott Fitzgerald, of course, *our* popular image of the artist.

The critic, on the other hand, is likely to become impatient with the lay indifference to the poetizing of life, and the "biographizing" of poetry; for he proceeds on the false assumption that the poet's life is primarily "given" and only illegitimately "made," while his work is essentially "made" and scarcely "given" at all. This is the source of endless confusion.

In perhaps the greatest periods of world literature, the "given" element in poetry is made clear by the custom of supplying, or more precisely, of *imposing* on the poet certain traditional bodies of story. The poet in such periods can think of himself only as "working with" materials belonging to the whole community, emending by a dozen or sixteen the inherited plot. Greek myths, the fairy tales and *novelle* of the Elizabethans, the Christian body of legend available to Dante are examples of such material. (In our world a traditionally restricted body of story is found only in sub-art: the pulp Western, or the movie Horse-opera.) In such situations, Archetype and "story" are synonymous; one remembers that for Aristotle, *mythos* was the word for "plot," and plot was, he insisted, the most important element in tragedy. That Aristotle makes his assertions on rationalistic grounds, with no apparent awareness of the importance of the Archetype as such, does not matter; it does not even matter whether the poet himself is aware of the implications of his material. As long as he works with such an inherited gift, he can provide the ritual satisfaction necessary to great art without self-consciousness.

A Shakespeare, a Dante, or a Sophocles, coming at a moment when the Archetypes of a period are still understood as "given," and yet are not considered too "sacred" for rendering through the individual Signature, possess immense initial advantages over the poet who comes earlier or later in the process. But the great poet is not simply the mechanical result of such an occasion; he must be able to rise to it, to be capable (like Shakespeare) of at once realizing utterly the archetypal implications of his material, and of formally embodying it in a lucid and unmistakable Signature. But the balance is delicate and incapable of being long maintained. The brief history of Athenian tragedy provides the classic instance. After the successes of Sophocles come the attempts of Euripides; and in Euripides one begins to feel the encounter of Signature and Archetype as a *conflict*—the poet and the collectivity have begun to lose touch with each other and with their common pre-conscious sources of value and behavior. Euripides seems to feel his inherited material as a burden, tucking it away in prologue and epilogue, so that he can get on with his proper business—the imitation of particulars. The poem begins to come apart; the acute critic finds it, however "tragic," sloppy, technically inept; and the audience raises the familiar cry of "incomprehensible and blasphemous!" Even the poet himself begins to distrust his own impulses, and writes, as Euripides did in his *Bacchae,* a mythic criticism of his own sacrilege.

After the Euripidean crisis, the Archetypes survive only in fallen form: as inherited and scarcely understood structures (the seeds of the *genres* which are structural Archetypes become structural platitudes); as type characters, less complex than the masks that indicate them; as "popular" stock plots. The "Happy Ending" arises as a kind of *ersatz* of the true reconciliation of society and individual in Sophoclean tragedy; and the audience which can no longer find essential reassurance in its poetry that the Super-Ego and the Id can live at peace with each other, content themselves with the demonstration that at least Jack has his Jill, despite the comic opposition of the Old Man. Still later, even the tension of Euripidean tragedy and New Comedy is lost, and the Archetype comes to be disregarded completely; poetry becomes either utterly "realistic," rendering the struggle between Ego and Super-Ego in terms of the imitation of particulars; or it strives to be "pure" in the contemporary sense, that is, to make the Signature its sole subject as well as its means.

Can the Archetype be redeemed after such a fall? There are various possibilities (short of the emergence of a new, ordered myth-system): the writer can, like Graham Greene or Robert Penn Warren, capture for serious purposes—that is, re-render through complex and subtle Signatures—debased "popular" Archetypes: the thriller, the detective story, the Western or science-fiction; or the poet can ironically manipulate the shreds and patches of out-lived mythologies, fragments shored against our ruins. Eliot, Joyce, Ezra Pound, and Thomas Mann have all made attempts of the latter sort, writing finally not archetypal poetry, but poetry *about* archetypes, in which plot (anciently *mythos* itself) founders under the burden of overt explication, or disappears completely. Or the poet can, like Blake or Yeats or Hart Crane, invent a private myth system of his own. Neither of the last two expedients can reach the popular audience, which prefers its archetypes rendered without self-consciousness of so intrusive a sort.

A final way back into the world of the Archetypes, available even in our atomized culture, is an extension of the way instinctively sought by the Romantics, down through the personality of the poet, past his particular foibles and eccentricities, to his unconscious core, where he becomes one with us all in the presence of our ancient Gods, the protagonists of fables we think we no longer believe. In fantasy and terror, we can return to our common source. It is a process to delight a Hegelian, the triple swing from a naive communal to the personal to a sophisticated communal.

We must be aware of the differences between the thesis and synthesis of our series. What cannot be recreated as Plot becomes reborn as Character—ultimately the character of the poet (what else is available to him?), whether directly or in projection. In the Mask of his life and the manifold masks of his work, the poet expresses for a whole society the ritual meaning of its inarticulate selves; the artist goes forth not to "recreate the conscience of his race," but to redeem its unconscious. We cannot get back into the primal Garden of the unfallen Archetypes, but we can yield ourselves to the dreams and images that mean paradise regained. For the critic who cannot only yield, but must also *understand,* there are available new methods of exploration. To understand the Archetypes of Athenian drama, he needs (above and beyond semantics) anthropology; to understand those of recent poetry, he needs (beyond "close analysis") depth analysis, as defined by Freud and, particularly, by Jung.

The biographical approach, tempered by such findings, is just now coming into its own. We are achieving new ways of connecting (or more precisely, of understanding a connection which has always existed) the Poet and the poem, the lived and the made, the Signature and the Archetype. It is in the focus of the poetic personality that *Dichtung* and *Wahrheit* become one; and it is incumbent upon us, without surrendering our right to make useful distinctions, to seize the principle of that unity. "Only connect!"

EDMUND WILSON

Historical Criticism

I want to talk about the historical interpretation of literature—that is, about the interpretation of literature in its social, economic and political aspects.

To begin with, it will be worth while to say something about the kind of criticism which seems to be furthest removed from this. There is a kind of comparative criticism which tends to be non-historical. The essays of T. S. Eliot, which have had such an immense influence in our time, are, for example, fundamentally non-historical. Eliot sees, or tries to see, the whole of literature, so far as he is acquainted with it, spread out before him under the aspect of eternity. He then compares the work of different periods and countries, and tries to draw from it general conclusions about what literature ought to be. He understands, of course, that our point of view in connection with literature changes, and he has what seems to me a very sound conception of the whole body of writing of the past as something to which new works are continually being added, and which is not thereby merely increased in bulk but modified as a whole—so that Sophocles is no longer precisely what he was for Aristotle, or Shakespeare what he was for Ben Jonson or for Dryden or for Dr. Johnson, on account of all the later literature that has intervened between them and us. Yet at every point of this continual accretion, the whole field may be surveyed, as it were, spread out before the critic. The critic tries to see it as God might; he calls the books to a Day of Judgment. And, looking at things in this way, he may arrive at interesting and valuable conclusions which could hardly be reached by approaching them in any other way. Eliot was able to see, for example—what I believe had never been noticed before—that the French Symbolist poetry of the nineteenth century had certain fundamental resemblances to the English poetry of the age of Donne. Another kind of critic would draw certain historical conclusions from these purely aesthetic findings, as the Russian D. S. Mirsky did; but Eliot does not draw them.

Another example of this kind of non-historical criticism, in a somewhat different way and on a somewhat different plane, is the work of the late George Saintsbury. Saintsbury was a connoisseur of wines; he wrote an entertaining book on the subject. And his attitude toward literature, too, was that of the connoisseur. He tastes the authors and tells

Reprinted, by permission, from *The Triple Thinkers*, New York: Oxford University Press, Inc., revised and enlarged edition, 1948. This essay was originally a lecture delivered at Princeton University, October 23, 1940.

you about the vintages; he distinguishes the qualities of the various wines. His palate was as fine as could be, and he possessed the great qualification that he knew how to take each book on its own terms without expecting it to be some other book and was thus in a position to appreciate a great variety of kinds of writing. He was a man of strong social prejudices and peculiarly intransigent political views, but, so far as it is humanly possible, he kept them out of his literary criticism. The result is one of the most agreeable and most comprehensive commentaries on literature that has ever been written in English. Most scholars who have read as much as Saintsbury don't have Saintsbury's discriminating taste. Here is a critic who has covered the whole ground like any academic historian, yet whose account of it is not merely a chronology but a record of fastidious enjoyment. Since enjoyment is the only thing he is looking for, he does not need to know the causes of things, and the historical background of literature does not interest him very much.

There is, however, another tradition of criticism which dates from the beginning of the eighteenth century. In the year 1725, the Neapolitan philosopher Vico published *La Scienza Nuova,* a revolutionary work on the philosophy of history, in which he asserted for the first time that the social world was certainly the work of man, and attempted what is, so far as I know, the first social interpretation of a work of literature. This is what Vico says about Homer: "Homer composed the *Iliad* when Greece was young and consequently burning with sublime passions such as pride, anger and vengeance—passions which cannot allow dissimulation and which consort with generosity; so that she then admired Achilles, the hero of force. But, grown old, he composed the *Odyssey,* at a time when the passions of Greece were already somewhat cooled by reflection, which is the mother of prudence—so that she now admired Ulysses, the hero of wisdom. Thus also, in Homer's youth, the Greek people liked cruelty, abuse, savagery, fierceness, ferocity; whereas, when Homer was old, they were already enjoying the luxuries of Alcinoüs, the delights of Calypso, the pleasures of Circe, the songs of the sirens and the pastimes of the suitors, who went no further in aggression and combat than laying siege to the chaste Penelope—all of which practices would appear incompatible with the spirit of the earlier time. The divine Plato is so struck by this difficulty that, in order to solve it, he tells us that Homer had foreseen in inspired vision these dissolute, sickly and disgusting customs. But in this way he makes Homer out to have been but a foolish instructor for Greek civilization, since, however much he may condemn them he is displaying for imitation these corrupt and decadent habits which were not to be adopted till long after the foundation of the nations of Greece, and accelerating the natural course which human events would take by spurring the Greeks on to corruption. Thus it is plain that the Homer of the *Iliad* must have preceded by many years the Homer who wrote the *Odyssey;* and it is plain that the former must belong to the northeastern part of Greece, since he celebrates the Trojan War, which took place in his part of the country, whereas the latter belongs to the southeastern part, since he celebrates Ulysses, who reigned there."

You see that Vico has here explained Homer in terms both of historical period and of geographical origin. The idea that human arts and institutions were to be studied and elucidated as the products of the geographical and climatic conditions in which the people who created them lived, and of the phase of their social development through which they were passing at the moment, made great progress during the eighteenth century. There are traces of it even in Dr. Johnson, that most orthodox and classical of critics—as, for example, when he accounts for certain characteristics of Shakespeare by the relative barbarity of the age in which he lived, pointing out, just as Vico had done, that "nations, like individuals, have their infancy." And by the eighties of the eighteenth century Herder, in his *Ideas on the Philosophy of History,* was writing of poetry that it was a kind of "Proteus among the people, which is always changing its form in response to the languages, manners, and habits, to the temperaments and climates, nay even to the accents of different nations." He said—what could still seem startling even so late as that— that "language was not a divine communication, but something men had produced themselves." In the lectures on the philosophy of history that Hegel delivered in Berlin in 1822–1823, he discussed the national literatures as expressions of the societies which had produced them—societies which he conceived as great organisms continually transforming themselves under the influence of a succession of dominant ideas.

In the field of literary criticism, this historical point of view came to its first complete flower in the work of the French critic Taine, in the middle of the nineteenth century. The whole school of historian-critics to which Taine belonged—Michelet, Renan, Sainte-Beuve—had been occupied in interpreting books in terms of their historical origins. But Taine was the first of these to attempt to apply these principles systematically and on a large scale to a work devoted exclusively to literature. In the Introduction to his *History of English Literature,* published in 1863, he made his famous pronouncement that works of literature were to be understood as the upshot of three interfusing factors: *the moment, the race and the milieu.* Taine thought he was a scientist and a mechanist, who was examining works of literature from the same point of view as the chemist in experimenting with chemical compounds. But the difference between the critic and the chemist is that the critic cannot first combine his elements and then watch to see what they will do: he can only ex-

amine phenomena which have already taken place. The procedure that
Taine actually follows is to pretend to set the stage for the experiment
by describing the moment, the race and the milieu, and then to say:
"Such a situation demands such and such a kind of writer." He now
goes on to describe the kind of writer that the situation demands, and
the reader finds himself at the end confronted with Shakespeare or Milton or Byron, or whoever the great figure is—who turns out to prove the
accuracy of Taine's prognosis by precisely fitting the description.

There is thus a certain element of imposture in Taine; but it is a
very good thing that there is. If he had really been the mechanist that
he thought he was, his work on literature would have had little value.
The truth was that Taine loved literature for its own sake—he was at
his best himself a brilliant artist—and he had very strong moral convictions which give his writing emotional power. His mind, to be sure, was
an analytic one, and his analysis, though terribly oversimplified, does
have an explanatory value. Yet his work was what we call creative. Whatever he may say about chemical experiments, it is evident when he writes
of a great writer that the moment, the race and the milieu have combined,
like the three sounds of the chord in Browning's poem about Abt Vogler,
to produce not a fourth sound but a star.

To Taine's set of elements was added, dating from the middle of
the century, a new element, the economic, which was introduced into
the discussion of historical phenomena mainly by Marx and Engels. The
non-Marxist critics themselves were at the time already taking into account the influence of the social classes. In his chapters on the Norman
conquest of England, Taine shows that the difference between the literatures produced respectively by the Normans and by the Saxons was partly
the difference between a ruling class, on the one hand, and a vanquished
and oppressed class, on the other. And Michelet in his volume on the
Regency, which was finished the same year that the *History of English
Literature* appeared, studies the *Manon Lescaut* of the Abbé Prévost as a
document representing the point of view of the small gentry before the
French Revolution. But Marx and Engels derived the social classes from
the way that people made or got their livings—from what they called the
methods of production; and they tended to regard these economic processes as fundamental to civilization.

The Dialectical Materialism of Marx and Engels was not really so
materialistic as it sounds. There was in it a large element of the Hegelian
idealism that Marx and Engels thought they had got rid of. At no time
did these two famous materialists take so mechanistic a view of things
as Taine began by professing; and their theory of the relation of works
of literature to what they called the *economic base* was a good deal less

simple than Taine's theory of the moment, the race and the milieu.
They thought that art, politics, religion, philosophy and literature belonged to what they called the *superstructure* of human activity; but
they saw that the practitioners of these various departments tended also
to constitute social groups, and that they were always pulling away from
the kind of solidarity based on economic classes in order to establish a
professional solidarity of their own. Furthermore, the activities of the
superstructure could influence one another, and they could influence
the economic base. It may be said of Marx and Engels in general that,
contrary to the popular impression, they were tentative, confused and
modest when it came down to fundamentals, where a materialist like
Taine was cocksure. Marx once made an attempt to explain why the
poems of Homer were so good when the society that produced them was
from his point of view—that is, from the industrial point of view—so
primitive; and this gave him a good deal of trouble. If we compare his
discussion of this problem with Vico's discussion of Homer, we see that
the explanation of literature in terms of a philosophy of social history is
becoming, instead of simpler and easier, more difficult and more complex.

Marx and Engels were deeply imbued, moreover, with the German
admiration for literature, which they had learned from the age of Goethe.
It would never have occurred to either of them that *der Dichter* was not
one of the noblest and most beneficent of humankind. When Engels
writes about Goethe, he presents him as a man equipped for "practical
life," whose career was frustrated by the "misery" of the historical situation in Germany in his time, and reproaches him for allowing himself
to lapse into the "cautious, smug and narrow" Philistinism of the class
from which he came; but Engels regrets this, because it interfered with
the development of the "mocking, defiant, world-despising genius," *"der
geniale Dichter," "der gewaltige Poet,"* of whom Engels would not even,
he says, have asked that he should have been a political liberal if Goethe
had not sacrificed to his bourgeois shrinkings his truer aesthetic sense.
And the great critics who were trained on Marx—Franz Mehring and
Bernard Shaw—had all this reverence for the priesthood of literature.
Shaw deplores the absence of political philosophy and what he regards
as the middle-class snobbery in Shakespeare; but he celebrates Shakespeare's poetry and his dramatic imagination almost as enthusiastically
as Swinburne did, describing even those potboiling comedies—*Twelfth
Night* and *As You Like It*—the themes of which seem to him most
contemptible—as "the Crown Jewels of English dramatic poetry." Such
a critic may do more for a writer by showing him as a real man dealing
with a real world at a definite moment of time than the impressionist
critic of Swinburne's type who flourished in the same period of the late
nineteenth century. The purely impressionist critic approaches the whole

of literature as an exhibit of belletristic jewels, and he can only write a rhapsodic catalogue. But when Shaw turned his spotlight on Shakespeare as a figure in the Shavian drama of history, he invested him with a new interest as no other English critic had done.

The insistence that the man of letters should play a political role, the disparagement of works of art in comparison with political action, were thus originally no part of Marxism. They only became associated with it later. This happened by way of Russia, and it was due to special tendencies in that country that date from long before the Revolution or the promulgation of Marxism itself. In Russia there have been very good reasons why the political implications of literature should particularly occupy the critics. The art of Pushkin itself, with its marvelous power of implication, had certainly been partly created by the censorship of Nicholas I, and Pushkin set the tradition for most of the great Russian writers who followed him. Every play, every poem, every story, must be a parable of which the moral is *implied.* If it were stated, the censor would suppress the book as he tried to do with Pushkin's *Bronze Horseman,* where it was merely a question of the packed implications protruding a little too plainly. Right down through the writings of Chekhov and up almost to the Revolution, the imaginative literature of Russia presents the peculiar paradox of an art that is technically objective and yet charged with social messages. In Russia under the Tsar, it was inevitable that social criticism should lead to political conclusions, because the most urgent need from the point of view of any kind of improvement was to get rid of the tsarist regime. Even the neo-Christian moralist Tolstoy, who pretends to be non-political, is as political in his implications as any, because his preaching will inevitably embroil him with the Church, and the Church is an integral part of the tsardom. Tolstoy's pamphlet called *What Is Art,* in which he throws overboard Shakespeare and a large part of modern literature, including his own novels, in the interest of his intransigent morality, is the example which is most familiar to us of the moralizing Russian criticism; but it was only the most sensational expression of a kind of approach which had been prevalent since Belinsky and Chernyshevsky in the early part of the century. The critics, who were usually journalists writing in exile or for a contraband press, were always tending to demand of the imaginative writers that they should dramatize bolder morals.

Even after the Revolution had destroyed the tsarist government, this situation did not change. The old habits of censorship persisted in the new socialist society of the Soviets, which was necessarily made up of people who had been stamped by the die of the despotism. We find the peculiar phenomenon of a series of literary groups attempting one after the other to obtain official recognition or to make themselves sufficiently powerful to establish themselves as arbiters of literature. Lenin and Trotsky and Lunacharsky had the sense to oppose these attempts: the comrade-dictators of Proletcult or Lev or Rapp would certainly have been just as bad as the Count Benckendorff who made Pushkin miserable, and when the Stalin bureaucracy, after the death of Gorky, got control of this department as of everything else, they instituted a system of repression that made Benckendorff and Nicholas I look like Lorenzo de' Medici. In the meantime, Trotsky, who was Commissar of War but himself a great political writer with an interest in belles-lettres, attempted in 1924, apropos of one of these movements, to clarify the situation. He wrote a brilliant and valuable book called *Literature and Revolution,* in which he explained the aims of the government, analyzed the work of the Russian writers and praised or rebuked the latter as they seemed to him in harmony or in conflict with the former. Trotsky is intelligent, sympathetic; it is evident that he is really fond of literature and that he knows that a work of art does not fulfill its function in terms of the formulas of party propaganda. But Mayakovsky, the Soviet poet, whom Trotsky had praised with reservations, expressed himself in a famous joke when he was asked what he thought about Trotsky's book—a pun which implied that a Commissar turned critic was inevitably a Commissar still; and what a foreigner cannot accept in Trotsky is his assumption that it is the duty of the government to take a hand in the direction of literature.

This point of view, indigenous to Russia, has been imported to other countries through the permeation of Communist influence. The Communist press and its literary followers have reflected the control of the Kremlin in all the phases through which it has passed, down to the wholesale imprisonment of Soviet writers which has been taking place since 1935. But it has never been a part of the American system that our Republican or Democratic administration should lay down a political line for the guidance of the national literature. A recent gesture in this direction on the part of Archibald MacLeish, who seemed a little carried away by his position as Librarian of Congress, was anything but cordially received by serious American writers. So long as the United States remains happily a non-totalitarian country, we can very well do without this aspect of the historical criticism of literature.

Another element of a different order has, however, since Marx's time been added to the historical study of the origins of works of literature. I mean the psychoanalysis of Freud. This appears as an extension of something which had already got well started before, which had figured even in Johnson's *Lives of the Poets,* and of which the great exponent had been Sainte-Beuve: the interpretation of works of literature in the light of the personalities behind them. But the Freudians made this interpretation more exact and more systematic. The great example of the psychoanalysis of an artist is Freud's own essay on Leonardo da Vinci; but this has little critical interest: it is an attempt to construct a case history. One of the best examples I know of the application of Freudian analysis to literature is in Van Wyck Brooks's book, *The Ordeal of Mark Twain*, in which Mr. Brooks uses an incident of Mark Twain's boyhood as a key to his whole career. Mr. Brooks has since repudiated the method he resorted to here on the ground that no one but an analyst can ever know enough about a writer to make a valid psychoanalytic diagnosis. This is true, and it is true of the method that it has led to bad results where the critic has built a Freudian mechanism out of very slender evidence, and then given us merely a romance exploiting the supposed working of this mechanism, in place of an actual study, keeping close to the facts and the documents, of the writer's life and work. But I believe that Van Wyck Brooks really had hold of something important when he fixed upon that childhood incident of which Mark Twain gave so vivid an account to his biographer—that scene at the deathbed of his father when his mother made him promise that he would not break her heart. If it was not one of those crucial happenings that are supposed to determine the complexes of Freudianism, it has certainly a typical significance in relation to Mark Twain's whole psychology. The stories that people tell about their childhood are likely to be profoundly symbolic even when they have been partly or wholly made up in the light of later experience. And the attitudes, the compulsions, the emotional "patterns" that recur in the work of a writer are of great interest to the historical critic.

These attitudes and patterns are embedded in the community and the historical moment, and they may indicate its ideals and its diseases as the cell shows the condition of the tissue. The recent scientific experimentation in the combining of Freudian with Marxist method, and of psychoanalysis with anthropology, has had its parallel development in criticism. And there is thus another element added to our equipment for analyzing literary works, and the problem grows still more complex.

The analyst, however, is of course not concerned with the comparative values of his patients any more than the surgeon is. He cannot tell you why the neurotic Dostoevsky produces work of immense value to his fellows while another man with the same neurotic pattern would become a public menace. Freud himself emphatically states in his study of Leonardo that his method can make no attempt to account for Leonardo's genius. The problems of comparative artistic value still remain after we have given attention to the Freudian psychological factor just as they do after we have given attention to the Marxist economic factor and to the racial and geographical factors. No matter how thoroughly and searchingly we may have scrutinized works of literature from the historical and biographical points of view, we must be ready to attempt to estimate, in some such way as Saintsbury and Eliot do, the relative degrees of success attained by the products of the various periods and the various personalities. We must be able to tell good from bad, the first-rate from the second-rate. We shall not otherwise write literary criticism at all, but merely social or political history as reflected in literary texts, or psychological case histories from past eras, or, to take the historical point of view in its simplest and most academic form, merely chronologies of books that have been published.

And now how, in these matters of literary art, do we tell the good art from the bad? Norman Kemp Smith, the Kantian philosopher, whose courses I was fortunate enough to take at Princeton twenty-five years ago, used to tell us that this recognition was based primarily on an emotional reaction. For purposes of practical criticism this is a safe assumption on which to proceed. It is possible to discriminate in a variety of ways the elements that in any given department go to make a successful work of literature. Different schools have at different times demanded different things of literature: *unity, symmetry, universality, originality, vision, inspiration, strangeness, suggestiveness, improving morality, socialist realism,* etc. But you could have any set of these qualities that any school of writing has demanded and still not have a good play, a good novel, a good poem, a good history. If you identify the essence of good literature with any one of these elements or with any combination of them, you simply shift the emotional reaction to the recognition of the element or elements. Or if you add to your other demands the demand that the writer must have *talent,* you simply shift this recognition to the talent. Once people find some grounds of agreement in the coincidence of their emotional reactions to books, they may be able to discuss these elements profitably; but if they do not have this basic agreement, the discussion will make no sense.

But how, you may ask, can we identify this élite who know what they are talking about? Well, it can only be said of them that they are self-appointed and self-perpetuating, and that they will compel you to accept their authority. Impostors may try to put themselves over, but these quacks will not last. The implied position of the people who know about literature (as is also the case in every other art) is simply that they know what they know, and that they are determined to impose their opinions by main force of eloquence or assertion on the people who do not know. This is not a question, of course, of professional workers in literature—such as editors, professors and critics, who very often have no real understanding of the products with which they deal—but of readers of all kinds in all walks of life. There are moments when a first-rate writer, unrecognized or out of fashion with the official chalkers-up for the market, may find his support in the demand for his work of an appreciative cultivated public.

But what is the cause of this emotional reaction which is the critic's divining rod? This question has long been a subject of study by the branch of philosophy called Aesthetics, and it has recently been made a subject of scientific experimentation. Both these lines of inquiry are likely to be prejudiced in the eyes of the literary critic by the fact that the inquiries are sometimes conducted by persons who are obviously deficient in literary feeling or taste. Yet one should not deny the possibility that something of value might result from the speculations and explorations of men of acute minds who take as their given data the aesthetic emotions of other men.

Almost everybody interested in literature has tried to explain to himself the nature of these emotions that register our approval of artistic works; and I of course have my own explanation.

In my view, all our intellectual activity, in whatever field it takes place, is an attempt to give a meaning to our experience—that is, to make life more practicable; for by understanding things we make it easier to survive and get around among them. The mathematician Euclid, working in a convention of abstractions, shows us relations between the distances of our unwieldy and cluttered-up environment upon which we are able to count. A drama of Sophocles also indicates relations between the various human impulses, which appear so confused and dangerous, and it brings out a certain justice of Fate—that is to say, of the way in which the interaction of these impulses is seen in the long run to work out—upon which we can also depend. The kinship, from this point of view, of the purposes of science and art appears very clearly in the case of the Greeks, because not only do both Euclid and Sophocles satisfy us by making patterns, but they make much the same kind of patterns. Euclid's *Elements* takes simple theorems and by a series of logical operations builds them up to a climax in the square on the hypotenuse. A typical drama of Sophocles develops in a similar way.

Some writers (as well as some scientists) have a different kind of explicit message beyond the kind of reassurance implicit in merely understanding life or in the harmony of artistic form. Not content with such an achievement as that of Sophocles—who has one of his choruses tell us that it is better not to be born, but who, by representing life as noble and based on law, makes its tragedies easier to bear—such writers attempt, like Plato, to think out and recommend a procedure for turning it into something better. But other departments of literature—lyric poetry such as Sappho's, for example—have *less* philosophical content than Sophocles. A lyric gives us nothing but a pattern imposed on the expression of a feeling; but this pattern of metrical quantities and of consonants and vowels that balance has the effect of reducing the feeling, however unruly or painful it may seem when we experience it in the course of our lives, to something orderly, symmetrical and pleasing; and it also relates this feeling to the more impressive scheme, works it into the larger texture, of the body of poetic art. The discord has been resolved, the anomaly subjected to discipline. And this control of his emotion by the poet has the effect at second hand of making it easier for the reader to manage his own emotions. (Why certain sounds and rhythms gratify us more than others, and how they are connected with the themes and ideas that they are chosen as appropriate for conveying, are questions that may be passed on to the scientist.)

And this brings us back again to the historical point of view. The experience of mankind on the earth is always changing as man develops and has to deal with new combinations of elements; and the writer who is to be anything more than an echo of his predecessors must always find expression for something which has never yet been expressed, must master a new set of phenomena which has never yet been mastered. With each such victory of the human intellect, whether in history, in philosophy or in poetry, we experience a deep satisfaction: we have been cured of some ache of disorder, relieved of some oppressive burden of uncomprehended events.

This relief that brings the sense of power, and, with the sense of power, joy, is the positive emotion which tells us that we have encountered a first-rate piece of literature. But stay! you may at this point warn: are not people often solaced and exhilarated by literature of the trashiest kind? They are: crude and limited people do certainly feel some such emotion in connection with work that is limited and crude. The man who is more highly organized and has a wider intellectual range will feel it in connection with work that is finer and more complex. The difference between the emotion of the more highly organized man and the emotion of the less highly organized one is merely a matter of gradation. You sometimes discover books—the novels of John Steinbeck, for example—that seem to mark precisely the borderline between work that is definitely superior and work that is definitely bad. When I was speaking a little while back of the genuine connoisseurs who establish the standards of taste, I meant, of course, the people who can distinguish Grade A and who prefer it to the other grades.

LIONEL TRILLING
Manners, Morals, and the Novel

The invitation that was made to me to address you this evening
was couched in somewhat uncertain terms. Time, place, and cordiality
were perfectly clear, but when it came to the subject our hosts were not
able to specify just what they wanted me to talk about. They wanted
me to consider literature in its relation to manners—by which, as they
relied on me to understand, they did not really mean *manners*. They did
not mean, that is, the rules of personal intercourse in our culture; and
yet such rules were by no means irrelevant to what they did mean. Nor
did they quite mean manners in the sense of *mores,* customs, although,
again, these did bear upon the subject they had in mind.

I understood them perfectly, as I would not have understood them
had they been more definite. For they were talking about a nearly in-
definable subject.

Somewhere below all the explicit statements that a people makes
through its art, religion, architecture, legislation, there is a dim mental
region of intention of which it is very difficult to become aware. We now
and then get a strong sense of its existence when we deal with the past,
not by reason of its presence in the past but by reason of its absence.
As we read the great formulated monuments of the past, we notice that
we are reading them without the accompaniment of something that
always goes along with the formulated monuments of the present. The
voice of multifarious intention and activity is stilled, all the buzz of
implication which always surrounds us in the present, coming to us from
what never gets fully stated, coming in the tone of greetings and the tone
of quarrels, in slang and humor and popular songs, in the way children
play, in the gesture the waiter makes when he puts down the plate, in
the nature of the very food we prefer.

Some of the charm of the past consists of the quiet—the great distracting buzz of implication has stopped and we are left only with what
has been fully phrased and precisely stated. And part of the melancholy
of the past comes from our knowledge that the huge, unrecorded hum of
implication was once there and left no trace—we feel that because it is
evanescent it is especially human. We feel, too, that the truth of the
great preserved monuments of the past does not fully appear without it.

From letters and diaries, from the remote, unconscious corners of the great works themselves, we try to guess what the sound of the multifarious implication was and what it meant.

Or when we read the conclusions that are drawn about our own culture by some gifted foreign critic—or by some stupid native one—who is equipped only with a knowledge of our books, when we try in vain to say what is wrong, when in despair we say that he has read the books "out of context," then we are aware of the matter I have been asked to speak about tonight.

What I understand by manners, then, is a culture's hum and buzz of implication. I mean the whole evanescent context in which its explicit statements are made. It is that part of a culture which is made up of half-uttered or unuttered or unutterable expressions of value. They are hinted at by small actions, sometimes by the arts of dress or decoration, sometimes by tone, gesture, emphasis, or rhythm, sometimes by the words that are used with a special frequency or a special meaning. They are the things that for good or bad draw the people of a culture together and that separate them from the people of another culture. They make the part of a culture which is not art, or religion, or morals, or politics, and yet it relates to all these highly formulated departments of culture. It is modified by them; it modifies them; it is generated by them; it generates them. In this part of culture assumption rules, which is often so much stronger than reason.

The right way to begin to deal with such a subject is to gather together as much of its detail as we possibly can. Only by doing so will we become fully aware of what the gifted foreign critic or the stupid native one is not aware of, that in any complex culture there is not a single system of manners but a conflicting variety of manners, and that one of the jobs of a culture is the adjustment of this conflict.

But the nature of our present occasion does not permit this accumulation of detail and so I shall instead try to drive toward a generalization and an hypothesis which, however wrong they turn out to be, may at least permit us to circumscribe the subject. I shall try to generalize the subject of American manners by talking about the attitude of Americans toward the subject of manners itself. And since in a complex culture there are, as I say, many different systems of manners and since I cannot talk about them all, I shall select the manners and the attitude toward manners of the literate, reading, responsible middle class of people who are ourselves. I specify that they be reading people because I shall draw my conclusions from the novels they read. The hypothesis I propose is that our attitude toward manners is the expression of a particular conception of reality.

All literature tends to be concerned with the question of reality—I mean quite simply the old opposition between reality and appearance, between what really is and what merely seems. "Don't you *see?*" is the question we want to shout at Oedipus as he stands before us and before fate in the pride of his rationalism. And at the end of *Oedipus Rex* he demonstrates in a particularly direct way that he now sees what he did not see before. "Don't you *see?*" we want to shout again at Lear and Gloucester, the two deceived, self-deceiving fathers: blindness again, resistance to the clear claims of reality, the seduction by mere appearance. The same with Othello—reality is right under your stupid nose, how *dare* you be such a gull? So with Molière's Orgon—my good man, my honest citizen, merely *look* at Tartuffe and you will know what's what. So with Milton's Eve—"Woman, watch out! Don't you see—anyone can see—that's a *snake!*"

The problem of reality is central, and in a special way, to the great forefather of the novel, the great book of Cervantes, whose four-hundredth birthday was celebrated in 1947. There are two movements of thought in *Don Quixote,* two different and opposed notions of reality. One is the movement which leads toward saying that the world of ordinary practicality *is* reality in its fullness. It is the reality of the present moment in all its powerful immediacy of hunger, cold, and pain, making the past and the future, and all ideas, of no account. When the conceptual, the ideal, and the fanciful come into conflict with this, bringing their notions of the past and the future, then disaster results. For one thing, the ordinary proper ways of life are upset—the chained prisoners are understood to be good men and are released, the whore is taken for a lady. There is general confusion. As for the ideal, the conceptual, the fanciful, or romantic—whatever you want to call it—it fares even worse: it is shown to be ridiculous.

Thus one movement of the novel. But Cervantes changed horses in midstream and found that he was riding Rosinante. Perhaps at first not quite consciously—although the new view is latent in the old from the very beginning—Cervantes begins to show that the world of tangible reality is not the real reality after all. The real reality is rather the wildly conceiving, the madly fantasying mind of the Don: people change, practical reality changes, when they come into its presence.

In any genre it may happen that the first great example contains the whole potentiality of the genre. It has been said that all philosophy is a footnote to Plato. It can be said that all prose fiction is a variation on the theme of *Don Quixote.* Cervantes sets for the novel the problem of appearance and reality: the shifting and conflict of social classes becomes the field of the problem of knowledge, of how we know and of how reliable our knowledge is, which at that very moment of history is vexing the philosophers and scientists. And the poverty of the Don suggests that the novel is born with the appearance of money as a social element—money, the great solvent of the solid fabric of the old society, the great generator of illusion. Or, which is to say much the same thing, the novel is born in response to snobbery.

Snobbery is not the same thing as pride of class. Pride of class may not please us but we must at least grant that it reflects a social function. A man who exhibited class pride—in the day when it was possible to do so—may have been puffed up about what he *was,* but this ultimately depended on what he *did.* Thus, aristocratic pride was based ultimately on the ability to fight and administer. No pride is without fault, but pride of class may be thought of as today we think of pride of profession, toward which we are likely to be lenient.

Snobbery is pride in status without pride in function. And it is an uneasy pride of status. It always asks, "Do I belong—do I really belong? And does he belong? And if I am observed talking to him, will it make me seem to belong or not to belong?" It is the peculiar vice not of aristocratic societies which have their own appropriate vices, but of bourgeois democratic societies. For us the legendary strongholds of snobbery are the Hollywood studios, where two thousand dollars a week dare not talk to three hundred dollars a week for fear he be taken for nothing more than fifteen hundred dollars a week. The dominant emotions of snobbery are uneasiness, self-consciousness, self-defensiveness, the sense that one is not quite real but can in some way acquire reality.

Money is the medium that, for good or bad, makes for a fluent society. It does not make for an equal society but for one in which there is a constant shifting of classes, a frequent change in the personnel of the dominant class. In a shifting society great emphasis is put on appearance—I am using the word now in the common meaning, as when people say that "a good appearance is very important in getting a job." To appear to be established is one of the ways of becoming established. The old notion of the solid merchant who owns far more than he shows increasingly gives way to the ideal of signalizing status by appearance, by showing more than you have: status in a democratic society is presumed to come not with power but with the tokens of power. Hence the development of what Tocqueville saw as a mark of democratic culture, what he called the "hypocrisy of luxury"—instead of the well-made peasant article and the well-made middle-class article, we have the effort of all articles to appear as the articles of the very wealthy.

And a shifting society is bound to generate an interest in appearance in the philosophical sense. When Shakespeare lightly touched on the matter that so largely preoccupies the novelist—that is, the movement from one class to another—and created Malvolio, he immediately involved the question of social standing with the problem of appearance and reality. Malvolio's daydreams of bettering his position present themselves to him as reality, and in revenge his enemies conspire to convince him that he is literally mad and that the world is not as he sees it. The predicament of the characters in *A Midsummer Night's Dream* and of Christopher Sly seems to imply that the meeting of social extremes and the establishment of a person of low class in the privileges of a high class always suggested to Shakespeare's mind some radical instability of the senses and the reason.

The characteristic work of the novel is to record the illusion that snobbery generates and to try to penetrate to the truth which, as the novel assumes, lies hidden beneath all the false appearances. Money, snobbery, the ideal of status, these become in themselves the objects of fantasy, the support of the fantasies of love, freedom, charm, power, as in *Madame Bovary,* whose heroine is the sister, at a three-centuries' remove, of Don Quixote. The greatness of *Great Expectations* begins in its title: modern society bases itself on great expectations which, if ever they are realized, are found to exist by reason of a sordid, hidden reality. The real thing is not the gentility of Pip's life but the hulks and the murder and the rats and decay in the cellarage of the novel.

An English writer, recognizing the novel's central concern with snobbery, recently cried out half-ironically against it. "Who cares whether Pamela finally exasperates Mr. B. into marriage, whether Mr. Elton is more or less than moderately genteel, whether it is sinful for Pendennis nearly to kiss the porter's daughter, whether young men from Boston can ever be as truly refined as middle-aged women in Paris, whether the District Officer's fiancée ought to see so much of Dr. Aziz, whether Lady Chatterley ought to be made love to by the gamekeeper, even if he was an officer during the war? Who cares?"

The novel, of course, tells us much more about life than this. It tells us about the look and feel of things, how things are done and what things are worth and what they cost and what the odds are. If the English novel in its special concern with class does not, as the same writer says, explore the deeper layers of personality, then the French novel in exploring these layers must start and end in class, and the Russian novel, exploring the ultimate possibilities of spirit, does the same—every situation in Dostoevski, no matter how spiritual, starts with a point of social pride and a certain number of rubles. The great novelists knew that manners indicate the largest intentions of men's souls as well as the smallest and they are perpetually concerned to catch the meaning of every dim implicit hint.

The novel, then, is a perpetual quest for reality, the field of its research being always the social world, the material of its analysis being always manners as the indication of the direction of man's soul. When we understand this we can understand the pride of profession that moved D. H. Lawrence to say, "Being a novelist, I consider myself superior to the saint, the scientist, the philosopher and the poet. The novel is the one bright book of life."

Now the novel as I have described it has never really established itself in America. Not that we have not had very great novels but that the novel in America diverges from its classic intention, which, as I have said, is the investigation of the problem of reality beginning in the social field. The fact is that American writers of genius have not turned their minds to society. Poe and Melville were quite apart from it; the reality they sought was only tangential to society. Hawthorne was acute when he insisted that he did not write novels but romances—he thus expressed his awareness of the lack of social texture in his work. Howells never fulfilled himself because, although he saw the social subject clearly, he would never take it with full seriousness. In America in the nineteenth century, Henry James was alone in knowing that to scale the moral and aesthetic heights in the novel one had to use the ladder of social observation.

There is a famous passage in James's life of Hawthorne in which James enumerates the things which are lacking to give the American novel the thick social texture of the English novel—no state; barely a specific national name; no sovereign; no court; no aristocracy; no church; no clergy; no army; no diplomatic service; no country gentlemen; no palaces; no castles; no manors; no old country houses; no parsonages; no thatched cottages; no ivied ruins; no cathedrals; no great universities; no public schools; no political society; no sporting class—no Epsom, no Ascot! That is, no sufficiency of means for the display of a variety of manners, no opportunity for the novelist to do his job of searching out reality, not enough complication of appearance to make the job interesting. Another great American novelist of very different temperament had said much the same thing some decades before: James Fenimore Cooper found that American manners were too simple and dull to nourish the novelist.

This is cogent but it does not explain the condition of the American novel at the present moment. For life in America has increasingly thickened since the nineteenth century. It has not, to be sure, thickened so much as to permit our undergraduates to understand the characters of Balzac, to understand, that is, life in a crowded country where the competitive pressures are great, forcing intense passions to express themselves fiercely and yet within the limitations set by a strong and complicated tradition of manners. Still, life here has become more complex and more pressing. And even so we do not have the novel that touches significantly on society, on manners. Whatever the virtues of Dreiser may be, he could not report the social fact with the kind of accuracy it needs. Sinclair Lewis is shrewd, but no one, however charmed with him as a social satirist, can believe that he does more than a limited job of social understanding. John Dos Passos sees much, sees it often in the great way of Flaubert, but can never use social fact as more than either backdrop or "condition." Of our novelists today perhaps only William Faulkner deals with society as the field of tragic reality and he has the disadvantage of being limited to a provincial scene.

It would seem that Americans have a kind of resistance to looking closely at society. They appear to believe that to touch accurately on the matter of class, to take full note of snobbery, is somehow to demean themselves. It is as if we felt that one cannot touch pitch without being defiled—which, of course, may possibly be the case. Americans will not deny that we have classes and snobbery, but they seem to hold it to be indelicate to take precise cognizance of these phenomena. Consider that Henry James is, among a large part of our reading public, still held to be at fault for noticing society as much as he did. Consider the conversation that has, for some interesting reason, become a part of our literary folklore. Scott Fitzgerald said to Ernest Hemingway, "The very rich are different from us." Hemingway replied, "Yes, they have more money." I have seen the exchange quoted many times and always with the intention of suggesting that Fitzgerald was infatuated by wealth and had received a salutary rebuke from his democratic friend. But the truth is that after a certain point quantity of money does indeed change into quality of personality: in an important sense the very rich *are* different from us. So are the very powerful, the very gifted, the very poor. Fitzgerald was right, and almost for that remark alone he must surely have been received in Balzac's bosom in the heaven of novelists.

It is of course by no means true that the American reading class has no interest in society. Its interest fails only before society as it used to be represented by the novel. And if we look at the commercially successful serious novels of the last decade, we see that almost all of them have been written from an intense social awareness—it might be said that our present definition of a serious book is one which holds before us some image of society to consider and condemn. What is the situation of the dispossessed Oklahoma farmer and whose fault it is, what situation the Jew finds himself in, what it means to be a Negro, how one gets a bell for Adano, what is the advertising business really like, what it means to be insane and how society takes care of you or fails to do so—these are the matters which are believed to be most fertile for the novelist, and certainly they are the subjects most favored by our reading class.

The public is probably not deceived about the quality of most of these books. If the question of quality is brought up, the answer is likely to be: no, they are not great, they are not imaginative, they are not "literature." But there is an unexpressed addendum: and perhaps they are all the better for not being imaginative, for not being literature—they are not literature, they are reality, and *in a time like this* what we need is reality in large doses.

When, generations from now, the historian of our times undertakes to describe the assumptions of our culture, he will surely discover that the word *reality* is of central importance in his understanding of us. He will observe that for some of our philosophers the meaning of the word was a good deal in doubt, but that for our political writers, for many of our literary critics, and for most of our reading public, the word did not open discussion but, rather, closed it. Reality, as conceived by us, is whatever is external and hard, gross, unpleasant. Involved in its meaning is the idea of power conceived in a particular way. Some time ago I had occasion to remark how, in the critical estimates of Theodore Dreiser, it is always being said that Dreiser has many faults but that it cannot be denied that he has great power. No one ever says "a kind of power." Power is assumed to be always "brute" power, crude, ugly, and undiscriminating, the way an elephant appears to be. It is seldom understood to be the way an elephant actually is, precise and discriminating; or the way electricity is, swift and absolute and scarcely embodied.

The word *reality* is an honorific word and the future historian will naturally try to discover our notion of its pejorative opposite, appearance, mere appearance. He will find it in our feeling about the internal; whenever we detect evidences of style and thought we suspect that reality is being a little betrayed, that "mere subjectivity" is creeping in. There follows from this our feeling about complication, modulation, personal idiosyncrasy, and about social forms, both the great and the small.

Having gone so far, our historian is then likely to discover a puzzling contradiction. For we claim that the great advantage of reality is its hard, bedrock, concrete quality, yet everything we say about it tends toward the abstract and it almost seems that what we want to find in reality is abstraction itself. Thus we believe that one of the unpleasant bedrock facts is social class, but we become extremely impatient if ever we are told that social class is indeed so real that it produces actual differences of personality. The very people who talk most about class and its evils think that Fitzgerald was bedazzled and Hemingway right. Or again, it might be observed that in the degree that we speak in praise of the "individual" we have contrived that our literature should have no individuals in it—no people, that is, who are shaped by our liking for the interesting and memorable and special and precious.

Here, then, is our generalization: that in proportion as we have committed ourselves to our particular idea of reality we have lost our interest in manners. For the novel this is a definitive condition because it is inescapably true that in the novel manners make men. It does not matter in what sense the word manners is taken—it is equally true of the sense which so much interested Proust or of the sense which interested Dickens or, indeed, of the sense which interested Homer. The Duchesse de Guermantes unable to delay departure for the dinner party to receive properly from her friend Swann the news that he is dying but able to delay to change the black slippers her husband objects to; Mr. Pickwick and Sam Weller; Priam and Achilles—they exist by reason of their observed manners.

So true is this, indeed, so creative is the novelist's awareness of manners, that we may say that it is a function of his love. It is some sort of love that Fielding has for Squire Western that allows him to note the great, gross details which bring the insensitive sentient man into existence for us. If that is true, we are forced to certain conclusions about our literature and about the particular definition of reality which has shaped it. The reality we admire tells us that the observation of manners is trivial and even malicious, that there are things much more important for the novel to consider. As a consequence our social sympathies have indeed broadened, but in proportion as they have done so we have lost something of our power of love, for our novels can never create characters who truly exist. We make public demands for love, for we know that broad social feeling should be infused with warmth, and we receive a kind of public product which we try to believe is not cold potatoes. The reviewers of Helen Howe's novel of a few years ago, *We Happy Few,* thought that its satiric first part, an excellent comment on the manners of a small but significant segment of society, was ill-natured and unsatisfactory, but they approved the second part, which is the record of the heroine's self-accusing effort to come into communication with the great soul of America. Yet it should have been clear that the satire had its source in a kind of affection, in a real community of feeling, and told the truth, while the second part, said to be so "warm," was mere abstraction, one more example of our public idea of ourselves and our national life. John Steinbeck is generally praised both for his reality and his warmheartedness, but in *The Wayward Bus* the lower-class characters receive a doctrinaire affection in proportion to the suffering and sexuality which define their existence, while the ill-observed middle-class characters are made to submit not only to moral judgment but to the withdrawal of all fellow-feeling, being mocked for their very misfortunes and almost for their susceptibility to death. Only a little thought or even less feeling is required to perceive that the basis of his creation is the coldest response to abstract ideas.

Two novelists of the older sort had a prevision of our present situation. In Henry James's *The Princess Casamassima* there is a scene in which the heroine is told about the existence of a conspiratorial group of revolutionaries pledged to the destruction of all existing society. She has for some time been drawn by a desire for social responsibility; she has wanted to help "the people," she has longed to discover just such a group as she now hears about, and she exclaims in joy, "Then it's real, it's solid!" We are intended to hear the Princess's glad cry with the knowledge that she is a woman who despises herself, "that in the darkest hour of her life she sold herself for a title and a fortune. She regards her doing so as such a terrible piece of frivolity that she can never for the rest of her days be serious enough to make up for it." She seeks out poverty, suffering, sacrifice, and death because she believes that these things alone are real; she comes to believe that art is contemptible; she withdraws her awareness and love from the one person of her acquaintance who most deserves them, and she increasingly scorns whatever suggests variety and modulation, and is more and more dissatisfied with the humanity of the present in her longing for the more perfect humanity of the future. It is one of the great points that the novel makes that with each passionate step that she takes toward what she calls the real, the solid, she in fact moves further away from the life-giving reality.

In E. M. Forster's *The Longest Journey* there is a young man named Stephen Wonham who, although a gentleman born, has been carelessly brought up and has no real notion of the responsibilities of his class. He has a friend, a country laborer, a shepherd, and on two occasions he outrages the feelings of certain intelligent, liberal, democratic people in the book by his treatment of this friend. Once, when the shepherd reneges on a bargain, Stephen quarrels with him and knocks him down; and in the matter of the loan of a few shillings he insists that the money be paid back to the last farthing. The intelligent, liberal, democratic people know that this is not the way to act to the poor. But Stephen cannot think of the shepherd as the poor nor, although he is a country laborer, as an object of research by J. L. and Barbara Hammond; he is rather a reciprocating subject in a relationship of affection —as we say, a friend—and therefore liable to anger and required to pay his debts. But this view is held to be deficient in intelligence, liberalism, and democracy.

In these two incidents we have the premonition of our present cultural and social situation, the passionate self-reproachful addiction to a "strong" reality which must limit its purview to maintain its strength, the replacement by abstraction of natural, direct human feeling. It is worth noting, by the way, how clear is the line by which the two novels descend from *Don Quixote*—how their young heroes come into life with large preconceived ideas and are knocked about in consequence; how both are concerned with the problem of appearance and reality, *The Longest Journey* quite explicitly, *The Princess Casamassima* by indirection; how both evoke the question of the nature of reality by contriving a meeting and conflict of diverse social classes and take scrupulous note of the differences of manners. Both have as their leading characters people who are specifically and passionately concerned with social injustice and both agree in saying that to act against social injustice is right and noble but that to choose to act so does not settle all moral problems but on the contrary generates new ones of an especially difficult sort.

I have elsewhere given the name of moral realism to the perception of the dangers of the moral life itself. Perhaps at no other time has the enterprise of moral realism ever been so much needed, for at no other time have so many people committed themselves to moral righteousness. We have the books that point out the bad conditions, that praise us for taking progressive attitudes. We have no books that raise questions in our minds not only about conditions but about ourselves, that lead us to refine our motives and ask what might lie behind our good impulses.

There is nothing so very terrible in discovering that something does lie behind. Nor does it need a Freud to make the discovery. Here is a publicity release sent out by one of our oldest and most respectable publishing houses. Under the heading "What Makes Books Sell?" it reads, "Blank & Company reports that the current interest in horror stories has attracted a great number of readers to John Dash's novel . . . because of its depiction of Nazi brutality. Critics and readers alike have commented on the stark realism of Dash's handling of the torture scenes in the book. The publishers originally envisaged a woman's market because of the love story, now find men reading the book because of the other angle." This does not suggest a more than usual depravity in the male reader, for "the other angle" has always had a fascination, no doubt a bad one, even for those who would not themselves commit or actually witness an act of torture. I cite the extreme example only to suggest that something may indeed lie behind our sober intelligent interest in moral politics. In this instance the pleasure in the cruelty is protected and licensed by moral indignation. In other instances moral indignation, which has been said to be the favorite emotion of the middle class, may be in itself an exquisite pleasure. To understand this does not invalidate moral indignation but only sets up the conditions on which it ought to be entertained, only says when it is legitimate and when not.

But, the answer comes, however important it may be for moral realism to raise questions in our minds about our motives, is it not at best a matter of secondary importance? Is it not of the first importance that we be given a direct and immediate report on the reality that is daily being brought to dreadful birth? The novels that have done this have effected much practical good, bringing to consciousness the latent feelings of many people, making it harder for them to be unaware or indifferent, creating an atmosphere in which injustice finds it harder to thrive. To speak of moral realism is all very well. But it is an elaborate, even fancy, phrase and it is to be suspected of having the intention of sophisticating the simple reality that is easily to be conceived. Life presses us so hard, time is so short, the suffering of the world is so huge, simple, unendurable—anything that complicates our moral fervor in dealing with reality as we immediately see it and wish to drive headlong upon it must be regarded with some impatience.

True enough: and therefore any defense of what I have called moral realism must be made not in the name of some highflown fineness of feeling but in the name of simple social practicality. And there is indeed a simple social fact to which moral realism has a simple practical relevance, but it is a fact very difficult for us nowadays to perceive. It is that the moral passions are even more willful and imperious and impatient than the self-seeking passions. All history is at one in telling us that their tendency is to be not only liberating but also restrictive.

It is probable that at this time we are about to make great changes in our social system. The world is ripe for such changes and if they are not made in the direction of greater social liberality, the direction forward, they will almost of necessity be made in the direction backward, of a terrible social niggardliness. We all know which of those directions we want. But it is not enough to want it, not even enough to work for it —we must want it and work for it with intelligence. Which means that we must be aware of the dangers which lie in our most generous wishes. Some paradox of our natures leads us, when once we have made our fellow men the objects of our enlightened interest, to go on to make them the objects of our pity, then of our wisdom, ultimately of our coercion. It is to prevent this corruption, the most ironic and tragic that man knows, that we stand in need of the moral realism which is the product of the free play of the moral imagination.

For our time the most effective agent of the moral imagination has been the novel of the last two hundred years. It was never, either aesthetically or morally, a perfect form and its faults and failures can be quickly enumerated. But its greatness and its practical usefulness lay in its unremitting work of involving the reader himself in the moral life, inviting him to put his own motives under examination, suggesting that reality is not as his conventional education has led him to see it. It taught us, as no other genre ever did, the extent of human variety and the value of this variety. It was the literary form to which the emotions of understanding and forgiveness were indigenous, as if by the definition of the form itself. At the moment its impulse does not seem strong, for there never was a time when the virtues of its greatness were so likely to be thought of as weaknesses. Yet there never was a time when its particular activity was so much needed, was of so much practical, political, and social use—so much so that if its impulse does not respond to the need, we shall have reason to be sad not only over a waning form of art but also over our waning freedom.

Evaluation

I. A. RICHARDS
Badness in Poetry

Il faut dissiper un malentendu: nous sommes pourris d'art!
LE CORBUSIER-SAUGNIER

The theory of badness in poetry has never received the study which it deserves, partly on account of its difficulty. For with bad art even more than with good unless we are careful to distinguish the communicative from the value aspects, even when these are connected, we shall find the issues obscured. Sometimes art is bad because communication is defective, the vehicle inoperative; sometimes because the experience communicated is worthless; sometimes for both reasons. It would perhaps be best to restrict the term bad art to cases in which genuine communication does to a considerable degree take place, what is communicated being worthless, and to call the other cases defective art. But this is not the usual practice of critics, any work which produces an experience displeasing to the critic being commonly called bad, whether or not this experience is like that responsible for the work.

Let us begin by considering an instance of defective communication; choosing an example in which it is likely that the original experience had some value.

From *Principles of Literary Criticism* by I. A. Richards. Reprinted by permission of Harcourt, Brace & World, Inc. and of Routledge & Kegan Paul, Ltd.

THE POOL

Are you alive?
I touch you.
You quiver like a sea-fish.
I cover you with my net.
What are you—banded one?

I take a complete work to avoid possible unfairness. Here we have the whole of the link which is to mediate between the experiences of the author and of the reader. Aristotle, in a different connection, it is true, and for different reasons, affirmed that a work of art must possess a certain magnitude, and we can adapt his remark here. Not the brevity only of the vehicle, but its simplicity, makes it ineffective. The sacrifice of metre in free verse needs, in almost all cases, to be compensated by length. The loss of so much of the formal structure leads otherwise to tenuousness and ambiguity. Even when, as here, the original experience is presumably slight, tenuous and fleeting, the mere correspondence of matter to form is insufficient. The experience evoked in the reader is not sufficiently specific. A poet may, it is true, make an unlimited demand upon his reader, and the greatest poets make the greatest claim, but the demand made must be proportional to the poet's own contribution. The reader here supplies too much of the poem. Had the poet said only, "I went and poked about for rocklings and caught the pool itself," the reader, who converts what is printed above into a poem, would still have been able to construct an experience of equal value; for what results is almost independent of the author.

To pass to a case in which communication is successful, where the objection lies to what is communicated:

After the fierce midsummer all ablaze
     Has burned itself to ashes and expires
     In the intensity of its own fires,
Then come the mellow, mild, St. Martin days
Crowned with the calm of peace, but sad with haze.
     So after Love has led us, till he tires
     Of his own throes and torments, and desires,
Comes large-eyed Friendship: with a restful gaze
He beckons us to follow, and across
     Cool, verdant vales we wander free from care.
     Is it a touch of frost lies in the air?
Why are we haunted with a sense of loss?
     We do not wish the pain back, or the heat;
     And yet, and yet, these days are incomplete.

As to the success of the communication there can be no question. Both the popularity of the author, Ella Wheeler Wilcox, of whose work this is a favourable specimen, and records of the response made by well-educated persons, who read it without being aware of the authorship, leave this beyond doubt. It reproduces the state of mind of the writer very exactly. With a very numerous class of readers pleasure and admiration ensue. The explanation is, probably, in the soothing effect of aligning the very active Love-Friendship groups of impulses with so settled yet rich a group as the Summer-Autumn simile brings in. The mind finds for a moment an attitude in which to contemplate a pair of situations (Love and Friendship) together, situations which are for many minds particularly difficult to see together. The heavy regular rhythm, the dead stamp of the rimes, the obviousness of the descriptions ("mellow, mild, St. Martin"; "cool verdant vales") their alliteration, the triteness of the close, all these accentuate the impression of conclusiveness. The restless spirit is appeased, one of its chief problems is made to seem as if, regarded from a lofty, all-embracing standpoint, it is no problem but a process of nature.

This reconciliation, this appeasement, is common to much good and to much bad poetry alike. But the value of it depends upon the level of organisation at which it takes place, upon whether the reconciled impulses are adequate or inadequate. In this case those who have adequate impulses as regards *any* of the four main systems involved, Summer, Autumn, Love, Friendship, are not appeased. Only for those who make certain conventional, stereotyped maladjustments instead, does the magic work.

The nature and source of these stock conventional attitudes is of great interest. Suggestion is very largely responsible for them. The normal child under the age of ten is probably free from them, or at least with him they have no fixity or privileged standing. But as general reflection develops the place of the free direct play of experience is taken by the deliberate organisation of attitudes, a clumsy and crude substitute. "Ideas," as they are commonly called, arise. A boy's "Idea" of Friendship or of Summer or of his Country is not, though the name would seem to imply it, primarily an intellectual affair. It is rather an attitude, or set of attitudes, of tendencies to act in certain fashions rather than others. Now reflection, unless very prolonged and very arduous, tends to fix the attitude by making us dwell in it, by *removing us from experience*. In the development of any attitude there are stages, points of rest, of relatively greater stability. These, as we dwell in them, become more and more difficult to pass, and it is not surprising that most people remain all their lives in various halfway houses.

These stages or levels of emotional adjustment seem, for the most part, to be fixed not by any special suitability to circumstances, certainly not to present circumstances, but much more by social suggestion and by accidents which withdraw us from actual experience, the one force which might push us further. At present bad literature, bad art, the cinema, etc., are an influence of the first importance in fixing immature and actually inapplicable attitudes to most things. Even the decision as to what constitutes a pretty girl or a handsome young man, an affair apparently natural and personal enough, is largely determined by magazine covers and movie stars. The quite common opinion that the arts have after all very little effect upon the community shows only that too little attention is being paid to the effects of bad art.

The losses incurred by these artificial fixations of attitudes are evident. Through them the average adult is worse, not better adjusted to the possibilities of his existence than the child. He is even in the most important things functionally unable to face facts: do what he will he is only able to face fictions, fictions projected by his own stock responses.

Against these stock responses the artist's internal and external conflicts are fought, and with them the popular writer's triumphs are made. Any combination of these general Ideas, hit at the right level or halting point of development, is, if suitably advertised, certain of success. Best-sellers in all the arts, exemplifying as they do the most general levels of attitude development, are worthy of very close study. No theory of criticism is satisfactory which is not able to explain their wide appeal and to give clear reasons why those who disdain them are not necessarily snobs.

The critic and the Sales Manager are not ordinarily regarded as of the same craft, nor are the poet and the advertising agent. It is true that some serious artists are occasionally tempted into poster designing. It is, however, doubtful whether their work pays. But the written appeals which have the soundest financial prospects as estimated by the most able American advertisers are such that no critic can safely ignore them. For they do undoubtedly represent the literary ideals present and future of the people to whom they are addressed.[1] They are tested in a way in which few other forms of literature are tested, their effects are watched by adepts whose livelihood depends upon the accuracy of their judgment, and they are among the best indices available of what is happening to taste. Criticism will justify itself as an applied science when it is able to indicate how an advertisement may be profitable without necessarily being crass. We shall see later under what conditions popularity and possible high value are compatible.

The strongest objection to, let us say, the sonnet we have quoted,

---

[1] A specimen: "The thoughtful man, the man on business bent, wends his way to Wembley with definite purpose. He seeketh knowledge, desireth increase of commerce or willeth to study new epoch-making inventions."— *Official Advertisement.*

is that a person who enjoys it, through the very organisation of his responses which enables him to enjoy it, is debarred from appreciating many things which, if he could appreciate them, he would prefer. We must not, of course, forget those variations in psychological efficiency discussed in Chapter XXII as degrees of vigilance. Even a good critic at a sufficiently low ebb of neural potency might mistake such a sonnet for one of Shakespeare's or with more ease for one of Rossetti's. But when vigilance was restored he would see, or at least feel, the differences. The point is that a reader who, at a high degree of vigilance, thoroughly enters into and enjoys this class of verse, is necessarily so organised that he will fail to respond to poetry. Time and much varied experience might change him sufficiently, but by then he would no longer be able to enjoy such verse, he would no longer be the same person.

A general statement such as this about the incompatibility of inexpressibly complex adjustments must naturally be incapable of strict proof. Individuals with alternating personalities and subject to fugues would have to be considered. So would the phenomena of "mutations of regime" unaccompanied by change of vigilance if such occur. None the less very much evidence substantiates the statement. The experience of all those who have passed through the stages in the development of attitudes presupposed by great poetry is probably conclusive.

Even though the intricacies of the nervous system should be capable of getting round this objection, there remain sufficient other reasons why indulgence in verse of this character should be condemned. There can be no doubt whatever that the value of the experience which results from it is small. On a pleasure theory of value there might well be doubt, since those who do enjoy it certainly appear to enjoy it in a high degree. But on the theory here maintained, the fact that those who have passed through the stage of enjoying the *Poems of Passion* to that of enjoying the bulk of the contents of the *Golden Treasury,* for example, do not return, settles the matter. We must bear in mind, of course, the conditions which have to be satisfied before this test is conclusive. That a man who has passed through the stage of drinking nothing but beer to the stage of drinking nothing but brandy rarely returns, does not prove that brandy is the better drink. It merely proves that it is the more efficient intoxicant. We have to ask in applying the test what the responses in question are, and in the case of poetry they are so varied, so representative of all the activities of life, that actual universal preference on the part of those who have tried both kinds fairly is the same (on our view) as superiority in value of the one over the other. Keats, by universal qualified opinion, is a more efficient poet than Wilcox, and that is the same thing as saying that his works are more valuable.

REUBEN A. BROWER

Light and Bright and Sparkling:
Irony and Fiction in *Pride and Prejudice*

The work is rather too light, and bright, and sparkling; it wants shade; it wants to be stretched out here and there with a long chapter of sense, if it could be had; if not, of solemn specious nonsense. . . .

JANE AUSTEN

Many pages of *Pride and Prejudice* can be read as sheer poetry of wit, as Pope without couplets. The antitheses are almost as frequent and almost as varied; the play of ambiguities is certainly as complex; the orchestration of tones is as precise and subtle. As in the best of Pope, the displays of ironic wit are not without imaginative connection; what looks most diverse is really most similar, and ironies are linked by vibrant reference to basic certainties. There are passages too in which the rhythmical pattern of the sentence approaches the formal balance of the heroic couplet:

> Mr. Bennet was so odd a mixture of quick parts, sarcastic humour, reserve, and caprice, that the experience of three and twenty years had been insufficient to make his wife understand his character. *Her* mind was less difficult to develope. She was a woman of mean understanding, little information, and uncertain temper. When she was discontented she fancied herself nervous. The business of her life was to get her daughters married; its solace was visiting and news.

The triumph of the novel—whatever its limitations may be—lies in combining such poetry of wit with the dramatic structure of fiction. In historical terms, to combine the traditions of poetic satire with those of the sentimental novel, that was Jane Austen's feat in *Pride and Prejudice.*

For the "bright and sparkling," seemingly centrifugal play of irony is dramatically functional. It makes sense as literary art, the sense with which a writer is most concerned. The repartee, while constantly amusing, delineates characters and their changing relations and points the way to a climactic moment in which the change is most clearly recognized. Strictly speaking, this union of wit and drama is achieved with complete success only in the central sequence of *Pride and Prejudice,* in the pres-

From *The Fields of Light: An Experiment in Reading* by Reuben A. Brower. Copyright 1951 by Oxford University Press, Inc. Reprinted by permission.

entation of Elizabeth's and Darcy's gradual revaluation of each other. Here, if anywhere, Jane Austen met James's demand that the novel should give its readers the maximum of "fun"; at the same time she satisfied the further standard implied in James's remark that the art of the novel is "above all an art of preparations." That she met these demands more continuously in *Emma* does not detract from her achievement in *Pride and Prejudice*.

Her blend of ironic wit and drama may be seen in its simplest form in the first chapter of the novel, in the dialogue between Mr. and Mrs. Bennet on the topic of Mr. Bingley's leasing Netherfield Park. Every remark which each makes, Mrs. Bennet petulantly, and Mr. Bennet perversely, bounces off the magnificent opening sentence:

> It is a truth universally acknowledged, that a single man in possession of a good fortune, must be in want of a wife.

The scene that follows dramatizes the alternatives implied in "universally," Mrs. Bennet reminding us of one; and Mr. Bennet, of the other:

> "My dear Mr. Bennet," said his lady to him one day, "have you heard that Netherfield Park is let at last?"
>
> Mr. Bennet replied that he had not.
>
> "But it is," returned she; "for Mrs. Long has just been here, and she told me all about it."
>
> Mr. Bennet made no answer.
>
> "Do not you want to know who has taken it?" cried his wife impatiently.
>
> "*You* want to tell me, and I have no objection to hearing it."
>
> This was invitation enough.
>
> "Why, my dear, you must know, Mrs. Long says that Netherfield is taken by a young man of large fortune from the north of England; that he came down on Monday in a chaise and four to see the place, and was so much delighted with it that he agreed with Mr. Morris immediately; that he is to take possession before Michaelmas, and some of his servants are to be in the house by the end of next week."
>
> "What is his name?"
>
> "Bingley."
>
> "Is he married or single?"
>
> "Oh! single, my dear, to be sure! A single man of large fortune; four or five thousand a year. What a fine thing for our girls!"
>
> "How so? how can it affect them?"
>
> "My dear Mr. Bennet," replied his wife, "how can you be so tiresome! You must know that I am thinking of his marrying one of them."
>
> "Is that his design in settling here?"
>
> "Design! nonsense, how can you talk so!"

A parallel appears in the opening of Pope's Epistle, "Of the Characters of Women":

> Nothing so true as what you once let fall,
> "Most Women have no Characters at all,"

a pronouncement immediately followed by a series of portraits showing that women have "characters" in one sense if not in another. It is also easy to find counterparts in Pope's satirical mode for Mr. Bennet's extreme politeness of address, his innocent queries, and his epigrammatic turns. The character that emerges from this dialogue is almost that of a professional satirist: Mr. Bennet is a man of quick parts and sarcastic humor, altogether a most unnatural father. Mrs. Bennet speaks another language; *her* talk does not crackle with irony and epigram; *her* sentences run in quite another mold. They either go on too long or break up awkwardly in impulsive exclamations; this is the talk of a person of "mean understanding" and "uncertain temper."

But though the blended art of this scene is admirable, a limitation appears. Mr. and Mrs. Bennet are so perfectly done that little more is left to be expressed. Variety or forward movement in the drama will almost surely be difficult, which obviously proves to be the case. The sequences that depend most closely on the opening scene—those concerned with the business of getting the Bennet daughters married—are all amusingly ironic, but relatively static as drama. As Mrs. Bennet contrives to join Jane and Bingley, to marry one daughter to Mr. Collins, and to further Lydia's exploits with the military, father, mother, and daughters remain in very nearly the same dramatic positions. True enough, the last of these sequences ends in a catastrophe. But the connection between Lydia's downfall and the earlier scenes of ironic comedy in which Mr. and Mrs. Bennet are opposed is not fully expressed. Lydia's behavior "leads to this" in a Richardsonian moral sense, but Lydia is too scantly presented in relation to her parents or to Wickham to prepare us adequately for her bad end. We accept it if at all as literary convention. Incidentally, we might conjecture that the marriage-market sequences belong to the early version of *Pride and Prejudice,* or at least that they are examples of Jane Austen's earlier manner. In the central sequence of *Pride and Prejudice,* especially in its more complex blend of ironic and dramatic design, we can see anticipated the more mature structure of both *Mansfield Park* and *Emma*.

In portraying the gradual change in Elizabeth's estimate of Darcy and in his attitude to her, Jane Austen achieves a perfect harmony between the rich ambiguity of ironic dialogue and the movement toward the climactic scenes in which the new estimate is revealed. I shall limit my discussion to scenes from the Elizabeth-Darcy narrative through the episode in which Elizabeth recognizes her "change in sentiment." Let us first read Jane Austen's dialogue as poetry of wit, disregarding for the time being any forward movement in the drama, and observing the variety of the irony and the unity of effect achieved through recurrent patterns and through assumptions shared by writer and reader. As in our reading of Pope, we may in this way appreciate the extraordinary richness of ironic texture and the imaginative continuity running through the play of wit. In analyzing the ironies and the assumptions, we shall see how intensely dramatic the dialogue is, dramatic in the sense of defining characters through the way they speak and are spoken about.

The aura of implications which surrounds many of the dialogues between Elizabeth and Darcy is complex enough to delight the most pure Empsonian. Take for example the dialogue in which Sir William Lucas attempts to interest Mr. Darcy in dancing:

> . . . Elizabeth at that instant moving towards them, he was struck with the notion of doing a very gallant thing, and called out to her,
>
> "My dear Miss Eliza, why are not you dancing?—Mr. Darcy, you must allow me to present this young lady to you as a very desirable partner.—You cannot refuse to dance, I am sure, when so much beauty is before you." And taking her hand, he would have given it to Mr. Darcy, who, though extremely surprised, was not unwilling to receive it, when she instantly drew back, and said with some discomposure to Sir William,
>
> "Indeed, Sir, I have not the least intention of dancing,—I entreat you not to suppose that I moved this way in order to beg for a partner."
>
> Mr. Darcy with grave propriety requested to be allowed the honour of her hand; but in vain. Elizabeth was determined; nor did Sir William at all shake her purpose by his attempt at persuasion.
>
> "You excel so much in the dance, Miss Eliza, that it is cruel to deny me the happiness of seeing you; and though this gentleman dislikes the amusement in general, he can have no objection, I am sure, to oblige us for one half hour."
>
> "Mr. Darcy is all politeness," said Elizabeth, smiling.
>
> "He is indeed—but considering the inducement, my dear Miss Eliza, we cannot wonder at his complaisance, for who would object to such a partner?"
>
> Elizabeth looked archly, and turned away.

"Mr. Darcy is all politeness": the statement, as Elizabeth might say, has a "teazing" variety of meanings. Mr. Darcy is polite in the sense indicated by "grave propriety," that is, he shows the courtesy appropriate to a gentleman—which is the immediate, public meaning of Elizabeth's compliment. But "grave propriety," being a very limited form of politeness, reminds us forcibly of Mr. Darcy's earlier behavior. His "gravity" at the ball had been "forbidding and disagreeable." "Grave propriety" may also mean the bare civility of "the proudest, most disagreeable man in the world." So Elizabeth's compliment has an ironic twist: she smiles and looks "archly." "All politeness" has also quite another meaning. Mr.

Darcy "was not unwilling to receive" her hand. He is polite in more than the public proper sense; his gesture shows that he is interested in Elizabeth as a person. Her archness and her smile have for the reader an added ironic value: Elizabeth's interpretation of Darcy's manner may be quite wrong. Finally, there is the embracing broadly comic irony of Sir William's action. "Struck with the notion of doing a very gallant thing," he is pleasantly unconscious of what he is in fact doing and of what Elizabeth's remark may mean to her and to Darcy.

A similar cluster of possibilities appears in another conversation in which Darcy asks Elizabeth to dance with him:

> . . . soon afterwards Mr. Darcy, drawing near Elizabeth, said to her—
>
> "Do not you feel a great inclination, Miss Bennet, to seize such an opportunity of dancing a reel?"
>
> She smiled, but made no answer. He repeated the question, with some surprise at her silence.
>
> "Oh!" said she, "I heard you before; but I could not immediately determine what to say in reply. You wanted me, I know, to say 'Yes,' that you might have the pleasure of despising my taste; but I always delight in overthrowing those kind of schemes, and cheating a person of their premeditated contempt. I have therefore made up my mind to tell you, that I do not want to dance a reel at all—and now despise me if you dare."
>
> "Indeed I do not dare."
>
> Elizabeth, having rather expected to affront him, was amazed at his gallantry; but there was a mixture of sweetness and archness in her manner which made it difficult for her to affront anybody; and Darcy had never been so bewitched by any woman as he was by her. He really believed, that were it not for the inferiority of her connections, he should be in some danger.
>
> Miss Bingley saw, or suspected enough to be jealous; and her great anxiety for the recovery of her dear friend Jane, received some assistance from her desire of getting rid of Elizabeth.
>
> She often tried to provoke Darcy into disliking her guest, by talking of their supposed marriage, and planning his happiness in such an alliance.

Again Mr. Darcy's request may be interpreted more or less pleasantly, depending on whether we connect it with his present or past behavior. Again Elizabeth's attack on Darcy and her archness have an irony beyond the irony intended by the speaker. But the amusement of this dialogue lies especially in the variety of possible tones which we detect in Darcy's speeches. Elizabeth hears his question as expressing "premeditated contempt" and scorn of her own taste. But from Mr. Darcy's next remark and the comment which follows, and from his repeating his question and showing "some surprise," we may hear in his request a tone expressive of some interest, perhaps only gallantry, perhaps, as Elizabeth later puts it, "somewhat of a friendlier nature." We could take his "Indeed I do not dare" as pure gallantry (Elizabeth's version) or as a sign of conventional "marriage intentions" (Miss Bingley's interpretation), if it were not for the nice reservation, "He really believed, that were it not for the inferiority of her connections, he should be in some danger." We must hear the remark as spoken with this qualification. This simultaneity of tonal layers can be matched only in the satire of Pope, where, as we have seen, the reader feels the impossibility of adjusting his voice to the rapid changes in tone and the difficulty of representing by a single sound the several sounds he hears as equally appropriate and necessary. Analysis such as I have been making shows clearly how arbitrary and how thin any stage rendering of *Pride and Prejudice* must be. No speaking voice could possibly represent the variety of tones conveyed to the reader by such interplay of dialogue and comment.

It would be easy enough to produce more of these dialogues, especially on the subject of music or dancing, each with its range of crisply differentiated meanings. Similar patterns of irony recur many times. Mr. Darcy makes his inquiries (polite or impolite), asking with a smile (scornful or encouraging) questions that may be interpreted as pompous and condescending or gallant and well-disposed. So Mr. Darcy cross-examines Elizabeth in the scene in which their "superior dancing" gives such pleasure to Sir William:

> "What think you of books?" said he, smiling.
> "Books—Oh! no.—I am sure we never read the same, or not with the same feelings."
> "I am sorry you think so; but if that be the case, there can at least be no want of subject.—We may compare our different opinions."
> "No—I cannot talk of books in a ball-room; my head is always full of something else."
> "The *present* always occupies you in such scenes—does it?" said he, with a look of doubt.

When connected with a hint of Darcy's changing attitude, that "look of doubt," Elizabeth's arch comments take on the added ironic value we have noted in other conversations.

Earlier in this dialogue, Darcy and Elizabeth run through the same sort of question and answer gamut, and with very nearly the same ironic dissonances:

> He smiled, and assured her that whatever she wished him to say should be said.
> "Very well.—That reply will do for the present.—Perhaps by and

bye I may observe that private balls are much pleasanter than public ones.—But *now* we may be silent."

"Do you talk by rule then, while you are dancing?"

"Sometimes. One must speak a little, you know. It would look odd to be entirely silent for half an hour together, and yet for the advantage of *some,* conversation ought to be so arranged as that they may have the trouble of saying as little as possible."

"Are you consulting your own feelings in the present case, or do you imagine that you are gratifying mine?"

"Both," replied Elizabeth archly; "for I have always seen a great similarity in the turn of our minds.—We are each of an unsocial, taciturn disposition, unwilling to speak, unless we expect to say something that will amaze the whole room, and be handed down to posterity with all the eclat of a proverb."

"This is no very striking resemblance of your own character, I am sure," said he.

When Darcy himself is being quizzed he frequently remarks on his own behavior in a way that may be sublimely smug or simply self-respecting, as for example in his comment on his behavior at the first of the Hertfordshire balls:

"I certainly have not the talent which some people possess," said Darcy, "of conversing easily with those I have never seen before. I cannot catch their tone of conversation, or appear interested in their concerns, as I often see done."

But these conversations are not simply sets of ironic meanings; they are in more than a trivial sense *jeux d'esprit,* the play of an adult mind. (The sophistication they imply is of a kind which, as John Jay Chapman once remarked, is Greek and French, rather than English.) The fun in Jane Austen's dialogue has a serious point; or rather, the fun *is* the point. The small talk is the focus for her keen sense of the variability of character, for her awareness of the possibility that the same remark or action has very different meanings in different relations. What most satisfies us in reading the dialogue in *Pride and Prejudice* is Jane Austen's awareness that it is difficult to know any complex person, that knowledge of a man like Darcy is an interpretation and a construction, not a simple absolute. Like the characters of Proust, the chief persons in *Pride and Prejudice* are not the same when projected through the conversation of different people. The *snobisme* of Darcy's talk, like Swann's, is measured according to the group he is with. Mr. Darcy is hardly recognizable as the same man when he is described by Mr. Wickham, by his housekeeper, or Elizabeth, or Mr. Bingley.

But it is only the complex persons, the "intricate characters," that require and merit interpretation, as Elizabeth points out in the pleasant conversation in which she tells Bingley that she "understands him perfectly":

> "You begin to comprehend me, do you?" cried he, turning towards her.
>
> "Oh! yes,—I understand you perfectly."
>
> "I wish I might take this for a compliment; but to be so easily seen through I am afraid is pitiful."
>
> "That is as it happens. It does not necessarily follow that a deep, intricate character is more or less estimable than such a one as yours."
>
> "Lizzy," cried her mother, "remember where you are, and do not run on in the wild manner that you are suffered to do at home."
>
> "I did not know before," continued Bingley immediately, "that you were a studier of character. It must be an amusing study."
>
> "Yes; but intricate characters are the *most* amusing. They have at least that advantage."
>
> "The country," said Darcy, "can in general supply but few subjects for such a study. In a country neighbourhood you move in a very confined and unvarying society."
>
> "But people themselves alter so much, that there is something new to be observed in them for ever."

Elizabeth's remark with its ironic application to Darcy indicates the interest that makes the book "go" and shows the type of awareness we are analyzing. "Intricate characters are the *most* amusing," because their behavior can be taken in so many ways, because they are not always the same people. The man we know today is a different man tomorrow. Naturally, we infer, people will not be equally puzzling to every judge. Mr. Bingley and Jane find Mr. Darcy a much less "teazing" man than Elizabeth does. It is only the Elizabeths, the adult minds, who will observe something new in the "same" people.

Such are the main assumptions behind the irony of *Pride and Prejudice,* as they are expressed through conversational studies of Darcy's character. In marked contrast with the opening scene of the novel, there is in these dialogues no nondramatic statement of the ironist's position, a further sign that in shaping the Elizabeth-Darcy sequence Jane Austen was moving away from the modes of satire toward more purely dramatic techniques.

While Jane Austen's irony depends on a sense of variability and intricacy of character, her vision is not one of Proustian relativity. The sense of variability is balanced by a vigorous and positive belief. Elizabeth, in commenting on Charlotte Lucas' choice of Mr. Collins, expresses very emphatically this combination of skepticism and faith:

> "My dear Jane, Mr. Collins is a conceited, pompous, narrow-minded silly man; you know he is, as well as I do; and you must feel, as well as

I do, that the woman who marries him, cannot have a proper way of thinking. You shall not defend her, though it is Charlotte Lucas. You shall not, for the sake of one individual, change the meaning of principle and integrity, nor endeavour to persuade yourself or me, that selfishness is prudence, and insensibility of danger, security for happiness."

Though as usual Elizabeth's affirmations have an ironic overtone for the reader, they express a belief that is implied throughout *Pride and Prejudice*. There are persons such as Mr. Collins and Mrs. Bennet and Lady Catherine, about whom there can be no disagreement among people who "have a proper way of thinking." These fixed characters make up a set of certainties against which more intricate exhibitions of pride and prejudice are measured. They are the "fools" which James says are almost indispensable for any piece of fiction. For Jane Austen there can be no doubt about the meaning of "principle and integrity" and similar terms of value. Right-thinking persons know what pride is and when to apply the term. In common with her contemporaries Jane Austen enjoys the belief that some interpretations of behavior are more reasonable than others. The climactic scene of the novel, in which Elizabeth arrives at a new view of Darcy, shows us what is meant by a more reasonable interpretation: it is a reasoned judgment of character reached through long experience and slow weighing of probabilities. The certainty is an achieved certainty.

So the local ironies in Jane Austen, as in Pope, are defined and given larger significance through assumptions shared by the writer and public. The trivial dialogues are constantly being illuminated by a fine sense of the complexity of human nature and by a steady belief in the possibility of making sound judgments. At the same time the playfulness is always serving for "the illustration of character." (The term is Elizabeth's, though in applying it to Darcy, she is as usual unaware of its aptness to her own behavior.) Both she and Darcy are "illustrated" by their ambiguous questions and answers and the alternate interpretations which are so deftly indicated: the poetry of wit in *Pride and Prejudice* is completely dramatic. Certainly nothing could be more dramatic than the assumptions we have been describing: they reflect the practical dramatist's interest in human beings and their behavior, his awareness that character is expressed by what men say and do. The assumption that more reasonable interpretations of conduct are attainable provides for the movement toward a decisive change in relationships at the climax of the novel. It also lays the ground for the resolution of ambiguities and the cancellation of irony at the same moment.

We can now appreciate how beautifully the ironies of the dialogue function in the curve of the main dramatic sequence. The conversations

have been skilfully shaped to prepare us for Elizabeth's revised estimate
of Darcy, for her recognition that Darcy regards her differently, and for
her consequent "change of sentiment" toward him. The preparation
for this climax is made mainly through the controlled use of ambiguity
that we have been observing. Though we are always being led to make
double interpretations, we are never in confusion about what the alternatives are. It is important also that in these ironic dialogues no comment is
included that makes us take Darcy's behavior in only an unpleasant sense.
When there is comment, it is mainly used to bring out the latent ambiguity without in any way resolving it. So in general the earlier Darcy
scenes are left open in preparation for a fresh estimate of his character.
The pleasanter interpretation of one of Darcy's or Elizabeth's remarks
or of one of the author's comments allows for the later choice and for
the consequent recognitions. The pleasanter possibility also gives in passing a hint of Darcy's changing attitude to Elizabeth. For instance, the
more favorable meaning of Elizabeth's "Mr. Darcy is all politeness" or
of the comment on his "grave propriety" points forward to Darcy's perfect courtesy at Pemberley and to Elizabeth's admission that he was
right in objecting to her family's "impropriety of conduct."

This exquisite preparation pays wonderfully at the climactic moment of the novel, when Elizabeth reconsiders the letter in which Darcy
justified his conduct toward Bingley and Jane and Wickham. Since
more kindly views of Darcy have been introduced through the flow of
witty talk, Darcy does not at that point have to be remade, but merely
reread. (The tendency to remake a character appears in an obvious form
only in the later and lesser scenes of the novel.)

The passages in which Elizabeth reviews the letter present an odd,
rather legalistic process. After the more obvious views of Darcy's behavior and the possible alternatives are directly stated, the evidence
on both sides is weighed and a reasonable conclusion is reached:

> After wandering along the lane for two hours, giving way to every
> variety of thought; re-considering events, determining probabilities, and
> reconciling herself as well as she could, to a change so sudden and so
> important, fatigue, and a recollection of her long absence, made her at
> length return home. . . .

To illustrate her manner of "determining probabilities" we might take
one of several examples of Darcy's pride. Immediately after Darcy has
proposed to her, she describes his treatment of Jane in rather brutal
language:

> . . . his pride, his abominable pride, his shameless avowal of what
> he had done with respect to Jane, his unpardonable assurance in ac-
> knowledging, though he could not justify it.

A little later, she rereads the passage in which Darcy explains that Jane
had shown no "symptom of peculiar regard" for Bingley. A second perusal reminds Elizabeth that Charlotte Lucas had a similar opinion, and
she acknowledges the justice of this account of Jane's outward behavior.
In much the same way she reviews other charges, such as Darcy's unfairness to Wickham or his objection to her family's "want of importance," and she is forced by the new evidence to draw "more probable"
conclusions.

Jane Austen does not make us suppose that Elizabeth has now
discovered the real Darcy or that an intricate person is easily known
or known in his entirety, as is very clearly shown by Elizabeth's reply
to Wickham's ironic questions about Darcy:

> "I dare not hope," he continued in a lower and more serious tone,
> "that he is improved in essentials."
> "Oh, no!" said Elizabeth. "In essentials, I believe, he is very much
> what he ever was."
> While she spoke, Wickham looked as if scarcely knowing whether
> to rejoice over her words, or to distrust their meaning. There was a
> something in her countenance which made him listen with an appre-
> hensive and anxious attention, while she added,
> "When I said that he improved on acquaintance, I did not mean
> that either his mind or manners were in a state of improvement, but
> that from knowing him better, his disposition was better understood."

It is wise not to be dogmatic about "essentials," since in any case they
remain "as they were." A sensible person contents himself with "better
understanding."

This process of judgment is not merely odd or legalistic, because
it is dramatically appropriate. It fits exactly the double presentation of
Darcy's character through ironic dialogue and comment, and it fits perfectly the picture of Elizabeth as "a rational creature speaking the truth
from her heart," one who adapts her statements to her knowledge. She
is quite clear about the meaning of "pride" and "vanity," and she judges
herself with complete honesty:

> "Had I been in love, I could not have been more wretchedly blind.
> But vanity, not love, has been my folly.—Pleased with the preference
> of one, and offended by the neglect of the other, on the very beginning
> of our acquaintance, I have courted prepossession and ignorance, and
> driven reason away, where either were concerned. Till this moment, I
> never knew myself."

We feel that Elizabeth's judgment of Darcy and of herself is right because the preparation for it has been so complete. The foundations for

Elizabeth's choices and her acknowledgment of error were laid in the ambiguous remarks of the earlier scenes of the novel.

The dialogue has been preparing us equally well and with perhaps greater refinement for Elizabeth's realization that she and Darcy now regard one another with very different feelings. The ironic remarks and commentary have included hints that revealed ever so gradually Darcy's developing interest in Elizabeth. Mr. Darcy's "politeness," his "repeated questions," his "gallantry," his "look of doubt," if interpreted favorably, indicate his increasing warmth of feeling. Elizabeth's pert remarks and impertinent questions bear an amusing relation to this change in Darcy's sentiments. Besides being more ambiguous than she supposes, they backfire in another way, by increasing Darcy's admiration. Her accusation of "premeditated contempt" brings out his most gallant reply, and her "mixture of sweetness and archness" leaves him more "bewitched" than ever. In this and other ways the repartee provides local "amusements" while pointing forward to the complete reversal of feeling that follows the meeting at Pemberley.

The judicial process by which Elizabeth earlier "determined probabilities" in judging Darcy's past conduct is matched by the orderly way in which she now "determines her feelings" toward him:

> . . . and the evening, though as it passed it seemed long, was not long enough to determine her feelings towards *one* in that mansion; and she lay awake two whole hours, endeavouring to make them out. She certainly did not hate him. No; hatred had vanished long ago, and she had almost as long been ashamed of ever feeling a dislike against him, that could be so called. The respect created by the conviction of his valuable qualities, though at first unwillingly admitted, had for some time ceased to be repugnant to her feelings; and it was now heightened into somewhat of a friendlier nature, by the testimony so highly in his favour, and bringing forward his disposition in so amiable a light, which yesterday had produced. But above all, above respect and esteem, there was a motive within her of good will which could not be overlooked. It was gratitude.—Gratitude, not merely for having once loved her, but for loving her still well enough, to forgive all the petulance and acrimony of her manner in rejecting him, and all the unjust accusations accompanying her rejection. He who, she had been persuaded, would avoid her as his greatest enemy, seemed, on this accidental meeting, most eager to preserve the acquaintance, and without any indelicate display of regard, or any peculiarity of manner, where their two selves only were concerned, was soliciting the good opinion of her friends, and bent on making her known to his sister. Such a change in a man of so much pride, excited not only astonishment but gratitude —for to love, ardent love, it must be attributed; and as such its im-

pression on her was of a sort to be encouraged, as by no means unpleas-
ing, though it could not be exactly defined. She respected, she esteemed,
she was grateful to him, she felt a real interest in his welfare. . . .

In this beautifully graded progress of feeling, from "hatred" or any
"dislike" to "respect" to "esteem" to "gratitude" and "a real interest" in
Darcy's "welfare," each sentiment is defined with an exactness that is
perfectly appropriate to Elizabeth's habit of mind as presented earlier in
the novel. She defines her sentiments as exactly as her moral judgments.

As all ambiguities are resolved and all irony is dropped, the reader
feels the closing in of a structure by its necessary end, the end implied
in the crude judgment of Darcy in the first ballroom scene. The harsh
exhibit of the way character is decided in this society prepares us to
view Mr. Darcy's later actions as open to more than one interpretation:

> . . . Mr. Darcy soon drew the attention of the room by his fine, tall
> person, handsome features, noble mien; and the report which was in
> general circulation within five minutes after his entrance, of his having
> ten thousand a year. The gentlemen pronounced him to be a fine figure
> of a man, the ladies declared he was much handsomer than Mr. Bing-
> ley, and he was looked at with great admiration for about half the eve-
> ning, till his manners gave a disgust which turned the tide of his popu-
> larity; for he was discovered to be proud, to be above his company, and
> above being pleased; and not all his large estate in Derbyshire could
> then save him from having a most forbidding, disagreeable countenance,
> and being unworthy to be compared with his friend.
> . . . His character was decided. He was the proudest, most disagree-
> able man in the world, and everybody hoped that he would never come
> there again.

These comments convey above all the aloof vision of the ironist,
of Jane Austen herself, who had been described years before as a little
girl "who is a judge of character and who remains silent." In the very
grammar of the sentences (the passive voice, the *oratio obliqua*), there
is an implication of a detached and superior mind that reports both judgments of Darcy, knowing quite well which is the more true, and fully
aware that true judgment is considerably more difficult than most people
suppose. The display of alternatives in ironic dialogue, the projection
by this means of intricate characters, and the movement toward a sounder
evaluation of first impressions—all this and more is implicit in the
initial view of Darcy and his judges.

Once we have reached the scenes in which the promise of the
introduction is fulfilled, the literary design of both ironic and dramatic
is complete. Thereafter, it must be admitted, *Pride and Prejudice* is not
quite the same sort of book. There are fewer passages of equally bright
and varied irony and consequently rarer exhibitions of intricacy of char-

acter. Mr. Darcy now appears as "humble," not "proud," and even as "perfectly amiable." There are single scenes of a broadly satiric sort, in which Mr. and Mrs. Bennet express characteristic opinions on their daughters' alliances and misalliances. But the close and harmonious relation between ironic wit and dramatic movement is disturbed. A great deal happens, from seductions and mysterious financial transactions to reunions of lovers and weddings. But these events seem to belong to a simpler world where outright judgments of good and bad or of happy and unhappy are in place. The double vision of the ironist is more rarely in evidence.

Occasionally, we feel a recovery of the richer texture of amusement and of the more complex awareness of character revealed in the central sequence. One glancing remark suggests that the final picture of Darcy might have been less simply ideal (Darcy has just been commenting on how well Bingley had taken his confession of having separated Bingley and Jane):

> Elizabeth longed to observe that Mr. Bingley had been a most delightful friend; so easily guided that his worth was invaluable; but she checked herself. She remembered that he had yet to learn to be laughed at, and it was rather too early to begin. In anticipating the happiness of Bingley, which of course was to be inferior only to his own, he continued the conversation till they reached the house.

It is perhaps not "rational," as Elizabeth would say, to expect the same complexity when a drama of irony has once arrived at its resolution. But it is probably wise for the novelist to finish up his story as soon as possible after that point has been reached. In *Emma,* the crucial scene of readjustment comes very near the end of the novel. Jane Austen does not run the risk of presenting many scenes in which Emma appears as a wiser and less fanciful young woman. To be sure, the risk is lessened somewhat because the initial and governing vision in Emma is less purely ironic than in *Pride and Prejudice.*

The triumph of *Pride and Prejudice* is a rare one, just because it is so difficult to balance a purely ironic vision with credible presentation of a man and woman undergoing a serious "change of sentiment." Shakespeare achieves an uneasy success in *Much Ado About Nothing,* and Fielding succeeds in *Tom Jones* because he does not expect us to take "love" too seriously. The problem for the writer who essays this difficult blend is one of creating dramatic speech which fulfils his complex intention. In solving this problem of expression, Jane Austen has her special triumph.

ROBERT PENN WARREN

Pure and Impure Poetry

Critics are rarely faithful to their labels and their special strategies. Usually the critic will confess that no one strategy—the psychological, the moralistic, the formalistic, the historical—or combination of strategies, will quite work the defeat of the poem. For the poem is like the monstrous Orillo in Boiardo's *Orlando Innamorato*. When the sword lops off any member of the monster, that member is immediately rejoined to the body, and the monster is as formidable as ever. But the poem is even more formidable than the monster, for Orillo's adversary finally gained a victory by an astonishing feat of dexterity: he slashed off both the monster's arms and quick as a wink seized them and flung them into the river. The critic who vaingloriously trusts his method to account for the poem, to exhaust the poem, is trying to emulate this dexterity: he thinks that he, too, can win by throwing the lopped-off arms into the river. But he is doomed to failure. Neither fire nor water will suffice to prevent the rejoining of the mutilated members to the monstrous torso. There is only one way to conquer the monster: you must eat it, bones, blood, skin, pelt, and gristle. And even then the monster is not dead, for it lives in you, is assimilated into you, and you are different, and somewhat monstrous yourself, for having eaten it.

So the monster will always win, and the critic knows this. He does not want to win. He knows that he must always play stooge to the monster. All he wants to do is to give the monster a chance to exhibit again its miraculous power.

With this fable, I shall begin by observing that poetry wants to be pure. And it always succeeds in this ambition. In so far as we have poetry at all, it is always pure poetry; that is, it is not non-poetry. The poetry of Shakespeare, the poetry of Pope, the poetry of Herrick, is pure, in so far as it is poetry at all. We call the poetry "higher" or "lower," we say "more powerful" or "less powerful" about it, and we are, no doubt, quite right in doing so. The souls that form the great rose of Paradise are seated in banks and tiers of ascending blessedness, but they are all saved, they are all perfectly happy; they are all "pure," for they have all been purged of mortal taint. This is not to say, however, that if we get poetry from one source, such a single source, say Shakespeare, should suffice us in as much as we can always appeal to it, or that, since all poetry is equally pure, we engage in a superfluous labor in trying to explore or create new sources of poetry. No, for we can remember that every soul in the great rose is precious in the eyes of God. No soul is the substitute for another.

Poetry wants to be pure, but poems do not. At least, most of them do not want to be too pure. The poems want to give us poetry, which is pure, and the elements of a poem, in so far as it is a good poem, will work together toward that end, but many of the elements, taken in themselves, may actually seem to contradict that end, or be neutral toward the achieving of that end. Are we then to conclude that, because neutral or recalcitrant elements appear in poems, even in poems called great, these elements are simply an index to human frailty, that in a perfect world there would be no dross in poems which would, then, be perfectly pure? No, it does not seem to be merely the fault of our world, for the poems include, deliberately, more of the so-called dross than would appear necessary. They are not even as pure as they might be in this imperfect world. They mar themselves with cacophonies, jagged rhythms, ugly words and ugly thoughts, colloquialisms, clichés, sterile technical terms, head work and argument, self-contradictions, clevernesses, irony, realism—all things which call us back to the world of prose and imperfection.

Sometimes a poet will reflect on this state of affairs, and grieve. He will decide that he, at least, will try to make one poem as pure as possible. So he writes:

> Now sleeps the crimson petal, now the white;
> Nor waves the cypress in the palace walk;
> Nor winks the gold fin in the porphyry font:
> The firefly wakens: waken thou with me.

We know the famous garden. We know how all nature conspires here to express the purity of the moment: how the milk-white peacock glimmers like a ghost, and how like a ghost the unnamed "she" glimmers on to her tryst; how earth lies "all Danaë to the stars," as the beloved's heart lies open to the lover; and how, in the end, the lily folds up her sweetness, "and slips into the bosom of the lake," as the lovers are lost in the sweet dissolution of love.

And we know another poet and another garden. Or perhaps it is the same garden, after all:

> I arise from dreams of thee
> In the first sweet sleep of night,
> When the winds are breathing low
> And the stars are shining bright.

> I arise from dreams of thee,
> And a spirit in my feet
> Hath led me—who knows how?
> To thy chamber window, Sweet!

We remember how, again, all nature conspires, how the wandering airs "faint," how the Champak's odors "pine," how the nightingale's complaint "dies upon her heart," as the lover will die upon the beloved's heart. Nature here strains out of nature, it wants to be called by another name, it wants to spiritualize itself by calling itself another name. How does the lover get to the chamber window? He refuses to say how, in his semi-somnambulistic daze, he got there. He blames, he says, "a spirit in my feet," and hastens to disavow any knowledge of how that spirit operates. In any case, he arrives at the chamber window. Subsequent events and the lover's reaction toward them are somewhat hazy. We only know that the lover, who faints and fails at the opening of the last stanza, and who asks to be lifted from the grass by a more enterprising beloved, is in a condition of delectable passivity, in which distinctions blur out in the "purity" of the moment.

Let us turn to another garden: the place, Verona; the time, a summer night, with full moon. The lover speaks:

> But soft! what light through yonder window breaks?
> It is the east. . . .

But we know the rest, and know that this garden, in which nature for the moment conspires again with the lover, is the most famous of them all, for the scene is justly admired for its purity of effect, for giving us the very essence of young, untarnished love. Nature conspires beneficently here, but we may chance to remember that beyond the garden wall strolls Mercutio, who can celebrate Queen Mab, but who is always aware that nature has other names as well as the names the pure poets and pure lovers put upon her. And we remember that Mercutio outside the wall, has just said:

> . . . 'twould anger him
> To raise a spirit in his mistress's circle
> Of some strange nature, letting it there stand
> Till she had laid it and conjured it down.

Mercutio has made a joke, a bawdy joke. That is bad enough, but worse, he has made his joke witty and, worst of all, intellectually complicated in its form. Realism, wit, intellectual complication—these are the enemies of the garden purity.

But the poet has not only let us see Mercutio outside the garden wall. Within the garden itself, when the lover invokes nature, when he spiritualizes and innocently trusts her, and says,

> Lady, by yonder blessed moon I swear,

the lady herself replies,

> O, swear not by the moon, the inconstant moon,
> That monthly changes in her circled orb.

The lady distrusts "pure" poems, nature spiritualized into forgetfulness. She has, as it were, a rigorous taste in metaphor, too; she brings a logical criticism to bear on the metaphor which is too easy; the metaphor must prove itself to her, must be willing to subject itself to scrutiny beyond the moment's enthusiasm. She injects the impurity of an intellectual style into the lover's pure poem.

And we must not forget the voice of the nurse, who calls from within, a voice which, we discover, is the voice of expediency, of half-measures, of the view that circumstances alter cases—the voice of prose and imperfection.

It is time to ask ourselves if the celebrated poetry of this scene, which as poetry is pure, exists despite the impurities of the total composition, if the effect would be more purely poetic were the nurse and Mercutio absent and the lady a more sympathetic critic of pure poems. I do not think so. The effect might even be more vulnerable poetically if the impurities were purged away. Mercutio, the lady, and the nurse are critics of the lover, who believes in pure poems, but perhaps they are necessary. Perhaps the lover can only be accepted in their context. The poet seems to say: "I know the worst that can be said on this subject, and I am giving fair warning. Read at your own risk." So the poetry arises from a recalcitrant and contradictory context; and finally involves that context.

Let us return to one of the other gardens, in which there is no Mercutio or nurse, and in which the lady is more sympathetic. Let us mar its purity by installing Mercutio in the shrubbery, from which the poet was so careful to banish him. You can hear his comment when the lover says:

> And a spirit in my feet
> Hath led me—who knows how?
> To thy chamber window, Sweet!

And we can guess what the wicked tongue would have to say in response to the last stanza.

It may be that the poet should have made his peace early with Mercutio, and have appealed to his better nature. For Mercutio seems to be glad to cooperate with a poet. But he must be invited; otherwise, he is apt to show a streak of merry vindictiveness about the finished product. Poems are vulnerable enough at best. Bright reason mocks them like sun from a wintry sky. They are easily left naked to laughter when leaves fall in the garden and the cold winds come. Therefore, they need all the friends they can get, and Mercutio, who is an ally of reason and who himself is given to mocking laughter, is a good friend for a poem to have.

On what terms does a poet make his peace with Mercutio? There are about as many sets of terms as there are good poets. I know that I have loaded the answer with the word *good* here, that I have implied a scale of excellence based, in part at least, on degree of complication. I shall return to this question. For the moment, however, let us examine a poem whose apparent innocence and simple lyric cry should earn it a place in any anthology of "pure poetry."

> Western wind, when wilt thou blow
>   That the small rain down can rain?
> Christ, that my love were in my arms
>   And I in my bed again!

The lover, grieving for the absent beloved, cries out for relief. Several kinds of relief are involved in the appeal to the wind. First there is the relief that would be had from the sympathetic manifestation of nature. The lover, in his perturbation of spirit, invokes the perturbations of nature. He exclaims,

> Western wind, when wilt thou blow

and Lear exclaims,

> Blow, winds, and crack your cheeks! rage! blow!

Second, there is the relief that would be had by the fulfillment of grief —the frost of grief, the drouth of grief broken, the full anguish expressed, then the violence allayed in the peace of tears. Third, there is the relief that would be had in the excitement and fulfillment of love itself. There seems to be a contrast between the first two types of relief and the third type; speaking loosely, we may say that the first two types are romantic and general, the third type realistic and specific. So much for the first two lines.

In the last two lines, the lover cries out for the specific solace of his case: reunion with his beloved. But there is a difference between the two lines. The first is general, and romantic. The phrase "in my arms" does not seem to mean exactly what it says. True, it has a literal meaning, if we can look close at the words, but it is hard to look close because of the romantic aura—the spiritualized mist about them.[1] But with the last line the perfectly literal meaning suddenly comes into sharp focus. The mist is rifted and we can look straight at the words, which, we discover with a slight shock of surprise, do mean exactly what they say. The last line is realistic and specific. It is not even content to say,

And I in bed again!

It is, rather, more scrupulously specific, and says,

And I in *my* bed again! [2]

All of this does not go to say that the realistic elements here are to be taken as cancelling, or negating, the romantic elements. There is no ironical leer. The poem is not a celebration of carnality. It is a faithful lover who speaks. He is faithful to the absent beloved, and he is also faithful to the full experience of love. That is, he does not abstract one aspect of the experience and call it the whole experience. He does not strain nature out of nature; he does not over-spiritualize nature. This nameless poet would never have said, in the happier days of his love, that he had been led to his Sweet's chamber window by "a spirit in my feet"; and he certainly would not have added the coy disavowal, "who knows how?" But because the nameless poet refused to over-spiritualize nature, we can accept the spirituality of the poem.

Another poem gives us another problem.

> Ah, what avails the sceptered race,
> Ah, what the form divine!
> What every virtue, every grace!
> Rose Aylmer, all were thine.

---

[1] It may be objected here that I am reading the phrase "in my arms" as a 20th Century reader. I confess the fact. Certainly, several centuries have passed since the composition of the little poem, and those centuries have thickened the romantic mist about the words, but it is scarcely to be believed that the 16th Century was the clear, literal Eden dawn of poetry when words walked without the fig leaf.

[2] In connection with the word *my* in this line, we may also feel it helps to set over the comfort and satisfaction there specified against the bad weather of the first two lines. We may also glance at the word *small* in the second line. It is the scrupulous word, the word that, realistically, makes us believe in the rain. But, too, it is broader in its function. The storm which the lover invokes will not rend the firmament, it will not end the world; it will simply bring down the "small" rain, a credible rain.

> Rose Aylmer, whom those wakeful eyes
> May weep, but never see,
> A night of memories and of sighs
> I consecrate to thee.

This is another poem about lost love: a "soft" subject. Now to one kind of poet the soft subject presents a sore temptation. Because it is soft in its natural state, he is inclined to feel that to get at its poetic essence he must make it softer still, that he must insist on its softness, that he must render it as "pure" as possible. At first glance, it may seem that Landor is trying to do just that. What he says seems to be emphatic, unqualified, and open. Not every power, grace, and virtue could avail to preserve his love. That statement insists on the pathetic contrast. And in the next stanza, wakefulness and tearfulness are mentioned quite unashamedly, along with memories and sighs. It is all blurted out, as pure as possible.

But only in the paraphrase is it "blurted." The actual quality of the first stanza is hard, not soft. It is a chiseled stanza, in which formality is insisted upon. We may observe the balance of the first and second lines; the balance of the first half with the second half of the third line, which recapitulates the structure of the first two lines; the balance of the two parts of the last line, though here the balance is merely a rhythmical and not a sense balance as in the preceding instances; the binders of discreet alliteration, repetition, and assonance. The stanza is built up, as it were, of units which are firmly defined and sharply separated, phrase by phrase, line by line. We have the formal control of the soft subject, ritual and not surrender.

But in the second stanza the rigor of this formality is somewhat abated, as the more general, speculative emphasis (why cannot pomp, virtue, and grace avail?) gives way to the personal emphasis, as though the repetition of the beloved's name had, momentarily, released the flood of feeling. The first line of the second stanza spills over into the second; the "wakeful eyes" as subject find their verb in the next line, "weep," and the *wake-weep* alliteration, along with the rest after *weep,* points up the disintegration of the line, just as it emphasizes the situation. Then with the phrase "but never see" falling away from the long thrust of the rhetorical structure to the pause after *weep,* the poem seems to go completely soft, the frame is broken. But, even as the poet insists on "memories and sighs" in the last two lines he restores the balance. Notice the understatement of "A night." It says: "I know that life is a fairly complicated affair, and that I am committed to it and to its complications. I intend to stand by my commitment, as a man of integrity, that is, to live despite the grief. Since life is complicated, I cannot, if

I am to live, spare too much time for indulging grief. I can give *a* night, but not all nights." The lover, like the hero of Frost's poem "Stopping by Woods on a Winter Evening," tears himself from the temptation of staring into the treacherous, delicious blackness, for he, too, has "promises to keep." Or he resembles the Homeric heroes who, after the perilous passage is made, after their energy has saved their lives, and after they have beached their craft and eaten their meal, can then set aside an hour before sleep to mourn the comrades lost by the way—the heroes who, as Aldous Huxley says, understand realistically a whole truth as contrasted with a half-truth.

Is this a denial of the depth and sincerity of the grief? The soft reader, who wants the poem pure, may be inclined to say so. But let us look at the last line to see what it gives us in answer to this question. The answer seems to lie in the word *consecrate*. The meter thrusts this word at us; we observe that two of the three metrical accents in the line fall on syllables of this word forcing it beyond its prose emphasis. The word is important and the importance is justified, for the word tells us that the single night is not merely a lapse into weakness, a trivial event to be forgotten when the weakness is overcome. It is, rather, an event of the most extreme and focal importance, an event formally dedicated, "set apart for sacred uses," an event by which other events are to be measured. So the word *consecrate* formalizes, philosophizes, ritualizes the grief; it specifies what style in the first stanza has implied.

But here is another poem of grief, grief at the death of a child:

> There was such speed in her little body,
> And such lightness in her footfall,
> It is no wonder that her brown study
> Astonishes us all.

> Her wars were bruited in our high window.
> We looked among orchard trees and beyond
> Where she took arms against her shadow,
> Or harried unto the pond

> The lazy geese, like a snow cloud
> Dripping their snow on the green grass,
> Tricking and stopping, sleepy and proud,
> Who cried in goose, Alas,

> For the tireless heart within the little
> Lady with rod that made them rise
> From their noon apple dreams, and scuttle
> Goose-fashion under the skies!

> But now go the bells, and we are ready;
> In one house we are sternly stopped
> To say we are vexed at her brown study,
> Lying so primly propped.*

Another soft subject, softer, if anything, than the subject of "Rose Aylmer," and it presents the same problem. But the problem is solved in a different way.

The first stanza is based on two time-honored clichés: first, "Heaven, won't that child ever be still, she is driving me distracted"; and second, "She was such an active, healthy-looking child, would you've ever thought she would just up and die?" In fact, the whole poem develops these clichés, and exploits, in a backhand fashion, the ironies implicit in their inter-relation. And in this connection, we may note that the fact of the clichés, rather than more original or profound observations, at the root of the poem is important; there is in the poem the contrast between the staleness of the clichés and the shock of the reality. Further, we may note that the second cliché is an answer, savagely ironical in itself, to the first: the child you wished would be still *is* still, despite all that activity which your adult occupations deplored.

But such a savage irony is not the game here. It is too desperate, too naked, in a word, too pure. And ultimately, it is, in a sense, a meaningless irony if left in its pure state, because it depends on a mechanical, accidental contrast in nature, void of moral content. The poem is concerned with modifications and modulations of this brute, basic irony, modulations and modifications contingent upon an attitude taken toward it by a responsible human being, the speaker of the poem. The savagery is masked, or ameliorated.

In this connection, we may observe, first, the phrase "brown study." It is not the "frosted flower," the "marmoreal immobility," or any one of a thousand such phrases which would aim for the pure effect. It is merely the brown study which astonishes—a phrase which denies, as it were, the finality of the situation, underplays the pathos, and merely reminds one of those moments of childish pensiveness into which the grown-up cannot penetrate. And the phrase itself is a cliché—the common now echoed in the uncommon.

Next, we may observe that stanzas two, three, and four simply document, with a busy yet wavering rhythm (one sentence runs through the three stanzas) the tireless naughtiness which was once the cause of rebuke, the naughtiness which disturbed the mature goings-on in the room with the "high window." But the naughtiness has been transmuted,

---

* From *Selected Poems* by John Crowe Ransom, copyright 1924, 1927, 1945 by Alfred A. Knopf, Inc.

by events just transpired, into a kind of fanciful story-book dream-world, in which geese are whiter than nature, and the grass greener, in which geese speak in goose language, saying "Alas," and have apple dreams. It is a drowsy, delicious world, in which the geese are bigger than life, and more important. It is an unreal (now unreal because lost), stylized world. Notice how the phrase "the little lady with rod" works: the detached, grown-up primness of "little lady"; the formal, stiff effect gained by the omission of the article before *rod;* the slightly unnatural use of the word *rod* itself, which sets some distance between us and the scene (perhaps with the hint of the fairy story, a magic wand, or a magic rod—not a common, every-day stick). But the stanzas tie back into the premises of the poem in other ways. The little girl, in her naughtiness, warred against her shadow. Is it crowding matters too hard to surmise that the shadow here achieves a sort of covert symbolic significance? The little girl lost her war against her "shadow," which was always with her. Certainly the phrase "tireless heart" has some rich connotations. And the geese which say "Alas!" conspire with the family to deplore the excessive activity of the child. (They do not conspire to express the present grief, only the past vexation—an inversion of the method of the pastoral elegy, or of the method of the first two garden poems.)

The business of the three stanzas, then, may be said to be twofold. First, they make us believe more fully in the child and therefore in the fact of the grief itself. They "prove" the grief, and they show the deliciousness of the lost world which will never look the same from the high window. Second, and contrariwise, they "transcend" the grief, or at least give a hint of a means for transcending the immediate anguish: the lost world is, in one sense, redeemed out of time; it enters the pages of the picture book where geese speak, where the untrue is true, where the fleeting is fixed. What was had cannot, after all, be lost. (By way of comparison—a comparison which, because extreme, may be helpful—I cite the transcendence in *La Récherche du Temps Perdu.*) The three stanzas, then, to state it in another way, have validated the first stanza and have prepared for the last.

The three stanzas have made it possible for us to say, when the bell tolls, "we are ready." Some kind of terms, perhaps not the best terms possible but some kind, have been made with the savage underlying irony. But the terms arrived at do not prevent the occasion from being a "stern" one. The transcendence is not absolute, and in the end is possible only because of an exercise of will and self-control. Because we control ourselves, we can say "vexed" and not some big word. And the word itself picks up the first of the domestic clichés on which the poem is based—the outburst of impatience at the naughty child who, by dying, has performed her most serious piece of naughtiness. But now the word comes to us charged with the burden of the poem, and further, as re-echoed here by the phrase "brown study," charged by the sentence in which it occurs: we are gathered formally, ritualistically, sternly together to say the word *vexed*.[3] *Vexed* becomes the ritualistic, the summarizing word.

I have used the words *pure* and *impure* often in the foregoing pages, and I confess that I have used them rather loosely. But perhaps it has been evident that I have meant something like this: the pure poem tries to be pure by excluding, more or less rigidly, certain elements which might qualify or contradict its original impulse. In other words, the pure poems want to be, and desperately, all of a piece. It has also been evident, no doubt, that the kinds of impurity which are admitted or excluded by the various little anthology pieces which have been analyzed, are different in the different poems. This is only to be expected, for there is not one doctrine of "pure poetry"—not one definition of what constitutes impurity in poems—but many. And not all of the doctrines are recent. When, for example, one cites Poe as the father of *the* doctrine of pure poetry, one is in error; Poe simply fathered *a* particular doctrine of pure poetry. One can find other doctrines of purity long antedating Poe. When Sir Philip Sidney, for example, legislated against tragi-comedy, he was repeating a current doctrine of purity. When Ben Jonson told William Drummond that Donne, for not keeping of accent, deserved hanging, he was defending another kind of purity, and when Dryden spoke to save the ear of the fair sex from metaphysical perplexities in amorous poems, he was defending another kind of purity, just as he was defending another when he defined the nature of the heroic drama. The 18th Century had a doctrine of pure poetry, which may be summed up under the word *sublimity,* but which involved two corollary doctrines, one concerning diction and the other concerning imagery. But at the same time that this century, by means of these corollary doctrines, was tidying up and purifying, as Mr. Monk and Mr. Henn have indicated, the doctrine de-

---

[3] It might be profitable, in contrast with this poem, to analyze "After the Burial," by James Russell Lowell, a poem which is identical in situation. But in Lowell's poem the savagery of the irony is unqualified. In fact, the whole poem insists, quite literally, that qualification is impossible: the scheme of the poem is to set up the brute fact of death against possible consolations. It insists on "tears," the "thin-worn locket," the "anguish of deathless hair," "the small-ness of the child's grave," the "little shoe in the corner." It is a poem which, we might say, does not progress, but ends where it begins, resting in the sav-age irony from which it stems; or we might say that it is a poem without any "insides" for the hero of the poem is not attempting to do anything about the problem which confronts him—it is a poem without issue, without conflict, a poem of unconditional surrender. In other words, it tries to be a pure poem, pure grief, absolutely inconsolable. It is a strident poem, and strident in its rhythms. The fact that we know this poem to be an expression of a bereave-ment historically real makes it an embarrassing poem, as well. It is a naked poem.

rived from Longinus, it was admitting into the drama certain impurities which the theorists of the heroic drama would not have admitted.[4]

But when we think of the modern doctrine of pure poetry, we usually think of Poe, as critic and poet, perhaps of Shelley, of the Symbolists, of the Abbé Brémond, perhaps of Pater, and certainly of George Moore and the Imagists. We know Poe's position: the long poem is "a flat contradiction in terms," because intense excitement, which is essential in poetry, cannot be long maintained; the moral sense and the intellect function more satisfactorily in prose than in poetry, and, in fact, "Truth" and the "Passions," which are for Poe associated with intellect and the moral sense, may actually be inimical to poetry; vagueness, suggestiveness, are central virtues, for poetry has for "its object an *indefinite* instead of a *definite* pleasure"; poetry is not supposed to undergo close inspection, only a cursory glance, for it, "above all things, is a beautiful painting whose tints, to minute inspection, are confusion worse confounded, but start out boldly to the cursory glance of the connoisseur"; poetry aspires toward music, since it is concerned with "indefinite sensations, to which music is an *essential,* since the comprehension of sweet sound is our most indefinite conception"; melancholy is the most poetical effect and enters into all the higher manifestations of beauty. We know, too, the Abbé Brémond's mystical interpretation, and the preface to George Moore's anthology, and the Imagist manifesto.

But these views are not identical. Shelley, for instance, delights in the imprecision praised and practiced by Poe, but he has an enormous appetite for "Truth" and the "Passions," which are, except for purposes of contrast, excluded by Poe. The Imagist manifesto, while excluding ideas, endorses precision rather than vagueness in rendering the image, and admits diction and objects which would have seemed impure to Poe and to many poets of the 19th Century, and does not take much stock in the importance of verbal music. George Moore emphasizes the objective aspect of his pure poetry, which he describes as "something which the poet creates outside his own personality," and this is opposed to the subjective emphasis in Poe and Shelley; but he shares with both an emphasis on verbal music, and with the former a distaste for ideas.

But more recently, the notion of poetic purity has emerged in other contexts, contexts which sometimes obscure the connection of the new theories with the older theories. For instance Max Eastman has a theory. "Pure poetry," he says in *The Literary Mind,* "is the pure effort to heighten consciousness." Mr. Eastman, we discover elsewhere in his book, would ban idea from poetry, but his motive is different from, say, the motive of Poe, and the difference is important: Poe would kick out the ideas

[4] Samuel Holt Monk: *The Sublime: a Study of Critical Theories in XVIII-Century England,* and T. R. Henn: *Longinus and English Criticism.*

because the ideas hurt the poetry, and Mr. Eastman would kick out the ideas because the poetry hurts the ideas. Only the scientist, he tells us, is entitled to have ideas on any subject, and the rest of the citizenry must wait to be told what attitude to take toward the ideas which they are not permitted to have except at secondhand. Literary truth, he says, is truth which is "uncertain or comparatively unimportant." But he assigns the poet a function—to heighten consciousness. But in the light of this context we would have to rewrite his original definition: pure poetry is the pure effort to heighten consciousness, but the consciousness which is heightened must not have any connection with ideas, must involve no attitude toward any ideas.

Furthermore, to assist the poet in fulfilling the assigned function, Mr. Eastman gives him a somewhat sketchy doctrine of "pure" poetic diction. For instance, the word *bloated* is not admissible into a poem because it is, as he testifies, "sacred to the memory of dead fish," and the word *tangy* is, though he knows not exactly how, "intrinsically poetic." The notion of a vocabulary which is intrinsically poetic seems, with Mr. Eastman, to mean a vocabulary which indicates agreeable or beautiful objects. So we might rewrite the original definition to read: pure poetry is the pure effort to heighten consciousness, but the consciousness which is heightened must be a consciousness exclusively of agreeable or beautiful objects—certainly not a consciousness of any ideas.

In a recent book, *The Idiom of Poetry*, Frederick Pottle has discussed the question of pure poetry. He distinguishes another type of pure poetry in addition to the types already mentioned. He calls it the "Elliptical," and would include in it symbolist and metaphysical poetry (old and new) and some work by poets such as Collins, Blake, and Browning. He observes—without any pejorative implication, for he is a critical relativist and scarcely permits himself the luxury of evaluative judgments— that the contemporary product differs from older examples of the elliptical type in that "the modern poet goes much farther in employing private experiences or ideas than would formerly have been thought legitimate." To the common reader, he says, "the prime characteristic of this kind of poetry is not the nature of its imagery but its obscurity: its urgent suggestion that you add something to the poem without telling you what that something is." This omitted "something" he interprets as the prose "frame," to use his word, the statement of the occasion, the logical or narrative transitions, the generalized application derived from the poem, etc. In other words, this type of pure poetry contends that "the effect would be more powerful if we could somehow manage to feel the images fully and accurately without having the effect diluted by any words put in to give us a 'meaning'—that is, if we could expel all the talk *about* the imaginative realization and have the pure realization itself." [5]

For the moment I shall pass the question of the accuracy of Mr. Pottle's description of the impulse of Elliptical Poetry and present the question which ultimately concerns him. How pure does poetry need to be in practice? That is the question which Mr. Pottle asks. He answers by saying that a great degree of impurity *may* be admitted, and cites our famous didactic poems, *The Faerie Queene, The Essay on Man, The Vanity of Human Wishes, The Excursion.* That is the only answer which the relativist, and nominalist, can give. Then he turns to what he calls the hardest question in the theory of poetry: what kind of prosaism is acceptable and what is not? His answer, which he advances very modestly, is this:

> . . . the element of prose is innocent and even salutary when it appears as—take your choice of three metaphors—a background on which the images are projected, or a frame in which they are shown, or a thread on which they are strung. In short, when it serves a *structural* purpose. Prose in a poem seems offensive to me when . . . the prosaisms are sharp, obvious, individual, and ranked coordinately with the images.

At first glance this looks plausible, and the critic has used the sanctified word *structural.* But at second glance we may begin to wonder what the sanctified word means to the critic. It means something rather mechanical—background, frame, thread. The structure is a showcase, say a jeweler's showcase, in which the little jewels of poetry are exhibited, the images. The showcase shouldn't be ornamental itself ("sharp, obvious, individual," Mr. Pottle says), for it would then distract us from the jewels; it should be chastely designed, and the jewels should repose on black velvet and not on flowered chintz. But Mr. Pottle doesn't ask what the relation among the bright jewels should be. Apparently, not only does the showcase bear no relation to the jewels, but the jewels bear no relation to each other. Each one is a shining little focus of heightened

[5] F. W. Bateson, in *English Poetry and the English Language,* discusses the impulse in contemporary poetry. Tennyson, he points out in connection with "The Sailor Boy," dilutes his poetry by telling a story as well as writing a poem, and "a shorter poem would have spoilt his story." The claims of prose conquer the claims of poetry. Of the Victorians in general: "The dramatic and narrative framework of their poems, by circumventing the disconcerting plunges into *medias res* which are the essence of poetry, brings it down to a level of prose. The reader knows where he is; it serves the purpose of introduction and note." Such introduction and notes in the body of the poem itself are exactly what Mr. Pottle says is missing in Elliptical Poetry. Mr. Bateson agrees with Poe in accepting intensity as the criterion of the poetic effect, and in accepting the corollary that a poem should be short. But he, contradicting Poe, seems to admire precise and complicated incidental effects.

consciousness, or pure realization, existing for itself alone. Or perhaps
he should desire that they be arranged in some mechanical pattern, such
a pattern, perhaps, as would make it easier for the eye to travel from one
little jewel to the next when the time comes to move on. Structure becomes here simply a device of salesmanship, a well-arranged showcase.

It is all mechanical. And this means that Mr. Pottle, after all, is
himself an exponent of pure poetry. He locates the poetry simply in the
images, the nodes of "pure realization." This means that what he calls
the "element of prose" includes definition of situation, movement of narrative, logical transition, factual description, generalization, ideas. Such
things, for him, do not participate in the poetic effect of the poem; in
fact, they work against the poetic effect, and so, though necessary as a
frame, should be kept from being "sharp, obvious, individual." [6]

I have referred to *The Idiom of Poetry,* first, because it is such an
admirable and provocative book, sane, lucid, generous-spirited, and second, because, to my mind, it illustrates the insidiousness with which a
doctrine of pure poetry can penetrate into the theory of a critic who is
suspicious of such a doctrine. Furthermore, I have felt that Mr. Pottle's
analysis might help me to define the common denominator of the various
doctrines of pure poetry.

That common denominator seems to be the belief that poetry is an
essence that is to be located at some particular place in a poem, or in
some particular element. The exponent of pure poetry persuades himself
that he has determined the particular something in which the poetry
inheres, and then proceeds to decree that poems shall be composed, as
nearly as possible, of that element and of nothing else. If we add up the
things excluded by various critics and practitioners, we get a list about
like this:

1. ideas, truths, generalizations, "meaning"
2. precise, complicated, "intellectual" images
3. unbeautiful, disagreeable, or neutral materials
4. situation, narrative, logical transition

[6] Several other difficulties concerning Mr. Pottle's statement may suggest themselves. First, since he seems to infer that the poetic essence resides in the image, what view would he take of meter and rhythm? His statement, strictly
construed, would mean that these factors do not participate in the poetic effect,
but are simply part of the frame. Second, what view of dramatic poetry is implied? It seems again that a strict interpretation would mean that the story
and the images bear no essential relation to each other, that the story is simply part of the frame. That is the story, characters, rhythms, and ideas, are on
one level and the images, in which the poetry inheres, are on another. But
Miss Spurgeon, Mr. Knight, and other critics have given us some reason for
holding that the images do bear some relation to the business of the other
items. In fact, all of the items, as M. Maritain has said, "feelings, ideas, representations, are for the artist merely materials and means, still symbols." That
is, they are all elements in a single expressive structure.

5. realistic details, exact descriptions, realism in general
6. shifts in tone or mood
7. irony
8. metrical variation, dramatic adaptations of rhythm, cacophony, etc.
9. meter itself
10. subjective and personal elements

No one theory of pure poetry excludes all of these items, and, as a matter of fact, the items listed are not on the same level of importance. Nor do the items always bear the same interpretation. For example, if one item seems to be central to discussions of pure poetry, it is the first: "ideas," it is said, "are not involved in the poetic effect, and may even be inimical to it." But this view can be interpreted in a variety of ways. If it is interpreted as simply meaning that the paraphrase of a poem is not equivalent to the poem, that the poetic gist is not to be defined as the statement embodied in the poem with the sugar-coating as bait, then the view can be held by opponents as well as exponents of any theory of pure poetry. We might scale down from this interpretation to the other extreme interpretation that the poem should merely give the sharp image in isolation. But there are many complicated and confused variations possible between the two extremes. There is, for example, the interpretation that "ideas," though they are not involved in the poetic effect, must appear in poems to provide, as Mr. Pottle's prosaisms do, a kind of frame, or thread, for the poetry—a spine to support the poetic flesh or a Christmas tree on which the baubles of poetry are hung.[7] T. S. Eliot has said something of this sort:

> The chief use of the "meaning" of a poem, in the ordinary sense, may be (for here again I am speaking of some kinds of poetry and not all) to satisfy one habit of the reader, to keep his mind diverted and quiet, while the poem does its work upon him: much as the imaginary burglar is always provided with a bit of nice meat for the house-dog.

Here, it would seem, Mr. Eliot has simply inverted the old sugar-coated pill theory: the idea becomes the sugar-coating and the "poetry" becomes the medicine. This seems to say that the idea in a poem does not participate in the poetic effect, and seems to commit Mr. Eliot to a theory of pure poetry. But to do justice to the quotation, we should first observe that the parenthesis indicates that the writer is referring to some sort of

---

[7] Such an interpretation seems to find a parallel in E. M. Forster's treatment of plot in fiction. Plot in his theory becomes a mere spine and does not really participate, except in a narrow, formal sense, in the fictional effect. By his inversion of the Aristotelian principle, the plot becomes merely a necessary evil.

provisional and superficial distinction and not to a fundamental one, and second observe that the passage is out of its context. In the context, Mr. Eliot goes on to say that some poets "become impatient of this 'meaning' [explicit statement of ideas in logical order] which seems superfluous, and perceive possibilities of intensity through its elimination." This may mean either of two things. It may mean that ideas do not participate in the poetic effect, or it may mean, though they do participate in the poetic effect, they need not appear in the poem in an explicit and argued form. And this second reading would scarcely be a doctrine of pure poetry at all, for it would involve poetic casuistry and not poetic principle.

We might, however, illustrate the second interpretation by glancing at Marvell's "Horatian Ode" on Cromwell. Marvell does not give us narrative; he does not give us an account of the issues behind the Civil War; he does not state the two competing ideas which are dramatized in the poem, the idea of "sanction" and the idea of "efficiency." But the effect of the poem does involve these two factors; the special reserved, scarcely resolved, irony, which is realized in the historical situation, is an irony derived from unstated materials and ideas. It is, to use Mr. Pottle's term again, a pure poem in so far as it is elliptical in method, but it is anything but a pure poem if by purity we mean the exclusion of idea from participation in the poetic effect. And Mr. Eliot's own practice implies that he believes that ideas do participate in the poetic effect. Otherwise, why did he put the clues to his ideas in the notes at the end of the *Waste Land* after so carefully excluding any explicit statement of them from the body of the poem? If he is regarding those ideas as mere bait—the "bit of nice meat for the house-dog"—he has put the ideas in a peculiar place, in the back of the book—like giving the dog the meat on the way out of the house with the swag or giving the mouse the cheese after he is in the trap. All this would lead one to the speculation that Marvell and Mr. Eliot have purged away statement of ideas from their poems, not because they wanted the ideas to participate less in the poetry, but because they wanted them to participate more fully, intensely, and immediately. This impulse, then, would account for the characteristic type of image, types in which precision, complication, and complicated intellectual relation to the theme are exploited; in other words, they are trying —whatever may be their final success—to carry the movement of mind to the center of the process. On these grounds they are the exact opposite of poets who, presumably on grounds of purity, exclude the movement of mind from the center of the poetic process—from the internal structure of the poem—but pay their respect to it as a kind of footnote, or gloss, or application coming at the end. Marvell and Eliot, by their cutting away of frame, are trying to emphasize the participation of ideas in the poetic process. Then Elliptical Poetry is not, as Mr. Pottle says it is, a pure poetry at all if we regard intention; the elliptical poet is elliptical for purposes of inclusion, not exclusion.

But waiving the question of Elliptical Poetry, no one of the other theories does—or could—exclude all the items on the list above. And that fact may instruct us. If all of these items were excluded, we might not have any poem at all. For instance, we know how some critics have pointed out that even in the strictest imagist poetry idea creeps in—when the image leaves its natural habitat and enters a poem it begins to "mean" something. The attempt to read ideas out of the poetic party violates the unity of our being and the unity of our experience. "For this reason," as Santayana puts it, "philosophy, when a poet is not mindless, enters inevitably into his poetry, since it has entered into his life; or rather, the detail of things and the detail of ideas pass equally into his verse, when both alike lie in the path that has led him to his ideal. To object to theory in poetry would be like objecting to words there; for words, too, are symbols without the sensuous character of the things they stand for; and yet it is only by the net of new connections which words throw over things, in recalling them, that poetry arises at all. Poetry is an attenuation, a rehandling, an echo of crude experience; it is itself a theoretic vision of things at arm's length." Does this not lead us to the conclusion that poetry does not inhere in any particular element but depends upon the set of relationships, the structure, which we call the poem?

Then the question arises: what elements cannot be used in such a structure? I should answer that nothing that is available in human experience is to be legislated out of poetry. This does not mean that anything can be used in *any* poem, or that some materials or elements may not prove more recalcitrant than others, or that it might not be easy to have too much of some things. But it does mean that, granted certain contexts, any sort of material, a chemical formula for instance, might appear functionally in a poem. It also may mean that, other things being equal, the greatness of a poet depends upon the extent of the area of experience which he can master poetically.

Can we make any generalizations about the nature of the poetic structure? First, it involves resistances, at various levels. There is the tension between the rhythm of the poem and the rhythm of speech (a tension which is very low at the extreme of free verse and at the extreme of verse such as that of "Ulalume," which verges toward a walloping doggerel); between the formality of the rhythm and the informality of the language; between the particular and the general, the concrete and the abstract; between the elements of even the simplest metaphor; between the beautiful and the ugly; between ideas (as in Marvell's poem); between the elements involved in irony (as in "Bells for John Whiteside's Daughter" or "Rose Aylmer"); between prosisms and poeticisms (as in "West-

ern Wind"). This list is not intended to be exhaustive; it is intended to
be merely suggestive. But it may be taken to imply that the poet is like
the jiujitsu expert; he wins by utilizing the resistance of his opponent—
the materials of the poem. In other words, a poem, to be good, must earn
itself. It is a motion toward a point of rest, but if it is not a resisted motion, it is motion of no consequence. For example, a poem which depends
upon stock materials and stock responses is simply a toboggan slide, or a
fall through space. And the good poem must, in some way, involve the
resistances; it must carry something of the context of its own creation;
it must come to terms with Mercutio. This is another way of saying that
a good poem involves the participation of the reader; it must, as Coleridge puts it, make the reader into "an active creative being." Perhaps
we can see this most readily in the case of tragedy: the definition of good
or evil is not a "given" in tragedy, it is something to be earned in the
process, and even the tragic villain must be "loved." We must kill him,
as Brutus killed Caesar, not as butchers but as sacrificers. And all of this
adds up to the fact that the structure is a dramatic structure, a movement through action toward rest, through complication toward simplicity
of effect.

In the foregoing discussion, I have deliberately omitted reference
to another type of pure poetry, a type which, in the context of the present war, may well become dominant. Perhaps the most sensible description of this type can be found in an essay by Herbert Muller:

> If it is not the primary business of the poet to be eloquent about these
> matters [faith and ideals], it still does not follow that he has more
> dignity or wisdom than those who are, or that he should have more
> sophistication. At any rate the fact is that almost all poets of the past
> did freely make large, simple statements, and not in their prosy or lax
> moments.

Mr. Muller then goes on to illustrate by quoting three famous, large,
simple statements:

> In la sua voluntade e nostra pace

and

> We are such stuff
> As dreams are made on; and our little lives
> Are rounded with a sleep

and

> The mind is its own place, and in itself
> Can make a heaven of hell, a hell of heaven.

Mr. Muller is here attacking the critical emphasis on ironic tension in
poetry. His attack really involves two lines of argument. First, the poet

is not wiser than the statesman, philosopher, or saint, people who are eloquent about faith and ideals and who say what they mean, without benefit of irony. This Platonic (or pseudo-Platonic) line of argument is, I think, off the point in the present context. Second, the poets of the past who have made large, simple affirmations have said what they meant. This line of argument is very much on the point.

Poets *have* tried very hard, for thousands of years, to say what they mean. But they have not only tried to say what they mean, they have tried to prove what they mean. The saint proves his vision by stepping cheerfully into the fires. The poet, somewhat less spectacularly, proves his vision by submitting it to the fires of irony—to the drama of his structure—in the hope that the fires will refine it. In other words, the poet wishes to indicate that his vision has been earned, that it can survive reference to the complexities and contradictions of experience. And irony is one such device of reference.

In this connection let us look at the first of Mr. Muller's exhibits. The famous line occurs in Canto III of the *Paradiso*. It is spoken by Piccarda Donati, in answer to Dante's question as to why she does not desire to rise higher than her present sphere, the sphere of the moon. But it expresses, in unequivocal terms, a central theme of the *Commedia,* as of Christian experience. On the one hand, it may be a pious truism, fit for sampler work, and on the other hand, it may be a burning conviction, tested and earned. Dante, in his poem, sets out to show how it has been earned and tested. One set of ironic tensions, for instance, which centers about this theme concerns the opposition between the notion of human justice and the notion of divine justice. The story of Paolo and Francesca is so warm, appealing, and pathetic in its human terms and their punishment so savage and unrelenting, so incommensurable, it seems, with the fault, that Dante, torn by the conflict, falls down as a dead body falls. Or Farinata, the enemy of Dante's house, is presented by the poet in terms of his human grandeur, which now, in Hell, is transmuted into a superhuman grandeur,

> com' avesse l'inferno in gran dispitto.

Ulysses remains a hero, a hero who should draw special applause from Dante, who defined the temporal end of man as the conquest of knowledge. But Ulysses is damned, as the great Brutus is damned, who hangs from the jaws of the fiend in the lowest pit of traitors. So divine justice is set over against human pathos, human dignity, human grandeur, human intellect, human justice. And we recall how Virgil, more than once, reminds Dante that he must not apply human standards to the sights he sees. It is this long conflict, which appears in many forms, this ironic tension, which finally gives body to the simple eloquence of the line in question; the statement is meaningful, not for what it says, but for what has gone before. It is earned. It has been earned by the entire poem.

I do not want to misrepresent Mr. Muller. He does follow his quotations by the sentence: "If they are properly qualified in the work as a whole, they may still be taken straight, they *are* [he italicizes the word] taken so in recollection as in their immediate impact." But can this line be taken so in recollection, and was it taken so in its "immediate impact"? And if one does take it so, is he not violating, very definitely, the poet's meaning, for the poet means the *poem,* he doesn't mean the line.

It would be interesting to try to develop the contexts of the other passages which Mr. Muller quotes. But in any case, he was simply trying, in his essay, to guard against what he considered to be, rightly or wrongly, a too narrow description of poetry; he was not trying to legislate all poetry into the type of simple eloquence, the unqualified statement of "faith and ideas." But we have already witnessed certain, probably preliminary, attempts to legislate literature into becoming a simple, unqualified, "pure" statement of faith and ideal. We have seen the writers of the 1920's called the "irresponsibles." We have seen writers such as Proust, Eliot, Dreiser, and Faulkner, called writers of the "death drive." Why are these writers condemned? Because they have tried, within the limits of their gifts, to remain faithful to the complexities of the problems with which they were dealing, because they refused to take the easy statement as solution, because they tried to define the context in which, and the terms by which, faith and ideals could be earned. But this method will scarcely satisfy the mind which is hot for certainties; to that mind it will seem merely an index to lukewarmness, indecision, disunity, treason. The new theory of purity would purge out all complexities and all ironies and all self-criticism. And this theory will forget that the hand-me-down faith, the hand-me-down ideals, no matter what the professed content, is in the end not only meaningless but vicious. It is vicious because as parody, it is the enemy of all faith.

DAVID DAICHES

The Criticism of Fiction: Some Second Thoughts

Fiction is today, as it has been for some time, the dominant literary form, and one might suppose, therefore, that modern criticism would have devoted itself particularly to the novel and the short story. The modern critic, however, has preferred to concentrate on poetry, for reasons which are not difficult to see. The abundance and variety of fiction makes the establishment of critical norms for that art a very difficult business; ideals of complexity and consistency of structure can be applied to lyrical poetry without too much strain, but the novel is often a more discursive form and rarely one in which the readers' main interest lies in the appreciation of structural artfulness. Not that structural artfulness is lacking in a good novel, but it is not often what the reader is primarily interested in seeing.

One can, of course, develop an ideal definition of a good novel which would recognize that, in the artistic handling of prose narrative, the total significance flowers cumulatively out of the handling of each unit of meaning at each point. If I may be allowed to quote from one of my own earlier attempts to grapple with this problem, I might give the following ideal definition: "Fiction as an art form is the narration of a series of situations that are so related to each other that a significant unity of meaning is achieved; the situations are presented in language such that at each point in the progress of the narrative the kind of relation between retrospect and anticipation is set up that continually and cumulatively reinforces the desired implications of the plot, so that plot becomes symbolic as well as literal in its meaning." And I added: "One definition of a 'bad novel' would therefore be a novel in which no adequate complex of meaning has been achieved, where the devices of style, structure, etc., which the author has employed have not been adequate to shape the work into an illuminating unity."[1] Symbolization, the development of new meanings out of situations by the way in which they are arranged, ordered and presented, would thus depend equally on style and structure—style being the handling of the presentation at each particular point, and plot the larger aspects of the same thing. On this definition, style would become a function of plot, and expression and structure would be part of a single complex of effective artistic communication.

The fact is, however, that such a definition, though useful as indicating an ideal towards which the art of fiction *tends,* is rarely if ever an accurate account of what goes on in a novel. Even in lyric poetry, where intensity of expression is at its maximum and the fusion of the different elements that make up the poem can almost achieve a unity which gets beyond chronological sequence to lie in the mind as a single

Reprinted, by permission, from *Literary Essays,* Edinburgh: Oliver & Boyd, Ltd., 1957. This essay was originally a lecture delivered at the University of Rochester, New York, in 1950.

[1] *A Study of Literature,* Cornell University Press and Oxford University Press, 1948, p. 55.

instantaneous pattern, this kind of unity is never wholly achieved, and the fact that the expression takes place in units that are deployed in a chronological sequence makes it impossible for the whole poem to burst into total meaning outside time, as it were. Indeed, it might be maintained that if a poem could achieve this kind of simultaneity it would cease to be a poem; for, after all, its medium is language and language depends on time, on the arrangement of a sequence, in order to communicate at all. One might say that lyrical poetry *tends towards* the escape from the time dimension, approaching ever nearer to this ideal as the poem becomes more finely wrought, but that if it were ever fully to achieve this ideal it would cease to exist.

With fiction, the unreality of the ideal definition is more clearly demonstrable. It can be applied with profit, though never wholly literally, to Flaubert, to some of James, to some of Stevenson; but what of Scott and Dickens and Trollope? A great deal of English fiction is much more muddied with life, much more crowded with boisterous irrelevancies, than any Flaubertian or Jamesian or Stevensonian definition of the art of fiction would allow. "Most people suppose," wrote Stevenson to James in 1884, ". . . that striking situations, or good dialogue, are got by studying life; they will not rise to understand that they are prepared by deliberate artifice and set off by painful suppression." But what is the relation between "deliberate artifice" and the knowledge of life in a novel of Dickens? Where did Scott get the vernacular dialogue which is what provides the true vitality in all his Scottish novels? The English tradition is rich in novels whose whole glory is their wealth of shouting and jostling characters who are brought vividly to the reader's eye by means of a superficial and not very craftsmanlike plot, and who are dismissed only when their creator has become exhausted. Dryden's famous remark on the *Canterbury Tales*—"Here is God's plenty"—has nothing to do with structure or pattern, yet it is a remark peculiarly applicable to the work of English novelists from Defoe to Joyce Carey.

Let us put the question another way. Few critics would deny that Willa Cather's *Alexander's Bridge,* a finely constructed but lifeless novel written under the influence of James, is much inferior to the same writer's *The Song of the Lark,* which is crowded with details that have no proper place in the plot, is structurally defective, and comes to an end only when the author has nothing more to say. In spite of its formal defects, *The Song of the Lark* is a rich and satisfying novel, pulsing with life, creating its own universe as it moves, picking out and presenting vividly freshly remembered incidents from the author's childhood. Language here has been made to *hold* life, and though there are moments in the novel which irritate or offend, the work as a whole has force and vitality and can be read with satisfaction by the most sophisticated reader.

Are there, then, two criteria, one drawn from art and one drawn from life? Must we distinguish between the kind of novelist who achieves an artful disposition of the pattern, and the kind who, disregarding the more purely aesthetic aspects of his work, creates a convincing and lively world of action? To do so would represent a complete abdication of the critic's function. The distinction here is surely not between the artful and the lively, but between different kinds of artfulness. James himself talked about the necessity of "the sense of felt life" in a novel, and it would never have occurred to him to sacrifice this to superficial neatness of form. To achieve the illusion of a living and pulsing world is not the work of the man who merely knows life and feels strongly about it; it is the work of the writer who can handle language in such a way that what he knows and feels can be carried alive into the reader's imagination. We most adequately face our problem by realizing that form manifests itself in a variety of ways, that an episodic novel may have an adequate form of its own even though its structure is neither complex nor consistent, that, in fact, the novel fulfills itself in many and various ways and no single definition of a good novel will do.

The richness of a Dickens novel has its own means of communicating itself, and it is not artless. The fact that Dickens wrote many of his novels for serial publication, that he did not always know what he was going to do with his characters once he had created them, that he sometimes had no notion of how he was going to end a novel until he had written a substantial part of it, would all mean eventual failure if he were writing *The Portrait of a Lady* or even *Treasure Island.* There are, of course, some Dickens novels—*Great Expectations,* for example—where structural unity does exist and is of the greatest importance in achieving the total effect; but *The Pickwick Papers* in one way and *Nicholas Nickleby* in another illustrate how a novel can move along in no particular direction once it has set up a world for it to move in, and what we enjoy here is not the movement but what it brings us to.

The universe of each of these two Dickens novels is both rich and consistent, even though the structure may not be consistent. The universe is created by character, not by plot, the only function of plot being to deploy the characters. (Character itself is created by art, working with the raw materials supplied by observation and imagination.) The death of little Nell in *The Old Curiosity Shop* is preposterously sentimental; it is a bad scene, and offends most of us, but it does not kill the novel, as it would kill another kind of novel, for as an ending it is not necessary to complete the novel's meaning, and as an episode it exists by itself, to be taken or left.

We turn to Trollope, not a great novelist but an agreeable one, and ask ourselves what is the "peculiar pleasure" we derive from his works. He, too, creates a fictional world, but it exists not so much in virtue of the fascinating and lively characters who inhabit it as in virtue of its concreteness and inclusiveness. Trollope's world is a "probable" world, and we enjoy living in it in a relaxed and even escapist way because it is easy to enter, pleasant to walk about in, and adequately credible. It is, of course, dangerous to generalise about Trollope, who wrote so many different kinds of novels: but at least it might be said that he is read today (and he is read surprisingly widely) because his world of muted crises, of human situations presented and worked out against a stable background, is both valid and self-contained. There are no passionate glimpses into the well-springs of human nature, nor do the plots build up cumulatively a unique insight which depends for its adequate presentation on the continuous relation between style and structure; there is little "symbolization" and clearly no searching for *le mot juste*. Trollope makes language carry conviction; the pressure is low and the craftsmanship is only adequate, but the fictional world does emerge, convincing, logical, agreeable and interesting to contemplate. This is doubtless a minor kind of art, but it is civilized and pleasant.

A very different kind of self-contained world is that created by Joyce's *Ulysses*. Here the structure *is* important, but not in the way that the structure of, say, *Madame Bovary* is important. More accurately, one might say that the structure of *Ulysses* is important the way it is in Flaubert, but it has a still more important function—to emphasize the completeness and logicality of the world which the novel creates as it moves. The more I read *Ulysses,* the less interested I am in the working out of the Homeric theme or in the organization of the plot as organization. I find myself more and more fascinated by the completeness of the world presented, by the fact than an incident on page 25 is explained and illuminated by another incident on page 300, that an unexplained gesture of Leopold Bloom in the fourth episode is given logic and meaning with reference to something that happens or is explained twenty episodes further on. This is a novel which cannot possibly be appreciated on first reading, not because we lack the Homeric clues (which are quite unimportant and can in fact be totally ignored by the reader without much loss) but because a great deal of the pleasure we get out of the book derives from our recognition when reading a passage on, say, page 20 that what is said here has richer meaning with reference to a fragment of conversation on page 200, an incident on page 250, or a character's recollection on page 300. This is not what we normally mean by adequacy of structure, for that kind of structure is cumulative, and builds up its meanings in chronological sequence, taking account of the fact that our memory of early incidents fades as we get further into the book. But *Ulysses* makes no concessions to memory; its effects are not achieved cumulatively but simultaneously; to enjoy the book fully we must have it all lying in our mind at once and see as we read any given part all the other parts which support and explain it and which in turn are supported and explained by this part. The simultaneity (which, as I have noted in discussing lyric poetry, can never be really achieved) is not, of course, present in the actual process of reading, which takes place in time, but if we know the book well and remember it in detail we can compensate for chronology by memory.

The richness of *Ulysses* is thus very different from that of *The Pickwick Papers*. It is not the gusto and vitality of Joyce's novel which impress us (as they so often do in Dickens) so much as the sheer completeness and self-consistency of the world in which the characters move. It all fits together; everything has a satisfying meaning if we are familiar enough with the novel to keep in mind all the relevant passages simultaneously. This is a kind of effect difficult to parallel elsewhere in fiction. The enjoyment to be derived from this savouring of the interrelationships between the different parts of the world created by the novel does not come from the appreciation of form as such, but from the pleasure of inhabiting a fictional universe so much more totally known to us in its interrelated parts than anything can be in real life. As far as I know, this kind of effect and value in fiction has not been recognized by critics.

The very completeness of Joyce's world prevents us from being overcome by a sense of its abundance, for a sense of abundance arises when we get glimpses of more characters than we can properly account for. Quaint or lively characters who emerge out of a dim background to reveal themselves as comic or picturesque and then return to the unknown from whence they came can add immensely to the sense of life in a work; one might consider the function of minor characters in Scott, for example. Scott's handling of minor characters, particularly of the dialogue he puts into their mouths, does have real relevance to the over-all structure of the novel, but we appreciate this aspect of his work not because we appreciate this relevance but because these characters help to make the world in which they dwell both more interesting and more human. *Interestingness* is a criterion no serious critic has dared to apply to art, but I can see no reason why it should not be applied. We must, of course, distinguish it from suspense and other ways of holding attention, which may be quite meretricious. By interestingness I mean the ability to intrigue and fascinate the reader the more he reads—not simply the ability to make him read on in order to find out what happens next, but the power to keep him absorbed in the individual incident. Mere truth is no more valid a criterion for art than for philosophy. What is obviously true is liable to be trite: what *might* be true and is at the same time suggestive, intriguing, attention-compelling, is a better criterion to apply to both philosophy and art. Devices for increasing the interestingness of a work of fiction may be quite independent of the conventionally accepted formal properties and may be successfully practised independently of them.

Aristotle, we all know, said that plot was the "soul" of drama, and in a sense this is certainly true for Greek drama and for much subsequent drama and fiction. But is plot the "soul" of Shakespeare's *Henry IV*, Part I? The story of that play is important; the patterning of events, with their causal connections, helps to give the play its meaning, to make the whole thing pleasingly comprehensive as a unit. But does the "peculiar pleasure" we derive from the play really derive from the manner in which the various incidents are arranged with respect to each other? There could be no play without the plot, true enough, but the richness of dialogue and incident, the bubbling vitality which is conveyed not by the *order* in which things happen but by the *way* in which they happen, by the life which springs from the characters in operation—this is what we most enjoy the play for, and this is achieved not by structural artfulness but by artfulness in the use of language to present the given incident. What Levin Schücking called, in a somewhat different connection, Shakespeare's "episodic intensification" can be usefully applied to any play or novel in which the life emerges through the energy and colour of the individual incident, and where the work as a whole is a series of such incidents linked by relatively flat passages whose function is to ensure that the nominal structure does not fall apart.

I am not trying to restore the old distinction between the novel of character and the novel of incident, though this has its uses, but I am maintaining that there are kinds of interest in fiction which do not depend on those qualities of organization which we like to think of as of basic significance in a work of art. Professor R. S. Crane, in a brilliant article in the *American Journal of General Education* for January 1950, has analysed the structure of *Tom Jones* in astonishing detail. He does not, however, raise the question of the part played by structure in the total impact of the novel. In what degree do the kinds of interest which we find in *Tom Jones* depend on this structure—a structure, it might be added, whose complexity nobody can see until Professor Crane has pointed it out? This is not a rhetorical question but one which deserves a careful and an honest answer.

I suppose that Professor Wimsatt of Yale would say that this line of argument is an example of the "affective fallacy," and that the whole notion of interestingness as a criterion is based on the erroneous assumption that the way in which the work affects the reader (albeit the experienced and sensitive reader) is critically relevant. But the ontological fallacy, which is the name I give to what he and others profess, is even more misleading, for it assumes that the essence of a work of art is something different from its capacity for being properly perceived. If Berkeley's theory of knowledge had been applied to art, Dr Johnson could never have refuted him by kicking a stone: for the *esse* of a work of art *is* its *percipi*. That being so, what we perceive is of the first importance, and the quality of the perception depends directly on the original creator who arranged things in terms of their perceptive potentialities. The artist, like God, works in a communicative medium, and the test of his success is the reactions of the qualified receiver. In examining the reactions of the qualified receiver (reader, in the case of novels) the critic can determine the kinds of appeal different kinds of work possess, and he can then proceed to find out what it is in them which accounts for the appeal. The most fruitful criticism always operates in this way: it clarifies and explains effects with reference to their causes in the work.

There are more types of artfulness at work in fiction than are dreamed of in our philosophy. How does Jane Austen, for example, achieve that sublime clarity of presentation which is a source of perpetual wonder to the reader, and what is the relation of that clarity to her characteristic irony? The analysis of the relation of style to plot in her novels will go only a little way in answering these questions, and the mere analysis of structure will not begin to answer them. The wit of Huxley's *Antic Hay* is part of the texture of the dialogue, and that texture cannot be discussed with the same critical tools which can demonstrate the cunning of James's *The Turn of the Screw*. Fiction is, in fact, a blanket term which covers many different kinds of skills, many different ways of handling narrative in language, for many different purposes.

There are even important differences in what might be called the unit of artifice. In some novelists it is possible to examine each phrase, noting the effectiveness of the smallest unit of expression and its contribution to the sum of significance. We all know—we have the author's word for it—that this can be done for Flaubert, where the slightest alteration in the form of expression can be disastrous to the shape of the whole paragraph and so to the rhythm of the total work. But in, say, Hardy's *The Return of the Native* the unit of artifice is large: it is not the individual word or phrase, but the swell of the whole paragraph, and as long as that swell is maintained one could change phrases and even whole sentences without impairing the work in the least. This is equally true of Scott, though not where he is working with vernacular dialogue, and indeed it is true of most nineteenth century English novelists except (odd juxtaposition!) Emily Brontë and Stevenson. It is quite unrealistic to suggest that in Hardy's novels the expression at each point is so perfectly subdued to the total intention that the smallest alteration would be fatal. One could alter or omit large passages without the most perceptive critic being aware that anything was wrong. Hardy's massive, flinty style is based on a large unit of artifice, not, as with Flaubert, on a small one, and differences of this kind must be noted by the critic if he is not to make a fool of himself by applying analytic techniques indiscriminately whether or not they are appropriate to the kind of craftsmanship the artist employed.

We are inclined to be hypnotized by the word "artist." If the writer is an artist, we maintain, then he *must* be aware all the time of the precise relation of each individual stroke to the total effect he is aiming at. But two things should be remembered: one is that artists are men, and therefore fallible, and their works are thus no more perfect than the highest kind of human achievement in other categories; the other is that the term "artist" covers a great many different ways of handling a communicative medium, and brilliant craftsmanship may be demonstrated by any one of an indefinite number of kinds of cunning. This is particularly true of the novel, which in English especially is an "impure" art form—or at least we have to consider it impure if we hold too narrow a definition of art. Our ideal definition of the novel is helpful if we consider it as an ideal towards which certain kinds of fiction tend; but if we allow it to determine in advance what we are going to see in a novel, it will end by obscuring the reasons why fiction is in fact enjoyed, and thus divorcing the critic wholly from the appreciative reader. A critic so divorced is engaged merely in a kind of pedantic play, which may be amusing to himself and his fellow professionals but has no further function. It is in order to avoid this that I have thought it worth while to emphasize certain distinctions between different kinds of novels and their "peculiar pleasures."

Index

OF CRITICAL TERMS AND TOPICS DISCUSSED IN CHAPTERS I–V